Essential Maths

Book 8 Core

Elmwood Education

First published 2020 by

Elmwood Education Ltd
Unit 5, Mallow Park
Watchmead
Welwyn Garden City
Herts.
AL7 1GX
Tel. 01707 333232

© David Rayner, Michael White
The moral rights of the authors have been asserted.
Database right Elmwood Education (maker).

ISBN 9781 906 622 794

Typeset and illustrated by Tech-Set Ltd., Gateshead, Tyne and Wear.

PREFACE

Essential Maths Book 8 Core has been written for pupils who are working in the middle ability range.

There is no set path through the book. The book has, however, been split into 6 units. Each unit of work can be used during one half-term with appropriate revision material at the end of the unit. Many topics are reviewed later in the book which is essential for consolidation.

Puzzles, activities and mental arithmetic tasks can be found between the units, to be used whenever appropriate. Investigations appear regularly throughout the book. Ideas for discussing and exploring themes from the 'history of mathematics' are included between each pair of units.

No textbook will have the 'right' amount of material for every class.
The authors believe that it is preferable to have too much material rather than too little. There are many opportunities for reasoning and for pupils to start to develop the skills to explain and to justify. Twelve 'Spot the mistakes' sections are included to encourage these aspects.

Very occasionally an exercise is labelled with an 'E'. This suggests that these questions may be particularly demanding. Each topic finishes with consolidation and extension questions to be used as appropriate.

Pupil self-assessment is very important. Regular 'check yourself' sections appear throughout the book. Answers to these parts only are provided at the back of the book for immediate feedback.

The authors are indebted to Hilary White and Jackie Mace for their invaluable contribution to this book.

Michael White and David Rayner

CONTENTS

UNIT 1

In section 1.1 you will practise:

- using cube numbers and higher powers
- multiplying and dividing indices

Cube numbers and higher powers

- The first three *cube numbers* are:
  $1^3 = 1 \times 1 \times 1 = 1$
  $2^3 = 2 \times 2 \times 2 = 8$
  $3^3 = 3 \times 3 \times 3 = 27$

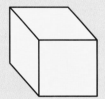

- Higher powers are written in a similar way.
  $3 \times 3 \times 3 \times 3 \times 3$ is written 3^5. 'Three to the power of 5'
  $2 \times 2 \times 2 \times 2 \times 2 \times 2$ is written 2^6. 'Two to the power of 6'

- The power button on a calculator is usually

Exercise 1M

1 Work out

(a) 4^3 (b) 5^3 (c) 6^3 (d) 10^3 (e) 7^3

2 Find the side length of each square.

(a)
area
$= 36\,cm^2$

(b)
area
$= 9\,cm^2$

(c)
area
$= 144\,cm^2$

3 Work out the following, without a calculator.

(a) 1^3 (b) 11^2 (c) $\left(\dfrac{1}{2}\right)^2$ (d) $\left(\dfrac{1}{2}\right)^3$ (e) 0.1^2

4　'1 is the only cube number which is also a square number.' True or false?

5　Copy and complete this table, using a calculator to help you obtain the answers.

We say	We write	We work out	Answer
2 to the power of 4	2^4	$2 \times 2 \times 2 \times 2$	
3 to the power of 4		$3 \times 3 \times 3 \times 3$	
	4^4		256
5 to the power of 2			
	6^5		7776
		$8 \times 8 \times 8 \times 8 \times 8$	
		$9 \times 9 \times 9$	
	3^9		
10 to the power of 2			
2 to the power of 10			

6　The numbers 10, 100, 1000 … form the basis of our number system.
Write each of the numbers 10, 100, 1000, 10 000, 100 000 and 1 million as a power of 10

7　Which is larger: 2^3 or 3^2?

8　Find the missing numbers so
that the answer is always 100

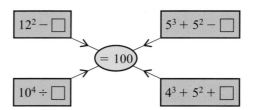

9　Write the numbers opposite in order of size,
starting with the smallest.

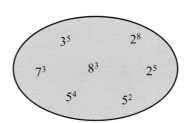

10 Read this letter which appeared recently in a newspaper.

How old was Tony at the time?

> ## In his prime
>
> Sir, The letters about age and numbers remind me of an incident that occurred some years ago when, after early retirement, I taught GCSE Maths part-time at a local college.
>
> One of a group of mature students asked me my age, to which I replied that I was currently a prime number and in three years' time would be a perfect square.
>
> Another student said I couldn't possibly be 13, to which another added that I could easily be 97.
>
> The matter was resolved when yet another pointed out that in three years' time my age would also be a perfect cube. Such is the delight of numbers.
>
> TONY HARWOOD
> Chandlers Ford, Hants

Multiplying indices

Consider 4^3 4 is the *base* number.

3 is the *index* (plural is '*indices*').

$5^2 \times 5^4 = (5 \times 5) \times (5 \times 5 \times 5 \times 5) = 5^6$

We observe that we add the powers when multiplying the same number with indices.

Dividing indices

$\dfrac{5^4}{5^2} = \dfrac{\cancel{5} \times \cancel{5} \times 5 \times 5}{\cancel{5} \times \cancel{5}} = 5^2$

We observe that we subtract the powers when dividing the same number with indices.

$a^m \times a^n = a^{m+n}$
$a^m \div a^n = a^{m-n}$

$6^3 \times 6^2 \times 6^4 = 6^{3+2+4} = 6^9$

$\dfrac{7^4 \times 7^5}{7^3 \times 7^3} = \dfrac{7^9}{7^6} = 7^{9-6} = 7^3$

Exercise 2M

1 Copy and complete the following, giving each answer in index form.

(a) $7^4 \times 7^2 = 7^{4+2} = 7^\square$
(b) $4^3 \times 4^5 = 4^\square$
(c) $3^7 \div 3^5 = 3^\square$
(d) $8^9 \div 8^7 = 8^{9-7} = 8^\square$
(e) $5^4 \times 5^8 = 5^\square$
(f) $6^{10} \div 6^5 = 6^\square$

4

2 Work out and write each answer as a number in index form.

(a) $8^4 \times 8^3$

(b) $9^{10} \div 9^3$

(c) $7^3 \times 7^3 \times 7^2$

(d) $6^5 \times 6^7$

(e) $5^4 \times 5^3 \times 5^6$

(f) $3^3 \times 3^3 \times 3^3$

(g) $\dfrac{3^7}{3^4}$

(h) $\dfrac{6^8}{6^3}$

(i) $7^2 \times 7^4 \times 7^4 \times 7^3$

3 Copy and complete

(a) $3^5 \times 3^2 = \square$

(b) $\square \times 4^5 = 4^8$

(c) $\square \times 6^4 = 6^9$

(d) $2^4 \times \square = 2^{11}$

(e) $3^8 \div 3^4 = \square$

(f) $2^9 \div \square = 2^2$

(g) $7^{20} \div \square = 7^8$

(h) $10^{15} \div \square = 10^6$

(i) $\square \div 4^7 = 4^4$

4 Beatrix says that $3^4 \times 3 = 3^{4+0} = 3^4$. Carl does not agree. Who is correct?
Give a reason for your answer.

5 Work out and write each answer as a number in index form.

(a) $\dfrac{6^5 \times 6^3}{6^2}$

(b) $\dfrac{5^8 \times 5^4}{5^7}$

(c) $\dfrac{3^8}{3^2 \times 3^3}$

(d) $\dfrac{7^6 \times 7^4}{7^2 \times 7^3}$

(e) $\dfrac{2^7 \times 2^3}{2^4 \times 2^4}$

(f) $\dfrac{9^6 \times 9^5}{9^3 \times 9^4}$

(g) $\dfrac{5^7 \times 5^4 \times 5^4}{5^6 \times 5^3}$

(h) $\dfrac{3^8 \times 3^7}{3^4 \times 3^2 \times 3^4}$

(i) $\dfrac{2^7 \times 2^4 \times 2^6}{2^5 \times 2^2 \times 2^4}$

6 Write down the area of this
rectangle in index form.

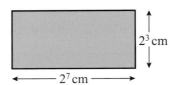

2^3 cm

2^7 cm

7 Which is smaller?
Give reasons for
your answer.

P $\boxed{\dfrac{7^2 \times 7^{10}}{7^3 \times 7^4}}$ or Q $\boxed{\dfrac{7^5 \times 7^9}{7^8}}$

8 Work out and write each answer as a number in index form.

(a) $2^3 \times 2$

(b) 5×5^6

(c) $3^4 \times 3 \times 3^2$

(d) $6^7 \times 6^4 \times 6$

(e) $7^2 \times 7 \times 7^5$

(f) $2 \times 2^4 \times 2$

(g) $\dfrac{3^6 \times 3}{3^2 \times 3^2}$

(h) $\dfrac{9^3 \times 9^5}{9^4 \times 9}$

(i) $\dfrac{5 \times 5 \times 5^3}{5^2 \times 5}$

9 In this question, give each answer as an ordinary number.
For example, $3^5 \div 3^3 = 3^2 = 3 \times 3 = 9$

(a) $5^6 \div 5^4$

(b) $2^3 \times 2$

(c) $7^8 \div 7^7$

(d) $3^9 \div 3^6$

(e) $10^8 \div 10^5$

(f) $1^6 \times 1^4$

(g) $2^2 \times 2^3$

(h) $\dfrac{5^6 \times 5^3}{5^7}$

(i) $\dfrac{4^7 \times 4^4}{4^5 \times 4^5}$

Need more practice with the rules of indices?

1 Work out

(a) 2^5

(b) 8^3

(c) 3^4

(d) $\left(\dfrac{1}{4}\right)^3$

(e) 0.2^3

2 What power of 2 gives the answer 16?

3 Which is larger: 4^3 or 2^6?

4 Find the missing number if $3^3 + 5^3 + \boxed{} = 200$

5 Work out and write each answer as a number in index form.

(a) $5^2 \times 5^6$

(b) $3^8 \div 3^2$

(c) $4^3 \times 4^5 \times 4^3$

(d) $10^{11} \div 10^7$

(e) $\dfrac{6^5 \times 6^7}{6^9}$

(f) $\dfrac{2^{24}}{2^7 \times 2^8}$

(g) $9^4 \times 9^8 \times 9^3$

(h) $\dfrac{8^3 \times 8^8}{8^5 \times 8^2}$

(i) $7^5 \times 7$

(j) $3 \times 3^5 \times 3$

(k) $\dfrac{2^5 \times 2^4}{2^3 \times 2^2 \times 2^2}$

(l) $\dfrac{9 \times 9^6}{9^2 \times 9^3}$

6 Match the questions below which give the same answer.

$\boxed{5^3 \times 5^3}$ $\boxed{\dfrac{5^8}{5^3}}$ $\boxed{5 \times 5^5}$ $\boxed{\dfrac{5^3 \times 5^7}{5^6}}$

         $\boxed{\dfrac{5^{20}}{5^6 \times 5^9}}$

$\boxed{\dfrac{5^4 \times 5^8}{5^5}}$ $\boxed{5^3 \times 5}$ $\boxed{\dfrac{5^9 \times 5^6}{5^3 \times 5^5}}$

7 Work out the actual difference between 4×4^2 and 3×3^3

8 $\dfrac{7^3 \times 7^\square}{7^8} = 7^6$ Write down the value missing from the box opposite.

9 3^4 can be written in index form as $3^2 \times 3^2$ or $3 \times 3 \times 3 \times 3$. Write down as many other ways as possible for writing 3^4 in index form.

10 The area of the rectangle opposite is $5^{10}\,\text{cm}^2$.

Write down the value of x in index form.

$5^6\,\text{cm}$

Extension questions with the rules of indices

Raising a power to a further power

$(2^3)^2 = 2^3 \times 2^3 = (2 \times 2 \times 2) \times (2 \times 2 \times 2) = 2^6$

$(5^2)^3 = 5^2 \times 5^2 \times 5^2 = (5 \times 5) \times (5 \times 5) \times (5 \times 5) = 5^6$

To raise a power to a further power, we multiply the powers.

$$(a^m)^n = a^{m \times n} = a^{mn}$$

Examples: $(7^3)^4 = 7^{3 \times 4} = 7^{12}$

$\dfrac{3^2 \times 3^8}{(3^2)^4} = \dfrac{3^{10}}{3^8} = 3^2$

1 Work out and write each answer as a number in index form.
   (a) $(3^2)^4$ (b) $(2^4)^2$ (c) $(7^4)^3$
   (d) $(5^4)^5$ (e) $(6^8)^{10}$ (f) $(8^2)^2 \times 8^2$
   (g) $(7^3)^4 \div 7^7$ (h) $(3^5)^2 \times (3^4)^6$ (i) $(5^4)^8 \times 5$

2 Which of the expressions below is the odd one out?

   $\boxed{(5^2)^4}$ $\boxed{5^5 \times 5^3}$ $\boxed{(5^3)^3 \div 5}$ $\boxed{5^4 + 5^4}$ $\boxed{5^{11} \div 5^3}$

3 In this question, give each answer as an ordinary number.
   (a) $(3^2)^2$ (b) $(4^3)^2 \div 4^4$ (c) $5^3 \times 5$
   (d) $(2^2)^3 \times 2^2$ (e) $(7^5)^2 \div (7^3)^3$ (f) $(1^2)^4 \times (1^3)^3$
   (g) $\dfrac{(8^5)^4}{(8^3)^6}$ (h) $\dfrac{(3^2)^4 \times 3^2}{3^7}$ (i) $\dfrac{(2^3)^4 \times (2^2)^5}{2^{14} \times (2^2)^2}$

4 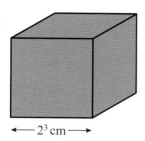 Work out the volume of this cube, giving the answer

(a) in index form

(b) as an ordinary number.

2^3 cm

5 Gary says that $(7^2)^4$ is equal to 7^6. *Explain clearly* the mistake that Gary has made.

6 Answer 'true' or 'false' for each statement below.

(a) $(3^2)^3 = 3^5$

(b) $(2^2)^3 > 8^2$

(c) $2^3 \times 3^3 = 6^6$

(d) $\dfrac{(7^3)^5}{(7^4)^2} = 7^7$

(e) $\dfrac{(6^2)^4 \times 6^3}{6^5 \times 6^2} = 6^2$

(f) $\dfrac{9^8 \times 9^6}{(9^3)^4} = 9^2$

Investigation – consecutive sums

- Consecutive numbers are whole numbers which appear next to each other on the number line: 4, 5 and 6 are consecutive.
  7 and 10 are not consecutive.

- Using only sets of consecutive numbers it is possible to form all the numbers from 1 to 40 except for the powers of 2 (1, 2, 4, 8, 16, 32).

- Copy and complete the table opposite to find the consecutive sums for every number from 1 to 40 except for the powers of 2

  Some target numbers can be formed in more than one way.

- Continue the pattern to 100. You should look at your results and use any patterns you can see to help you.

Target	Consecutive sum
1	Impossible
2	Impossible
3	1 + 2
4	Impossible
5	2 + 3
6	1 + 2 + 3
☐	
40	6 + 7 + 8 + 9 + 10

Investigation – power sums

A Here is a list of the first six powers of 2

$$2^0 = 1$$
$$2^1 = 2$$
$$2^2 = 4$$
$$2^3 = 8$$
$$2^4 = 16$$
$$2^5 = 32$$

(Yes! 2^0 really is 1. Check it on a calculator. We will discuss the power zero in a later book.)

- Using only the numbers 1, 2, 4, 8, 16 and 32 it is possible to form all the whole numbers from 1 to 32 inclusive, by adding and subtracting.

  (We call them 'power *sums*' even though we sometimes subtract.)

Target	Power sum
1	1
2	2
3	4 − 1
4	4
5	4 + 1
6	2 + 4
7	1 + 2 + 4
☐	☐
32	32

- You may use each of 1, 2, 4, 8, 16 and 32 only once.

  E.g. 5 = 2 + 2 + 1 is not allowed.

  5 = 4 + 1 is allowed.

- Copy and complete the table above to find power sums for every number from 1 to 32

- Can you continue the patterns to 63? 127? …

B

$$3^0 = 1$$
$$3^1 = 3$$
$$3^2 = 9$$
$$3^3 = 27$$

Here are the first four powers of 3. Using only these numbers it is possible to form all the whole numbers between 1 and 40. Copy and complete the table, again using each number (1, 3, 9 and 27) only *once*.

Target	Power sum
1	1
2	3 − 1
3	3
4	1 + 3
5	9 − 3 − 1
☐	☐
40	?

1.2 Prime factors, HCF and LCM

In section 1.2 you will:

- review prime numbers, factors and multiples
- express a number as the product of its prime factors
- use Venn diagrams to find HCFs and LCMs

Prime numbers, factors and multiples

- A *prime* number has two factors only. It is divisible exactly by just two different numbers: itself and 1.

  Note that 1 has only one factor so is not a prime number.

  Here are some prime numbers: $\boxed{7}$ $\boxed{23}$ $\boxed{11}$

- The *factors* of 15 divide into 15 exactly.

  $\boxed{1 \times 15}$ $\boxed{3 \times 5}$ The factors of 15 are 1, 3, 5 and 15

- The first four *multiples* of $\boxed{6}$ are $\boxed{6, 12, 18, 24}$

  The first four multiples of $\boxed{11}$ are $\boxed{11, 22, 33, 44}$

Exercise 1M

1 Write down the first four multiples of

    (a) 4   (b) 6   (c) 20   (d) 25

2 Which of these are prime numbers? $\boxed{21}$ $\boxed{5}$ $\boxed{49}$ $\boxed{81}$ $\boxed{13}$ $\boxed{65}$

3 Find *all* the factors of

    (a) 12   (b) 30   (c) 17   (d) 50

4 7 is a factor of which numbers between 20 and 30?

5

    (a) From the balls shown, which two balls add up to 24? There are three answers.

    (b) Which two prime number balls add up to 18? There are two answers.

6 'All prime numbers are odd.' True or false?

7 Add together all the prime numbers less than 16

8 Mia says that the largest factor of 32 is 16. Is she correct? Give a reason for your answer.

9 60 is mid-way between two prime numbers. What are they?

10 (a) List the factors of 28

   (b) List the factors of 36

   (c) List the common factors of 28 and 36

   (d) Write down the highest common factor (HCF) of 28 and 36

11 Find the HCF of

   (a) 24 and 42   (b) 35 and 49

12 True or false?
   'The total number of cubes in the pyramid is a multiple of 5.'
   Give a reason for your answer.

13 Here are the first six multiples of 12 and 15

12 : 12	24	36	48	60	72
15 : 15	30	45	60	75	90

   Write down the lowest common multiple (LCM) of 12 and 15 [i.e. the lowest number which is in both lists].

14 Copy and complete the first five multiples of 6 and 8

   6 : 6, 12, ☐ , ☐ , ☐

   8 : 8, ☐ , ☐ , ☐ , ☐

   Write down the LCM of 6 and 8

15 Find the LCM of

   (a) 8 and 10   (b) 25 and 40   (c) 9, 12 and 15

16 The LCM of n and 18 is 72. Suggest a possible value for the number n.

Expressing a number as the product of its prime factors

Factors of a number which are also prime numbers are called prime factors. We can find these prime factors using a 'factor tree'. Here are two examples.

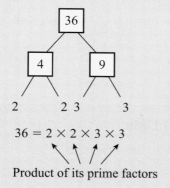

$$36 = 2 \times 2 \times 3 \times 3$$

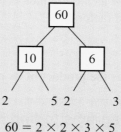

$$60 = 2 \times 2 \times 3 \times 5$$

Product of its prime factors

Exercise 2M

1 Copy and complete these factor trees.

(a)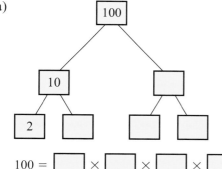

(b)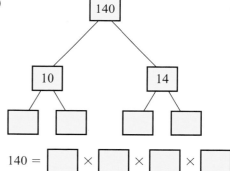

2 Draw a factor tree for 108. Remember that you only stop when you get to prime factors.

3 Draw factor trees for the following numbers.
   (a) 24   (b) 72   (c) 110   (d) 300   (e) 126   (f) 630   (g) 392   (h) 3960

4 Find a number with prime factors of only 7, 11 and 17

5 Copy and fill in the missing numbers in the answer shown opposite.

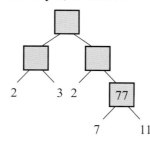

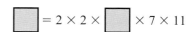

6 A factor tree for 364 is shown opposite.

   (a) *Explain clearly* a mistake
       that has been made.

   (b) Express 364 as the product
       of its prime factors.

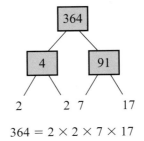

$364 = 2 \times 2 \times 7 \times 17$

7 Express 5775 as the product of its prime factors.

Using Venn diagrams to find HCFs and LCMs

The prime factors of two numbers can be written in a Venn diagram.

For example, $924 = 2 \times 2 \times 3 \times 7 \times 11$
and $1386 = 2 \times 3 \times 3 \times 7 \times 11$

Venn diagram

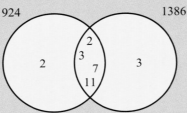

Multiply the numbers in the intersection to find the HCF.

$HCF = 2 \times 3 \times 7 \times 11 = 462$

Multiply *all* the numbers in the Venn diagram to find the LCM.

$LCM = 2 \times 2 \times 3 \times 3 \times 7 \times 11 = 2772$

Exercise 3M

1 The Venn diagram opposite shows the
   prime factors of 30 and 165.
   Work out

   (a) the HCF of 30 and 165

   (b) the LCM of 30 and 165

2 The Venn diagram opposite shows the
   prime factors of 105 and 330.
   Work out

   (a) the HCF of 105 and 330

   (b) the LCM of 105 and 330

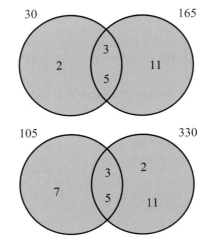

3 975 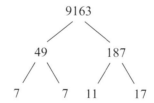 550   The Venn diagram opposite shows the prime factors of 975 and 550.
Work out

(a) the HCF of 975 and 550

(b) the LCM of 975 and 550

4 (a) If $315 = 3 \times 3 \times 5 \times 7$ and $273 = 3 \times 7 \times 13$, draw a Venn diagram for the prime factors of 315 and 273

(b) Work out the HCF of 315 and 273

(c) Work out the LCM of 315 and 273

5 (a) If $1386 = 2 \times 3 \times 3 \times 7 \times 11$ and $858 = 2 \times 3 \times 11 \times 13$, draw a Venn diagram for the prime factors of 1386 and 858

(b) Work out the HCF of 1386 and 858

(c) Work out the LCM of 1386 and 858

6 Draw factor trees then Venn diagrams to find the HCF and LCM of

(a) 126 and 210   (b) 90 and 165   (c) 650 and 1365

7 Use the factor tree for 9163
to help you find the HCF and
LCM of 231 and 9163

```
          9163
         /    \
       49      187
      /  \     /  \
     7    7  11    17
```

8 Find the HCF and LCM of 399 and 455

Need more practice with prime factors, HCF and LCM?

1 Write down *all* the factors of

(a) 44   (b) 54   (c) 29

2 Write down the first ten prime numbers.

3 'All multiples of 9 are multiples of 3.' True or false?

4   (a) List the factors of 24

     (b) List the factors of 40

     (c) List the common factors of 24 and 40 [i.e. the numbers which are in list (a) and list (b)].

     (d) Write down the HCF of 24 and 40

5   The number in the square is the product of the two numbers on either side of it.
Copy and complete.

(a)   (b)   (c)

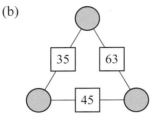 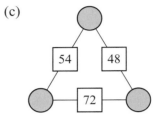

6   Write down the LCM of 12 and 25

7   How many prime numbers have 5 as their last digit?

8   'Modelkit' makes kits for model planes in its factory. Martin has to check every 40th box to make sure the glue is present. Nina has to check every 50th box to make sure the paint is present. Which is the first box that both Martin and Nina have to check?

9   Complete these factor trees, then write each of 110 and 150 as the product of its prime factors.

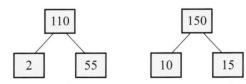

10   Draw factor trees, then write each number below as the product of its prime factors.

     (a) 30   (b) 120   (c) 230   (d) 250

Extension questions with prime factors, HCF and LCM

1    $385 = 5 \times 7 \times 11$ and $2145 = 3 \times 5 \times 11 \times 13$

     A Venn diagram is drawn.

     (a) Work out the HCF of 385 and 2145

     (b) Work out the LCM of 385 and 2145

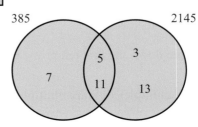

2 $154 = 2 \times 7 \times 11$ and $714 = 2 \times 3 \times 7 \times 17$

(a) Draw a Venn diagram for the prime factors of 154 and 714

(b) Work out the HCF of 154 and 714

(c) Work out the LCM of 154 and 714

3 Bus A and bus B both leave the Town Hall at 08:30. Bus A returns to the Town Hall every 20 minutes and bus B returns to the Town Hall every 24 minutes. How many times do bus A and bus B return to the Town Hall at the same time between 09:00 and 17:00?

4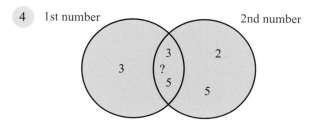

1st number   2nd number

The prime factors of two numbers are shown in the Venn diagram opposite. One factor is missing. Work out the LCM of the two numbers if the HCF is 45.

5 Some prime numbers can be written as the sum of two square numbers, e.g. $1^2 + 2^2 = 5$ Find four 2-digit prime numbers that can be written as the sum of two square numbers. [Hint: start by listing the square numbers.]

6 Draw factor trees then a Venn diagram to find the HCF and LCM of 147 and 1254

7 Does every whole number between 20 and 30 have an even number of factors? Give a reason for your answer.

8 Find the HCF and LCM of 3094 and 3549

9 A chiropodist visits an elderly person every 5 weeks and a hairdresser visits every 6 weeks. The chiropodist and hairdresser both visit the elderly person on 3rd March. What will be the date when they both arrive again on the same day?

10 Pencils can only be bought in whole boxes. Mr Davies buys 36 pencils, Ms Jones buys 90 pencils and Mrs Patel buys 180 pencils. What is the largest possible number of pencils in one box?

1.3 Using algebra

In section 1.3 you will:

- simplify algebraic expressions
- use letters for numbers

Simplifying algebraic expressions

An algebraic *expression* is formed from letter symbols and numbers. For example, $3n$, $4n + 5$ and $1 - 2x$ are all expressions. Notice that there is no equals sign in an expression.

$4 \times n = 4n$

$m \times n = mn$

$(m + n) \div y = \dfrac{m + n}{y}$

$m \times m = m^2$

Like terms can be added:

$2m + n + 3m + 5n = 5m + 6n$

$5n + 4 - 2n - 6 = 3n - 2$

$n^2 + 4n^2 = 5n^2$

Cancelling fractions:

$\dfrac{\cancel{6} \times 2}{\cancel{6}} = 2 \qquad \dfrac{2 \times \cancel{n}}{\cancel{n}} = 2 \qquad \dfrac{8n}{2} = 4n$

Exercise 1M

Simplify the following expressions as far as possible by collecting like terms.

1. $6x + 2y + 3x$
2. $3m + 3m + n$
3. $4a + b + 2b + a$

4. $4m + 3n - 2m - n$
5. $7p + 5q - 3p - 4q$
6. $8x + y + 5y$

7. $a + 7 + 3a - 4$
8. $5p - 3p - 4 + p$
9. $4n + 1 - 3n - 6$

10. Which two expressions below are equivalent? (This means they give the same answer when the like terms are collected.)

    (a) $5m + 6n + m + 3 - 2n$ (b) $3n + 6 + 4m - 2 + 3n$ (c) $4n + 7 + 4m + 2n - 3$

11. Write down an expression for the perimeter of each shape below. Collect like terms where possible.

    (a)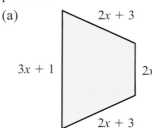

    (b)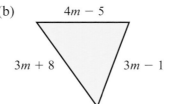

    (c)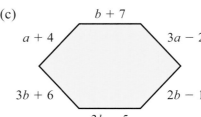

Simplify the expressions in questions ⑫ to ⑳ as far as possible.

⑫ $3a + b - 2a + 6b$

⑬ $8 + m - 11 + m$

⑭ $3x + 2 - 5x + 3$

⑮ $5n + 3n - 1 - 7n$

⑯ $2y - 4y + 3 - 2$

⑰ $9a + 4 - 6 - 7a$

⑱ $3 + 6q - 2 - 9q$

⑲ $16 - 3n + 1 + 2n + m$

⑳ $3m - 6m + 2 - 6$

㉑ Find three matching pairs.

A $\boxed{2a + 3 - a}$ B $\boxed{b + 3 + a + 1}$ C $\boxed{a + 3b + 3 - 2b}$

D $\boxed{b + 2a + 3 - a}$ E $\boxed{3 + a}$ F $\boxed{a + 4 + b}$

㉒ Martin says that $4n^2 + 3n^2 + n = 8n^2$.
Explain clearly the mistake that Martin has made.

㉓ Simplify
(a) $3n^2 + 4n^2$

(b) $8m^2 - 3m$

(c) $2y^2 + 3y + 2y^2$

(d) $6x^2 - 3x^2 + 5x^2$

(e) $2x^2 + 3x + 1$

(f) $5a^2 - 3a^2 + 7a$

(g) $4m + 3 + 2m - 3m^2$

(h) $4 + 3y^2 + 2 - y^2$

(i) $3n + 7n^2 + 3 - 2n$

㉔ Draw a rectangle with the same perimeter
as the triangle shown opposite.
Show clearly the length and width of
the rectangle.

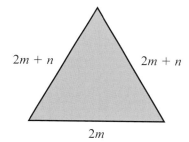

$2m + n$ $2m + n$

$2m$

Exercise 2M

① Write down any pairs of expressions from below that are equal to each other.

$\boxed{4 + 4}$ $\boxed{4 \times 3}$ $\boxed{4 + 3}$ $\boxed{4 - 3}$

$\boxed{3 \times 4}$ $\boxed{4^2}$ $\boxed{3 - 4}$ $\boxed{4 \times 4}$

② Write down any pairs of expressions from below that are equal to each other.

$\boxed{n - 3}$ $\boxed{n^2}$ $\boxed{n + 3}$ $\boxed{3 - n}$

$\boxed{3 + n}$ $\boxed{\frac{n}{3}}$ $\boxed{3 \div n}$ $\boxed{n \times n}$

In questions ③ to ⑰, answer 'true' or 'false'.

③ $a + b = b + a$

④ $a \times a = a^2$

⑤ $7 \times n = n \times 7$

⑥ $m \times m = 2m$

⑦ $h \times 3 = 3h$

⑧ $a - b = b - a$

⑨ $4n - n = 4$

⑩ $n \div 6 = 6 \div n$

⑪ $a \div 4 = \dfrac{a}{4}$

⑫ $\dfrac{6a}{2} = 3a$

⑬ $a \times a \times a = a^3$

⑭ $mn = nm$

⑮ $m \times m \times m = 3m$

⑯ $(a + b) \div n = \dfrac{a + b}{n}$

⑰ $\dfrac{5n}{n} = 5$

In questions ⑱ to ㉖, simplify each expression.

⑱ $4a \times 3b$

⑲ $7m \times 4n$

⑳ $5p \times 6q$

㉑ $5m \times 3n \times 2p$

㉒ $5a \times 7 \times 2b$

㉓ $n \times n$

㉔ $4n \times 4n$

㉕ $7p \times 3p$

㉖ $8a \times 2 \times 3a$

㉗ Here are some cards.

| 3n | n + 2 | n + n | n |

| n² | 2n ÷ 2 | n³ |

| n − 2 | 3n − n | 2 ÷ n | n × n |

(a) Which cards will always be the same as ?

(b) Which card will always be the same as $n \times n \times n$?

(c) Which card will always be the same as $\dfrac{2}{n}$?

(d) Draw a new card which will always be the same as $2n + 2n$.

㉘ Maurice has £$(3n + 2)$ and Jo has £$(5n + 7)$. How much more money does Jo have than Maurice?

㉙ Carol weighs $(3a + 1)$ kg and Lee weighs $(6a - 3)$ kg. By how much more does Lee weigh than Carol if Lee is heavier?

㉚ Write down a question which gives the answer $20mnp$.

Using letters for numbers

Find the expressions you are left with.

(a) Start with n, multiply by 5 and then add 8 $n \rightarrow 5n \rightarrow 5n + 8$

(b) Start with a, subtract b and then add 10 $a \rightarrow a - b \rightarrow a - b + 10$

(c) Start with p, add 3 and then multiply the result by 4 $p \rightarrow p + 3 \rightarrow 4(p + 3)$

(d) Start with m, subtract t and then square the result. $m \rightarrow m - t \rightarrow (m - t)^2$

Notice that *brackets* are needed in parts (c) and (d).

Exercise 3M

Write down the expression you get. If any of your answers contain brackets, do not remove them.

1   Start with n, multiply by 5 and then add x.

2   Start with n, add x and then multiply the result by 5

3   Start with h, multiply by 6 and then subtract t.

4   Start with h, subtract t and then multiply the result by 6

5   Start with b, add x and then multiply the result by 5

6   Start with b, multiply by a and then add x.

7   Start with y, square it and then multiply the result by 3

8   Start with n, multiply by d and then subtract 3

9   Start with a, double it and then add A.

10   Start with h, subtract H and then multiply the result by 5

11   Start with x, subtract 8 and then multiply the result by 5

12   Start with x, square it and then add 2

13   Start with y, double it and then subtract 3

14   Start with a, add 10 and then square the result.

15 Here is a flow diagram for the expression $2(3n + 7)$.

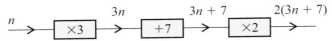

$n \rightarrow \boxed{\times 3} \xrightarrow{3n} \boxed{+7} \xrightarrow{3n + 7} \boxed{\times 2} \xrightarrow{2(3n + 7)}$

Find the expression for each of the following flow charts.

(a) $n \rightarrow \boxed{\times 2} \rightarrow \boxed{-4} \rightarrow \boxed{\times 5} \rightarrow$

(b) $n \rightarrow \boxed{\times 5} \rightarrow \boxed{+7} \rightarrow \boxed{\times 3} \rightarrow$

(c) $n \rightarrow \boxed{+2} \rightarrow \boxed{\times 5} \rightarrow \boxed{-3} \rightarrow$

(d) $n \rightarrow \boxed{\div 2} \rightarrow \boxed{+6} \rightarrow \boxed{\times 4} \rightarrow$

(e) $n \rightarrow \boxed{\text{square}} \rightarrow \boxed{+7} \rightarrow \boxed{\times 8} \rightarrow$

(f) $n \rightarrow \boxed{+3} \rightarrow \boxed{\text{square}} \rightarrow \boxed{\times 6} \rightarrow$

16 Draw the flow diagram for the following expressions.

(a) $2n + 7$

(b) $3(5n - 3)$

(c) $\dfrac{6n + 1}{5}$

(d) $n^2 - 3$

(e) $(n + 5)^2$

(f) $3(n^2 - 1)$

17 Ricky is bowling. There are 10 pins standing. On her first throw she knocks down m pins and on her second throw she knocks down n pins. How many pins are still standing?

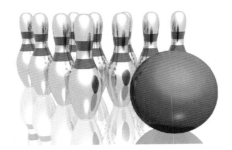

18 Terry has 90 pence. His father gives him another t pence and then he spends h pence. How much money does Terry now have?

19 Zara has £n. Her mother gives her the same amount of money again. Zara then spends £7 on a book and £2 on a magazine. How much money does Zara now have?

20 An orange costs 40p and a lemon costs 30p. Write down an expression for the total cost of n oranges and m lemons.

21 Faye used to earn £d per week. She then had a rise of £9 per week. How much will she now earn in 7 weeks?

22

Monday to Friday	£6 per hour
Saturday	£7 per hour
Sunday	£9 per hour

The rate of pay at Pollock's fish store is shown in this table.

(a) Ed works for n hours on Wednesday. How much does he earn?

(b) Beatrice works for p hours on Friday and q hours on Sunday. How much does she earn?

(c) Sam works for m hours on each day of the weekend. How much does he earn in total?

Exercise 4M

1 A small bag of peanuts contains y nuts and a large bag contains 5 times as many. If a boy buys a large bag and then eats 9 nuts, how many nuts are left in his bag?

2 A tile weighs t kg. How much do n tiles weigh?

3 Rowena has £m. She spends £9 then divides the remaining money equally between her 3 brothers. How much money does each brother get?

4 Phil has 3 bags of coins.
Each bag has n coins inside.

Write an expression to show the total number of coins in Phil's 3 bags after the following.

(a) Phil took 4 coins out of one bag.

(b) Phil took 1 coin out of *each* bag.

(c) Phil took 3 coins out of each of *two* of the bags and *none* out of the other bag.

(d) Phil took 5 coins out of one bag and 2 coins out of each of the other two bags.

5 Alex has a large number of cards. Altogether there are $4n + 12$ cards.

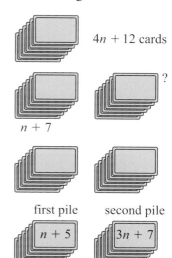

(a) Alex sorts the cards into two piles. One pile has $n + 7$ cards. Write an expression for the number of cards in the second pile.

(b) Now Alex takes all the cards and puts them into two equal piles. How many cards are in each pile?

(c) Finally Alex puts the cards into two piles as shown. There are 18 cards in the first pile. How many cards are in the second pile?

6 Adalee has $(2n + 9)$ socks in her top drawer and $(3n + 5)$ socks in her bottom drawer. She takes 3 socks out of her top drawer and puts them in the bottom drawer. How many socks does she have in total in the 2 drawers?

7. In number walls, each brick is made by adding the two bricks underneath it.

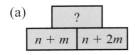

Draw the walls below and fill in the missing expressions.

(a)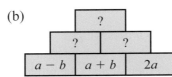

(b)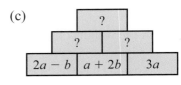

(c)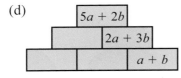

(d)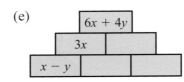

(e)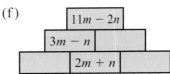

(f)

Need more practice with using algebra?

Simplify the following expressions as far as possible.

1. $5a + 3a + 4b$

2. $6m + 4n - 2n + 3m$

3. $7p + 2 - p$

4. $4n + 2m - 3n + 1$

5. $3y - y + 4x - x$

6. $8a + 1 - 3a + a$

7. $6m \times 3n$

8. $4a \times 3b \times 5c$

9. $9p \times 3p$

10. $8a \times a \times 3$

11. $\dfrac{9m}{m}$

12. $\dfrac{4a^2}{2}$

13. Connor buys 12 satsumas. He eats n satsumas on Friday, 2 satsumas on Saturday and m satsumas on Sunday. How many satsumas does he now have?

14. A football weighs x kg and a cricket bat weighs y kg. How much do 3 footballs and n cricket bats weigh in total?

15. Which expression below is the odd one out when the like terms have been collected?

| $4m + 3n - 1 - n$ | $2n + 5 + 4m - 6$ | $2m - 1 + 2n + 2m - n$ | $m + 5n + 3m - 3n - 1$ |

16. Milena says that $3a \times 8a$ is equal to $24aa$. Rufus says that the answer is $24a^2$. Who is correct?

17. Mrs Edgar has 3 boxes of Christmas decorations. The number of decorations in each box is shown on the front of the box. Write an expression to show the total number of decorations in all 3 boxes after each of the following.

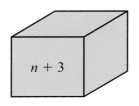

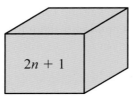

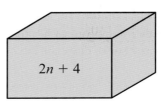

(a) *n* decorations are taken out of each box.

(b) 4 decorations are taken out of one box, 2 decorations are taken out of a second box and no decorations are taken out of the remaining box.

(c) 3 decorations are taken out of each box.

18 Sarah eats *n* chicken drumsticks. Her sister eats 3 times more drumsticks than Sarah. Her brother eats 2 drumsticks less than Sarah. How many drumsticks do they all eat in total?

19 *Explain clearly* why $\frac{n}{3}$ is not equal to $\frac{3}{n}$ (Hint: choose a value for *n*).

20 Which expressions below are the same as 4*n*?

| $n + 4$ | $5n - n$ | $n + n + n + n$ | $2 \times n \times 2$ | $8n \div 4$ |

21 What must be added to $3n - 4 + n + 4m$ to give $7n + 2m$?

22 What must be added to $2a + 8 + 3b + 3a - 1$ to give $7a + 2b + 3$?

Extension questions with using algebra

Investigation – Number squares

1 Draw your own addition square like the one shown here.

+	1	2	3	4	5	6	7	8	9
1	2	3	4	5	6	7	8	9	10
2	3	4	5	6	7	8	9	10	11
3	4	5	6	7	8	9	10	11	12
4	5	6	7	8	9	10	11	12	13
5	6	7	8	9	10	11	12	13	14
6	7	8	9	10	11	12	13	14	15
7	8	9	10	11	12	13	14	15	16
8	9	10	11	12	13	14	15	16	17
9	10	11	12	13	14	15	16	17	18

(2) Here are some 2 by 2 squares taken from the main square.

4	5
5	6

9	10
10	11

14	15
15	16

Add up the four numbers in each square. What do you notice?

(3) In this 2 by 2 square the smallest number is 8.
Draw the square and fill in the missing numbers.

8	?
?	?

(4) In another 2 by 2 square the *largest* number is 8. Draw the square and fill in the missing numbers.

(5) In a 2 by 2 square the four numbers add up to 44. Draw the square and fill in the numbers.

(6) Here is a 3 by 3 square taken from the main square.
Add up the nine numbers in the square.
What do you notice?

4	5	6
5	6	7
6	7	8

(7) Add up the four *corner* numbers in a 3 by 3 square. Copy and complete this sentence: 'In a 3 by 3 square, the sum of the four corner numbers is _____ times the middle number.'

(8) (a) Here is a 2 by 2 square.
The top left number is x.

The other three numbers are shown.

x	$x + 1$
$x + 1$	$x + 2$

(b) Draw the three squares shown and use x's to write down the other three numbers in each square.

(9) This is harder. Draw the square shown and use x's to fill in the other eight numbers.

(10) Draw this square and use x's to write down the other three *corner* numbers.

11 We do not always use *x*. What are the
four corner numbers in this square?

	N	

12 A large 'T' comprising five numbers can be drawn inside the number square.

1	2	3	4	5	6	7	8
9	10	11	12	13	14	15	16
17	18	19	20	21	22	23	24
25	26	27	28	29	30	31	32
33	34	35	36	37	38	39	40
41	42	43	44	45	46	47	48
49	50	51	52	53	54	55	56
57	58	59	60	61	62	63	64

The T can be moved around but it must stay upright. The 'T-number' is the number in the middle of the top row. In the example below, the T-number is T18

17	18	19		
	36			
	34			

(a) What is the smallest possible T-number?

(b) Work out the total of the numbers in T21

(c) Work out, as *quickly* as you can (Total of numbers in T37) – (Total of numbers in T36).

(d) Fill in the numbers for T75

	75	

(e) Use *x*'s to write the numbers for T*x*

	x	

✖ Spot the mistakes 1 ✖

Indices, prime factors, HCF, LCM and using algebra

Work through each question below and *explain clearly* what mistakes have been made.
Beware – some questions are correctly done.

1 Simplify $\dfrac{7^4 \times 7^3}{7^2}$

    Answer: $\dfrac{7^4 \times 7^3}{7^2} = \dfrac{7^{12}}{7^2} = 7^{12} \div 7^2 = 7^6$

2 Simplify $8a + 3b - a + 2b + 3a + 4$

    Answer: $11a + 5b + 4$

3 Express 858 as a product of its prime factors.

    Answer:

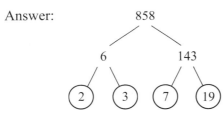

    $858 = 2 \times 3 \times 7 \times 19$

4 A circus act lasts for n minutes.
The act performs once each day
on Mondays to Fridays but twice
daily on Saturdays and Sundays.
Write down an expression for
the total number of minutes
performed by the act during one
complete week.

    Answer: 9 performances each week
              lasting n minutes, so total
              number of minutes $= 9n$.

5 Simplify $6m \times 3n \times 3p$

    Answer: $12mnp$

6 List all the factors of 48

    Answer: Factor pairs are $1 \times 48, 2 \times 24, 4 \times 12, 6 \times 8$
              so the factors of 48 are 1, 2, 4, 6, 8, 12, 24 and 48

7 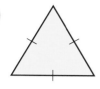 The equilateral triangle has the same perimeter as this rectangle.

Write down an expression for the length of each side of the triangle.

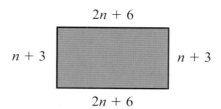

Answer: Perimeter of rectangle $= 2n + 6 + n + 3 + 2n + 6 + n + 3$
$= 6n + 18$

All three sides of the triangle are equal.

$6n \div 3 = 2n$ $18 \div 3 = 6$

Each side is $2n + 6$

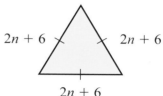

8 Work out the value of n if $5^n \times 5^4 = 5^8$

Answer: $n = 2$ because $2 \times 4 = 8$

9 The prime factors of 1050 and 375 are shown in the Venn diagram.
Work out the LCM of 1050 and 375

Answer: LCM $= 3 \times 5 \times 5 = 75$

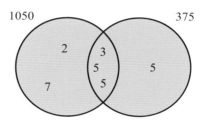

10 Misha has n sweets. Kate has twice as many sweets as Misha. Kate gives 5 sweets to her brother. Kate then eats 2 sweets. Write down an expression for how many sweets Kate now has.

Answer: Kate starts with $2n$ sweets. She gives 5 sweets to her brother, so now has $(2n - 5)$ sweets. Kate now eats 2 sweets, so has $(2n - 5 - 2)$ sweets. She has $(2n - 3)$ sweets.

CHECK YOURSELF ON SECTIONS 1.1, 1.2 and 1.3

1   Using cube numbers and higher powers

(a) Write down the value of 3^4

(b) Which is larger: 10^2 or 5^3?

2   Multiplying and dividing indices

Work out and write each answer as a number in index form.

(a) $7^8 \div 7^3$

(b) $5^2 \times 5 \times 5^6$

(c) $\dfrac{3^4 \times 3^5}{3^2 \times 3^3}$

3   Prime numbers, factors and multiples

(a) Write down all the factors of 28

(b) Add together all the prime numbers between 10 and 20

(c) Write down the first six multiples of 15

4   Expressing a number as the product of its prime factors

Complete the factor trees and write each number as the product of its prime factors.

(a)

(b)

5   Using Venn diagrams to find HCFs and LCMs

(a) The prime factors for 140 and 154 are shown in the Venn diagram opposite. Work out the HCF and LCM of 140 and 154

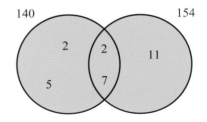

(b) Work out the HCF and LCM of 210 and 189

6   Simplifying algebraic expressions

Simplify

(a) $5m + 3n - 3m + 4$

(b) $3x - 2x + 4y - y$

(c) $7m \times 6n$

(d) $6 + 3p + 2p - 10$

(e) $4n \times 4n$

(f) $\dfrac{12m}{3}$

(g) Find the matching pair.

A $\boxed{2m + 3n - m}$ B $\boxed{2n - m + n}$ C $\boxed{n + m + n + n}$

(h) $m - 5 = 5 - m$. True or false?

7   Using letters for numbers

(a) Max earns £m each week. How much does he earn in p weeks?

(b) Janice is three times older than Alf. Mary is five years younger than Janice. How old is Mary if Alf is n years old?

(c) Ralph is 'bulking' up at the gym. Each week he puts on q kilograms. If he weighs 70 kg at the start of February, how much will he weigh four weeks later?

(d) David has $(6n + 18)$ DVDs.
   Rosie has $(2n + 5)$ DVDs.
   David gives Rosie half of his DVDs.
   Write an expression for the number of DVDs Rosie now has.

1.4 Construction and locus

In section 1.4 you will:

- review constructing triangles with a ruler, protractor and compasses
- learn to draw and describe the locus of a point
- draw constructions with a ruler and compasses only

Constructing triangles

Using a ruler, protractor and compasses you can construct the triangles below.

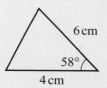
Two sides and the included angle are given.

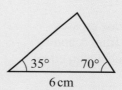
Two angles and a side are given.

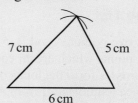
Three sides are given.

Exercise 1M

Construct each shape and measure the side or angle x.

1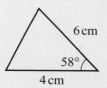

2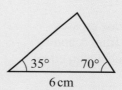

3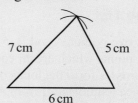

4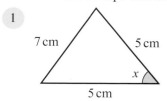

5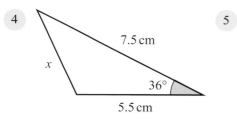

6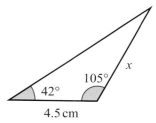

30

7 Construct this shape and
   measure the angle *x*.

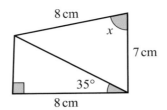

8 cm

x

7 cm

35°

8 cm

Locus

The *locus* of a point is the path traced out by the point as it moves.

(a) An athlete runs around a track.
    The locus looks like this:

(b) Alan throws a ball to Ben.

    The locus is the curve

Exercise 1E

1 Mark two points, A and B, 5 cm apart. Draw crosses
   at six points which are an equal distance from A and B.
   The crosses form the locus of points which are an equal
   distance [equidistant] from A and B.

   •   •
   A   B

2 Mark a point C with a dot. Draw crosses at ten points which are all 5 cm from C. The crosses
   form the locus of points which are 5 cm from C. Join up the crosses with a pair of compasses.
   Describe the locus.

3 With a dot, mark the bottom right corner of the page you are on. Draw crosses at six points
   which are the same distance from the two edges of the page.
   Describe the locus of the crosses you have drawn.

4

   (a) Describe the locus of the tip of the minute hand as the time
       goes from 10:10 to 11:10

   (b) Describe the locus of the tip of the *hour* hand as the time goes
       from 2 o'clock to 8 o'clock.

5 On a clock, the time goes from 9:00 to 9:05. Describe the locus of the tip of the *seconds* hand.

6 Mark a point O with a dot. Imagine that a tiny insect can wander around on your page up to
   2 cm from O. Draw the locus of points where the insect could be.

7 Draw a straight line, AB, 5 cm long. Imagine that a tiny insect can crawl so that it is always 2 cm from the straight line. Draw the locus of points where the insect could crawl.

8

   The corner A of a house is shown. A trench is to be dug so that it is always 2 metres from the corner A. Describe or sketch what the trench would look like from above.

9 Here is a spiral shape. Write simple instructions describing how to draw the spiral so that another person would be able to draw it.

10 Work with a partner.

   (a) Each draw a fairly simple shape without showing it to your partner. Now write instructions so that your partner can draw the shape.

   (b) Each follow the written instructions to draw your partner's shape.

Standard constructions (using compasses)

Constructing the perpendicular bisector of a line segment AB

With centres A and B, draw two arcs.

The perpendicular bisector is shown as a broken line.

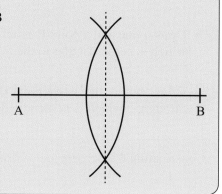

Exercise 2M

In this Exercise, construct using only a pencil, a straight edge, a protractor and a pair of compasses.

1 Draw a horizontal line AB of length 6 cm. Construct the perpendicular bisector of AB.

2 Draw a vertical line CD of length 8 cm. Construct the perpendicular bisector of CD.

3 (a) Use a protractor and ruler to draw the right-angled triangle ABC, as shown. For greater accuracy, draw lines slightly longer than 8 cm and 6 cm and *then* mark the points A, B and C.

(b) *Construct* the perpendicular bisector of AB.

(c) Construct the perpendicular bisector of AC.

(d) If done accurately, your two lines from (b) and (c) should cross exactly on the line BC.

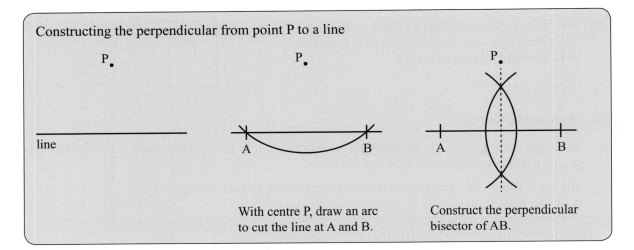

Constructing the perpendicular from point P to a line

With centre P, draw an arc to cut the line at A and B.

Construct the perpendicular bisector of AB.

4 Draw a line and a point P about 4 cm from the line. Construct the line which passes through P which is perpendicular to the line.

5 Draw another line and a point Q about 3 cm from the line. Construct the line which passes through Q which is perpendicular to the line.

Constructing the perpendicular from point P on a line

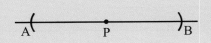

With centre P, draw arcs to cut the line at A and B.
Now bisect AB.

6 Draw a line and a point R on the line. Construct the perpendicular from the point R.

7 Draw another line and a point S on the line. Construct the perpendicular from the point S.

Exercise 3M

Constructing the bisector of an angle

With centre A, draw arc PQ.

With centres at P and Q, draw two more arcs.

The angle bisector is then drawn.

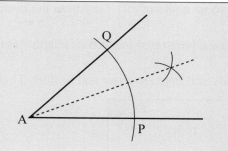

1   Draw an angle of about 50°. Construct the bisector of the angle.

2   Draw an angle of about 120°. Construct the bisector of the angle.

3   Draw an angle of about 70°. Construct the bisector of the angle.

4   Draw any triangle PQR and construct the bisectors of
    angles P and Q to meet at point X.

    With centre at X, draw a circle which just touches the sides
    of the triangle, as shown.

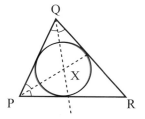

5   Draw a completely different triangle and repeat question 4 .

6   Use a ruler and compasses only to construct an angle of 45°

7   (a) Construct an equilateral triangle with each side 6 cm.
        This has produced a 60° angle.

    (b) Using a ruler and compasses only, construct an angle of 30°

Need more practice with construction and locus?

1   Construct each shape and measure the side or angle x.

(a)

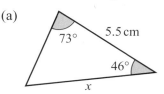

(b)

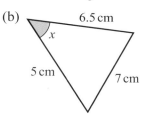

(c)

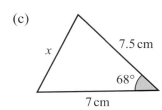

2 Draw the locus of all the points which are 4 cm away from a fixed point P.

3 Draw an angle of 80°. Construct the bisector of the angle.

4 Draw a horizontal line AB of length 7 cm. Construct the perpendicular bisector of AB.

5 Sally and Pete are sister and brother. There are two bedrooms in their house, as shown below.

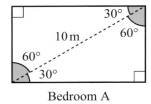

Bedroom A

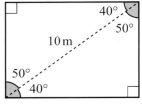

Bedroom B

They each want the bedroom with the larger area. Like all brothers and sisters they agree in a very friendly manner by tossing a coin. Sally wins. Which bedroom does she choose? (You need to construct each bedroom using a scale of 1 cm to 1 m then work out each area with a calculator.) How much larger is the area of Sally's bedroom compared with Pete's bedroom?

6 Mark two points, P and Q, 6 cm apart. Draw the locus of points which are an equal distance from P and Q.

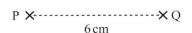

7 (a) Draw a 'faint' equilateral triangle with each side 8 cm.

(b) Use the diagram from part (a) to draw the triangle shown opposite.

(Hint: bisect one of the angles in the equilateral triangle.)

(c) Measure the length h.

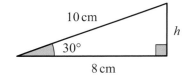

Extension questions with construction and locus

1 (a) Use a ruler and compasses only to construct triangle ABC as shown.

(b) Construct the perpendicular bisector of AC.

(c) Construct the bisector of angle A.

(d) Let the two bisectors meet at point X. Measure the length AX.

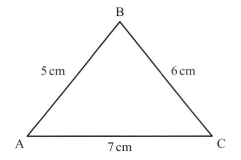

2 Draw a line and a point P about 5 cm from the line.
   Construct the line that passes through P which is
   perpendicular to the line.

P.

_____

3 Construct the shape
   opposite and measure *x*.

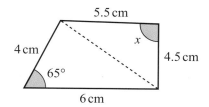

4 Draw a 6 cm line, AB. Draw the locus of all points which are 2 cm from the line AB.

5 A bicycle moves forward on level ground in a straight line.
   Sketch the locus of the valve on one of the wheels.

6 Draw *any* triangle KLM and construct
   (a) the perpendicular bisector of KM
   (b) the perpendicular bisector of KL.
   Mark the point of intersection X.

   Take a pair of compasses and, with centre
   at X and radius KX, draw a circle through
   the points K, L and M.
   This is the *circumcircle* of triangle KLM.
   Repeat the construction for another triangle of different shape.

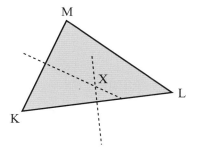

1.5 Angles

In section 1.5 you will:

- review calculating angles with parallel lines
- prove angle rules
- calculate angles in a quadrilateral
- solve mixed angle problems

Angle facts reminder

On a straight line

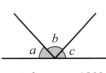

$a + b + c = 180°$

In a triangle

$a + b + c = 180°$

At a point

$m + n + p = 360°$

Angles and parallel lines

In this diagram, all the arrow lines are parallel.

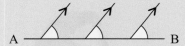

The arrows all make the same angle with the line AB. These angles are called **corresponding** angles.

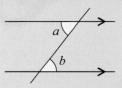

angle a = angle b
These are called **alternate** angles.

Many people think of corresponding angles as 'F' angles.

Many people think of alternate angles as 'Z' angles.

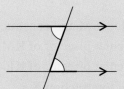

Find the angles marked with letters.

(a)

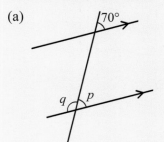

$p = 70°$ (corresponding angles)
$q = 110°$ (angles on a straight line)

(b)

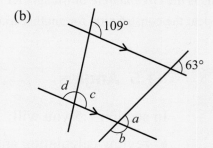

$a = 63°$ (corresponding angles)
$b = 117°$ (angles on a straight line)
$c = 109°$ (corresponding angles)
$d = 71°$ (angles on a straight line)

Exercise 1M

Find the angles marked with letters.

1
37°
a
65°

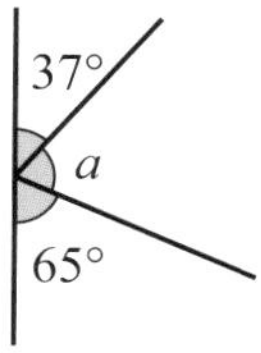

2
49°
75° b

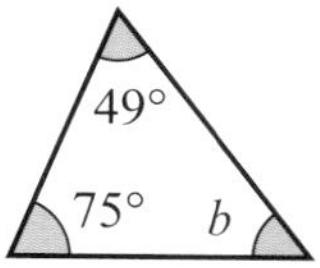

3
53°
c
d
e

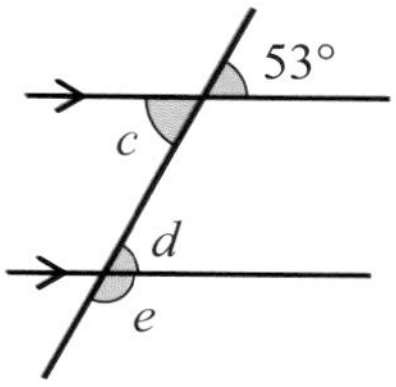

4
64° f
h g

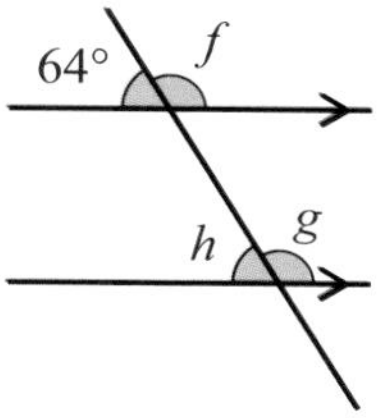

5
125°
i
j k

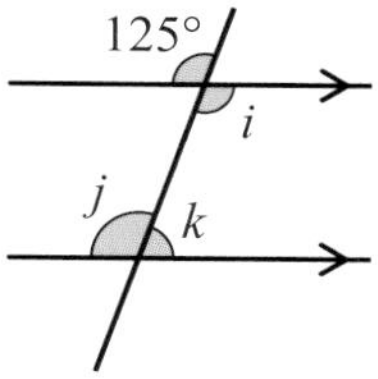

6
84°
139° l

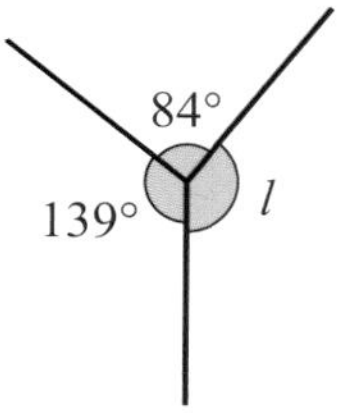

7
n
m 126°

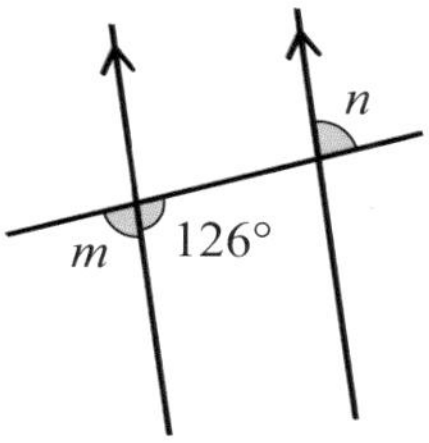

8
74° q 45°
p r

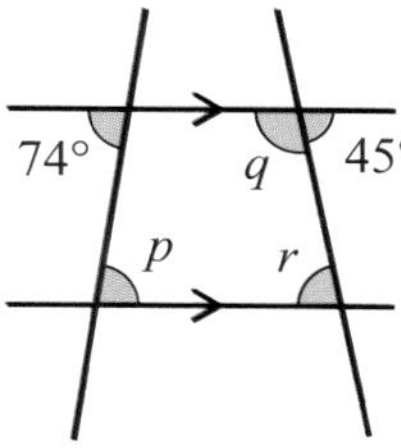

9
135°
s t
u 37°

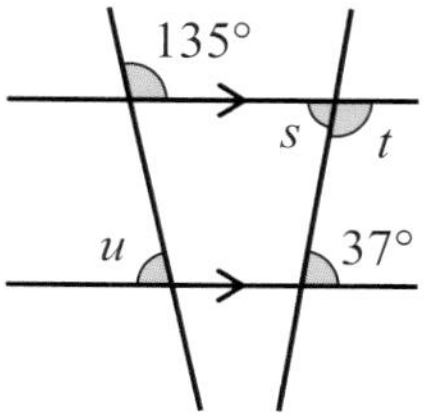

10
w
69° v
x
y
102°

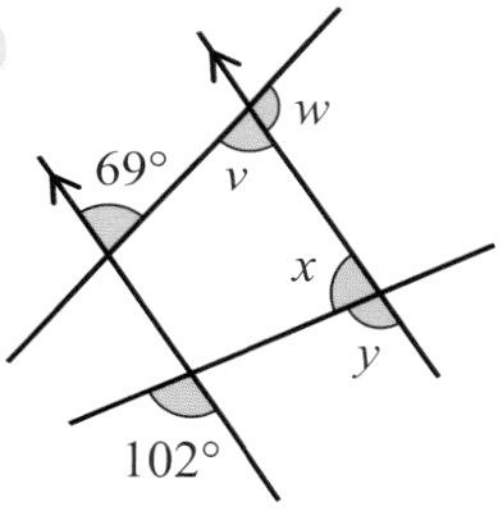

11
44° a
110°

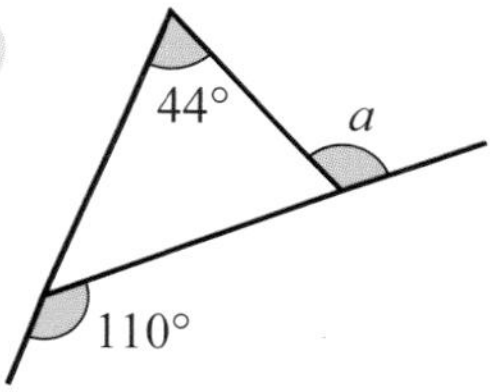

12
b
38°
c

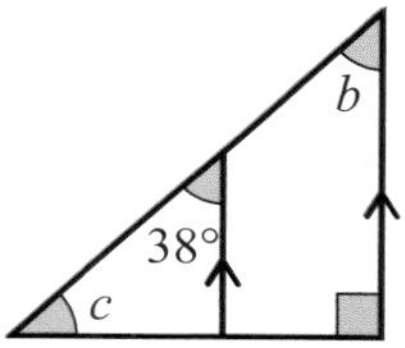

13
48°
e
70° f d

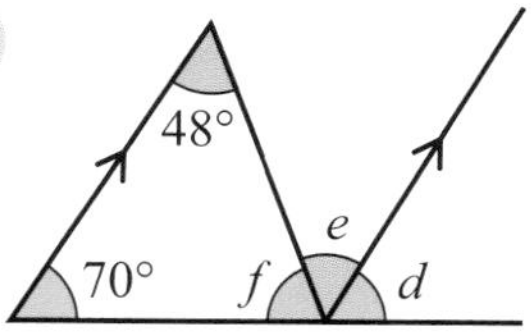

14
28° 65°
g h
i

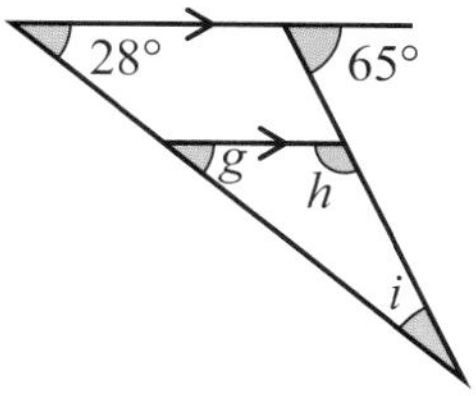

15
69° j

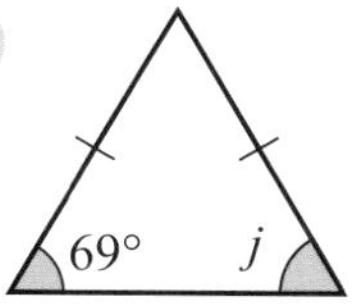

16
70° m k
l
32°

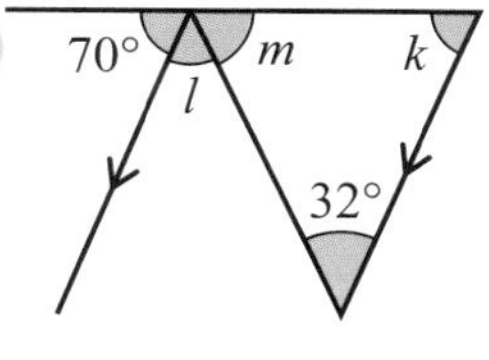

17

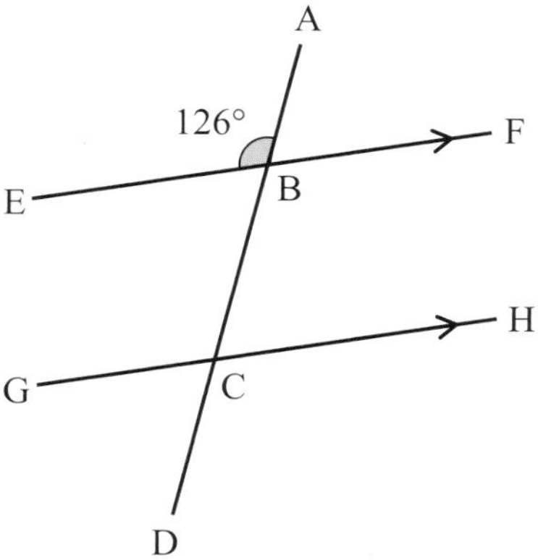

A
126°
E ——— B ——→ F
G ——— C ——→ H
D

Work out the value of DĈH by completing
the answer below.

CB̂F = 126°

(vertically o _ _ _ _ _ _ _ angles are equal)

DĈH = 126°

(c _ _ _ _ _ _ _ _ _ _ _ _ angles are equal)

18 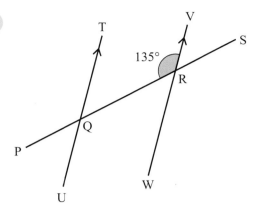 Work out the value of PQ̂U, giving reasons as shown in question 17 .

19 Work out the value of BÂC, giving full reasons for your answer.

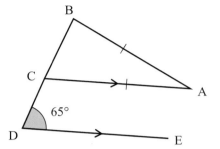

Proving angle rules

We need to prove that angle rules are true for every possible shape. We often prove one simple result and then use that result to prove further results (and so on).

Example:

When straight lines intersect, opposite angles are equal.

By definition, the angle on one whole turn is 360°

$$a + b + a + b = 360°$$

so

$$a + b = 180°$$

This proves that the sum of the angles on a straight line is 180°

Exercise 1E

1 Copy and complete this proof for the sum of the angles in a triangle.

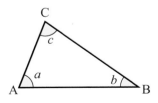 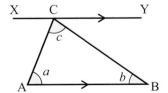 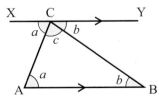

Here is △ABC.

Draw line XCY parallel to AB.

AB̂C = YĈB (alternate angles)

BÂC = ☐ (alternate angles)

$a + b + c = $ ☐ (angles on a straight line)

angles in a triangle: $a + b + c = 180°$

2 Copy and complete this proof for the sum of the angles in a quadrilateral.

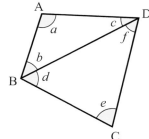

Draw any quadrilateral ABCD with diagonal BD.

Now $a + b + c = \boxed{}$ (angles in a $\triangle$)

and $d + e + f = \boxed{}$ (angles in a $\triangle$)

$\therefore a + b + c + d + e + f = \boxed{}$

This shows that the sum of the angles in a quadrilateral is 360°

3 To prove that the exterior angle of a triangle is equal to the sum of the two interior opposite angles.

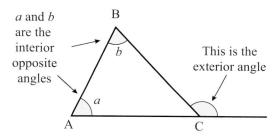

a and b are the interior opposite angles

This is the exterior angle

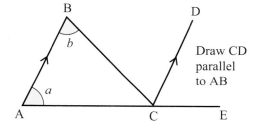

Draw CD parallel to AB

Copy and complete the proof.

$\hat{BAC} = \hat{DCE}$ (corresponding angles) ('F' angles)

$\hat{ABC} = \boxed{}$ (alternate angles) ('Z' angles)

$\therefore \boxed{} = \boxed{} + \boxed{}$

4 Explain why opposite angles of a parallelogram are equal.
[Use alternate and corresponding angles.]

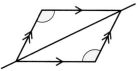

Angles in a quadrilateral

Question ② in the previous Exercise 1E proved that:

The angles in a quadrilateral add up to 360°

This is illustrated below:

Draw a quadrilateral of any shape on a piece of paper or card and cut it out.
Mark the four angles a, b, c and d and tear them off.

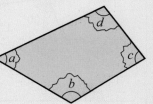

Arrange the four angles about a point.

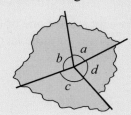

40

Exercise 2M

Find the angles marked with letters.

1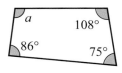

2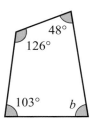

3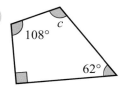

4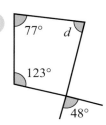

5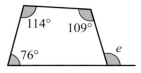

6

7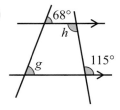

8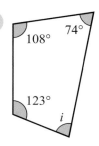

9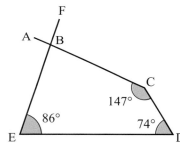

Work out the value of $A\widehat{B}F$ by copying and completing the answer below.

$E\widehat{B}C =$ ☐

(angles in a q _ _ _ _ _ _ _ _ _ _ _ _ add up to 360°)

$A\widehat{B}F =$ ☐

(vertically o _ _ _ _ _ _ _ angles are equal)

10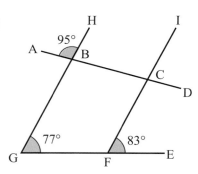

Work out the value of $B\widehat{C}F$, giving reasons as shown in question 9 .

11 Explain why at least one of the angles shown opposite must be incorrect.

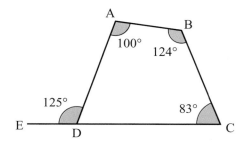

12 Work out the values of *x* and *y*.

(a)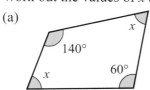

(b)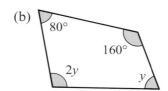

Mixed questions

Exercise 3M

1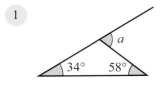

2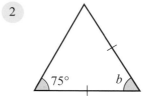

3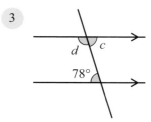

4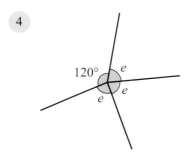

5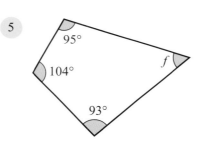

6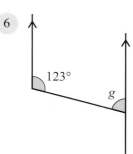

7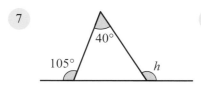

8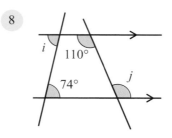

9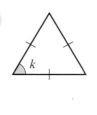

10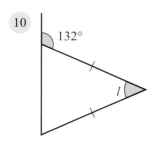

11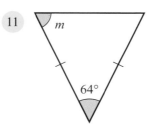

12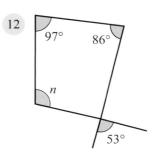

42

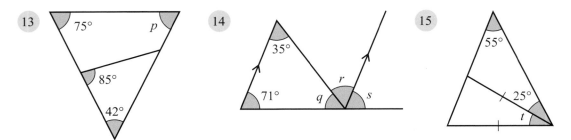

13 75° p 85° 42°

14 35° 71° q r s

15 55° 25° t

16

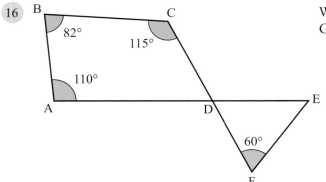

Work out the value of DÊF.
Give full reasons for your answer.

17

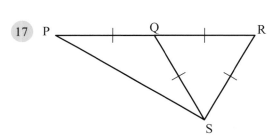

Give full reasons for
why PŜQ = 30°

Need more practice with angles?

Find the angles marked with letters.

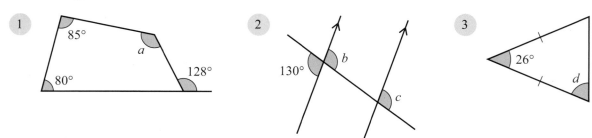

1 85° a 80° 128°

2 130° b c

3 26° d

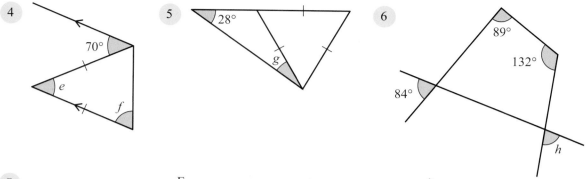

4

70°

e

f

5

28°

g

6

89°

132°

84°

h

7

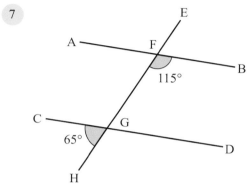

Work out the value of CĜF then *explain clearly* why we know that lines AB and CD are parallel.

8

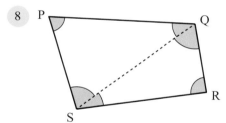

Use this diagram to explain why we know that the angles in a quadrilateral add up to 360°

9 Work out the value of AD̂C in the diagram opposite. Give full reasons for your answer.

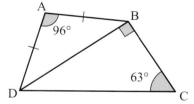

10 Prove that triangle PST is isosceles. *Explain clearly* each stage of your working out.

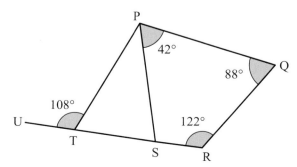

Extension questions with angles

Find the angles marked with letters.

1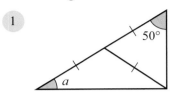

2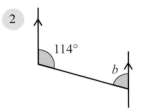

3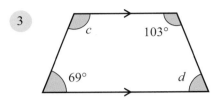

4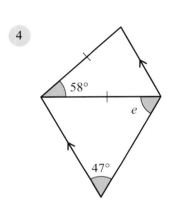

5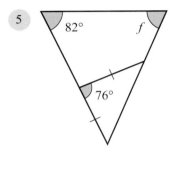

6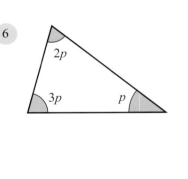

7   One of the angles in an isosceles triangle is 30°. Heather says that the other two angles must be 30° and 120°. Dai thinks that this may not be true. *Explain clearly* why Dai might think this.

8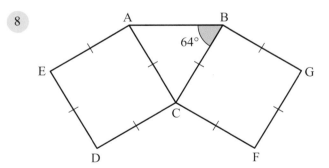

Triangle ABC has two identical squares attached to it, as shown.
Work out the value of DĈF.

9   Work out the value of CB̂E.
Give full reasons for your answer.

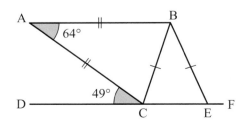

10 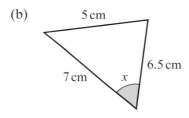 PQ̂R is twice the size of QP̂R.

Work out the value of QP̂R.

CHECK YOURSELF ON SECTIONS 1.4 and 1.5

1   Constructing triangles with a ruler, protractor and compasses

Construct each shape and measure the side or angle x.

(a)

x 7 cm   44°   5.5 cm

(b)

5 cm   6.5 cm   7 cm x

2   Drawing and describing the locus of a point

(a) Draw a point and label it P.
Draw the locus of all points which are 4 cm from P.

(b) Draw a 6 cm line and label it AB.
Draw crosses at six points which are 2 cm from the line AB.
Draw the whole locus of points which are 2 cm from the line AB.

3   Drawing constructions with a ruler and compasses only

(a) Draw a vertical line of length 7 cm. Construct the perpendicular bisector of this line.

(b) Use a protractor to draw an angle of 80°. Construct the bisector of this angle.

4   Calculating angles with parallel lines

Find the angles marked with letters.

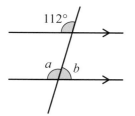

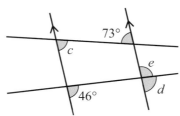

5 Proving angle rules

Use this diagram to prove that the angles
in a triangle add up to 180°

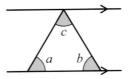

6 Calculating angles in a quadrilateral

Find the angles marked with letters.

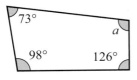

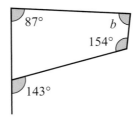

7 Solving mixed angle problems

Find the angles marked with letters.

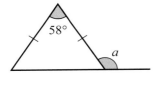

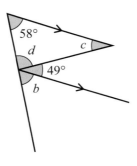

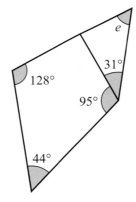

1.6 Fractions

In section 1.6 you will:

- convert improper fractions and mixed numbers
- add and subtract fractions (including mixed numbers)
- multiply and divide fractions (including mixed numbers)

Proper and improper fractions

proper fraction ⬇

numerator is less than denominator.

examples: $\frac{3}{7}$, $\frac{17}{59}$

improper fraction ⬇

numerator is larger than denominator.

examples: $\frac{4}{3}$, $\frac{17}{5}$

mixed number ⬇

contains both a whole number and a fraction.

examples: $4\frac{1}{2}$, $7\frac{3}{4}$

(often called 'top-heavy' fractions)

(a) Change $\frac{11}{4}$ to a mixed number.

Divide numerator by denominator. $11 \div 4 = 2$ rem. 3

Put remainder over denominator. $\frac{11}{4} = 2\frac{3}{4}$

(b) Change $3\frac{4}{7}$ to an improper fraction.

Multiply whole number by denominator. $3 \times 7 = 21$

Add the numerator. $21 + 4 = 25$

Put sum over denominator. $3\frac{4}{7} = \frac{25}{7}$

$+$

Exercise 1M

Change the following improper fractions to mixed numbers or whole numbers only.

1      $\frac{7}{2}$ 2 $\frac{8}{3}$

3   $\frac{5}{4}$ 4 $\frac{13}{7}$ 5 $\frac{28}{7}$ 6 $\frac{12}{5}$ 7 $\frac{22}{7}$ 8 $\frac{73}{10}$

9   How many halves are there in $6\frac{1}{2}$?

10   How many quarters are there in $7\frac{3}{4}$?

11   Write the purple areas as both mixed numbers and improper fractions.

(a)

(b)

(c)

(d)

48

In questions 12 to 21 , change the mixed numbers to improper fractions.

12 $2\frac{1}{3}$ 13 $5\frac{2}{3}$ 14 $6\frac{3}{4}$ 15 $4\frac{2}{5}$ 16 $7\frac{1}{8}$

17 $4\frac{3}{7}$ 18 $2\frac{4}{5}$ 19 $4\frac{7}{9}$ 20 $5\frac{3}{8}$ 21 $7\frac{4}{9}$

22 John has painted $\frac{91}{8}$ Warhammer warriors. Kat has painted $11\frac{5}{8}$ Warhammer warriors. Who has painted the larger amount?

23 Which fraction in this grid is *not* written as both an improper fraction and a mixed number?

$\frac{45}{7}$	$\frac{41}{7}$	$6\frac{6}{7}$
$5\frac{6}{7}$	$6\frac{3}{7}$	$\frac{43}{7}$
$\frac{37}{7}$	$\frac{48}{7}$	$5\frac{2}{7}$

Adding and subtracting fractions – reminder

Remember: $\frac{6}{9} = \frac{2}{3}$ $\frac{10}{15} = \frac{2}{3}$ We say that $\frac{2}{3}$, $\frac{6}{9}$ and $\frac{10}{15}$ are *equivalent fractions*.

Fractions can be added or subtracted when they have the same denominator.
$\frac{1}{7} + \frac{3}{7} = \frac{4}{7}$ Only add the numerators, *not* the denominators.

If fractions do not have the same denominator, change them into *equivalent fractions* that do have the same denominator, then add or subtract.

(a) $\frac{1}{12} + \frac{1}{4}$

$= \frac{1}{12} + \frac{3}{12}$

$= \frac{4}{12} = \frac{1}{3}$

(b) $\frac{9}{10} - \frac{3}{5}$

$= \frac{9}{10} - \frac{6}{10}$

$= \frac{3}{10}$

(c) $\frac{1}{3} + \frac{2}{5}$

$= \frac{5}{15} + \frac{6}{15}$

$= \frac{11}{15}$

Cancel the final answer if you can

Exercise 2M

1. Find the missing number to make these fractions equivalent.

   (a) $\dfrac{3}{8} = \dfrac{\square}{16}$

   (b) $\dfrac{1}{4} = \dfrac{\square}{20}$

   (c) $\dfrac{20}{48} = \dfrac{\square}{12}$

   (d) $\dfrac{6}{15} = \dfrac{\square}{5}$

   (e) $\dfrac{5}{9} = \dfrac{\square}{45}$

   (f) $\dfrac{5}{7} = \dfrac{\square}{42}$

   (g) $\dfrac{3}{11} = \dfrac{\square}{44}$

   (h) $\dfrac{18}{21} = \dfrac{\square}{7}$

2. Write four fractions equivalent to $\dfrac{2}{5}$

3. Cancel down each fraction to its simplest terms.

   (a) $\dfrac{7}{21}$

   (b) $\dfrac{6}{24}$

   (c) $\dfrac{18}{45}$

   (d) $\dfrac{40}{64}$

   (e) $\dfrac{24}{42}$

   (f) $\dfrac{60}{144}$

   (g) $\dfrac{20}{1000}$

   (h) $\dfrac{34}{40}$

   (i) $\dfrac{33}{121}$

   (j) $\dfrac{30}{75}$

4. Work out

   (a) $\dfrac{1}{4} + \dfrac{1}{3}$

   (b) $\dfrac{1}{2} + \dfrac{2}{5}$

   (c) $\dfrac{1}{3} + \dfrac{2}{5}$

   (d) $\dfrac{3}{4} + \dfrac{1}{5}$

   (e) $\dfrac{1}{5} - \dfrac{1}{6}$

   (f) $\dfrac{2}{3} - \dfrac{1}{4}$

   (g) $\dfrac{7}{12} - \dfrac{1}{8}$

   (h) $\dfrac{1}{2} - \dfrac{2}{11}$

   (i) $\dfrac{2}{5} + \dfrac{1}{6}$

   (j) $\dfrac{5}{6} - \dfrac{3}{4}$

   (k) $\dfrac{7}{8} - \dfrac{3}{5}$

   (l) $\dfrac{2}{7} + \dfrac{2}{5}$

5. Troy watches $\dfrac{3}{5}$ of a film then makes a cup of tea. He then watches another $\dfrac{1}{4}$ of the film. What total fraction of the film has he now watched?

6. In an election, everyone voted for A, B or C. If A got $\dfrac{1}{4}$ of the votes and B got $\dfrac{3}{8}$ of the votes, what fraction of the votes did C get?

7.  Trevor blows his trumpet for $\dfrac{1}{6}$ of the day and plays the drums for $\dfrac{3}{8}$ of the day. What fraction of the day does Trevor spend playing a musical instrument?

8. Davina reads $\dfrac{3}{8}$ of her book one day and $\dfrac{2}{5}$ the next day. What fraction of her book does she still have to read?

9 Work out the perimeter of the triangle.

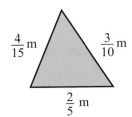

$\frac{4}{15}$ m $\frac{3}{10}$ m

$\frac{2}{5}$ m

10 Rebecca and Chris went on a short expedition. They were given equal rations of food. The chart shows what fraction of their food they ate each day. Who had the larger fraction of food left for Thursday and by how much?

	Rebecca	Chris
Monday	$\frac{1}{10}$	$\frac{1}{6}$
Tuesday	$\frac{1}{3}$	$\frac{1}{2}$
Wednesday	$\frac{2}{5}$	$\frac{1}{5}$
Thursday	?	?

Adding and subtracting mixed numbers

Change mixed numbers into improper fractions first.

$$1\frac{1}{4} + 2\frac{2}{3} = \frac{5}{4} + \frac{8}{3} = \frac{15}{12} + \frac{32}{12} = \frac{47}{12}$$

$$= 3\frac{11}{12} \quad \text{change to a mixed number at the end}$$

Exercise 3M

1 Copy and complete these calculations.

(a) $1\frac{1}{4} + 1\frac{2}{3}$

$$= \frac{5}{4} + \frac{5}{3}$$

$$= \frac{\square}{12} + \frac{\square}{12}$$

$$= \frac{\square}{12}$$

$$= 2\frac{\square}{12}$$

(b) $2\frac{3}{5} + 1\frac{1}{2}$

$$= \frac{\square}{5} + \frac{\square}{2}$$

$$= \frac{\square}{10} + \frac{\square}{10}$$

$$= \frac{\square}{10}$$

$$= \square\frac{\square}{10}$$

(c) $3\frac{1}{3} - 1\frac{3}{4}$

$$= \frac{\square}{3} - \frac{\square}{4}$$

$$= \frac{\square}{12} - \frac{\square}{12}$$

$$= \frac{\square}{12}$$

$$= \square\frac{\square}{12}$$

2 Work out, leaving each answer as a mixed number.

(a) $1\frac{2}{5} + 2\frac{1}{3}$

(b) $2\frac{1}{2} + 2\frac{5}{8}$

(c) $1\frac{1}{3} + 2\frac{1}{4}$

(d) $3\frac{1}{2} - 1\frac{5}{6}$

(e) $4\frac{5}{6} - 2\frac{1}{2}$

(f) $3\frac{3}{4} - 1\frac{7}{8}$

3 Find the perimeter of this rectangle.

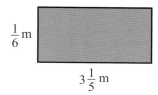

$\frac{1}{6}$ m

$3\frac{1}{5}$ m

4 A brother and sister are given $2\frac{1}{2}$ pizzas to eat. The brother dives in first and eats $1\frac{2}{5}$ pizzas. How many pizzas are left for his sister?

5 Work out

(a) $2\frac{3}{5} + 1\frac{3}{4}$

(b) $3\frac{1}{6} - 1\frac{3}{8}$

(c) $4\frac{1}{2} - 2\frac{4}{5}$

(d) $2\frac{5}{8} + 1\frac{3}{10}$

(e) $3\frac{1}{4} - 1\frac{7}{10}$

(f) $4\frac{3}{5} - 2\frac{7}{8}$

6 Caroline travels $4\frac{2}{5}$ km and Gabriel travels $2\frac{3}{4}$ km. How much further does Caroline travel than Gabriel?

7 $3\frac{5}{6} + \square = 5\frac{1}{2}$ What is the missing number?

Multiplying fractions

The pink shaded strip is $\frac{1}{5}$ of the rectangle

The black section is $\frac{1}{4}$ of $\frac{1}{5}$ of the rectangle

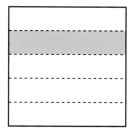

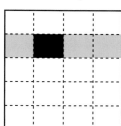

The rectangle on the right is divided into 20 equal parts, so the black section is $\frac{1}{20}$ of the rectangle.

So $\frac{1}{4}$ of $\frac{1}{5}$ of the rectangle $= \frac{1}{20}$ of the rectangle.

Notice that $\frac{1}{4} \times \frac{1}{5} = \frac{1}{20}$

The word 'of' can be replaced by a multiplication symbol.

Look at these multiplications

(a) $\frac{2}{3} \times \frac{1}{5} = \frac{2}{15}$

(b) $\frac{3}{7} \times \frac{1}{4} = \frac{3}{28}$

(c) $\frac{3}{4} \times \frac{1}{6} = \frac{3^1}{24_8} = \frac{1}{8}$

(d) $\frac{6}{7} \times \frac{2}{3} = \frac{12^4}{21_7} = \frac{4}{7}$

Multiply the numerators, multiply the denominators and then cancel down.

Exercise 4M

1. Work out each question below. Remember to cancel down the answers if possible.

   (a) $\frac{2}{5} \times \frac{3}{5}$ (b) $\frac{3}{7} \times \frac{1}{4}$ (c) $\frac{3}{8} \times \frac{2}{5}$ (d) $\frac{3}{4} \times \frac{1}{6}$

   (e) $\frac{5}{8} \times \frac{1}{2}$ (f) $\frac{5}{6} \times \frac{3}{4}$ (g) $\frac{2}{7} \times \frac{3}{4}$ (h) $\frac{1}{8} \times \frac{3}{5}$

   (i) $\frac{2}{9} \times \frac{3}{5}$ (j) $\frac{3}{11} \times \frac{1}{2}$ (k) $\frac{4}{9} \times \frac{3}{4}$ (l) $\frac{5}{12} \times \frac{8}{10}$

2. The diagram shows a square of side 1 m divided into four rectangles A, B, C and D.
   Find the areas of A, B, C and D in m².

   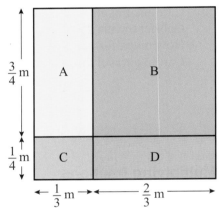

3. Work out each question below. Remember: 4 is the same as $\frac{4}{1}$
   Use cancelling.

   (a) $\frac{2}{3} \times \frac{6}{1}$ (b) $\frac{2}{5} \times \frac{20}{1}$ (c) $\frac{1}{8} \times \frac{10}{1}$ (d) $\frac{3}{7} \times 14$

   (e) $\frac{7}{10} \times 5$ (f) $\frac{5}{6} \times 4$ (g) $\frac{1}{20} \times 15$ (h) $\frac{3}{4} \times 6$

4. The petrol tank of a car holds 60 litres.
   How much petrol is in the tank when it is $\frac{4}{5}$ full?

5. Justin works 54 hours a week and he spends $\frac{5}{6}$ of his time on the phone. How many hours is that?

6 Work out

(a) $\frac{5}{9}$ of 27

(b) $\frac{5}{6}$ of 204

(c) $\frac{8}{9}$ of 108

(d) $\frac{3}{4}$ of 4.28

(e) $\frac{1}{4}$ of $\frac{1}{3}$

(f) $\frac{3}{5}$ of $\frac{1}{4}$

(g) $\frac{2}{3}$ of $\frac{3}{4}$

(h) $\frac{2}{5}$ of $\frac{10}{11}$

7 $\frac{5}{9}$ of Carl's photos are taken while he is holidaying.

$\frac{3}{7}$ of these holiday photos are taken while he is in Italy. What fraction of *all* Carl's photos are taken while he is in Italy?

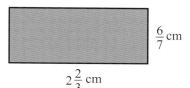

8 Work out $\frac{2}{5} \times \frac{1}{2} \times \frac{3}{8} \times \frac{4}{9}$

We can multiply mixed numbers by changing them to improper fractions ('top-heavy fractions').

(a) $2\frac{1}{2} \times \frac{3}{4}$

$= \frac{5}{2} \times \frac{3}{4}$

$= \frac{15}{8} = 1\frac{7}{8}$

(b) $1\frac{2}{3} \times 1\frac{1}{4}$

$= \frac{5}{3} \times \frac{5}{4}$

$= \frac{25}{12} = 2\frac{1}{12}$

Exercise 5M

1 Work out (a) $3\frac{1}{2} \times \frac{2}{3}$ (b) $1\frac{3}{4} \times \frac{1}{5}$

2 Work out the area of this rectangle.

$\frac{6}{7}$ cm

$2\frac{2}{3}$ cm

3 Work out

(a) $2\frac{1}{2} \times \frac{1}{4}$

(b) $2\frac{1}{2} \times \frac{1}{6}$

(c) $3\frac{1}{2} \times \frac{3}{10}$

(d) $1\frac{1}{2} \times \frac{2}{3}$

(e) $3\frac{1}{4} \times \frac{1}{10}$

(f) $\frac{3}{5} \times 4\frac{1}{4}$

(g) $2\frac{1}{2} \times 1\frac{1}{2}$

(h) $3\frac{1}{2} \times 3\frac{1}{2}$

4 Work out $2\frac{1}{2} \times 1\frac{3}{5} \times 2\frac{2}{9}$. Remember to cancel down the answer fully.

5   A photograph is $3\frac{1}{4}$ inches tall and $2\frac{1}{2}$ inches wide. Calculate the area of the photograph.

6   Which answer is the odd one out below? Show all your working out.

$$3\frac{1}{3} \times 1\frac{1}{2}$$ $$2\frac{4}{5} \times 2\frac{1}{7}$$ $$4\frac{2}{7} \times 1\frac{1}{6}$$

Dividing an integer by a fraction

•   How many quarters are there in 3?
    Answer: 12

• $2 \div \frac{1}{3}$ 'How many thirds are there in 2?'   Answer: 6

• $5 \div \frac{1}{2}$ 'How many halves are there in 5?'   Answer: 10

Exercise 6M

1   (a) How many quarters are there in 1?

    (b) How many quarters are there in 3?

    (c) How many quarters are there in 6?

2   (a) How many tenths are there in 2?

    (b) How many fifths are there in 3?

    (c) How many sevenths are there in 2?

3   Work out

    (a) $1 \div \frac{1}{5}$ (b) $3 \div \frac{1}{2}$ (c) $1 \div \frac{1}{10}$

    (d) $2 \div \frac{1}{2}$ (e) $9 \div \frac{1}{3}$ (f) $12 \div \frac{1}{3}$

4 Copy and complete this pattern.

$$60 \times \frac{1}{6} = 10 \qquad\qquad 10 \div \frac{1}{6} = 60$$

$$30 \times \frac{2}{6} = 10 \qquad\qquad 10 \div \frac{2}{6} = \square$$

$$20 \times \frac{3}{6} = 10 \qquad\qquad 10 \div \frac{3}{6} = \square$$

$$15 \times \frac{4}{6} = \square \qquad\qquad 10 \div \frac{4}{6} = \square$$

$$12 \times \frac{5}{6} = \square \qquad\qquad 10 \div \frac{5}{6} = \square$$

5 Copy and complete

(a) $10 = \square \times \frac{1}{2}$ (b) $\square \times \frac{1}{3} = 8$ (c) $\square \times \frac{1}{4} = 5$

(d) $\square \times \frac{1}{3} = 2$ (e) $11 = \square \times \frac{1}{2}$ (f) $\square \times \frac{1}{5} = 5$

Dividing a fraction by a fraction

How many $\frac{1}{8}$s are there in $\frac{1}{2}$?

The answer is 4

Notice that $\frac{1}{2} \div \frac{1}{8} = \frac{1}{2} \times \frac{8}{1} = 4$.

$\frac{1}{2}$ is shaded

To divide by a fraction, turn the fraction you are dividing by upside down and then multiply.

(a) $\frac{3}{5} \div \frac{1}{4} = \frac{3}{5} \times \frac{4}{1}$

$= \frac{12}{5}$

$= 2\frac{2}{5}$

(b) $1\frac{1}{4} \div 2\frac{2}{3}$ change to 'top-heavy' fractions first

$= \frac{5}{4} \div \frac{8}{3}$

$= \frac{5}{4} \times \frac{3}{8} = \frac{15}{32}$

Exercise 7M

1 Copy and complete

(a) $\frac{2}{5} \div \frac{3}{4}$

$= \frac{2}{5} \times \frac{\square}{3}$

$= \frac{\square}{15}$

(b) $\frac{1}{4} \div \frac{5}{7}$

$= \frac{1}{4} \times \frac{\square}{\square}$

$= \frac{\square}{20}$

(c) $\frac{3}{10} \div \frac{2}{3}$

$= \frac{3}{10} \times \frac{\square}{\square}$

$= \frac{\square}{\square}$

Work out

2 $\dfrac{1}{2} \div \dfrac{1}{4}$

3 $\dfrac{1}{3} \div \dfrac{1}{2}$

4 $\dfrac{3}{4} \div \dfrac{1}{3}$

5 $\dfrac{2}{3} \div \dfrac{1}{2}$

6 $\dfrac{1}{5} \div \dfrac{1}{2}$

7 $\dfrac{1}{2} \div \dfrac{1}{5}$

8 $\dfrac{3}{4} \div \dfrac{4}{5}$

9 $\dfrac{1}{2} \div \dfrac{1}{6}$

10 $\dfrac{5}{6} \div \dfrac{1}{3}$

11 $\dfrac{2}{5} \div \dfrac{2}{3}$

12 $\dfrac{5}{7} \div \dfrac{9}{10}$

13 $\dfrac{5}{12} \div \dfrac{1}{8}$

14 A cocktail glass holds $\dfrac{1}{7}$ of a litre. How many times can the glass be filled from 2 litres of cocktail?

15 A dog has $\dfrac{1}{8}$ kg of meat added to each meal. Exactly how many meals are covered by $\dfrac{2}{3}$ kg of meat?

Work out

16 $1\dfrac{3}{4} \div 3\dfrac{1}{3}$

17 $2\dfrac{1}{3} \div \dfrac{3}{8}$

18 $2\dfrac{2}{5} \div 5\dfrac{1}{2}$

19 $1\dfrac{1}{2} \div 2\dfrac{3}{4}$

20 $1\dfrac{5}{6} \div 3\dfrac{1}{2}$

21 $6 \div \dfrac{2}{5}$

22 Some children were each given $\dfrac{2}{5}$ of a bar of chocolate. How many children were there if $6\dfrac{4}{5}$ bars of chocolate were given out in total?

23 Work out $\dfrac{2}{3} \times \dfrac{1}{4} \div \dfrac{2}{5}$

24 Jamie has $4\dfrac{1}{2}$ litres of paint in total. Each tin contains $\dfrac{3}{8}$ litre of paint. How many tins of paint does Jamie have?

Need more practice with fractions?

Work out

1 $\dfrac{2}{3}$ of 15

2 $\dfrac{5}{6}$ of 24

3 $\dfrac{3}{4}$ of 16

4 $\dfrac{3}{8}$ of 24

5 $\dfrac{9}{10}$ of 60

6 $\dfrac{2}{5}$ of 100

7 $\dfrac{5}{6}$ of 36

8 $\dfrac{3}{5}$ of 120

9 Work out

(a) $\frac{1}{6} + \frac{2}{3}$

(b) $\frac{3}{4} + \frac{1}{8}$

(c) $\frac{3}{5} - \frac{1}{10}$

(d) $\frac{5}{8} + \frac{1}{16}$

(e) $\frac{5}{6} - \frac{2}{3}$

(f) $\frac{3}{4} - \frac{3}{8}$

(g) $\frac{5}{18} + \frac{1}{9}$

(h) $\frac{1}{10} + \frac{1}{20}$

10 Christine throws away $\frac{1}{4}$ of her shoes.
She gives $\frac{1}{8}$ of her shoes to her sister.
During July Christine wears $\frac{1}{2}$ of her shoes.
What fraction of her shoes does Christine
still have but remain unworn in July?

11 Work out and cancel down if necessary.

(a) $\frac{5}{7} \times \frac{3}{10}$

(b) $\frac{8}{9} \times \frac{3}{4}$

(c) $\frac{5}{11} \times 2$

(d) $\frac{3}{20} \times \frac{5}{9}$

12 Find each missing number below.

(a) $\frac{\square}{4}$ of 32 = 24

(b) $\frac{\square}{7}$ of 21 = 9

(c) $\frac{3}{\square}$ of 20 = 12

(d) $\frac{3}{\square}$ of 14 = 6

(e) $\frac{4}{5}$ of $\square$ = 16

(f) $\frac{3}{10}$ of $\square$ = 18

13 On each bounce a ball rises to $\frac{3}{4}$ of its previous height. How high will a ball bounce if it is
dropped from a height of 2 metres?

14 Work out

(a) $\frac{2}{3} - \frac{2}{5}$

(b) $\frac{1}{8} + \frac{5}{6}$

(c) $\frac{2}{5} + \frac{3}{7}$

(d) $\frac{7}{8} - \frac{3}{5}$

(e) $\frac{7}{10} - \frac{2}{9}$

(f) $\frac{3}{10} + \frac{1}{7}$

(g) $\frac{7}{9} - \frac{1}{4}$

(h) $\frac{2}{11} + \frac{5}{9}$

15 Each card has a fraction and a letter. Find the cards which contain equivalent fractions and
arrange the letters to make the name of a capital city.

(a)

M	A	R	E	O	T
$\frac{6}{10}$	$\frac{15}{24}$	$\frac{21}{35}$	$\frac{12}{20}$	$\frac{30}{50}$	$\frac{10}{16}$

(b)

S	C	E	M	O	W	A	O
$\frac{9}{21}$	$\frac{33}{77}$	$\frac{9}{24}$	$\frac{27}{63}$	$\frac{24}{56}$	$\frac{60}{140}$	$\frac{15}{45}$	$\frac{6}{14}$

16 Work out

(a) $\frac{3}{8} \div \frac{2}{3}$ 　　　(b) $\frac{5}{6} \div \frac{8}{9}$ 　　　(c) $\frac{1}{5} \div \frac{7}{10}$ 　　　(d) $\frac{3}{7} \div \frac{5}{8}$

17 Noel has £60. He spends two fifths of his money on a shirt. He spends three quarters of the remaining money on some trousers. How much money has he got left?

18 A footballer scores $\frac{4}{9}$ of his team's goals during one season. $\frac{3}{7}$ of his goals are headers. What fraction of his team's goals did he head?

Extension questions with fractions

Work out

1 $3\frac{1}{2} - 2\frac{2}{3}$ 　　　2 $1\frac{3}{4} + 2\frac{2}{5}$ 　　　3 $3\frac{1}{3} - 1\frac{7}{8}$

4 $2\frac{3}{4} \times 1\frac{1}{3}$ 　　　5 $3\frac{2}{3} \times 2\frac{5}{6}$ 　　　6 $1\frac{1}{4} \div 4\frac{1}{6}$

7 Danny eats $\frac{5}{8}$ of his crisps. Rae eats $\frac{2}{3}$ of the remaining crisps. What fraction of the crisps is left over?

8 Copy and complete the addition square.

+		$\frac{1}{6}$		$\frac{2}{3}$
	$\frac{7}{12}$			1
$\frac{3}{8}$				
			$\frac{7}{10}$	
	$\frac{3}{4}$		1	

9 A TV programme in a series lasts for $\frac{2}{3}$ of an hour. How many episodes of the programme can be watched in $7\frac{1}{3}$ hours?

10 Colin has to work out $1\frac{2}{3} \times 3\frac{2}{3}$. He says that $1 \times 3 = 3$ and $\frac{2}{3} \times \frac{2}{3} = \frac{4}{9}$ so the answer is $3\frac{4}{9}$. Explain why Colin is not correct by working out the answer yourself.

11 Which rectangle has the larger area and by how much?

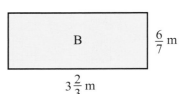

$\frac{2}{5}$ m 　A　 $\frac{6}{7}$ m 　B

$2\frac{1}{2}$ m 　　$3\frac{2}{3}$ m

12 Work out $\left(\frac{2}{5} \times \frac{3}{8}\right) + \left(\frac{7}{10} \times \frac{1}{2}\right)$

1.7 Probability 1

In section 1.7 you will:

- find the probability of events occurring or not occurring
- find the expected number of times an event will occur
- find experimental probabilities

Events occurring or not occurring

- If the probability of an event occurring is p, then the probability of it not occurring is $1 - p$.

- Ten discs numbered 1, 2, 3, 4, 5, 6, 7, 8, 9, 10 are put into a bag. One disc is selected at random.

  In this example, there are 10 possible equally likely outcomes of a trial.

  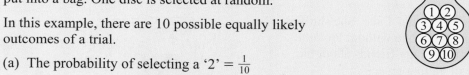

  (a) The probability of selecting a '2' $= \frac{1}{10}$

   This may be written p(selecting a '2') $= \frac{1}{10}$

  (b) p(not selecting a '2') $= 1 - \frac{1}{10}$

   $= \frac{9}{10}$

  (c) p(selecting a number greater than 7) $= \frac{3}{10}$

  (d) p(not selecting a number greater than 7) $= 1 - \frac{3}{10} = \frac{7}{10}$

Exercise 1M

1   Seven discs numbered 3, 4, 5, 7, 9, 11, 12 are placed in a bag. One disc is selected at random. Find the probability that it is

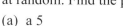

(a) a 5   (b) not a 5

(c) an odd number   (d) an even number.

2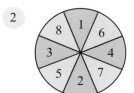

With this spinner, find the probability of getting

(a) a 7   (b) not a 7   (c) a prime number

(d) a number greater than 6

3   A dice has its faces numbered 2, 3, 3, 3, 4, 7. Find the probability of rolling

(a) a 7   (b) an even number.

4   One card is selected at random from the
    nine cards shown.

    Find the probability of selecting

    (a) the king of diamonds

    (b) a 9 or 10

    (c) a picture card

    (d) a card with a number less than 9

5   The probability that Mr Williams will buy a newspaper in the morning is 0.73. What is the
    probability that Mr Williams will not buy a newspaper in the morning?

6   If Mala throws a 3 or a 5 on her next throw when playing 'Snakes and Ladders' she will slide
    down a snake on the board. What is the probability that she will avoid a snake on her next throw?

7   Nicole has 3 kings and 1 ace. She shuffles
    the cards and takes one without looking.
    Nicole asks two of her friends about the
    probability of getting an ace.

    Angie says: Syline says:
    'It is $\frac{1}{3}$ because there are   'It is $\frac{1}{4}$ because there are

    3 kings and 1 ace.'   4 cards and only 1 ace.'

    Which of her friends is right?

8   A shopkeeper is keen to sell his stock of left-handed scissors. He has read that 9% of the
    population is left-handed. What is the probability that the next person to enter his shop is
    right-handed?

9   Penny throws a fair coin and gets a head. Her brother then throws the same coin. Write down
    the probability that her brother will get a head.

10 A bag contains the balls shown. One ball is taken out at random.
    Find the probability that it is

    (a) red   (b) not red   (c) blue.

    One more red ball and one more blue ball are added to the bag.

    (d) Find the new probability of selecting a red ball from the bag.

11 A box contains 15 balls which are either yellow or pink. There are 11 yellow balls.

    (a) One ball is randomly selected from the box. What is the probability of taking a pink ball?

    (b) If one pink ball has been removed, what is the probability of taking a pink ball if another
        ball is randomly selected?

12 Steve has taken a number of cards at random from a pack.
    The probability of picking a red card from Steve's cards is $\frac{3}{5}$

    (a) How many cards of each colour *could* there be in Steve's cards?

    (b) Write down another possibility for the number of cards of each colour that are in Steve's cards.

Expected number of successes

When an experiment (such as rolling a dice or tossing a coin) is repeated several times, we can calculate the number of times we expect an event to occur. We call the event in which we are interested a 'success'.

Expected number of successes = (probability of a success) × (number of trials)

(a) A fair dice is rolled 540 times. How many times would you expect to roll a '2'?

$p(\text{rolling a 2}) = \frac{1}{6}$

Expected number of 2s $= \frac{1}{6} \times 540$

$= 90$

(b) On a spinner, the probability of getting a 7 is $\frac{2}{9}$. How many times would you expect to score a 7 if you make 225 spins?

Expected number of 7s $= \frac{2}{9} \times 225$

$= 50$

Exercise 2M

1 A fair dice is rolled 480 times. How many times would you expect to roll
   (a) a 2   (b) an odd number?

2 This spinner, with 12 equal sectors, is spun 600 times. How often would you expect to spin
   (a) a pink sector   (b) an even number
   (c) a vowel   (d) a prime number?

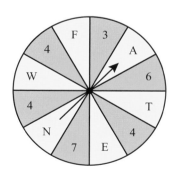

3 One ball is selected at random from the bag shown and then replaced. This procedure is repeated 400 times. How many times would you expect to select
   (a) a blue ball
   (b) a green ball?

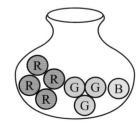

4   The probability of Russell having an egg for breakfast is $\frac{3}{5}$. The probability of Sabina having an egg for breakfast is $\frac{2}{3}$. Who is likely to eat more eggs over a period of 60 days and how many more eggs will that person have eaten?

5   A coin is biased so that the probability of tossing a 'head' is 0.4
   (a) How many 'heads' would you expect when the coin is tossed 200 times?
   (b) How many 'tails' would you expect when the coin is tossed 1000 times?

6   One quarter of the cards in a pack are 'hearts'. A card is randomly selected from a pack then replaced.
   (a) If this is repeated 240 times, how many 'hearts' would you expect to get?
   (b) If this is repeated 420 times, how many cards would you expect to get which are not 'hearts'?

7   People at a fair pay 50p to spin the pointer on this board. They win the amount shown. The game is played 600 times.
   (a) How much money would you expect to be paid out?
   (b) How much money would you expect the fair organisers to keep? This money is then given to a charity.

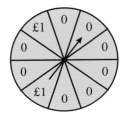

Experimental probability

Experimental probability $= \dfrac{\text{number of trials in which an event occurs}}{\text{total number of trials made}}$

Exercise 3M

Carry out experiments to work out the experimental probability of some of the following events.

Use a computer to simulate throwing two dice. Record the total score on a frequency diagram.

Toss two coins. What is the chance of tossing two heads?

Pick a card from a pack. What is the chance of picking an ace?

Make an eight-sided spinner numbered 1 to 8. What is the chance of spinning an eight?

Drop a drawing pin on the floor. What is the chance of it landing point up?

Exercise 4M

You may use a calculator.

1   A bag contains coloured balls. Rajiv randomly selects a ball from the bag and then replaces it. Here are the results.

Colour	White	Green	Blue
Frequency	10	31	19

Estimate the probability that on his next draw he will select

(a) a white ball   (b) a green ball.

2   Dimpna and Jenny both did the 'dropping a drawing pin' experiment. Here are their results.

Dimpna

Trials	20
'Point up'	10

Jenny

Trials	150
'Point up'	61

Another drawing pin is dropped.

(a) For Dimpna, what is the probability of getting 'point up'?

(b) For Jenny, what is the probability of getting 'point up'?

(c) Whose result is likely to be more reliable? Why?

3   Roll a fair dice 60 times. How many 'ones' would you expect to roll?
Compare your experimental result with the theoretical one.
Suppose you do the experiment again (i.e. roll the dice another 60 times).
Would you expect to get the same result?

4   Sean collected the results of 40 Liverpool home games.
Estimate the probability that in their next home game

Won	18
Lost	10
Drawn	12

(a) Liverpool will win

(b) Liverpool will lose.

For Liverpool's next 40 games, the results were
as shown opposite:

Won	23
Lost	11
Drawn	6

Using all 80 results, estimate the probability of

(c) Liverpool winning their next game

(d) Liverpool drawing their next game.

Would you expect these probabilities to be more accurate than those based on the first 40 matches? Why?

64

5   Martina throws a dice many times. She records the scores obtained in the table below.

Score	1	2	3	4	5	6
Frequency	20	50	22	18	55	23

Do you think that this dice is fair? Give a reason for your answer.

Need more practice with probability?

1 | W | E | L | O | V | E | T | H | E | S | E |

One card is randomly selected from the cards above. What is the probability that the card is

(a) the letter 'T'   (b) the letter 'E'   (c) a vowel?

2   The probability of a drawing pin landing 'point up' is 0.61

Find the probability of the drawing pin landing 'point down'.

3   One card is picked at random from a pack of 52.
There are 13 diamonds in a pack and 1 king of hearts.
Find the probability that the card chosen is

(a) a diamond   (b) not a diamond

(c) the king of hearts   (d) not the king of hearts.

4   This spinner is spun 140 times.
How many times would you expect
the spinner to land on a '2'?

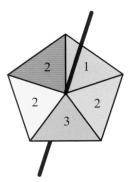

5   The 26 letters of the alphabet are written on discs. The five discs with vowels are put in bag A and the other discs are put in bag B. Find the probability of selecting

(a) an 'o' from bag A

(b) a 'z' from bag B

(c) a 'w' from bag A.

6   A box of chocolates contains the following:

8 toffee	7 truffle
12 marzipan	13 nut

A chocolate is taken at random.
Which type has a probability of $\frac{3}{10}$ of being chosen?
Justify your answer.

7   Dominic and Aditi are due to take their driving tests. Dominic says he has the same chance of passing the test as Aditi. Comment on Dominic's statement.

8   One card is selected at random from the eight cards shown. Find the probability of selecting

(a) the ace of diamonds   (b) a king

(c) an ace   (d) a red card.

(e) If a card is selected then replaced 200 times, how many times would you expect a '2' to be chosen?

Extension questions with probability

1

A bag contains 9 balls: 3 red, 4 blue and 2 yellow.

(a) Find the probability of selecting a red ball.

(b) The 2 yellow balls are replaced by 2 blue balls. Find the probability of selecting a blue ball.

2   A South Seas diver collected 965 oysters. Just one of the oysters contained a pearl. One oyster is chosen at random. Find the probability that

(a) it contains a pearl

(b) it does not contain a pearl.

3   A box contains 12 balls: 3 red, 2 yellow, 4 green and 3 white.

(a) Find the probability of selecting
    (i) a red ball
    (ii) a yellow ball.

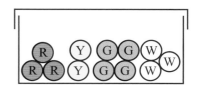

(b) The 3 white balls are replaced by 3 yellow balls. Find the probability of selecting
    (i) a red ball
    (ii) a yellow ball.

4   A researcher records the colours of cars on the high street during a four-hour period one day. The results are recorded below.

	Red	Blue	Silver	Other
Frequency	179	115	130	76

Estimate how many of the next 6000 cars to travel down the high street will be blue.

5   In one part of Africa there are 80 lions and 50 leopards.

(a) What is the probability of seeing a leopard first when visiting this part of Africa?

(b) 8 lions and 5 leopards are born in this area. What is the probability of seeing a leopard first now when visiting this part of Africa?

6   Mo puts these numbered balls in a bag.

(a) He shakes the bag and takes one ball without looking. What is the probability of getting a '2'?

(b) Mo wants to put more balls in the bag so that the chance of getting a '4' is *twice* the chance of getting a '3'. What balls could he put in the bag?

7   The tables below show the probabilities of two football teams winning, drawing or losing a football game.

Hatton United	win	draw	lose
Probability	?	0.15	0.3

Melby City	win	draw	lose
Probability	?	0.2	0.2

Which team is more likely to win its next game?
Give a reason for your answer.

8   One ball is selected at random from a bag containing m white balls and n green balls. What is the probability of selecting a green ball?

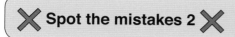

Spot the mistakes 2

Construction, locus, angles, fractions and probability

Work through each question below and *explain clearly* what mistakes have been made. Beware – some questions are correctly done.

1   Work out $\dfrac{2}{7} + \dfrac{3}{5}$

   Answer: $\dfrac{2}{7} + \dfrac{3}{5} = \dfrac{10}{35} + \dfrac{19}{35} = \dfrac{29}{35}$

2

Calculate, with reasons, the value of $C\widehat{B}E$.

   Answer: $A\widehat{B}G = 75°$ (corresponding angles $D\widehat{E}H$ and $A\widehat{B}G$ are equal)

   $C\widehat{B}E = 75°$ (vertically opposite angles $A\widehat{B}G$ and $C\widehat{B}E$ are equal)

3   Each Saturday Emily goes to the cinema or swims. The probability of Emily going to the cinema is 0.45. What is the probability that Emily goes swimming?

   Answer: probability of swimming $= 1 - 0.45$
   $= 0.55$

4   Construct the angle bisector of $A\widehat{B}C$ using a ruler and compasses only.

   Answer:

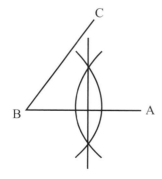

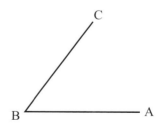

5   Work out $2\frac{1}{2} \times 3\frac{2}{3}$

   Answer: $2 \times 3 = 6$ and $\dfrac{1}{2} \times \dfrac{2}{3} = \dfrac{1}{3}$
   so $2\frac{1}{2} \times 3\frac{2}{3} = 6\frac{1}{3}$

6

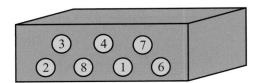

In this diagram, DE = DF.

Work out the value of $A\hat{B}C$, giving full reasons for your answer.

Answer: $E\hat{D}F = 35°$ (isosceles triangle).

$A\hat{D}C = 35°$ ($A\hat{D}C$ and $E\hat{D}F$ are vertically opposite angles which are equal).

$A\hat{B}C = 360° - 80° - 35° - 75°$ (angles in a quadrilateral add up to 360°).

$A\hat{B}C = 170°$

7 A box contains the 7 balls shown opposite. A ball is randomly chosen then replaced. This happens 35 times. How many times would you expect a prime number to be chosen?

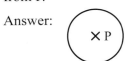

Answer: Probability of a prime number being chosen $= \dfrac{4}{7}$

Number of times a prime number should be chosen $= \dfrac{4}{7}$ of 35

$= 20$

8 Draw a point P then draw the locus of all the points which are less than or equal to 1 cm away from P.

Answer:

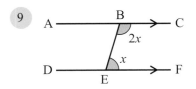

9

Work out the value of x.

Answer: $A\hat{B}E = x$ ($A\hat{B}E = B\hat{E}F$ because they are alternate angles which are equal).

$x + 2x = 180°$ (angles on a straight line add up to 180°)

$3x = 180°$, so $x = 60°$

10 A chef has two bags of flour. One bag contains $\frac{2}{5}$ kg of flour and the other bag contains $\frac{3}{4}$ kg of flour. The chef now uses $\frac{1}{3}$ kg of flour. How much flour does the chef have left?

Answer: Total flour $= \dfrac{2}{5} + \dfrac{3}{4} = \dfrac{5}{9}$ kg

Flour left over $= \dfrac{5}{9} - \dfrac{1}{3} = \dfrac{4}{6}$ kg

so the chef has $\dfrac{2}{3}$ kg of flour left.

CHECK YOURSELF ON SECTIONS 1.6 and 1.7

1   Converting improper fractions and mixed numbers

Convert into mixed numbers: (a) $\dfrac{7}{3}$ (b) $\dfrac{35}{6}$

Convert into improper fractions: (c) $3\frac{4}{5}$ (d) $2\frac{3}{4}$

2   Adding and subtracting fractions

Work out   (a) $\dfrac{1}{6} + \dfrac{2}{5}$ (b) $\dfrac{7}{8} - \dfrac{2}{3}$ (c) $1\frac{1}{2} + 2\frac{2}{3}$ (d) $3\frac{1}{5} - 1\frac{3}{4}$

3   Multiplying and dividing fractions

Work out   (a) $\dfrac{5}{8} \times \dfrac{4}{7}$ (b) $3\frac{1}{2} \times \dfrac{4}{5}$ (c) $\dfrac{7}{9} \div \dfrac{14}{15}$ (d) $1\frac{2}{5} \div 2\frac{1}{3}$

4   Finding the probability of events occurring or not occurring

(a) During the winter the probability of Amy's car starting in the morning is 0.9.
    What is the probability that Amy's car will *not* start in the morning?

(b) A box contains 2 yellow balls, 3 blue balls and 3 pink balls.
    Find the probability of
    (i) selecting a blue ball
    (ii) *not* selecting a pink ball.

(c) The 2 yellow balls are replaced by 2 pink balls.
    Find the probability of *not* selecting a pink ball.

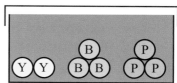

5   Finding the expected number of times an event will occur

(a) A fair dice is rolled 720 times.
    How many times would you
    expect to roll a '5'?

(b) This spinner is spun 60 times.
    How many times would you
    expect to score a '3'?

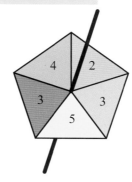

6	Finding experimental probabilities

Steve takes 25 penalties and scores 18 goals.

Estimate the probability that with his next penalty

(a) he will score a goal

(b) he will *not* score a goal.

(c) Would you expect the probabilities to be more accurate if Steve took 100 penalties and these results were used?

1.8 Applying mathematics 1

In section 1.8 you will apply maths in a variety of situations.

1. A village panto sells 57 tickets at £11 each and 132 tickets at £16 each. The panto costs £1887 to stage. Do the ticket sales cover this cost?

2. Look at the pattern of paving stones and count the number of stones in the first three rings around the centre stone.

   Assuming the pattern continues, how many stones will there be altogether in a circular pattern of seven rings around the centre stone?

3. Lucas and Zoe visit their mother on April 7th. From then on, Lucas visits his mother every fifth day and Zoe visits every eighth day. On what date will Lucas and Zoe both next visit their mother at the same time?

4. Elijah is given a birthday cake. He is rather selfish and does not share this cake with anyone else. On the first day he eats $\frac{2}{5}$ of the cake and on the second day he eats $\frac{3}{7}$ of the cake. What fraction of the cake is now left?

5. Copy each calculation and find the missing numbers.

   (a)
   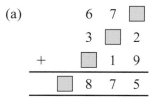

   (b)
   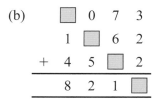

6. It costs 35p per minute to hire a powerful computer. How much will it cost to hire the computer from 07:40 to 08:15?

7 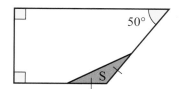 This diagram is a plan of Ava's living room. She wants to make a corner shelf as shown.

Write down how large the three angles will need to be for this shelf to fit correctly in the corner.

8 A scientific formula $v = u + at$ can be used to work out how fast something is travelling. Work out the value of u if $v = 29$, $a = 3$ and $t = 4$

9 The skateboard sequence was taken by a camera with a delay of 0.14 seconds between pictures. How long did the jump take?

10 Amelia spends $\frac{2}{3}$ of her monthly money on rent, bills and food. She saves $\frac{1}{4}$ of the remaining money each month. What fraction of her total monthly money does Amelia save?

UNIT 1   MIXED REVIEW

Part one

1 Work out

(a) $\frac{1}{2} - \frac{1}{3}$ (b) $\frac{2}{5} + \frac{1}{6}$ (c) $\frac{1}{2} \times \frac{3}{4}$ (d) $\frac{2}{5} \div \frac{7}{8}$

2 The number n has six factors only, including 1 and n. Two of its factors are 2 and 5. What is n?

3 Answer 'true' or 'false'.

(a) $3 \times n = 3 + n$ (b) $a \times 5 = 5a$ (c) $a + b + a = 2a + b$

(d) $n + 2n = 2n^2$ (e) $n \div 3 = \frac{n}{3}$ (f) $n \times n = n^2$

4 Find the angles marked with letters.

(a)    (b) 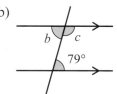   (c)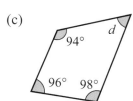

5 Ten discs numbered 1, 3, 3, 3, 4, 7, 8, 9, 11, 11 are placed in a bag. One disc is selected at random.

Find the probability that it is

(a) an even number

(b) a 3

(c) less than 6

6 Work out and write each answer as a number in index form.

(a) $7^3 \times 7^2$ (b) $3^8 \div 3^3$ (c) $5^4 \times 5$ (d) $\dfrac{2^5 \times 2^4}{2^2 \times 2^3}$

7 (a) Write an expression for the cost of n packets at 20p each.

(b) Write an expression for the cost of n stamps at 10p each.

8 (a) *Construct* the perpendicular bisector of AB.

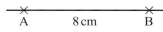

(b) *Construct* the bisector of the angle A.

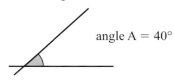

angle A = 40°

9 Work out, without a calculator

(a) 4^2 (b) 2^3 (c) 1^5 (d) 10^3 (e) 5^4

10 Look at these numbers.

12	18	30	35	51	70	80

(a) Which numbers divide exactly by 7?

(b) Which numbers divide exactly by both 5 and 2?

(c) Which numbers are multiples of 3?

11 Copy and complete this factor tree then express 270 as a product of its prime factors.

12 One day a quarter of the class is absent and 21 children are present. How many children are there in the class when no one is away?

13 Find two matching expressions.

A $\boxed{a + 2 + 3b - b}$ B $\boxed{3a + 2 - a + 2b}$ C $\boxed{2 + b + a + b}$

14 When playing Monopoly, Philip knows that the probability of throwing a 'double' with two dice is $\frac{1}{6}$. What is the probability that he does *not* throw a double with his next throw?

Part two

1. Avram's age is a multiple of 9. Next year it will be a multiple of 8. How old is Avram?

2. Jenny is on holiday. She spends n hours each day on the beach. How many hours does she spend on the beach during seven days? (your answer should be an expression containing n)

3. Simplify each expression by collecting like terms.

   (a) $3m + 5n - 2m + 2n$ (b) $6p + 3 + 2p - 1$ (c) $4w - w + 5q + 2w$

4. Construct an accurate copy of each triangle and find the length x and the angle y.

   (a)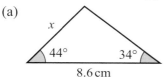

   (b)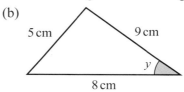

5. Copy and complete the addition square.

+		$\frac{2}{5}$
$\frac{1}{6}$	$\frac{1}{2}$	$\frac{17}{30}$
$\frac{3}{8}$		

6. John has two bags of toffees, each containing n toffees. He also has a tube of mints containing m mints.

   He gives his sister three toffees from each bag and he eats y mints.

   Write down an expression for the *total* number of toffees and mints that John now has.

7. Work out, without a calculator.

   (a) $1\frac{3}{4} \div \frac{1}{3}$ (b) $3\frac{2}{3} - 1\frac{4}{5}$ (c) $2\frac{1}{2} \times 1\frac{1}{4}$ (d) $2\frac{1}{5} \div 3\frac{1}{2}$

8.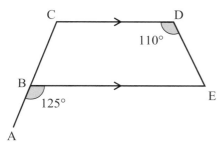

   Find the value of

   (a) $B\hat{C}D$

   (b) $B\hat{E}D$

9. Which number has more factors: 12 or 16? Give full reasons for your answer.

10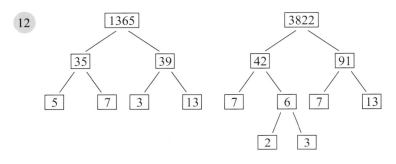

Copy this diagram. An ant crawls from B so that it is always the same distance from AB as BC. It stops when it is 3 cm from BC.

Draw the path taken by the ant.

11 A fair dice is thrown 90 times. How many times would you expect the dice to land on a square number?

12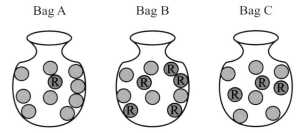

Use the factor trees to draw a Venn diagram then work out the HCF and LCM of 1365 and 3822

13 Karen is going to play a game called 'Lucky Dip'.
There are three bags labelled A, B and C.
Each bag contains red and green balls.
You win if you draw out a red ball from a bag.

Bag A   Bag B   Bag C

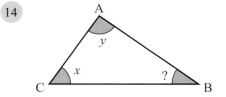

(a) Write down the probability of winning from bag A, from bag B, and from bag C.

(b) What is the probability of *not* winning from bag A?

14

Write down an expression for the size of $A\widehat{B}C$.
(your answer will have the letters x and y in it)

Puzzles and problems 1

1. Villages A, B, C, D, E, F, G, H, I are joined by a network of roads.
   The lengths of the roads are in miles.

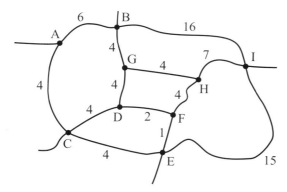

   (a) Find the shortest route from A to I.

   (b) Find the shortest route from B to E.

   (c) A family on a sight-seeing tour wish to visit all of the
       villages as they go from A to I. Find the shortest route
       passing through all the villages.

2. This network shows the roads joining towns A, B, … L.

   (a) Find the shortest route from B to K.

   (b) Find the shortest route from G to L.

   (c) Find the shortest route for a waste disposal lorry
       which has to visit every town as it travels
       from A to L.

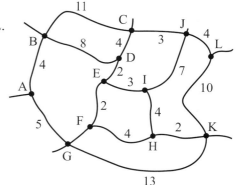

3. A class is electing five girls as captains of the following teams:
   swimming; gymnastics; netball; athletics; tennis.

   It is clearly best if the girl elected is good at the sport for
   which she is to be captain.

   Vera is good at swimming and gymnastics.
   Wilma is good at gymnastics, netball and tennis.
   Xenia is good at swimming and athletics.
   Yasmin is good at netball.
   Zara is good at netball and athletics.

   Work out the five games captains.

4 Four travellers W, X, Y, Z have to make a journey, for
which four tickets are available: by plane; by train;
by car; by boat.

    W prefers to go by plane or car.
    X prefers to go by boat.
    Y prefers to go by train or boat.
    Z prefers to go by train, car or boat.

Work out who should take each ticket so that
everyone is happy with their method of transport.

5 Six actors A, B, C, D, E, F are trying to decide who should play
the six parts in a play. The parts are:
the hero (H); the princess (P); the villain (V); the reporter
(R); the tree (T); the nurse (N).

    A would like to be the princess or the reporter.
    B would like to be the hero or the villain.
    C would like to be the hero or the nurse.
    D would like to be the villain or the tree.
    E would like to be the nurse or the tree.
    F would like to be the villain, the reporter or the tree.

Work out who should play each part.
Find two different solutions.

Mental arithmetic practice 1

Ideally a teacher will read out each question twice with pupils' books closed.

Test 1

1 Add together 5, 4 and 19

2 Write the number that is 8 less than
300.

3 What is 546 to the nearest hundred?

4 What is nine multiplied by six?

5 Write the number 8006 in figures.

6 Write 0.7 as a fraction.

7 Change seven and a half metres into
centimetres.

8 What is 4.6 multiplied by 1000?

9 How many thirds are there in two whole
ones?

10 26% of the people in a survey did not like
cheese. What percentage liked cheese?

11 The side of a square is 5 cm.
What is the area of the square?

12 A bus journey starts at six fifty. It lasts for
35 minutes. At what time does it finish?

13 How many groups of 5 can be made from
100?

14 At midday the temperature is 7°C.
By midnight it has fallen 12 degrees.
What is the temperature at midnight?

15 Write down a factor of 27 that is greater than 1.

16 What is 6000 divided by 10?

17 What number is eight squared?

18 How many seventeens are there in 340?

19 What is the difference between 3.3 and 5.5?

20 How much does each person receive when a prize of £200 is shared between 5 people?

21 How many more than 27 is 40?

22 20% of a number is 12. What is the number?

23 Find the change from a £10 note if you spend £3.20

24 How many altogether are 7, 6 and 5?

25 What is the remainder when 40 is divided by 7?

Test 2

1 What are two eighteens?

2 Add together 7, 8 and 9

3 Divide 8 into 48

4 Multiply 15 by 4

5 Write $\frac{3}{4}$ as a percentage.

6 Work out 13 divided by 10 as a decimal.

7 What number is 40 less than 75?

8 Share a cost of £56 between 7 people.

9 What four coins make 67p?

10 What is the product of 60 and 3?

11 I have two dogs and five cats. What fraction of my pets are cats?

12 What is the cost of 2 DVDs at £6.99 each?

13 Subtract the sum of 7 and 8 from 40

14 One quarter of a number is 3.5. What is the number?

15 I have one 10p coin, three 5p coins and one 50p coin. How much money do I have?

16 Lemons cost 12p each. What is the cost of 7 lemons?

17 Apples cost 75p for five. What is the cost of one apple?

18 A bunch of grapes costs 64p. What is the change from £1?

19 How many 20p coins do I need for £2.80?

20 A shirt costs £15.95 new. I get a discount of £4. How much do I pay?

21 I share 60 sweets equally among 5 people. How many sweets does each receive?

22 The area of a square is 36 cm^2. How long is each side?

23 What must I spend from £20 to leave £14.50?

24 How many millimetres are there in 10 metres?

25 Write 5.30 a.m. in 24-hour clock time.

A long time ago! 1

The Eye of Horus

In Ancient Egypt, Horus was represented as the falcon-headed god. He was the ultimate god of mathematics.

All Egyptian fractions were unit fractions, such as $\frac{1}{2}$, $\frac{1}{3}$ and $\frac{1}{8}$

The Eye of Horus represented the sacred unit fractions. The 'Eye of Horus' symbol was used to protect from evil.

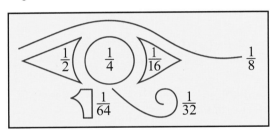

The Eye of Horus is shown opposite.

Each symbol represents the fraction shown.

By adding together different parts of the eye, other fractions are created.

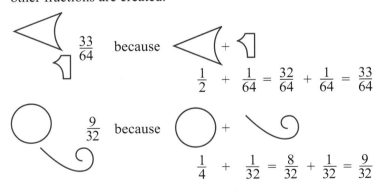

$$\frac{1}{2} \ + \ \frac{1}{64} = \frac{32}{64} \ + \ \frac{1}{64} = \frac{33}{64}$$

$$\frac{1}{4} \ + \ \frac{1}{32} = \frac{8}{32} \ + \ \frac{1}{32} = \frac{9}{32}$$

Exercise

1 Work out the value of each of these fractions.

(a)

(b)

(c)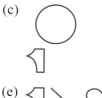

(d)

(e)

(f)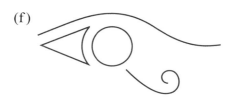

2 Use the symbols from the Eye of Horus to show the following fractions.

(a) $\dfrac{1}{16}$ (b) $\dfrac{3}{16}$ (c) $\dfrac{3}{4}$ (d) $\dfrac{7}{8}$

3 (a) What is the total of all the fractions in the Eye of Horus?

(b) What extra fraction is needed to make the total equal to 1?

4 **RESEARCH:**

(a) Find out more about the god Horus.

(b) Find out how the Egyptians represented the fraction $\dfrac{1}{3}$

UNIT 2

2.1 Percentages 1

In section 2.1 you will:

- express one number as a percentage of another number
- find percentage increases and decreases

Expressing one number as a percentage of another number

25 children are in a quiz. 9 are boys.

What percentage of the children in the quiz are boys?

9 out of 25 $= \dfrac{9}{25} = \dfrac{36}{100} = 36\%$ Write as a fraction then change to a percentage.

Exercise 1M

1   Tom has 20 pieces of fruit. 7 pieces of fruit are apples. What percentage of the pieces of fruit are the apples?

2   50 children watch a school football match. 22 are girls. What percentage of the children are girls?

3   500 people were asked to name their favourite film. 85 of them said 'Lord of the Rings'. What percentage of the people chose 'Lord of the Rings'?

4   One of these bags is red.

   What percentage of these bags are red?

5   Danny plays 25 games of pool and wins 16 of them. What percentage of the games did he *not* win?

6. Mark spent $\frac{3}{5}$ of his money on a computer game and $\frac{3}{20}$ of his money on food. What percentage of his money has he got left?

7. Three tenths of Lorna's books were science fiction. What percentage of her books were *not* science fiction?

8. Change each of the following into a percentage then put them in order of size, starting with the smallest.

A. 7 out of 25	B. 13 out of 20	C. 18 out of 60	D. 50 out of 200

9. Tania scored 60 out of 150 in a test. What percentage did she score?

10. Two groups of people were asked if they preferred EastEnders or Coronation Street. 11 out of 20 people in group A preferred EastEnders. 12 out of 25 people in group B preferred Coronation Street. Which group had the greater percentage of people who preferred EastEnders? Give full reasons for your answers.

11. It is reported that 43% of home owners have had ant invasions in their homes at some point. 3 groups of people in the town of Malby are asked if they have ever had an ant invasion at home. 31 out of 80 say yes, 18 out of 50 say yes and 27 out of 70 say yes. Do these figures support the 43% statement? Give full reasons for your answer.

To change more 'tricky' numbers into a percentage of each other, write the two numbers as a fraction of each other, then multiply by 100

23 people are asked if they can drive a car. 14 of them say 'yes'. What percentage of the people asked can drive?

14 out of 23 $= \dfrac{14}{23} \times 100 = 60.87$ (using a calculator)

$\qquad\qquad = 60.9\%$ (to one decimal place)

Exercise 2M

You may use a calculator. Give all answers to one decimal place.

1. There are 31 children in a class. 17 of them are girls. What percentage of the class are girls?

2. What percentage of the letters in the box are
   (a) vowels?
   (b) the letter R?

S	M	O	K	I	N	G	I	S
N	O	T	P	A	R	T	I	C
U	L	A	R	L	Y	G	O	O
D	F	O	R	Y	O	U	O	K

3. 16 children were playing in the park. 9 of them were wearing sandals. What percentage of the children were *not* wearing sandals?

4

	Men	Women	Total
Colour blind	55	37	92
Not colour blind	473	394	867
Total	528	431	959

The table shows the results of a test for colour blindness conducted on 959 people.

(a) What percentage of the men were colour blind?

(b) What percentage of the colour blind people were women?

5 A breakfast cereal contains the following ingredients by weight: toasted oat flakes 720 g, raw sugar 34 g, oat bran 76 g, honey 26 g, banana 57 g, hazelnuts 12 g.
What percentage of the packet is oat bran?

6 Four friends create kebabs for a barbecue. They decide to work out which kebab has the lowest fat content.

Jack's kebab	43.1 g fat in a 122 g portion
Gabby's kebab	29.6 g fat in an 85 g portion
Tom's kebab	48.2 g fat in a 149 g portion
Kate's kebab	31.8 g fat in a 98 g portion

Which kebab has the lowest percentage of fat in it?

7 There are 262 students in Year 11 at East Acre High School and 185 students in Year 11 at Redminster School. 147 of these students at East Acre High School get a grade 5 or above in their Maths GCSE. 107 of these students at Redminster School get a grade 5 or above in their Maths GCSE. Which school had the higher percentage of students gaining a grade 5 or above in their Maths GCSE and what was the difference in the percentages?

8

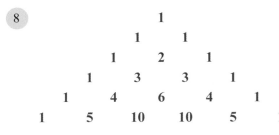

This triangle is known as Pascal's triangle. What percentage of the numbers are prime numbers? (remember: 1 is *not* prime)

9 Change these fractions into percentages then put them in order of size, starting with the smallest.

$$\frac{7}{11} \quad \frac{9}{13} \quad \frac{5}{9} \quad \frac{15}{26} \quad \frac{20}{37} \quad \frac{12}{21}$$

10 The table gives details of the ages of 884 pupils in a school.

(a) What percentage of the under-15s are boys?

(b) What percentage of the pupils in the whole school are girls?

(c) What percentage of the girls are 15 and over?

	Boys	Girls
Under 15	215	184
15 and over	223	262

'Simple' percentages in your head

Remember: Use multiples of 10% and 1%

10% of £30 = $\frac{1}{10}$ of 30 = 3, so 40% of £30 = 3 × 4 = £12

1% of £900 = $\frac{1}{100}$ of 900 = 9, so 7% of £900 = 9 × 7 = £63

> If a calculator may be used, make use of the $\boxed{\%}$ button.

Percentage increase or decrease

In 2020 the cost of taxing a car increased from £220 by 70%. What is the new cost?

70% of £220

$= \frac{70}{100} \times \frac{220}{1} = £154$

New cost of taxing car = £220 + £154

$= £374$

Exercise 3M

1   Work out without a calculator.
    (a) 20% of £80   (b) 5% of £40   (c) 30% of £70
    (d) 70% of £20   (e) 90% of £120   (f) 5% of £50

2   Steve has 280 toy soldiers. He gives 20% of the soldiers to his younger sister. How many soldiers does he have left?

3   Use a calculator to work out
    (a) 8% of £450   (b) 4% of £660   (c) 85% of £400
    (d) 6.5% of £200   (e) 7% of £6   (f) 17% of £175

4   A diving holiday priced at £860 is increased by 5%. What is the new price?

5   A lottery prize of £65 000 is divided between Steve, Pete and Phil so that Steve receives 22%, Pete receives 32% and Phil the rest. How much money does Phil receive?

6   A dog normally weighs 28 kg. After being put on a diet for three months its weight is reduced by 35%. How much does it weigh now?

7   The length of a new washing line is 21 m. After being used it stretches by 3%. Find the new length.

Do not use a calculator for the remainder of this exercise.

8   A marathon runner weighs 70 kg at the start of a race. During the race his weight is reduced by 5%. How much does he weigh at the end of the race?

9   (a) Increase £70 by 40%   (b) Decrease £320 by 15%

(c) Decrease £180 by 20%   (d) Increase £120 by 35%

10 A shop increases all its prices by 5%.
What are the new prices of these two items?

A
£90

B
£65

11 Gemma has £3600. She spends 45% of her money. How much money does she have left?

12 A car costs £8600. During the first year it loses 15% of its value. How much is the car now worth?

13
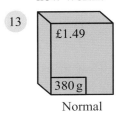
£1.49
380 g
Normal

£1.49
35% extra
FREE!
g
Offer

As part of a special promotion, the weight of breakfast cereal sold in a packet is increased by 35%, while the price remains the same. Calculate the weight of the breakfast cereal in the special 'offer' size.

14 In ten years the population of a town increases by 7% from its original number of 55 400 people. What is the new population?

Exercise 4M

You may use a calculator.

In questions 1 to 8 , work out each percentage and give the answer correct to the nearest penny.

1   13% of £2.13   2   27% of £5.85

3   15.1% of £7.87   4   11% of £6.27

5   13% of £6.17   6   16% of £0.87

7   37% of £5.20   8   15% of £11.23

> Example
> Work out 8% of £11.99 to the nearest penny.
> $$\frac{8}{100} \times \frac{11.99}{1}$$
> $= 0.95{\scriptstyle|}92$
> $= £0.96$ to the nearest penny

9   A hen weighs 2.7 kg. After laying an egg her weight is reduced by 1%. How much does she weigh now?

10 A mouse weighs 630 g. While escaping from a cat the mouse loses its tail and its weight is reduced by 4%. How much does the mouse weigh now?

11 Cheryl weighs 56 kg. After a month of hard work in the gym and 'sensible' eating, her weight decreases by 6%. How much does she weigh now?

12 Find the new price of a necklace costing £85, after the price is reduced by 7%

13

5 cm

8 cm

(a) Calculate the area of the rectangle shown.
(b) Calculate the new area when the length and width of the rectangle are each increased by 10%

14

Coopers
£85
watch
20% discount
less a further £15

Which shop offers the best deal and how much money would you save if you bought the watch from this shop?

Tanners
£85
watch
35% discount

15 The average daily attendance at a museum is 620 people. One Tuesday the attendance is down 5% on the average. On the Wednesday the attendance is up 15% on the average. How many more people visited the museum on the Wednesday compared with the Tuesday?

16 The price of a jacket is £70. This price is reduced by 20%. After 3 weeks the new price is increased by 20%. How much does the jacket now cost?

17 A bike costs £240. There are two payment schemes available from a shop, as shown opposite. What is the difference in the monthly payments between the two schemes?

Deposit 15%	Deposit 20%
plus 12 equal monthly payments	plus 24 equal monthly payments

18 Factory A makes 8500 radios each month and factory B makes 9000 radios each month. If factory A increases production by 12% and factory B increases production by 8%, how many more radios does factory B now produce each month compared with factory A?

Need more practice with percentages?

1. The price of a phone is £390. It is increased by 5%. What is the new price?

2. Meryl and Lee are playing 'pick a stick'.
   There are 40 sticks. Lee ends up picking 35%
   of the sticks. Meryl gets the rest of the sticks.
   How many sticks does Meryl get?

3. At a garage 140 cars were given a safety test and 65% of the cars passed the test.
   (a) How many cars passed the test?
   (b) How many cars failed the test?

4. Of the 980 children at a school, 45% cycle to school, 15% go by bus and the rest walk.
   (a) How many children cycle to school?
   (b) How many children walk to school?

5. The number of barrels of beer produced by a brewery
   last year was 8000. This year production has increased
   by 12%. How many barrels have been produced
   this year?

6.

Subject	Mark
Maths	$\frac{43}{50}$
English	$\frac{32}{40}$
Science	$\frac{17}{20}$
History	$\frac{21}{25}$

Edith sits 4 tests.
Her marks are shown in the table.
In which subject did she get the
highest percentage score?
Write down this percentage.

7. Which is larger? 15% of £80 or 4% of £300

8. There are 17 girls and 14 boys in a class. What percentage of the class are girls?
   Give the answer to one decimal place.

9   The island state of Gandia is divided between
    3 tribes, A, B and C, as shown.
    Tribe A subsequently starts a war and increases
    its land area by 15%. The area controlled by
    tribe B is reduced by 5%
    Draw a possible new map of Gandia and state
    the area now controlled by each tribe.

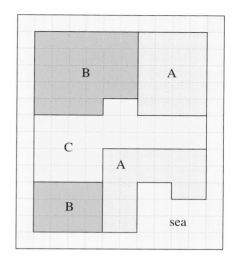

10 Last season the average home crowd watching
    Manchester United was 77 600 and the average
    price paid for admission was £45.
    This season the average crowd was 3% less
    but the average admission price was increased by 8%.
    How much money was paid for admission to the
    19 home games this season? Give your answer
    correct to the nearest thousand pounds.

11 Rob has £3239 in savings. During the year his savings increase by 6.2%.
    How much money does Rob now have in savings?

12 Two swimmers each have a personal best swimming
    time for a race of 185 seconds. During the season,
    one swimmer reduces their personal best time by 7%
    and the other swimmer reduces their personal best
    time by 3%. What is now the difference in their
    personal best times?

Extension questions with percentages

For increases, $\text{percentage increase} = \left(\dfrac{\text{actual increase}}{\text{original value}} \right) \times 100$

Example: A baker makes cakes costing £2.10 each and sells each cake for £3.78.
Work out the percentage profit.

actual profit = £3.78 − £2.10 = £1.68

$\text{percentage profit} = \left(\dfrac{1.68}{2.10} \right) \times 100 = 80\%$

↗
original cost price

1   The price of a jacket is increased from £48 to £62.40. Work out the percentage increase.

2   A baby's weight increases from 4 kg to 6.6 kg. Work out the percentage increase.

3   The number of medals won by a country at a sporting event decreases from 32 to 28. Find the percentage decrease in the number of medals won.

4   Darryl normally walks 2 km from his home to the shop then 2 km back again. One day he takes a short cut across the fields and his total journey is 3.12 km. Work out the percentage decrease in the distance he has walked.

5   Ariana's grandfather was 180 cm tall but is now 179.1 cm tall. Work out the percentage loss in his height.

6   A collector buys old phone boxes then sells them on. If the collector buys a phone box for £220 and sells it for £297, work out the percentage profit.

7   Work out the percentage profit or loss in each case.

	cost price	selling price
(a)	£70	£80.50
(b)	£640	£588.80
(c)	£8	£20

8   Rayaan buys 6 chairs at £15 each, 2 tables at £40 each and 1 wardrobe for £55. He then manages to sell 5 chairs at £35 each, 1 table for £118 and the wardrobe for £95. Work out the overall percentage profit.

9   Josiah invests £20 000 in a share of a sports company. Three years' later he sells his share for £22 240. What percentage profit did Josiah make?

10 A market stallholder buys 80 teddy bears at £1.99 each. The stallholder sells 42 of the bears for £6 each, 20 of the bears for £3 each and the remaining bears for £1 each. Work out the stallholder's percentage profit.

2.2 Rounding off and estimating

In section 2.2 you will:

- round numbers to decimal places and significant figures
- calculate using estimates

Rounding off to decimal places

- Using a calculator, $3.19^3 = 32.461759$

We can *round off* this number to either one or two decimal places.

- Rounding to one decimal place

If the figure in the 2nd decimal place is 5 *or more*, round up. Otherwise do not.

$32.461759 = 32.5$ to 1 d.p.

Also
$17.85 = 17.9$ to 1 d.p.

- Rounding to two decimal places

If the figure in the 3rd decimal place is 5 *or more*, round up. Otherwise do not.

$32.461759 = 32.46$ to 2 d.p.

$0.035 = 0.04$ to 2 d.p.

Exercise 1M

1 Round off these numbers to one decimal place.
   - (a) 7.32
   - (b) 8.276
   - (c) 0.873
   - (d) 14.18
   - (e) 0.462
   - (f) 6.832
   - (g) 12.629
   - (h) 0.949

2 Write the following numbers correct to two decimal places.
   - (a) 4.368
   - (b) 7.062
   - (c) 18.333
   - (d) 5.073
   - (e) 0.2657
   - (f) 28.759
   - (g) 0.7584
   - (h) 3.086

3 Work out these answers on a calculator and then round off the numbers correct to two decimal places.
   - (a) $14.96 \div 7$
   - (b) $3186 \div 429$
   - (c) 0.63×5.4
   - (d) $\sqrt{19}$
   - (e) $\sqrt{6.8}$
   - (f) 0.73×0.89
   - (g) 2.65^2
   - (h) 0.56^2

4   Find the difference between the perimeter of the rectangle and the perimeter of the triangle, giving the answer to two decimal places. All lengths are in cm.

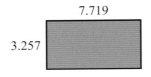

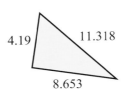

5   Work out these answers on a calculator and then round off the numbers correct to one decimal place.

(a) $\sqrt{83.6}$

(b) $\dfrac{7.14}{6.3}$

(c) $\dfrac{7.4^2}{3}$

(d) $0.9 \div 0.017$

(e) $\dfrac{3.6}{0.7} + 4.6$

(f) $\dfrac{\sqrt{63}}{9}$

(g) $\dfrac{3.2 \times 1.6}{2.9}$

(h) $\dfrac{7.8}{\sqrt{47}}$

6   A company makes 20 spheres. The diameter, in cm, of each sphere is listed below:

5.173	5.1761	5.168	5.1709
5.1634	5.1648	5.1762	5.167
5.1746	5.1639	5.1722	5.1753
5.1683	5.1717	5.1759	5.1628
5.172	5.1743	5.163	5.1664

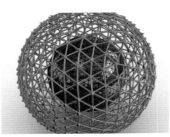

The company can only sell spheres which have a diameter of 5.17 cm when rounded off to two decimal places. How many of these spheres can the company *not* sell?

7   Jack was measured as being 1.7 m tall, correct to one decimal place. What is the shortest possible height Jack could be?

8   Cicely rounds off 15.49999 to two decimal places. She writes the answer 15.49. Is this correct?

9   A number is 27.8, rounded to one decimal place. Write down the smallest number greater than this number that rounds off to 27.9 to one decimal place.

Rounding off to significant figures

The most significant figure is the digit on the left of a number, excluding zeros. We can round off numbers to *significant figures*. We approach from the left and start counting as soon as we come to the first non-zero digit. Once we have started counting, we count any digits, zeros included.

$8\underline{2}.163 = 82.2$ to 3 s.f.
↑
round up

$6\underline{1}94.3 = 6200$ to 2 s.f.
↑
round up

$0.03\underline{0}714 = 0.0307$ to 3 s.f.
↑
round down

We need the two zeros after the '2' as the original number is approximately 6200

Exercise 2M

1 Write the following numbers to 3 significant figures.

(a) 59.6621   (b) 0.061943   (c) 32 791   (d) 586.08

(e) 7.6839   (f) 2468   (g) 5712.3   (h) 0.70285

(i) 5.00283   (j) 0.090407   (k) 74 628   (l) 0.08375

2 Kurt says that 6 and 4 are the first 2 significant figures in the number 0.604019. Is he correct?

3 Work out the area of this rectangle, giving the answer to 2 significant figures.

6.9 cm

16.18 cm

4 Write the following numbers to the amount of significant figures (s.f.) indicated.

(a) 8.392 (2 s.f.)   (b) 74.618 (1 s.f.)   (c) 7821 (1 s.f.)

(d) 0.07312 (2 s.f.)   (e) 0.10078 (3 s.f.)   (f) 5138.7 (1 s.f.)

(g) 0.90815 (4 s.f.)   (h) 24.638 (3 s.f.)   (i) 0.030849 (2 s.f.)

5 What is the smallest number that would be rounded to 28 500 correct to 3 significant figures?

6 What is the smallest number that would be rounded to 0.17 correct to 2 significant figures?

7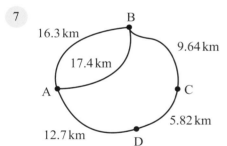

Olivia travels from B to C twice and along every other road once. How far does she travel in total, correct to 2 significant figures?

8 Work out these questions on a calculator and then round off the answers to 2 significant figures.

(a) $\sqrt{69.7}$ (b) $\dfrac{8.4 + 7.21}{3.2}$ (c) $\dfrac{11.6}{3.4} + 14$ (d) $\dfrac{8.4}{11} + \dfrac{4.21}{0.5}$

Estimating and checking answers

(a) Look at these calculations.

$4 \times 6, 4 \times 60, 40 \times 60, 40 \times 600$

$4 \times 6 = 24$

$4 \times 60 = 240$

$40 \times 60 = 2400$

$40 \times 600 = 24\,000$

(b) Work out a rough estimate for 382×12

Instead of 382 use 400

Instead of 12 use 10

382×12 is roughly 400×10, which is 4000

Exercise 3M

1. Work out
   (a) 30×2 (b) 30×20 (c) 30×2000 (d) 3×200
   (e) 6×70 (f) 60×700 (g) 40×9 (h) 400×90
   (i) 60×60 (j) 80×300 (k) 7×5000 (l) 40×70

2. Work out a rough estimate for the following.
   (a) 21×58 (b) 42×19 (c) 607×3 (d) 98.3×41

3. Do not use a calculator. Decide, by estimating, which of the three answers is closest to the exact answer. Write the calculation and the approximate answer for each question (use $\approx$).

	Calculation	A	B	C
(a)	97.9×11.3	90	500	1000
(b)	6.73×9.65	30	70	300
(c)	1.03×60.6	6	60	200
(d)	2.3×96	200	90	20
(e)	18.9×21.4	200	400	4000
(f)	5.14×5.99	15	10	30
(g)	811×11.72	8000	4000	800
(h)	99×98	1 million	100 000	10 000
(i)	1.09×29.6	20	30	60
(j)	$81\,413 \times 10.96$	8 million	1 million	800 000
(k)	$601 \div 3.92$	50	100	150
(l)	$402 \div 4.97$	8	0.8	80
(m)	$58.4 \div 0.98$	60	300	600
(n)	0.2×111.3	10	20	180
(o)	$217 \div 201.4$	0.2	1	10
(p)	$88.4 + 95 + 141$	300	100	3000

4. Petrol costs €1.09 per litre in Spain.
   Estimate the total cost of 48 litres.

Exercise 4M

Do not use a calculator for these questions.

1. Kate pays £25 per week for her electricity. Estimate the amount she spends on electricity in one year.

2. A school buys 69 tables. Estimate the total cost if each table is priced at £18.95

3. At a fun fair, customers pay 95p for a ride on a giant spinning wheel. The operator sells 2483 tickets during the weekend and his costs for electricity and rent are £114. Estimate his profit over the weekend.

In questions 4 and 5 there are six calculations and six answers. Write down each calculation and insert the correct answer from the list given. Use estimation.

4. (a) 5.9×6.1 (b) $19.8 \div 5$ (c) 32×9.9
   (d) $0.89 + 14.7$ (e) 4.5×44 (f) $4141 \div 40$

   | Answers: | 198, | 35.99, | 103.5, | 15.59, | 316.8, | 3.96 |

5. (a) $102.8 \div 5$ (b) $11.2 \div 98.6$ (c) 3×0.41
   (d) 34×2.9 (e) 51×3.9 (f) $238.6 \div 4.7$

   | Answers: | 50.76, | 20.56, | 1.23, | 198.9, | 98.6, | 0.114 |

6. A quick way of adding lots of prices on a shopping bill is to round every number to the nearest pound.

   So £2.43 becomes £2, £0.91 becomes £1, £0.24 becomes £0, and so on.

   (a) Use this method to estimate the totals below:

(i) WSKAS COCKTAIL	0.85	(ii) PLN BAGUETTE	0.49
H/EATING MINCE	3.95	FOIL	0.65
HAWAIIAN CRN	1.85	LETTUCE ROUND	0.24
PAIN AU CHOC	0.54	JW TUNA MAYO	0.75
PAIN AU CHOC	0.54	SOYA MILK	0.47
PAIN AU CHOC	0.54	SOYA MILK	0.47
BUTTER	0.89	ORNGE MRMLDE	0.74
BUTTER	0.89	YOGHURT	0.99
EGGS	0.78	SPGHTI/HOOPS	0.26
PORK/CHICK/PIE	2.03	CHEESE	1.34
MED.MAT.CHDR.	1.21	CAT FOOD	0.45
HOT PIES	1.47	CAT FOOD	0.45
POT. WAFFLES	1.39	VINEGAR	0.68
WHOLE BRIE	1.01	KING EDWARDS.	0.99
MUFFINS	0.49	UHT H/FAT MILK	0.26
BACON RASHERS	0.65	APPLES	1.89
BEETROOT	0.99	CAT FOOD	0.45
LOOSE CHEESE	0.99	PEACHES	0.24
		FROM. FRAIS	0.72

(b) Use a calculator to work out the exact total for part (i) and (ii).
Compare the answers with your estimates above.

Need more practice with rounding off and estimating?

1. Round off these numbers to the amount of decimal places (d.p.) indicated.
   (a) 0.618 (2 d.p.)   (b) 3.764 (1 d.p.)   (c) 20.65 (1 d.p.)   (d) 4.167 (1 d.p.)
   (e) 41.873 (2 d.p.)   (f) 0.0704 (3 d.p.)   (g) 7.7839 (2 d.p.)   (h) 0.0318 (1 d.p.)

2.  An estimated 50 000 people took 20 years to build the Great Wall of China. This number of people has been rounded off to the nearest thousand. What is the least number of people that may have built the Great Wall of China?

3. Work out these answers on a calculator and then round off the numbers correct to one decimal place.
   (a) $7.12 \div 4.6$ (b) $\dfrac{5.7}{0.7^2}$ (c) $(3.8 \div 1.3)^2$ (d) $\dfrac{\sqrt{(7.1 \times 2.6)}}{1.19}$

4. Write the decimal point in the correct place.
   (a) width of this book   1831 mm   (c) diameter of a football   3140 cm
   (b) weight of an 'average' new   (d) weight of a packet of sugar   100 kg
       born baby   3124 kg

5.  Some time ago a rather aggressive shark attacked a house in England. Estimate the following.
   (a) The length of the shark.
   (b) The cost of repairing the damage to the house.

6. What is the smallest number that would be rounded to 18.2 to one decimal place?

7. Answer true or false (the sign ≈ means 'is roughly equal to').
   (a) 27.8×3.2 (b) 904×23 (c) $4267 \div 38$
       $\approx 30 \times 3$ $\approx 900 \times 20$ $\approx 4000 \div 40$
       ≈ 90 $\approx 180\,000$ ≈ 100

8 Work out the answers, giving the numbers to 2 decimal places.

(a) 3.7×0.836 (b) $15.18 \div 16$ (c) $\sqrt{(2.8 \times 4.2)}$ (d) $(13 \div 8)^2$

9 A tablet costs £309. Roughly how much will 68 tablets cost?

Extension questions with rounding off and estimating

1 Write the following numbers to 2 significant figures.

(a) 61.87 (b) 0.8193 (c) 0.07128 (d) 5163

(e) 0.08018 (f) 0.00526 (g) 86 399 (h) 217.14

2

pot of paint	£15.95
box of tiles	£8.90
paintbrush	£2.99
piece of sandpaper	46p
2 m piece of wood	£3.12

Marie is decorating. She estimates that she needs 3 pots of paint, 4 paintbrushes, 5 pieces of wood, 12 pieces of sandpaper and 6 boxes of tiles.

(a) Estimate the total cost of her decorating supplies.

(b) Marie has a budget of £125. Can she afford everything?

3 A DVD is sold at £8.90 per copy. Estimate the total cost of 32 copies.

4 David had a three week holiday in Greece. On average he spent £58 each day. Estimate the total amount he spent during his holiday.

5 A boxer earned a fee of $8 million for a fight which lasted 1 minute 35 seconds. Estimate the money he earned per second of the fight.

6 $0.070537 = 0.07054$ to 3 significant figures. True or false?

7 Write down the smallest number that would be rounded to 8.17 correct to 3 significant figures.

8 Work out these questions, giving the answers to 3 significant figures.

(a) $\dfrac{71.67 \times 18.7}{11.6}$ (b) $\dfrac{15.6}{0.8} + \dfrac{7.19}{0.2}$ (c) $\dfrac{506.5 + 3.196}{17.3 + 31.6}$

9 (a) In 1989 thousands of people formed a human chain right across the USA, a distance of about 4300 km.
Estimate the number of people in the chain.

(b) Estimate the number of people needed to form a chain right around the equator. (Assume you have enough people volunteering to float for a while in the sea.) The distance right around the equator is about 40 000 km

10 Estimate

(a) the number of times your heart beats in one day (24 h)

(b) the thickness of one page in this book.

11 The number 0.0301825 is rounded off to both 3 decimal places and 3 significant figures. Which answer is larger and by how much?

Estimating game

- This is a game for two players. On squared paper, draw an answer grid with the numbers shown.

Answer grid

198	1089	99	100	360	18
180	450	22	440	155	1980
1240	200	45	62	100	550
40	620	495	279	800	55
2000	80	220	10	891	250
4950	1550	1000	3960	3069	341

- Take turns to choose two numbers from the question grid below and multiply them on a calculator.

Question grid

2	5	9
11	20	31
40	50	99

The number obtained is crossed out on the answer grid, using the player's own colour.

- The game continues until all the numbers in the answer grid have been crossed out. The object is to get four answers in a line (horizontally, vertically or diagonally). The winner is the player with most lines of four.

- A line of *five* counts as *two* lines of four.

- A line of *six* counts as *three* lines of four.

CHECK YOURSELF ON SECTIONS 2.1 and 2.2

1   Expressing one number as a percentage of another number

(a) John has 25 books. Nineteen of the books are about history. What percentage of the books are about history?

(b) A man earns £10 400 and pays £1768 in tax. What percentage of his earnings does he pay in tax?

2   Finding percentage increases and decreases

(a) Ali earns £540 each week.
She gets a pay rise of 15%.
How much money does she earn now?

(b) (i) Calculate the area of this picture.

    (ii) Calculate the new area when the length of each side is decreased by 5%

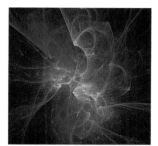

12 cm

12 cm

3   Rounding numbers to decimal places and significant figures

Round off

(a) 418.619 (to 1 d.p.)   (b) 0.081065 (to 3 s.f.)   (c) 3184.68 (to 2 s.f.)

Work out these questions, giving the answers correct to the number of decimal places or significant figures shown.

(d) $\dfrac{53.1^2}{0.7} - \dfrac{6.4}{1.18}$ (to 2 s.f.)   (e) $\dfrac{\sqrt{6}}{0.109}$ (to 2 d.p.)   (f) $\dfrac{15.6 + 7.5}{0.23^2}$ (to 3 s.f.)

4   Calculating using estimates

Work out a rough estimate for the following

(a) 19.7×41.2

(b) $804 \div 3.98$

(c) 6.09^2

(d) The label on a jar of jelly beans claims to contain 118 jelly beans. Estimate how many jelly beans there are in 21 jars.

2.3 Drawing graphs

In section 2.3 you will:

- review using lines which are parallel to the axes
- draw graphs
- use graphs
- find the equation of a line

Lines parallel to the axes

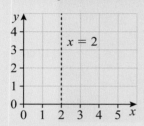

A line parallel to the
y-axis has an equation
$x = $ 'a number'

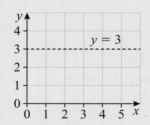

A line parallel to the
x-axis has an equation
$y = $ 'a number'

Exercise 1M

1　Copy the graph and then write down
　the coordinates for each point.

　A (2, 1)　H (,)
　B (,)　I (,)
　C (,)　J (,)
　D (,)　K (,)
　E (,)　L (,)
　F (,)　M (,)
　G (,)　N (,)

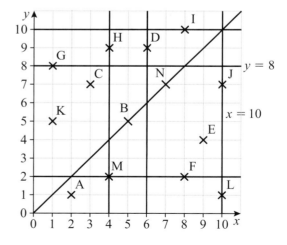

2　L lies on the line $x = 10$.
　Which other letter lies on $x = 10$?

3　Which letter lies on $x = 6$?

4　Which letters lie on $x = 4$?

5　G lies on the line $y = 8$.
　Which letter lies on $y = 10$?

6 Which letters lie on $y = 2$?

7 Which letters lie on $y = 5$?

8 Which letters lie on $y = 7$?

9 Which letter lies on $x = 9$?

10 The x coordinate of B is the same as the y coordinate. We say that B lies on the line $y = x$ (or $x = y$). Which other letter lies on $y = x$?

11 Letter M lies on $x = 4$ *and* $y = 2$. Which letter lies on $x = 8$ and $y = 2$?

12 Which letter lies on $x = 2$ and $y = 1$?

13 Which letter lies on $x = 10$ and $y = 7$?

In questions 14 and 15 there is a line of dots (A), a line of crosses (B) and a line of circles (C).

Write down the equations of the lines in each question.

14

15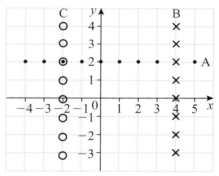

16 On squared paper, draw axes like those in questions 14 and 15 .
(a) Draw the lines $y = 2$ and $x = 3$.
Write down the coordinates of the point where the two lines meet.
(b) Draw the lines $y = -2$ and $x = 1$.
Write down the coordinates of the point where the two lines meet.

17 Name two lines which pass through each of the following points.
(a) $(4, 3)$ (b) $(6, 2)$ (c) $(7, -3)$ (d) $(-2, -8)$

18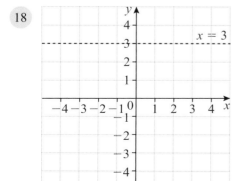

Max draws the line $x = 3$, as shown. He says that the point $(3, 1)$ lies on his line, which means the x value is equal to 3 (i.e. $x = 3$).

Explain clearly what is wrong with the graph and with what Max says.

Drawing graphs

Draw the graph of $y = 3x + 2$
for x-values from 0 to 5
by first completing the table below.

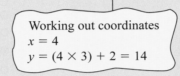

$3x + 2$ means $x \rightarrow \boxed{\times 3} \rightarrow \boxed{+2}$

For each x-value from 0 to 5,
use the equation to find the y-value.

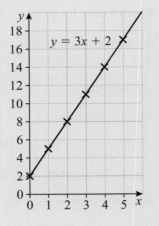

x	0	1	2	3	4	5
y	2	5	8	11	14	17
coordinates	(0, 2)	(1, 5)	(2, 8)	(3, 11)	(4, 14)	(5, 17)

Working out coordinates
$x = 4$
$y = (4 \times 3) + 2 = 14$

Note:

(a) Start both axes at 0 and take care with scales around 0

(b) Label the axes 'x' and 'y'

(c) Label the graph with its equation

Exercise 2M

For each question, copy and complete the table then draw the graph using the scales given.

1    $y = 2x + 4$ for x-values from 0 to 5

$2x + 4$ means $x \rightarrow \boxed{\times 2} \rightarrow \boxed{+4}$

x	0	1	2	3	4	5
y				10		
coordinates				(3, 10)		

(x-axis: use 1 cm for 1 unit
y-axis: use 1 cm for 2 units)

2    $y = 3x$ for x-values from 0 to 5

$3x$ means $x \rightarrow \boxed{\times 3}$

x	0	1	2	3	4	5
y		3				
coordinates		(1, 3)				

(x-axis: use 1 cm for 1 unit
y-axis: use 1 cm for 2 units)

3 $y = 2x + 1$ for x-values from 0 to 6

$2x + 1$ means $\boxed{x} \rightarrow \boxed{\times 2} \rightarrow \boxed{+1}$

x	0	1	2	3	4	5	6
y					9		
coordinates					(4, 9)		

(x-axis: use 1 cm for 1 unit
y-axis: use 1 cm for 1 unit)

4 $y = 6 - x$ for x-values from 0 to 6

$6 - x$ means $\boxed{6} \rightarrow \boxed{-x}$

x	0	1	2	3	4	5	6
y		5					
coordinates		(1, 5)					

(x-axis: use 1 cm for 1 unit
y-axis: use 1 cm for 1 unit)

5 $y = 3(x + 1)$ for x-values from 0 to 5

$3(x + 1)$ means $\boxed{x} \rightarrow \boxed{+1} \rightarrow \boxed{\times 3}$

(x-axis: 1 cm for 1 unit, y-axis: 1 cm for 2 units)

6 $y = 12 - 2x$

for x-values from 0 to 6

(x-axis: 1 cm for 1 unit,
y-axis: 1 cm for 1 unit)

7 $y = 20 - 3x$

for x-values from 0 to 6

(x-axis: 1 cm for 1 unit,
y-axis: 1 cm for 2 units)

Curved graphs

Draw the graph of $y = x^2 - 2$ for x-values from -3 to $+3$

$x^2 - 2$ means $\boxed{x} \rightarrow \boxed{\times x} \rightarrow \boxed{-2}$

For each x-value from -3 to $+3$, use the equation to find the y-value.

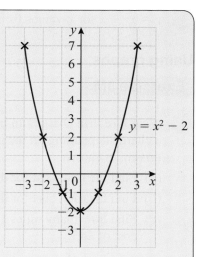

x	-3	-2	-1	0	1	2	3
y	7	2	-1	-2	-4	2	7
coordinates	$(-3, 7)$	$(-2, 2)$	$(-1, -1)$	$(0, -2)$	$(1, -1)$	$(2, 2)$	$(3, 7)$

Remember: a negative multiplied by a negative gives a positive
$y = (-3 \times -3) - 2 = 9 - 2 = 7$

Draw a *smooth* curve through the points.

Exercise 2E

For each question, copy and complete the table then draw the graph using a scale of 2 cm to 1 unit on the x-axis and 1 cm to 1 unit on the y-axis.

1 $y = x^2$ for x-values from -3 to $+3$

x^2 means $x \rightarrow \boxed{\times x}$

x	-3	-2	-1	0	1	2	3
y			1				
coordinates			$(-1, 1)$				

2 $y = x^2 + 4$ for x-values from -3 to $+3$

$x^2 + 4$ means $x \rightarrow \boxed{\times x} \rightarrow \boxed{+4}$

x	-3	-2	-1	0	1	2	3
y		8					
coordinates		$(-2, 8)$					

3 $y = x^2 - 3$ for x-values from -3 to $+3$

4 $y = (x - 2)^2$ for x-values from -1 to $+5$

5 $y = (x + 1)^2$ for x-values from -4 to $+2$

6 $y = x^2 + x$ for x-values from -3 to $+3$

Using graphs

Exercise 3M

1   A car hire firm charges an initial fee plus a charge depending on the number of miles driven, as shown.

(a) Find the total cost for driving 140 miles.

(b) Find the total cost for driving 600 miles.

(c) Find how many miles I can drive for a cost of £45

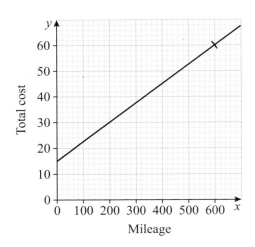

2 In June 2008, the pound (£) was worth 1.6 US dollars ($).

This graph converts pounds into dollars.

(a) What does one little square on the 'Pounds' axis show you?

(b) What does one little square on the 'Dollars' axis show you?

Use the graph to find out how many dollars are the same as

(c) £50   (d) £25

(e) £35   (f) £60

Use the graph to find out how many pounds are the same as

(g) $48   (h) $70

(i) $16   (j) $136

(k) On holiday in the USA, Chad bought a meal for $40. How many pounds did the meal cost?

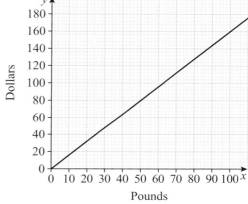

3 A teacher has marked a test out of 80 and wishes to convert the marks into percentages. Draw axes as shown and draw a straight line through the points (0, 0) and (80, 100).

(a) Use your graph to convert

    (i) 63 marks into a percentage

    (ii) 24 marks into a percentage.

(b) The pass mark was 60%. How many marks out of 80 were needed for a pass?

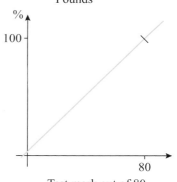

4 Temperature is usually measured in °C (Celsius) but can be measured in °F (Fahrenheit).

(a) Draw axes, as shown, with a scale of 1 cm to 10°
Draw a '×' where °F = 32 and °C = 0
Draw another '×' where °F = 86 and °C = 30

(b) Draw a long straight line through the two points above and use your graph to convert

    (i) 20°C into °F   (ii) −10°C into °F

    (iii) 50°F into °C

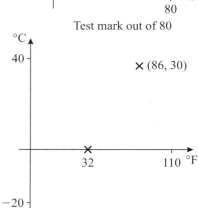

(c) The normal body temperature of a healthy person is 98°F. Sue's temperature is 39°C. Should she stay at home today or go to school as usual?

5 Selmin and Katie make different charges for people wanting pages typed professionally.

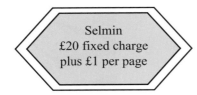

(a) How much would Selmin charge to type 30 pages?

(b) How much would Katie charge to type 10 pages?

(c) Draw axes for the number of pages typed and the total cost, using the scales given.

(d) On the same diagram, draw a graph for each typist to show their charges for up to 60 pages.

(e) Use your graphs to decide for what number of pages Selmin is the cheaper typist to choose.

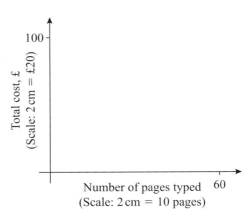

Drawing graphs using a computer or graphical calculator

Exercise 4M

Use a *graphical calculator* or a *graph plotter* on a *computer*.

1 Draw the graphs of $y = 2x + 6$,

$y = 2x + 1$, $y = 2x - 2$ and $y = 2x - 5$

Write down what you notice about each line and its equation.

(Clue: look at the points where the lines cut the y-axis)

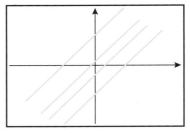

2 Draw the graphs of $y = x + 2$, $y = x + 5$, $y = x - 1$ and $y = x - 3$.
Write down what you notice about each line and its equation.

3 Draw the graphs of $y = 3x$, $y = 3x + 2$, $y = 3x - 4$ and $y = 3x - 2$.
Write down what you notice about each line and its equation.

4 (a) Where do you expect the line $y = 2x + 5$ to cut the y-axis?

(b) Where do you expect the line $y = 4x - 3$ to cut the y-axis?

5 Write down which of the two lines below are parallel.

$y = 6x - 3$ $y = 2x - 3$ $y = 6x + 1$

6 Write down the equation of any line parallel to $y = 5x + 3$

7 Draw the graphs of

$y = x^2$ $\qquad$ $y = 4 \div x$ $\qquad$ $y = x^2 + 3$ $\qquad$ $y = x^2 - 4$

8 Do you think the graph of $y = x^2 + 1$ would be a straight line?

Finding the equation of a line

- This line passes through:

  $(0, 2), (1, 3), (2, 4), (3, 5), (4, 6)$.

  For each point the y coordinate is two more than the x coordinate. The equation of the line is $y = x + 2$

  We could also say that the x coordinate is always two less than the y coordinate. The equation of the line could then be written as $x = y - 2$

  [Most mathematicians use the equation beginning '$y = $'].

- This line slopes the other way and passes through:

  $(0, 4), (1, 3), (2, 2), (3, 1), (4, 0)$.

  The sum of the x coordinate and the y coordinate is always 4. The equation of the line is $x + y = 4$

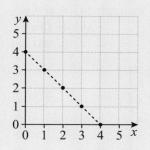

Exercise 5M

1 For each part write down the coordinates of the points marked, then write down the equation of the line that the points pass through.

(a)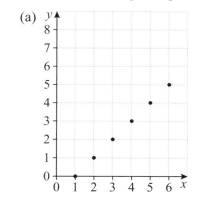

(b)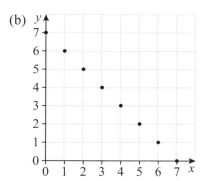

In questions ② to ⑨ you are given the coordinates of several points on a line. Find the equation of each line.

2

x	1	2	3	4	5	6
y	4	5	6	7	8	9

3

x	1	2	3	4	5	6
y	6	7	8	9	10	11

4

x	1	3	5	7
y	8	10	12	14

5

x	2	4	6	8
y	0	2	4	6

6

x	10	12	14	16
y	4	6	8	10

7

x	1	2	3	4	5
y	2	4	6	8	10

8

x	2	4	5	6
y	6	12	15	18

9

x	8	7	6	5	4	3
y	0	1	2	3	4	5

10 Find the equation of the line
through (a) A and B
        (b) B and C
        (c) C and A

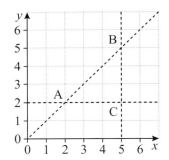

11 Find the equation of the line
through (a) D and E
        (b) E and F
        (c) D and F

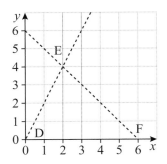

12

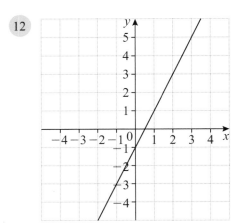

Which equation below belongs to the line shown opposite?

$$y = 2x + 3 \qquad y = 2x - 1 \qquad y = \tfrac{1}{2}x - 1$$

Need more practice with drawing graphs?

1. Write down the coordinates for each point.

   A (2, 4)

   B (5, 2)

   C (−2, 5)

   □

   N (5, −3)

2. Point A lies on the line $x = 2$. Which other letter lies on $x = 2$?

3. Point N lies on the line $y = -3$. Which other letter lies on $y = -3$?

4. Which letters lie on the line $x = -5$?

5. Which letter lies on the line $y = 5$?

6. Which letters lie on the line $y = x$?

7. Which line passes through B and N?

8. Which line passes through A and J?

9. Which line passes through L and I?

10. Which line passes through C, F and K?

For questions 11 and 12, complete a table of x and y values then draw the graph using the scales given.

11. $y = 4x + 1$ for x-values from 0 to 6

x	0	1	2	3	4	5	6
y					17		
coordinates					(4, 17)		

(x-axis: use 1 cm for 1 unit, y-axis: use 2 cm for 1 unit)

12. $y = \dfrac{x}{2}$ for x-values from 0 to 7

x	0	1	2	3	4	5	6	7
y						$2\frac{1}{2}$		
coordinates						$(5, 2\frac{1}{2})$		

(x-axis: use 1 cm for 1 unit, y-axis: use 2 cm for 1 unit)

13 The graph converts kilometres (km) into miles.

Use this graph to convert

(a) 40 km into miles

(b) 15 miles into km

(c) 45 miles into km

(d) 64 km into miles.

(e) Which is further – 30 km or 20 miles?

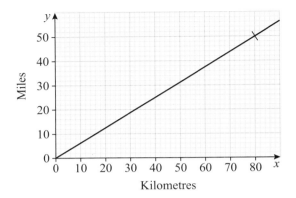

In questions **14** to **17** you are given the coordinates of several points on a line. Find the equation of each line.

14

x	1	2	3	4	5
y	5	6	7	8	9

15

x	0	1	2	3	4
y	−5	−4	−3	−2	−1

16

x	5	4	3	2	1	0
y	0	1	2	3	4	5

17

x	4	3	2	1	0
y	0	1	2	3	4

Extension questions with drawing graphs

1 Amelia says that the point (2, 5) lies on the line $y = 4x - 3$. *Explain clearly* whether she is correct or not.

2

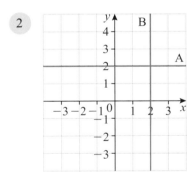

Which line opposite is the line $y = 2$: A or B?

3 For each equation, copy and complete the table then draw the graph using a suitable scale for the x and y axes.

(a) $y = x^2 + 2x$

x	−4	−3	−2	−1	0	1	2
y		3					
coordinates		(−3, 3)					

(b) $y = x^2 - 2x + 1$

x	-2	-1	0	1	2	3	4
y		4					
coordinates		$(-1, 4)$					

4 Write down the equations of lines A, B and C shown opposite.

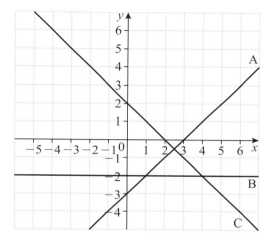

5 Using the same axes, draw the graphs of $y = x + 1$ and $x + y = 7$.
Take values of x from 0 to 6.
Write down the coordinates of the point where the lines meet.

6 In each part you are given the coordinates of several points on a line.
Find the equation of each line (each answer will be of the form $y = mx + c$, where m and c are numbers to be found).

(a)

x	1	2	3	4	5
y	3	5	7	9	11

(b)

x	0	1	2	3	4
y	1	4	7	10	13

(c)

x	0	1	2	3	4
y	6	8	10	12	14

(d)

x	1	2	3	4	5
y	6	10	14	18	22

7 On the same graph, draw the lines $x + y = 8$
$y = 2x + 2$
$y = 2$

Take values of x from 0 to 8. Find the area of the triangle formed.

✖ Spot the mistakes 3 ✖

Percentages, rounding, estimating and drawing graphs

Work through each question below and *explain clearly* what mistakes have been made.
Beware – some questions are correctly done.

1   Draw the lines $x = 4$ and $y = 2$. Write down the coordinates where the two lines meet.

Answer: 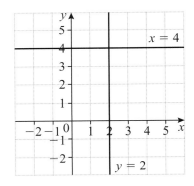   The lines meet at (2, 4).

2   Fiona earns £525 each week. She is given a 5% pay rise.
How much does Fiona now earn each week?

Answer: 5% of $525 = \dfrac{525}{5} = 105$

Fiona now earns $525 + 105 = £630$ each week.

3   There are 20 people on a bus. 13 of these people have a bag.
What percentage of the people do not have a bag?

Answer:

$$\frac{13}{20} = \frac{65}{100} = 65\%$$

$\times 5$

$\times 5$

65% of the people do not have a bag.

4   Work out $\dfrac{7.13 + 0.086}{4}$, giving the answer to 1 decimal place.

Answer:
```
    7 . 1 3
 +  0 . 0 8 6
 _____
    7 . 2 1 6
        1
```
```
      1 . 8 0 4
 4 ) 7 . ³2 1 ¹6
```
Now round off 1.804 to
1 decimal place.

Final answer = 1.8 to 1 d.p.

5

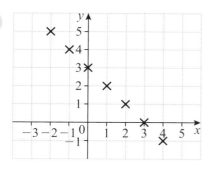

Write down the equation of the line which passes through all the crosses.

Answer: $y = x + 3$

6 Estimate the value of $\dfrac{9.98^2 - 89}{0.501}$

Answer: $\dfrac{9.98^2 - 89}{0.501} \approx \dfrac{10^2 - 90}{0.5} = \dfrac{100 - 90}{0.5}$

$= \dfrac{10}{0.5} = 5$

7 A short break to Rome costs £550. In January the cost of the holiday is reduced by 20%. Unfortunately the new cost of the holiday is increased by 20% in May.

How much does the holiday now cost?

Answer: 10% of 550 = 55

so 20% of 550 = 110

Cost after 20% decrease = 550 − 110 = £440

10% of 440 = 44

so 20% of 440 = 88

Cost after 20% increase = 440 + 88

Final cost = £528

8 Calculate the value of $\dfrac{3^2 - 7.3332}{8^2 + 4^2}$, giving the answer to 2 significant figures.

Answer: Calculator gives 0.020835, which equals 0.0208 to 2 significant figures.

9 Anya scores $\frac{29}{40}$ in a maths test and Kabir scores $\frac{42}{60}$ in a maths test.

Who scores the higher percentage and by how much?

Answer: Anya scores $\dfrac{29}{40} \times 100 = 72.5\%$

Kabir scores $\dfrac{42}{60} \times 100 = 70\%$

Anya scores 2.5% more than Kabir.

10 Draw a table of values for $y = x^2 + 3$ using x-values from -3 to $+3$.
Use these values to draw the graph of $y = x^2 + 3$.

Answer:

x	-3	-2	-1	0	1	2	3
y	-3	-1	1	3	5	7	9
coordinates	$(-3, -3)$	$(-2, -1)$	$(-1, 1)$	$(0, 3)$	$(1, 5)$	$(2, 7)$	$(3, 9)$

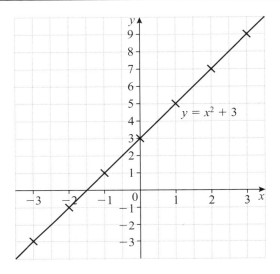

2.4 Sequences 1

In section 2.4 you will:

- find and use a rule for a sequence
- solve problems using differences in sequences

Sequences are very important in mathematics. Scientists carrying out research will often try to find patterns or rules to describe the results they obtain from experiments.

Here is a sequence 3, 6, 12, 24

- A number sequence is a set of numbers in a given order.
- Each number in a sequence is called a *term*.

Exercise 1M

Find the next number in each sequence.

1 4, 9, 14, 19

2 5, 8, 11, 14

3 17, 13, 9, 5

4	32, 25, 18, 11	5	2, 4, 8, 16	6	$2, 2\frac{1}{2}, 3, 3\frac{1}{2}$

7   0.6, 0.8, 1, 1.2   8   1, 4, 8, 13   9   3, 30, 300

10 80, 79, 77, 74   11 1, 3, 9, 27   12 11, 7, 3, −1

13 100, 10, 1, 0.1   14 −5, −2, 1, 4   15 $\frac{1}{16}, \frac{1}{8}, \frac{1}{4}, \frac{1}{2}$

16 Write down each sequence and find the missing numbers.

(a) | 2 | 6 | 18 | 54 | |

(b) | 9 | 5 | | −3 | −7 |

(c) | | 8 | | | 17 | 20 |

(d) | 1 | 2 | 4 | | 11 |

17 The first term of a sequence is 7 and the *term-to-term rule* is 'add 8'. The next term is 7 'add 8', which equals 15. Write down the next five terms of the sequence.

18 The first term of a sequence is 19 and the term-to-term rule is 'subtract 3'.
Write down the first five terms of the sequence.

19 Write down the term-to-term rule for each sequence.
(a) 11, 13, 15, 17, 19   (b) 62, 57, 52, 47
(c) 5, 10, 20, 40   (d) 81, 27, 9, 3

20 This picture shows ten piles of coins.

(a) Another row of piles is placed on the bottom. How many piles of coins are there now?

(b) Another two rows of piles are now added onto the bottom. How many piles of coins are there now?

21 Write down the rule for each sequence.
(a) 4.3, 4.5, 4.7, 4.9   (b) 86, 43, 21.5   (c) 0.02, 0.2, 2, 20
(d) 4, 1, −2, −5   (e) 1.6, 0.8, 0.4, 0.2   (f) 2.01, 2.05, 2.09

22 You are given the first term and the rule of several sequences.
Write down the first five terms of each sequence.

	First term	Rule
(a)	26	add 5
(b)	5	subtract 2
(c)	6	double
(d)	8000	divide by 10

Differences in sequences

Different numbers of lines are drawn below and the maximum number of crossovers for each arrangement is shown.

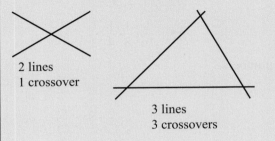

2 lines
1 crossover

3 lines
3 crossovers

4 lines
6 crossovers

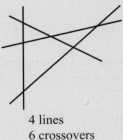

Lines	Crossovers
2	1
3	3
4	6
5	10

One method for predicting further results is to look at the *differences* between the numbers in the 'crossovers' column.

The differences form an easy pattern so that we can predict that there will be a maximum of 15 crossovers when 6 lines are drawn.

Lines	Crossovers	Differences
2	1	
		2
3	3	
		3
4	6	
		4
5	10	
		(5)
6	(15)	

predictions

Exercise 2M

1 Predict the next two terms in each sequence.

(a) 10, 12, 15, 19, …, …

(b) 1, 8, 17, 28, 41, …, …

(c) 5, 11, 19, 29, 41, …, …

2 Here is a sequence: 3   4   6   9

Write the numbers in a table as shown.

Predict the numbers shown with ? to find the next two terms in the sequence 3, 4, 6, 9, …

Terms	Differences
3	
	1
4	
	2
6	
	3
9	
	(?)
(?)	
	(?)
(?)	

3 Below are three sequences. Use differences to predict the next two numbers in each sequence.

(a) | 6 | 7 | 9 | 12 | 16 | ? | ? |

(b) | 7 | 11 | 16 | 22 | 29 | ? | ? |

(c) | 5 | 8 | 12 | 17 | 23 | ? | ? |

4 Here is a sequence of matchstick squares

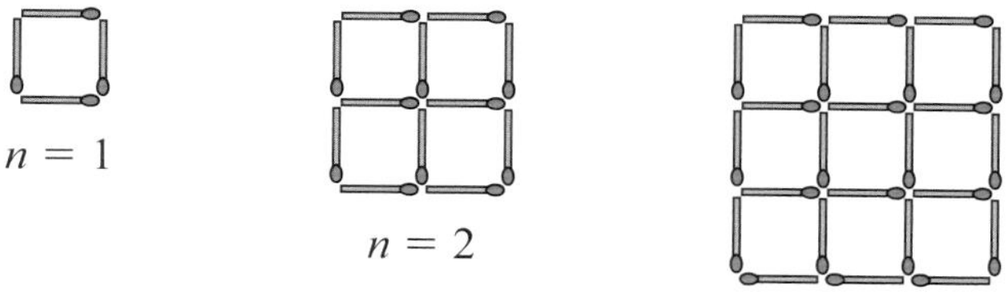

$n = 1$

$n = 2$

$n = 3$

Shape number, n	No. of matches	Differences
1	4	
		8
2	12	
		12
3	24	
		16
4	40	
5	?	

Use the differences to predict the number of matches in shape number 5.

Need more practice with sequences?

1 In an arithmetic sequence the terms go up or go down in equal steps.
For example 5, 9, 13, 17, … or 20, 17, 14, 11, …
Find the missing numbers in these arithmetic sequences.

(a)   2,   ☐ ,   12,   17,   ☐ , ☐

(b)   ☐ ,   32,   ☐ ,   20,   14

(c)   ☐ ,   27,   ☐ ,   21,   ☐

(d)   ☐ ,   41,   ☐ , ☐ , ☐ ,   17

116

2 The following are arithmetic sequences.

(a)
The 2nd term is 7
The 3rd term is 12
What is the 6th term?

(b)
The 2nd term is 17
The 4th term is 31
What is the 6th term?

3 The rule for the number sequences below is

'*double and add 1*'

Find the missing numbers.

(a) 3 $\longrightarrow$ 7 $\longrightarrow$ 15 $\longrightarrow$ 31 $\longrightarrow$ ☐   (b) ☐ $\longrightarrow$ 9 $\longrightarrow$ 19 $\longrightarrow$ 39

(c) ☐ $\longrightarrow$ 7 $\longrightarrow$ ☐ $\longrightarrow$ ☐

4 The rule for the sequences below is

'*multiply by 3 and take away 1*'

Find the missing numbers.

(a) 1 $\longrightarrow$ 2 $\longrightarrow$ 5 $\longrightarrow$ ☐   (b) ☐ $\longrightarrow$ 8 $\longrightarrow$ 23 $\longrightarrow$ ☐

(c) 4 $\longrightarrow$ ☐ $\longrightarrow$ ☐ $\longrightarrow$ ☐

5 Find the rule for each sequence. Each rule has two operations (similar to the rules in questions 3 and 4 above).

(a) 4 $\longrightarrow$ 7 $\longrightarrow$ 13 $\longrightarrow$ 25   (b) 2 $\longrightarrow$ 7 $\longrightarrow$ 22 $\longrightarrow$ 67

6 Look at this sequence $3^2 = 9$

$$33^2 = 1089$$
$$333^2 = 110\,889$$
$$3333^2 = 11\,108\,889$$

Write down the value of $33\,333^2$ and the value of $33\,333\,333^2$

7 Copy and complete the following sequence.

$$2 \times 99 = 198$$
$$3 \times 99 = 297$$
$$4 \times 99 = 396$$
$$5 \times 99 = ☐$$
$$☐ \times 99 = ☐$$

Extension questions with sequences

1   Below are three sequences. Use differences to predict the next two numbers in each sequence.

(a) 1
     6
     13
     22
     33
     (?)
     (?)

(b) 3
     6
     13
     24
     39
     (?)
     (?)

(c) 11
     14
     22
     35
     53
     (?)
     (?)

2   Below are the first three members of a sequence of patterns of hexagons made with sticks.

Diagram 1   Diagram 2   Diagram 3

Draw diagram 4 and count the number of sticks it contains. Write your results in a table and then predict the number of sticks needed to make diagram 6.

3   Find the next term in each sequence.

(a) $0.4, \frac{3}{5}, 0.8$ (b) $n, 2n, 3n, 4n$ (c) $\frac{1}{4}, 0.3, \frac{7}{20}$ (d) $21m, 17m, 13m, 9m$

4   (a) Look at the pattern below and then continue it for a further three rows.

$2^2 + 2 + 3 = 9$
$3^2 + 3 + 4 = 16$
$4^2 + 4 + 5 = 25$
☐   ☐   ☐   ☐

(b) Write down the line which starts
$12^2 + \ldots$

(c) Write down the line which starts
$20^2 + \ldots$

118

5   Below is a sequence of rectangles where each new diagram is obtained by drawing around the outside of the previous diagram, leaving a space of 1 unit.

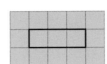

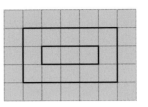

Diagram 1
3 squares

Diagram 2
15 squares

Diagram 3
35 squares

(a) Draw diagram 4 and count the number of squares it contains. Enter the number in a table and use differences to *predict* the number of squares in diagram 5.

(b) Now draw diagram 5 to check if your prediction was correct.

Diagram	Squares	Differences
1	3	
		12
2	15	
		20
3	35	
4		

6   The term-to-term rule for a sequence is 'divide by 10'.
Write down the first six terms of the sequence if the third term is 70

7   Some patterns are made from matchsticks.

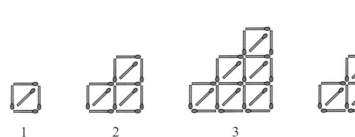

Pattern   1   2   3   4

(a) How many matchsticks will be in pattern number 6?

(b) Describe the term-to-term rule for this sequence.

CHECK YOURSELF ON SECTIONS 2.3 and 2.4

1 Using lines which are parallel to the axes

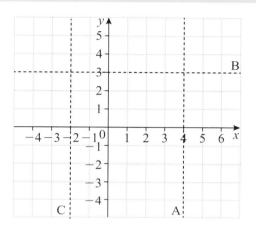

Write down the equation of

(a) line A

(b) line B

(c) line C.

(d) On which line is the point $(4, -2)$?

2 Drawing graphs

Copy and complete the table for $y = 4 - x$ then draw the graph using 1 cm for 1 unit on each axis.

x	0	1	2	3	4
y					
coordinates					

3 Using graphs

In the UK, petrol consumption for cars is usually quoted in 'miles per gallon'. In other countries, the metric equivalent is 'km per litre'.

(a) Convert 20 mpg. into km per litre.

(b) Convert 5 km per litre into mpg.

(c) A car travels 9 km on one litre of petrol. Convert this consumption into miles per gallon. Work out how many gallons of petrol the car will use, if it is driven a distance of 100 miles.

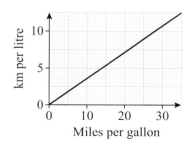

4 Finding the equation of a line

(a) The coordinates of several points on a line are given opposite. Write down the equation of the line.

x	1	2	3	4	5	6
y	7	8	9	10	11	12

(b)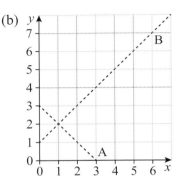

Write down the equation of line A and the equation of line B.

(Look at the coordinates of the points on each line carefully)

5 Finding and using a rule for a sequence

Write down the term-to-term rule for each sequence.

(a) 3, 12, 48, 192   (b) 5, 11, 17, 23   (c) 5, 2, −1, −4

(d) The first term of a sequence is 9 and the term-to-term rule is 'multiply by 3 then subtract 1'. Write down the first four terms of the sequence.

6 Using differences in sequences

Use differences to predict the next two numbers in each sequence.

(a) 6, 9, 13, 18, 24, ☐, ☐   (b) 4, 7, 12, 19, 28, ☐, ☐

2.5 Reflection and enlargement

In section 2.5 you will:

- draw reflections with and without using coordinates
- enlarge shapes
- use centres of enlargement

Drawing reflections

Take great care when the mirror line lies along a diagonal. Notice that the line PP′ is perpendicular to the mirror line.

Triangle P′Q′R′ is the *image* of triangle PQR under reflection in the mirror line. Similarly triangle PQR is the *image* of triangle P′Q′R′ under reflection in the same line.

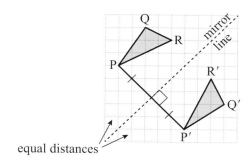

equal distances

The mirror line can pass through the shape which is being reflected, as shown here.

Exercise 1M

In questions ① to ⑨ , copy each shape onto squared paper and draw the image after reflection in the broken line.

1

2
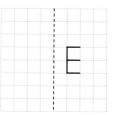

3
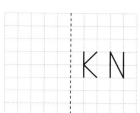

4
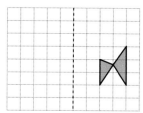

5
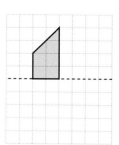

6
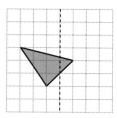

7
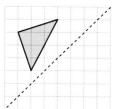

8
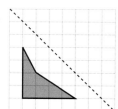

9
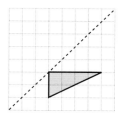

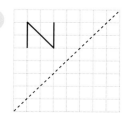

10 Write your name in capital letters and then reflect the letters in a mirror horizontal line.

11 Part of the sign for a taxi firm has snapped off. The missing part of the first letter is a reflection in a line drawn from P to Q.

On squared paper, draw an accurate picture of all the taxi sign before the corner part snapped off.

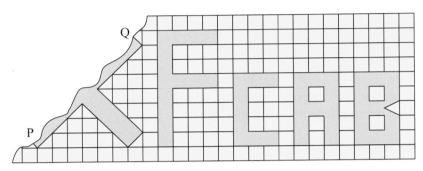

In questions 12 to 14 , first reflect the shape in line 1 and then reflect the image in line 2.

12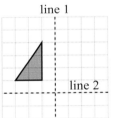

13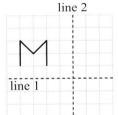

14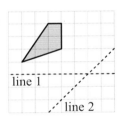

Using coordinates

(a) Triangle 2 is the image of triangle 1 under reflection in the *x-axis*.
    We will use the shorthand '△' for 'triangle'.

(b) △3 is the image of △2 under reflection in the line $x = -1$

(c) △4 is the image of △1 under reflection in the line $y = x$.

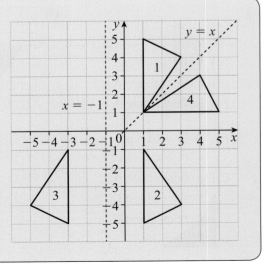

Exercise 2M

1. Copy the diagram onto squared paper.

   (a) Reflect the shaded triangle in the line $y = 2$. Label the image A.

   (b) Reflect the shaded triangle in the line $x = 1$. Label the image B.

   (c) Reflect the shaded triangle in the x-axis. Label the image C.

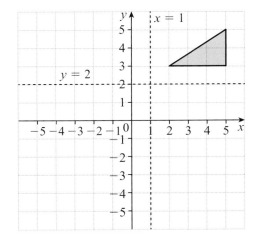

2. Copy the diagram onto squared paper. Draw the image of the shaded triangle under reflection in

   (a) $y = 1$, label it $\triangle$A

   (b) $x = -1$, label it $\triangle$B

   (c) $y = x$, label it $\triangle$C

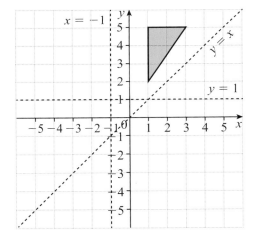

3. (a) Draw x and y axes with values from -6 to $+6$ and draw shape A which has vertices at $(3, 1)$, $(5, 3)$, $(5, 1)$, $(4, 0)$.

   (b) Reflect shape A in the x-axis onto shape B.

   (c) Reflect shape A in the y-axis onto shape C.

   (d) Reflect shape A in the line $y = x$ onto shape D.

4. (a) Draw x and y axes with values from -6 to $+6$ and draw shape A which has vertices at $(1, -2)$, $(3, -3)$, $(3, -4)$, $(1, -6)$.

   (b) Reflect shape A in the y-axis onto shape B.

   (c) Reflect shape B (not shape A!) in the line $y = x$ onto shape C.

   (d) Reflect shape C in the line $y = 1\frac{1}{2}$ onto shape D.

   (e) Write down the coordinates of the vertices of shape D.

124

5 Write down the equation of the mirror line for the following reflections

(a) △A → △C

(b) △A → △B

(c) △D → △G

(d) △F → △E

(e) △F → △D

Remember:

The x-axis is also the line y = 0
The y-axis is also the line x = 0

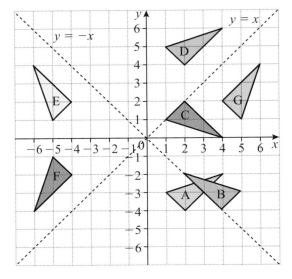

6 (a) Draw x and y axes with values from −6 to +6 and draw △1 with vertices at (3, 1), (6, 1), (6, 3).

(b) Reflect △1 in the line y = x onto △2

(c) Reflect △1 in the y-axis onto △3

(d) Reflect △2 in the y-axis onto △4

(e) Find the equation for the reflection △3 onto △4

7 The word 'AMBULANCE' is to be printed on the front of an ambulance so that a driver in front of the ambulance will see the word written the right way round, when viewed in the driver's mirror. How should the word be printed on the front of the ambulance?

8 (a) In what country did Napoleon live?
    Write your answer in "mirror" writing.

(b) Whose statue is on top of a column in Trafalgar Square?

(c) Which famous mathematician made a discovery after an apple fell on his head?

Enlargement

The original picture here has been enlarged by a scale factor of 2

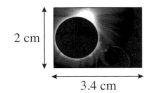

2 cm

3.4 cm

4 cm

6.8 cm

Notice that both the height *and* the width have been doubled.

- For an enlargement, the original and the enlargement must be exactly the same shape. All angles in both shapes are preserved.

-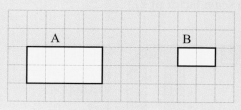

  Length of A = 2 × length of B

  Width of A = 2 × width of B

  ∴ A *is* an enlargement of B

Exercise 3M

Look at each pair of diagrams and decide whether or not one diagram is an enlargement of the other. For each question, write the scale factor of the enlargement or write 'not an enlargement'.

1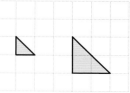

2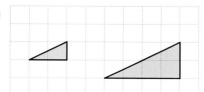

3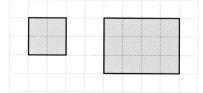

4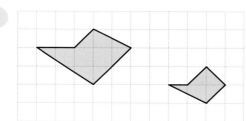

5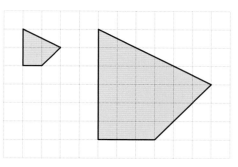

6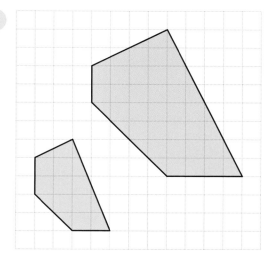

126

7 Here are some letters of the alphabet.

(a) Enlarge them by a scale factor of 2

(b) Draw your own initials and enlarge them by a scale factor of 2

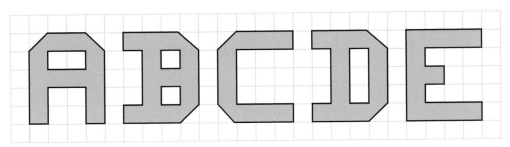

8 A photograph measuring 5 cm by 3.5 cm is enlarged so that it fits exactly into a frame measuring 20 cm by x cm. Calculate the value of x.

5 cm

3.5 cm

20 cm

x

9 This is a challenge! Draw an enlargement of this picture with scale factor 2. Shade in the numbers with different colours.

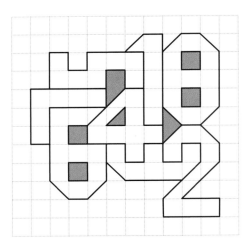

Centre of enlargement

(a) Draw an enlargement of triangle 1 with scale factor 3 and centre of enlargement O.

(b) Draw an enlargement of shape P with scale factor 2 and centre of enlargement O.

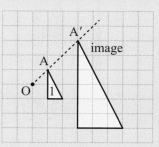

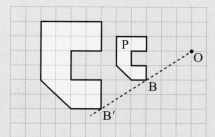

Notice that OA′ = 3 × OA.

Notice that OB′ = 2 × OB.

In both diagrams, just one point on the image has been found by using a construction line or by counting squares. When one point is known the rest of the diagram can easily be drawn, since the size and shape of the image is known.

Exercise 4M

In questions 1 to 6 , copy the diagram and then draw an enlargement using the scale factor and centre of enlargement given.

Leave room for enlargement!

1

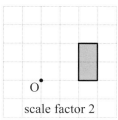

scale factor 2

2

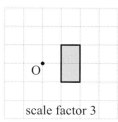

scale factor 3

3

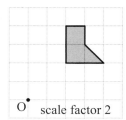

scale factor 2

4

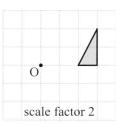

scale factor 2

5

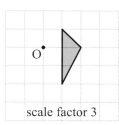

scale factor 3

6

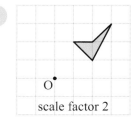

scale factor 2

7 Copy the diagram. Draw an enlargement of the triangle with scale factor 2 and centre of enlargement (0, 0).

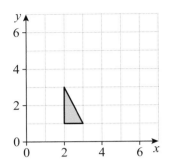

8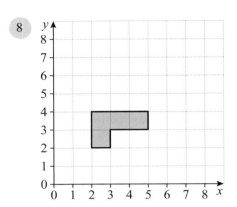

Copy this diagram. Draw an enlargement of the shape with scale factor 2 and centre of enlargement (2, 1).

Finding the centre of enlargement

A mathematical enlargement always has a *centre of enlargement* as well as a scale factor. The centre of enlargement is found by drawing lines through corresponding points on the object and image and finding where they intersect. For greater accuracy, it is better to count squares between points because it is difficult to draw construction lines accurately over a long distance.

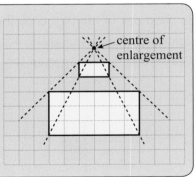

Exercise 5M

Draw the shapes and then draw lines through corresponding points to find the centre of enlargement. Don't draw the shapes too near the edge of the page!

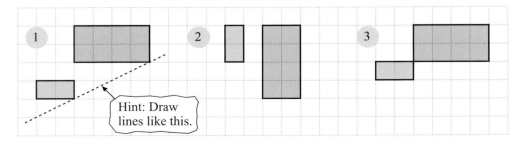

Hint: Draw lines like this.

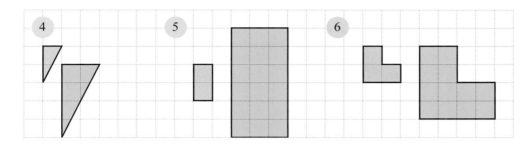

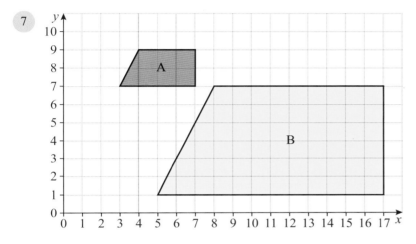

Shape A has been enlarged by scale factor 3 to make shape B.

Draw the diagram and find the coordinates of the centre of enlargement.

8 Shape P is enlarged by scale factor 4 about the centre of enlargement (3, 2) to give shape Q. What will be the coordinates of the centre of enlargement if shape Q is enlarged by scale factor $\frac{1}{4}$ to give shape P?

Need more practice with reflection and enlargement?

1

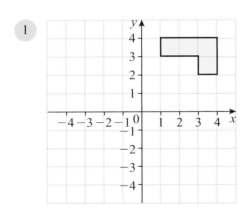

Copy the diagram.

(a) Reflect the shape in the x-axis. Label the image A.

(b) Reflect the shape in the y-axis. Label the image B.

130

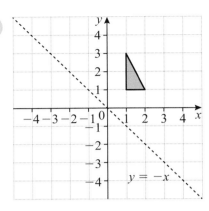

2

Copy the diagram.

Reflect the triangle in the line $y = -x$.

3 Look at each pair of diagrams and decide whether or not one diagram is an enlargement of the other. For each question, write the scale factor of the enlargement or write 'not an enlargement'.

(a)

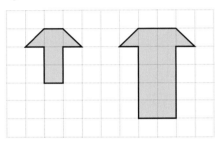

(b)

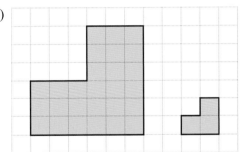

(c)

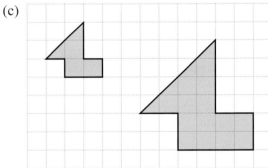

(d)

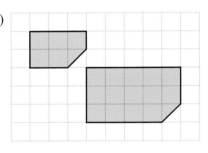

(e)

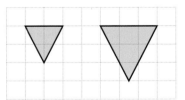

(f)

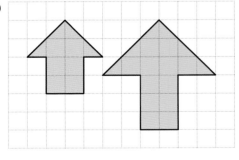

4 (a) Draw x and y axes with values from -6 to $+6$ and draw shape
   P which has vertices at $(-4, 2)$, $(-4, 3)$, $(-3, 5)$, $(-3, 2)$.

(b) Reflect shape P in the line $y = 2$ onto shape Q.

(c) Reflect shape Q in the y-axis onto shape R.

(d) Reflect shape R in the line $y = x$ onto shape S.

(e) Write down the coordinates of the vertices of shape S.

Enlarge the shapes in questions 5 to 7 by the scale factor given. Make sure you leave room on your page for the enlargement.

5 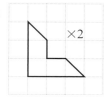 ×2

6 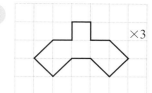 ×3

7 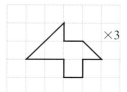 ×3

8 This picture is to be enlarged to fit the frame. Find the height of the frame.

60 mm

40 mm

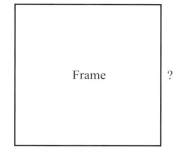

Frame ?

50 mm

Extension questions with reflection and enlargement

Copy each shape in questions 1 to 3 and draw the image after reflection in the broken line.

1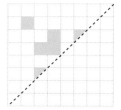

2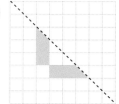

3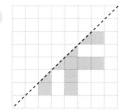

132

4   A photograph measuring 6 cm by 4 cm is reduced to fit frame A and another copy of the photograph is enlarged to fit frame B.

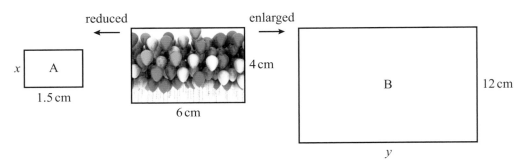

reduced   enlarged

x | A | 4 cm

1.5 cm   6 cm

B   12 cm

y

Calculate the value of x and the value of y.

5   The photo shows the captain of a ship holding a clock as his ship is slowly sinking.

The clock face has just 12 marks to show the hours. Draw the clock face, showing the hands as they would appear when looked at in a mirror, when the time was

(a) 2.30

(b) 5.45

6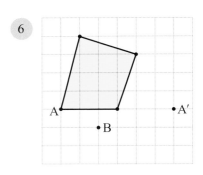

The yellow shape is reflected so that the image of A is A′.

(a) Copy the diagram and draw the mirror line for this reflection.

(b) Draw the image of the yellow shape after reflection in the mirror line.

(c) Draw a new mirror line which passes through point B and is at right angles to the first mirror line.
Draw the image of the yellow shape in this new mirror line.

7   (a) Draw x and y axes from -6 to $+6$

(b) Draw △1 with vertices at $(-4, 4)$, $(-4, 6)$, $(-1, 6)$.

(c) Reflect △1 in the line $x = -\frac{1}{2}$ onto △2

(d) Reflect △2 in the line $y = x$ onto △3

(e) Reflect △1 in the line $y = x$ onto △4

(f) Find the equation of the mirror line for the reflection △3 onto △4

8   For each of parts (a), (b) and (c), draw this grid.
    Draw an enlargement of the shape given in each part.

	Shape	Centre of enlargement	Scale factor
(a)	(1, 1) (2, 1) (2, 2) (1, 2)	(0, 0)	3
(b)	(2, 1) (4, 2) (2, 2)	(0, 0)	2
(c)	(4, 5) (6, 5) (6, 6) (4, 6)	(8, 8)	2

9   Shape A has been enlarged to make shape B.
    Copy the diagram then work out

    (a) the scale factor

    (b) the coordinates of the centre of
         enlargement.

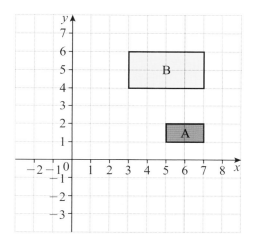

2.6 Rotation and combined transformations

In section 2.6 you will:

- rotate shapes

- find the centre of a rotation

- combine transformations

Rotation

Rotate the triangle through 90° anticlockwise about the point O.

The diagram on the right shows how tracing paper may be used.

Notice that we need three things to describe fully a rotation:

(a) the angle
(b) the direction (clockwise or anticlockwise)
(c) the centre of rotation.

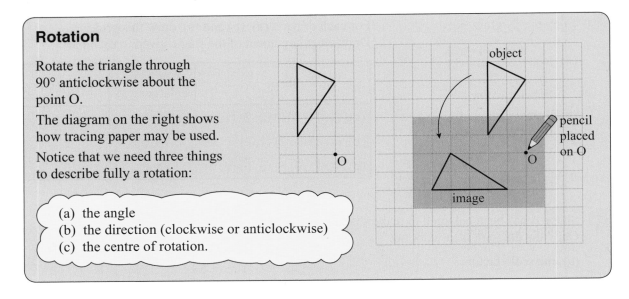

Exercise 1M

You may use tracing paper in this Exercise.

In questions ① to ⑥, draw the shape and then draw and shade its new position (the image) under the rotation given. Take O as the centre of rotation in each case.

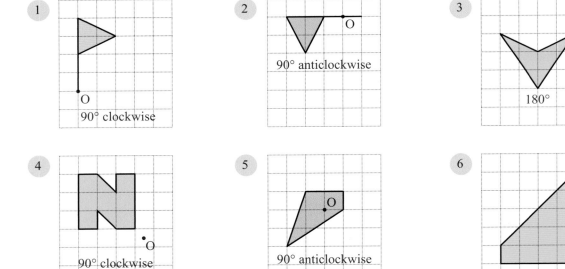

1 90° clockwise

2 90° anticlockwise

3 180°

4 90° clockwise

5 90° anticlockwise

6 45° anticlockwise

7 Copy the diagram shown, using axes from −6 to +6.

(a) Rotate triangle A 90° clockwise about (0, 0).
Label the new triangle P.

(b) Rotate triangle B 180° about (0, 0).
Label the new triangle Q.

(c) Rotate shape C 90° anticlockwise about (2, 2).
Label the new shape R.

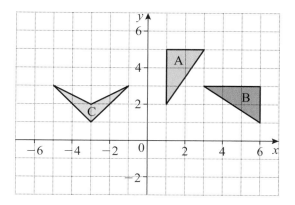

8 Triangle A is rotated 180° about (1, 3). Its image is triangle B. Triangle B is now rotated 180° about (1, 3). The new image is triangle C. What is the connection between triangle C and triangle A?

9 Copy the diagram shown.

(a) Rotate shape A 90° anticlockwise about (−3, −4). Label the new shape P.

(b) Rotate triangle B 90° clockwise about (1, 0). Label the new shape Q.

(c) Rotate shape C 90° clockwise about (2, 1). Label the new shape R.

(d) Rotate shape C 180° about (−2, 3). Label the new shape S.

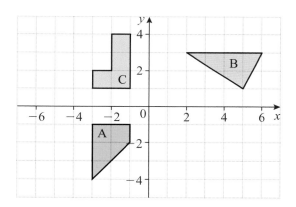

Finding the centre of a rotation

Exercise 2M

In questions 1 to 4 , copy each diagram. Draw the coloured shape on tracing paper. Place the tip of a pencil on different points until the shape can be rotated onto the white shape. Mark the centre of rotation with a dot.

1
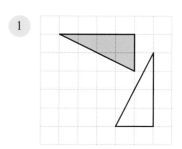

2
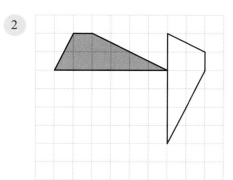

3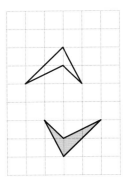

4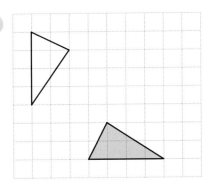

5 Find the coordinates of the centres of the following rotations

   (a) $\triangle 1 \rightarrow \triangle 2$

   (b) $\triangle 1 \rightarrow \triangle 3$

   (c) $\triangle 1 \rightarrow \triangle 4$

   (d) $\triangle 3 \rightarrow \triangle 5$

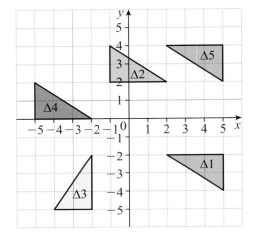

6 Copy the two squares carefully. It is possible to rotate the blue square onto the white square using three different centres of rotation. Find and mark these three points.

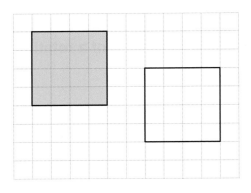

Making rotation patterns – a design activity

1 • On *tracing paper*, draw this pattern. The angle between
each pair of long lines must be 120°. Each long line is
marked every $\frac{1}{2}$ cm, as shown. We will call this pattern a
spoke pattern.

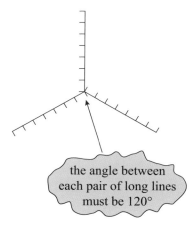

the angle between
each pair of long lines
must be 120°

• In your book or on squared paper copy, this design.
We will call this a *spoke*.

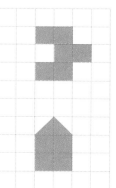

• Trace this spoke onto your *tracing paper*, as shown
opposite.

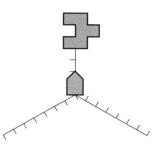

• Turn the tracing paper and trace the spokes, as shown, on the tracing paper.

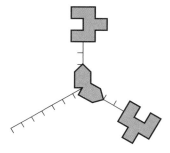 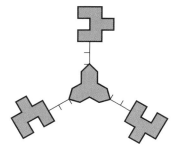

138

2 Using the method above, or a method of your own, draw these rotation patterns.

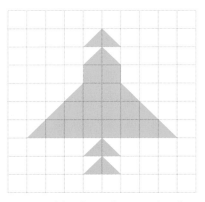

Draw this shape in your book.

Draw this on the tracing paper.

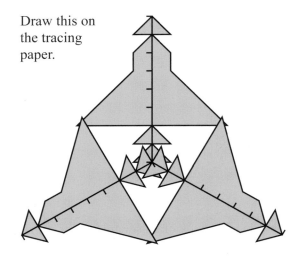

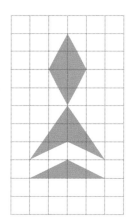

The angles between the lines on the spoke pattern will be 360° ÷ 5 = 72°

3   Experiment with patterns of your own. Here are some you could try.

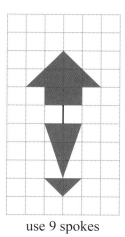

use 9 spokes

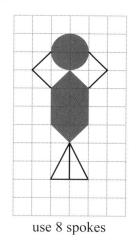

use 8 spokes

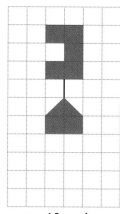

use 12 spokes

Combinations of two transformations

Reflection, rotation, translation and enlargement are all transformations. Sometimes we need a combination of transformations to move a shape where we want it.

Translation reminder: every point of the object moves the same distance in a parallel direction. Translation vectors are used to describe translations.

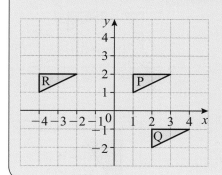

The translation of P to Q is $\begin{pmatrix} 1 \\ -3 \end{pmatrix}$ 1 to the right 3 down

The translation of Q to R is $\begin{pmatrix} -6 \\ 3 \end{pmatrix}$ 6 to the left 3 up

The translation of P to R is $\begin{pmatrix} -5 \\ 0 \end{pmatrix}$ 5 to the left 0 up or down

Exercise 3M

1   Copy this diagram.

(a) Reflect shape A in line 1 onto shape B.

(b) Reflect shape B in line 2 onto shape C.

(c) What single transformation will move shape A onto shape C?

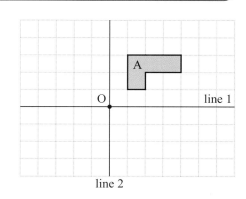

140

2 Copy this diagram.

(a) Rotate triangle D 90° clockwise about (0, 0). Label the new triangle E.

(b) Rotate triangle E 90° clockwise about (0, 0). Label the new triangle F.

(c) What single transformation will move triangle D onto triangle F?

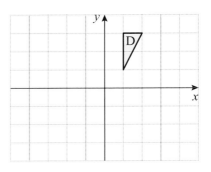

3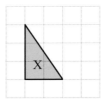

(a) Draw triangle X.

(b) Translate triangle X $\begin{pmatrix} 4 \\ 0 \end{pmatrix}$ onto triangle Y.

(c) Translate triangle Y $\begin{pmatrix} 1 \\ 2 \end{pmatrix}$ onto triangle Z.

(d) What single translation will move triangle X onto triangle Z?

4 Copy the diagram opposite. Describe the transformations below. Mark any points and lines necessary to find the answers.

(a) Triangle A onto triangle B in one move.

(b) Triangle B onto triangle C in one move.

(c) Triangle D onto triangle C in one move.

(d) Triangle A onto triangle C in two moves.

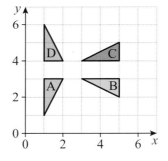

5 Describe fully the following transformations.

(a) Triangle A onto triangle B.

(b) Triangle B onto triangle C.

(c) Triangle A onto triangle D.

(d) Triangle C onto triangle E.

(e) Triangle A onto triangle C. (in two transformations)

(f) Triangle A onto triangle E. (in two or three transformations)

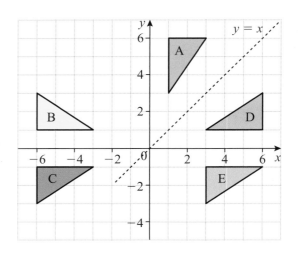

Need more practice with rotation and combined transformations?

1

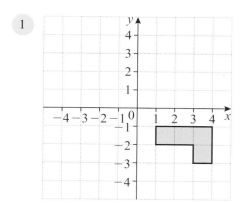

Copy this diagram then rotate the shape 90° clockwise about (1, 1).

2

Describe the rotation which

(a) moves the red piece onto the yellow piece

(b) moves the green piece onto the yellow piece.

3 (a) Copy the diagram opposite.

(b) Translate shape A by $\begin{pmatrix} 1 \\ -5 \end{pmatrix}$.

Label the new shape B.

(c) Reflect shape B in the y-axis.
Label the new shape C.

(d) Translate shape C by $\begin{pmatrix} 3 \\ 5 \end{pmatrix}$.

Label the new shape D.

(e) Describe fully the transformation
(i.e. reflection, rotation, translation or
enlargement) which moves shape D to shape A.

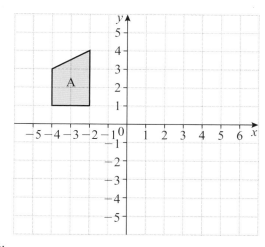

4 A shape A is translated by $\begin{pmatrix} 2 \\ 4 \end{pmatrix}$ then by $\begin{pmatrix} 1 \\ -2 \end{pmatrix}$ then by $\begin{pmatrix} 4 \\ 1 \end{pmatrix}$.

The final shape is labelled B.

Write down the translation vector which will translate shape B back to shape A.

5

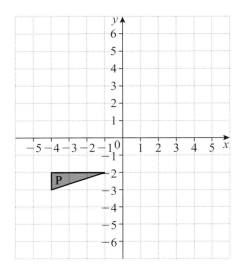

(a) Copy the diagram opposite.

(b) Rotate triangle P 180° about (0, 0). Label the new shape Q.

(c) Translate shape Q by $\begin{pmatrix} -1 \\ -4 \end{pmatrix}$. Label the new shape R.

(d) Rotate shape R 90° anticlockwise about (4, −2). Label the new shape S.

(e) The coordinates of one corner of triangle P are (−1, −2). Write down the coordinates of the corresponding corner in triangle S.

Extension questions with rotation and combined transformations

1

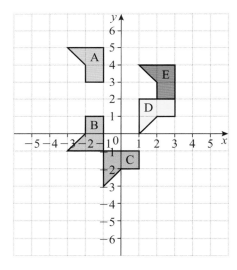

Describe fully the following transformations:

(a) shape A → shape B

(b) shape B → shape C

(c) shape C → shape D

(d) shape D → shape E

(e) shape E → shape A

2 Copy the diagram opposite then enlarge the shape by scale factor 3 about the centre (2, 0).

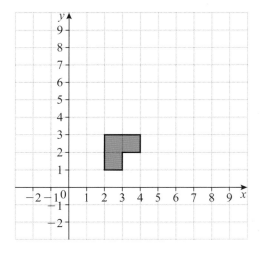

3 (a) Draw axes with values from −6 to +6 and draw triangle A with vertices at (2, 6), (6, 6), (6, 4).

    (b) Rotate triangle A 90° clockwise about (2, 6). Draw and label the new triangle B.

    (c) Rotate triangle B 180° about (2, 0). Draw and label the new triangle C.

    (d) Rotate triangle C 90° clockwise about (1, 0). Draw and label the new triangle D.

    (e) Rotate triangle D 90° anticlockwise about (−1, 4). Draw and label the new triangle E.

    (f) If triangle E is in the correct position you can now easily rotate triangle E onto triangle A. Write down the angle, direction and centre for this rotation.

4 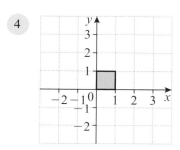 Describe fully four consecutive transformations that will move the square shown opposite into three new positions then back to its starting position.

5 Draw axes with values from −7 to +7 and draw triangles with the following vertices:

△1:	(3, 1)	(7, 1)	(7, 3)
△2:	(1, 3)	(1, 7)	(3, 7)
△3:	(7, −1)	(3, −1)	(3, −3)
△4:	(−1, −7)	(−3, −7)	(−3, −3)
△5:	(−2, 2)	(−6, 2)	(−6, 0)
△6:	(3, −4)	(3, −6)	(7, −6)

Describe fully the following rotations or reflections:

(a) △1 → △2   (b) △1 → △3   (c) △1 → △4

(d) △1 → △5   (e) △3 → △6

✖ Spot the mistakes 4 ✖

Sequences and transformations

Work through each question below and *explain clearly* what mistakes have been made. Beware – some questions are correctly done.

144

1 Copy then rotate shape P 90° anticlockwise about (0, 0).

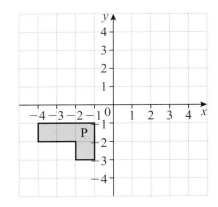

Answer: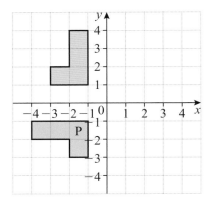

2 Copy then reflect triangle A in the line $x = -1$

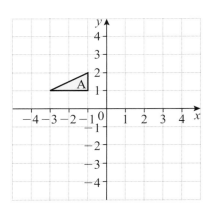

Answer: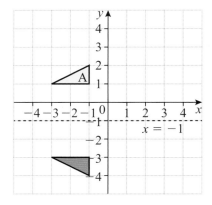

3 Predict the next 2 terms in this sequence.

33, 24, 15, 6, …, …

Answer: 33, 24, 15, 6, $\boxed{-2}$, $\boxed{-11}$

4 Copy then reflect shape M in
  the line $y = x$.

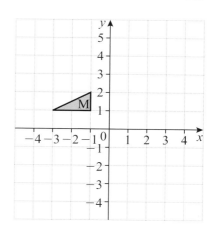

Answer:

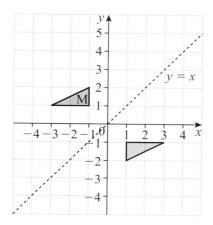

5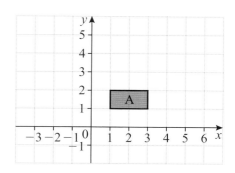

The rule for this sequence is ×2 and +1.
Find the missing numbers.

Answer: 7   13   27   55   111

6 Copy then enlarge shape A by
  scale factor 2 about the centre
  of enlargement (0, 1).

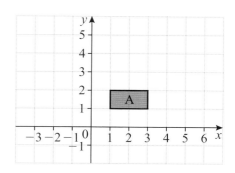

Answer:

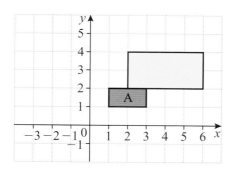

7   The point (2, 3) is reflected in the line $y = 3$.
    Write down the coordinates of the image
    of this point.

    Answer: (2, 3) is on the line $y = 3$ so does not
              move when reflected in the line $y = 3$.
              The coordinates of the image are
              therefore (2, 3).

8   Triangle P opposite is rotated
    180° onto triangle Q.
    Write down the coordinates of
    the centre of rotation.

    Answer: (2, 0)

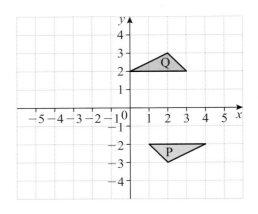

9   Use differences to predict the next term in the sequence 8, 11, 18, 29, 44, …

    Answer: 61

10

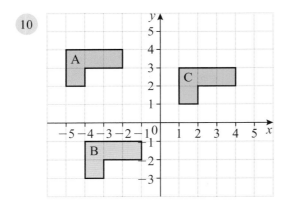

Shape B is translated to shape A.
Write down the translation vector.

Answer: $\begin{pmatrix} 1 \\ 5 \end{pmatrix}$

CHECK YOURSELF ON SECTIONS 2.5 and 2.6

1   Drawing reflections

(a) Copy the diagram.

(b) Draw the image of triangle 1 after reflection in the *y*-axis.

(c) Draw the image of triangle 2 after reflection in the line $x = 3$

(d) Write down the equation of the mirror line for the reflection of triangle 2 onto triangle 3

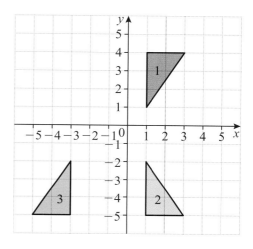

2   Enlarging shapes

Draw an enlargement of the shape shown opposite using scale factor 2

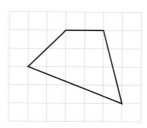

3   Using centres of enlargement

(a) Copy the diagram onto squared paper.

(b) Draw the enlargement of the pink triangle with centre of enlargement A and scale factor 2

(c) Draw the enlargement of the pink triangle with centre of enlargement B and scale factor 3

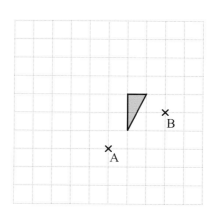

4   Rotating shapes

Copy the diagram shown. Use tracing paper to

(a) rotate triangle A 180° about (0, 0).
Draw and label the new triangle B.

(b) rotate triangle A 90° clockwise about (4, −1).
Draw and label the new triangle C.

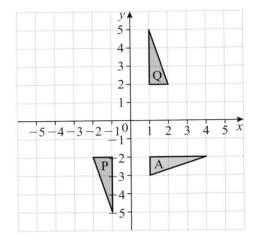

5   Finding the centre of a rotation

(a) On the diagram above, triangle A is rotated 90° clockwise onto triangle P.
Use tracing paper to find the centre of rotation.

(b) Triangle A is rotated 90° anticlockwise onto triangle Q. Use tracing paper to
find the centre of rotation.

6   Combining transformations

Copy the diagram.

(a) Describe the transformation which moves
triangle P onto triangle Q.

(b) Describe how triangle P is moved onto
triangle R using two transformations.

(c) Reflect triangle A in the y-axis.
Label this new triangle B.

(d) Reflect triangle B in the x-axis.
Label this new triangle C.

(e) What single transformation will move
triangle A onto triangle C?

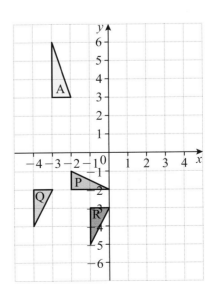

2.7 Applying mathematics 2

In section 2.7 you will apply maths in a variety of situations.

1. The costs for a Year 8 trip to the theatre are shown below. 105 students go on the trip.

ticket £16.50	(one free ticket for every 10 tickets bought)
1 coach (55 seats)	£375

   Each Year 8 student pays £22.50. How much money is left over when all the tickets and coaches have been paid for?

2. Rio has the same number of 20p and 50p coins. The total value of the coins is £7.
   How many of each coin does he have?

3. At a players' meeting at Mill End Football Club all the players can speak French or English or both.
   If 72% can speak English and 45% can speak French, what percentage of the players can speak both languages?

4. Toni has a furniture shop and on 20th September has 42 chairs in stock.
   Each week she sells 3 chairs.

   Edgar makes chairs. On 20th September he has 1 chair but then makes 6 chairs each week.
   During which week does Edgar first have more chairs than Toni?

5. Martian creatures are either tripods or octopods.
   Tripods have three legs. Octopods have eight legs.
   The Martians, on an exploratory visit to Earth, have 60 legs between them. How many are tripods and how many are octopods? Find both possible answers.

6. Work out the value of $B\hat{D}E$.
   Give reasons for your answer.

   A   B   C
   38°
   E   *Not drawn to scale*   D

7   It costs Christine £18 to make a dress. She sells each dress for £30.60.
    How many dresses does Christine sell in total if she makes a profit of £252?

8   The students in a school were given
    a spelling test. Some of the results
    are given in the table. How many
    girls passed the spelling test?

	Passed	Failed	Total
Boys		311	589
Girls		257	
Total		568	914

9

150 dominoes are each stood on their ends.
One domino is flicked and $\frac{2}{5}$ of the dominoes end
up being knocked over. Another domino is flicked
and 40% of the remaining dominoes are knocked
over. How many dominoes are still standing on
their ends?

10 Gavin wants to provide bacon and egg sandwiches at a local fête. He will use
    one rasher of bacon, one egg and two slices of bread for each sandwich.

    He can buy bread in packs of 24 slices, bacon in packs of 16 rashers and eggs
    in boxes of 6. Every slice of bread, rasher of bacon and egg must be used.

    What are the fewest number of packs of each of the bread, bacon and eggs that
    must be bought so that Gavin can definitely make sandwiches for more than
    120 people?

UNIT 2   MIXED REVIEW

Part one

1   A survey of 400 people reveals that 28% of people like 'Minty Fresh' toothpaste.
    Work out the number of people who like 'Minty Fresh'.

2   The rule for the sequences below is 'double and add 3'. Find the missing numbers.

    (a) 1 $\longrightarrow$ 5 $\longrightarrow$ 13 $\longrightarrow$ ☐

    (b) 2 $\longrightarrow$ ☐ $\longrightarrow$ ☐

    (c) ☐ $\longrightarrow$ 9 $\longrightarrow$ ☐

3   Vinny has a terrible diet. On average he eats 21 burgers each week. Estimate how many
    burgers he eats in one year.

4 (a) Copy the diagram.

   (b) Reflect the L shape in the x-axis.

   (c) Reflect the L shape in the line $y = x$.

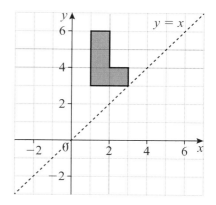

5 Draw the graph of $y = 6 - x$ for values of x from 0 to 6

x	0	1	2	3	4	5	6
y							

6 Write down the next number in each sequence.

(a) 3 9 15 21 ☐   (b) 1 2 4 7 ☐

7 (a) Copy the diagram onto squared paper.

   (b) Use tracing paper to make the centre of the rotation which rotates shape A onto shape B.

   (c) Describe *fully* the rotation.

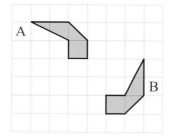

8 A DVD is sold at £10.95 per copy. Estimate the total cost of 485 copies.

9 Norman works out $198 \div 4.03$ and gets the answer 4.91 correct to two decimal places. Use estimation to decide if Norman is likely to be correct.

10 A dog weighs 25 kg. After a strict diet, the weight of the dog decreases by 8%. How much does the dog weigh now?

11 (a) Copy the pattern below and continue it to the line for 10^2

$$2^2 = 1^2 + 1 + 2 = 4$$
$$3^2 = 2^2 + 2 + 3 = 9$$
$$4^2 = 3^2 + 3 + 4 = 16$$

   (b) Without a calculator, use the pattern to work out

   (i) 31^2 (ii) 71^2 (iii) 101^2 (iv) 19^2

12 The number 0.040825 rounds off to 0.041, correct to 2 significant figures. True or false?

13 The numbers 1 to 12 are arranged on the star so that the sum of the numbers along each line is the same.

Copy and complete the star.

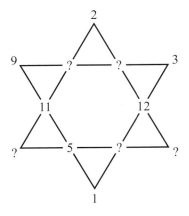

14 Draw axes with x and y values from 0 to 6

Plot   A(1, 4)   B(1, 1)   C(3, 1)

Plot   D(5, 4)   E(5, 1)   F(3, 1)

Write down the equation of the mirror line which reflects triangle ABC onto triangle DEF.

15 Work out $62\% - \dfrac{7}{20}$. Give the answer as a percentage.

Part two

1   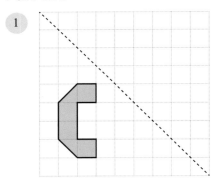   Copy this diagram onto squared paper and then draw its reflection in the broken line.

2 The pattern 24680 24680 24680 ..., is continued to form a number with one hundred digits. What is the sum of all one hundred digits?

3 13 out of 80 cars failed their annual MOT test. What percentage of the cars failed?

4 Copy each shape and then enlarge it using the centre of enlargement and the scale factor shown.

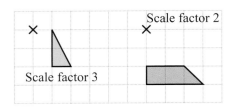

5　(a) Use a calculator to work out　(i)　350 ÷ 99

(ii)　350 ÷ 999

(iii) 350 ÷ 9999

(b) Use your answers to *predict* the answer to 350 ÷ 99 999, correct to 9 decimal places.

(c) Predict the answer to 350 ÷ 999 999, correct to 11 decimal places.

6　Find three numbers which add up to 10 and multiply to give 30

 +  +  = 10　　　 ×  ×  = 30

7　Here are six calculations and six answers. Write down each calculation and insert the correct answer from the list below. Use estimation.

(a)　79.6 ÷ 4　　　　　(b)　145 ÷ 150　　　　　(c)　288.2 ÷ 6

(d)　52.2 + 47.6　　　　(e)　10.4 ÷ 97　　　　　(f)　416 ÷ 1.97

Answers:	0.97,　99.8,　19.9,　0.11,　211.2,　48.0

8　Photograph B is an enlargement of photograph A. Calculate the height of photograph B.

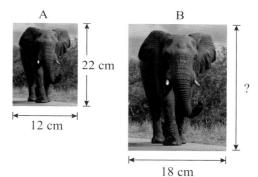

9　Draw the graph of $y = 2x + 3$ for values of x from 0 to 4

x	0	1	2	3	4
y					

10　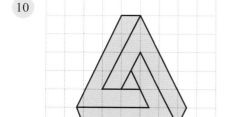　Enlarge this shape on squared paper by scale factor 2

11 Copy this diagram then enlarge the shape
    by scale factor 2 about the centre (0, 0).

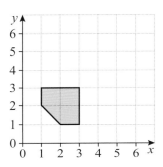

12

For his prize-winning three-dimensional puzzle of planet Earth
the inventor received £10 000 plus 3% of the profits made by the
distributor. In ten years the distributor's profit was £8 795 400.
How much did the inventor receive altogether?

13 Copy the diagram.
    Describe fully the following transformations:
    (a) triangle 1 onto triangle 3
    (b) triangle 1 onto triangle 4
    (c) triangle 3 onto triangle 2

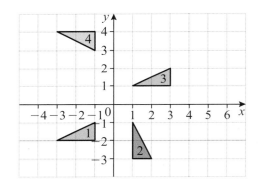

14

Plan A

£12.99 fixed charge

3.3p per unit used

Lisa uses 2140 units of
electricity one month and is charged
using Plan A opposite.

Plan B

No fixed charge

4.6p per unit used

Her mother uses 1870 units
of electricity and is charged
using Plan B opposite.
Who pays more money and by how much?

15 The photo shows objects reflected in a mirror
    with colours changed also.
    (a) Draw a diagram of your own design with
         black sections and white sections.
    (b) Draw a reflection of your design in a similar
         way to that shown in the photo.

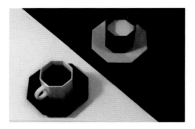

Puzzles and Problems 2

Cross numbers without clues

Here are cross number puzzles with a difference. There are no clues, only answers, and you have to find where the answers go.

(a) Copy out the cross number pattern.

(b) Fit all the given numbers into the correct spaces. Work logically and tick off the numbers from lists as you write them in the squares.

1

2 digits	3 digits	4 digits	5 digits
23	146	2708	25404
26	235	2715	25814
42	245		37586
57	337		
59	539		
87	695		

2

2 digits	3 digits	4 digits	5 digits
18	244	2163	36918
21	247	4133	46514
31	248	4213	54374
33	332	4215	54704
47	333	4283	87234
63	334	4317	
64	608	4394	
77			

3

2 digits	3 digits	4 digits	5 digits	7 digits
36	145	2286	16145	4235824
52	185	5235	66145	
56	245	5248	66152	
63	246	5249	66272	
65	374	5452	91671	
77	437	6241		
90	646			
	896			

4

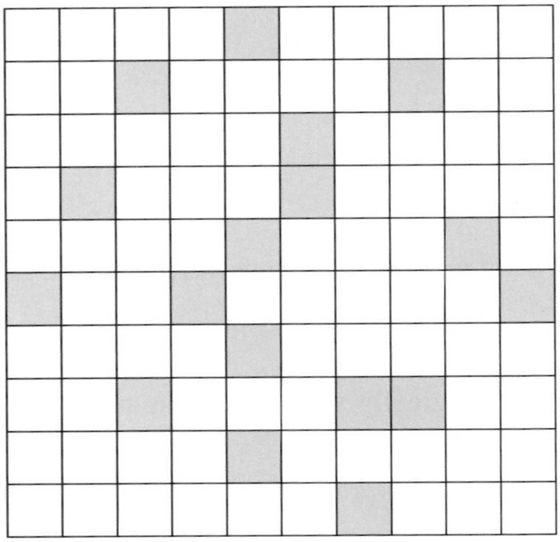

2 digits	3 digits	4 digits	5 digits
14	123	1325	14251
22	231	1478	29163
26	341	1687	29613
43	439	1976	29872
65	531	2523	34182
70	670	4798	54875
81		5601	63712
82		5611	67358
		5621	82146
		6109	84359
		8171	97273

6 digits	7 digits
145026	9354234
740136	
983514	

5

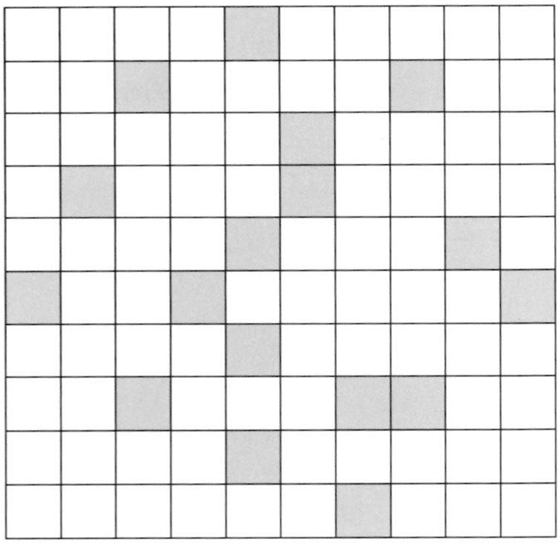

2 digits	3 digits	4 digits	5 digits
15	137	2513	29666
19	206	3048	31873
21	276	3214	40657
22	546	3244	43104
28	592	3437	43158
31	783	3514	54732
77		3517	60783
90		3544	62114
		4122	80751
		4127	82614
		6934	93654

6 digits	7 digits
235785	9733764
235815	
452705	

A long time ago! 2

Binary numbers

1 0 1 1 0 1 1 1 0 1 1 0 0 1 1 0 1 0 0 1

Decimal numbers use 10 digits:

0, 1, 2, 3, 4, 5, 6, 7, 8, 9

Binary numbers use only 2 digits: 0 and 1

A binary number uses powers of 2 to give its value.

$2^0 = 1$　　　$2^1 = 2$　　　$2^2 = 4$　　　$2^3 = 8$

What is the decimal value of the binary number 1101?

1　1　0　1　　　　　　　$= 8 + 4 + 0 + 1 = 13$

units
2
4
8

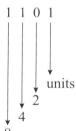

A switch can be 'on' or 'off'. The digit 1 can be used for 'on' and the digit 0 for 'off', so circuits can be built using binary numbers.

George Boole in the 19th century developed a 'true' or 'false' logic system called Boolean algebra.

Without binary numbers, there might never have been any computers, then where would we be?

The first mention of binary numbers was more than two thousand years ago by an Indian called Pingala.

Exercise

1　Look at the example above then change these binary numbers into decimal numbers.

(a) 101　　　　(b) 11　　　　(c) 110　　　　(d) 1001

(e) 10　　　　(f) 1010　　　　(g) 1100　　　　(h) 1111

2　What is the decimal value of the binary number 10000?

3　Write 32 as a binary number.

4　Write 64 as a binary number.

5   Write the following numbers in binary form.

     (a) 17   (b) 24   (c) 4   (d) 14   (e) 44

6   Add these binary numbers to get a binary answer.

$$
\text{(a)} \quad \begin{array}{r} 101 \\ + \ 11 \\ \hline \end{array} \qquad
\text{(b)} \quad \begin{array}{r} 1011 \\ + \ 1001 \\ \hline \end{array} \qquad
\text{(c)} \quad \begin{array}{r} 1010 \\ + \ 1111 \\ \hline \end{array}
$$

Mental arithmetic practice 2

Ideally a teacher will read out each question twice, with pupils' books closed.

Test 1

1   What is the perimeter of a square with sides 8 cm?

2   Write one fifth as a percentage.

3   What number is half way between 4.2 and 4.8?

4   I have six 20p coins, one 5p coin and one 2p coin. How much money do I have?

5   A poster costs three pounds. Andrew saves sixty pence per week. How many weeks will it be before he can buy the poster?

6   Screws cost 8 pence each. What is the cost of 25 screws?

7   Hooks cost 70 pence for five. What is the cost of 1 hook?

8   A pair of earrings costs £1.23. What is the change from £2?

9   How many 5p coins do I need for 85p?

10   A drill costs £34 new. I get a discount of £8.50. How much do I pay?

11   A TV programme starts at 9.50 and ends at 10.40. How long is the programme?

12   I travel at 60 mph for 4 hours. How far do I travel?

13   Work out 10 per cent of £65

14   Susie has 3 red pens and 4 black pens. What fraction of her pens are black?

15   Jacqui makes a phone call from 18.40 until 19.21. How long is the call in minutes?

16   What five coins make 62p?

17   Write the number fifty thousand and six in figures.

18   The product of two numbers is 39. One of the numbers is 3. What is the other?

19   Change four and a half metres into centimetres.

20   Subtract 18 from 150

21   Write three fifths as a decimal.

22   Increase £40 by 25%

23   I buy three magazines at 99p each. What change do I get from £10?

24   How many lengths of 8 cm can be cut from 50 cm?

25   How many minutes are there in $2\frac{3}{4}$ hours?

Test 2

1. What are 37 twos?

2. What is the smaller angle between the hands of a clock at 8 o'clock?

3. Two angles of a triangle are 55° and 30°. What is the third angle?

4. What is 50% of £44?

5. How many 5p coins are needed to make £10?

6. A car costing £8500 is reduced by £120. What is the new price?

7. What number is twice as big as 69?

8. On a tray, fourteen out of fifty peaches are rotten. What percentage is that?

9. Add together 11, 18 and 9

10. A book costs £13.55. Find the change from a £20 note.

11. What five coins make 51p?

12. What is $\frac{2}{3}$ of £186?

13. Write one twentieth as a decimal.

14. How many minutes are there between 8.15 p.m. and 10.20 p.m.?

15. A pools prize of six million pounds is shared equally between one hundred people. How much does each person receive?

16. If June 14th is a Tuesday, what day of the week is June 23rd?

17. True or false: 1 kg is about 2 pounds?

18. How many millimetres are there in 3.5 metres?

19. A daily newspaper costs 85p from Monday to Saturday and 95p on Sunday. What is the total cost for the seven days?

20. Write $\frac{3}{4}$ as a decimal.

21. A clock ticks once every second. How many times does it tick between six o'clock and seven o'clock?

22. Add eleven to nine times eight.

23. A rectangular piece of wood measures 15 cm by 10 cm. What is its area?

24. An egg box holds six eggs. How many boxes are needed for 100 eggs?

25. How many 79p stamps can I buy with £5?

UNIT 3

3.1 Area and perimeter

In section 3.1 you will:

- review finding areas and perimeters using rectangles and triangles
- find areas of parallelograms and trapeziums

Rectangles and triangles

Remember:

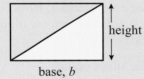 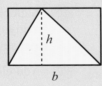 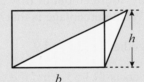

For each shaded triangle, area of triangle $= \dfrac{1}{2} b \times h$

Exercise 1M

1 Calculate the area of each shape. The lengths are in cm.

(a)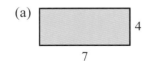

(b)

(c)

2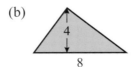
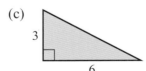

(a) Find the area of the lawn.

(b) Find the area of the yard.

(c) What is the total area of the yard and the lawn?

3   Calculate the area of each shape. The lengths are in cm.

(a)

(b)

(c)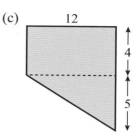

4      Here is a 4 × 6 rectangle made using 24 squares.
What other rectangles can be made using 24 squares?

5   Suzy has enough small squares to make exactly five different rectangles
(including a large square). How many squares does she have?

6   What metric unit would you use for the area of

(a) a tennis court

(b) the Isle of Man

(c) a 5p coin?

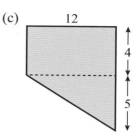

7      Des says that the area of this
triangle is $\frac{1}{2} \times 12 \times 20$, which
equals $120\,cm^2$. *Explain clearly*
whether he is correct or not.

8   Work out the perimeter
of the shape opposite.

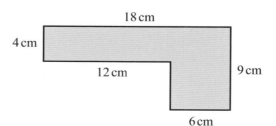

9 A photo has a border around it which is 3 cm wide.
Work out the area of the border.

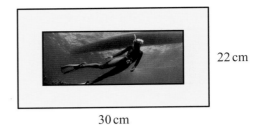

22 cm

30 cm

10

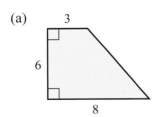

A

Which shape has the larger area and by how much?

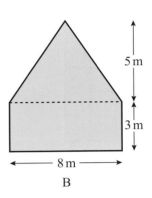

B

Exercise 2M

1 Calculate the area of each shape. The lengths are in cm.

(a)

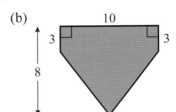

(b)

(c)

2

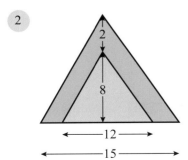

Calculate the pink area. The lengths are in cm.

3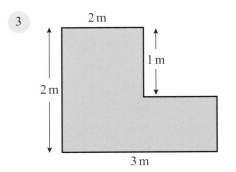

Tanya is going to tile this wall. Each tile is a square 10 cm by 10 cm. The tiles come in boxes of 25. Each box costs £18.

(a) How many tiles are needed?

(b) How much will the tiles cost?

(c) Tanya may break some of the tiles. She has to buy an extra 10% of tiles to allow for breakages. What is the total cost of the tiles now?

4 Work out the perimeter of

(a) a regular octagon of side 5 cm

(b) a square of area 100 cm²

5 Calculate the length of each side marked x. The area is written inside each shape.

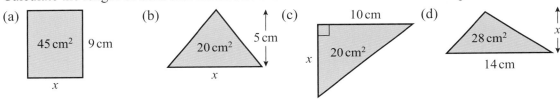

6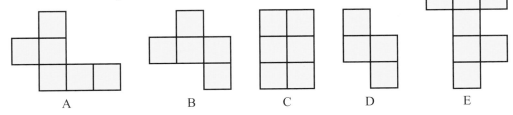

Eve wants to put skirting board around the edge of the room shown opposite. She can buy 3 m of skirting board for £12.50 and 2 m of skirting board for £9.50.

She does not want to cut any piece of skirting board. What is the least amount of money she could spend on the skirting board?

7 Here are some shapes made with centimetre squares.

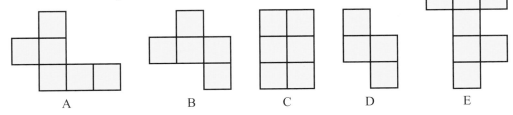

A   B   C   D   E

(a) Which shape has an area of 4 cm²?

(b) Which shape has a perimeter of 12 cm?

(c) Which two shapes have the same perimeter?

8 Draw a shape similar to those in question 7

(a) with area 7 cm² and perimeter 14 cm

(b) with area 11 cm² and perimeter 16 cm.

164

Parallelograms and trapeziums

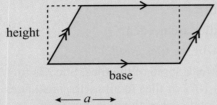

area of parallelogram = base × height

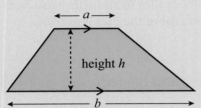

area of trapezium = $\frac{1}{2}h(a + b)$

area of trapezium = $\frac{1}{2}$ × height × sum of the parallel sides

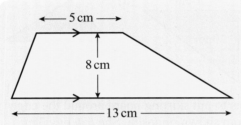

area of trapezium = $\frac{1}{2}h(a + b)$

$= \frac{1}{2} \times 8 \times (5 + 13)$

$= 4 \times 18$

$= 72 \text{ cm}^2$

Exercise 3M

Calculate the area of each shape. The lengths are in cm.

1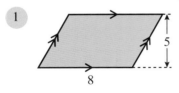

2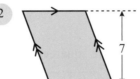

3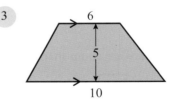

4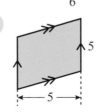

5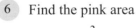

6 Find the pink area

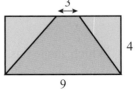

7 Sketch a trapezium with parallel sides of length 5 cm and 7 cm. The distance between the parallel sides is 4 cm. Calculate the area of the trapezium.

8 A parallelogram has a base of length 10 cm and an area of 60 cm². Calculate the height of the parallelogram.

9   The area of the parallelogram is
    equal to the area of the triangle.
    Find the height of the parallelogram.

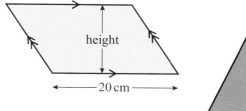

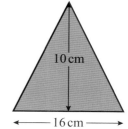

10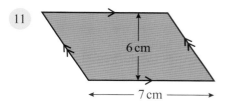

    The area of the trapezium shown is 12 cm². Find a possible set of values for
    a, b and h.

11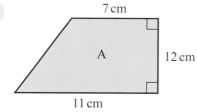

    Work out the area of
    the parallelogram as a
    percentage of the area of
    the trapezium.

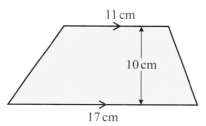

12

    Find the length x if the
    area of shape B is equal
    to the area of shape A.

Need more practice with area and perimeter?

1   The area of a triangle is 56 cm². What is the height of the triangle if its base is 14 cm?

2   Look at these shapes made with equilateral triangles.

      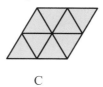   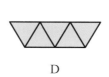

   A   B   C   D   E

    (a) Which shape has the largest area?
    (b) Which shape has the same area as shape A?
    (c) Which shape has the same perimeter as shape C?

166

3 Calculate the blue area.

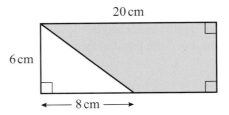

4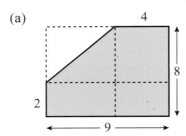

The area of square C is equal to the sum of the areas of rectangles A and B. How long is the side of square C?

5 A wall measuring 2 m by 6 m is covered with tiles which are 20 cm squares.
A box of 10 tiles costs £25.95. How much will it cost to buy the tiles for this wall?

6 Here are two shapes *both* with a perimeter of 32 cm.
Calculate the *area* of each shape.

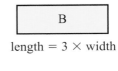

7 Find the total area of each shape. Lengths are in cm.

(a)

(b)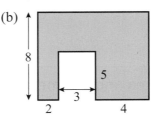

(c)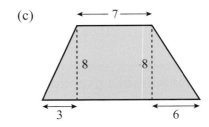

8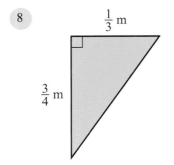

Which shape has the greater area and by how much? Give the answer as a fraction.

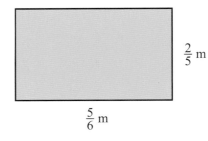

Extension questions with area and perimeter

Calculate the area of each shape. The lengths are in cm.

1
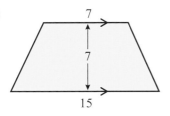

2
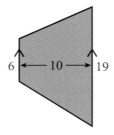

3
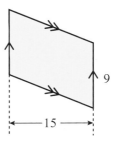

4
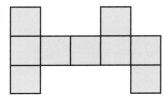

This shape has an area of 225 cm². Calculate its perimeter.

5 This photo of Hannah has height 5 cm greater than its width. The area of the photo is 84 cm². Find the dimensions of the photo.

6 The area of a parallelogram is 10 cm². How long is the base of the parallelogram if its height is 20 cm?

7 The diagram shows a garden with two crossing paths. Calculate the total area of the paths.

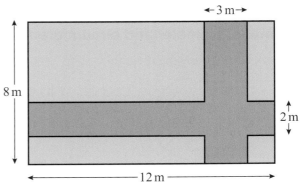

8 How many panes of glass 30 cm by 20 cm can be cut from a sheet which is 1 metre square?

9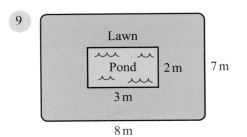

A gardener is spreading fertilizer on his lawn (but not the pond in the middle!). The instructions only say that 2 measures of the fertilizer will treat 10 m² of lawn. Each measure of fertilizer costs £8.60. Find the cost of the fertilizer required.

10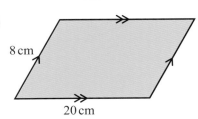

Tina says that the area of this parallelogram is 160 cm². *Explain clearly* why Tina is not correct.

11 The blue area is to be painted red. One tin of red paint can cover 9 m². How many tins of red paint are needed? Show all your working out.

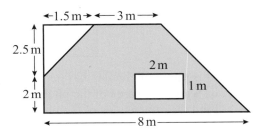

3.2 Circles

In section 3.2 you will:

- find the circumference of a circle

- find the area of a circle

Radius, diameter and circumference

Look at the following diagrams.

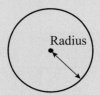

- The radius is half the diameter.
- The diameter is twice the radius.
- The length of the perimeter of a circle is called its *circumference*.

169

Exercise 1M   (Oral or written exercise)

For each of the circles shown below, write down

(a) the radius   (b) the diameter.

Remember to give the units in your answers!

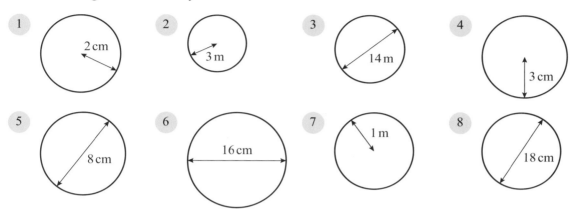

1. 2 cm
2. 3 m
3. 14 m
4. 3 cm
5. 8 cm
6. 16 cm
7. 1 m
8. 18 cm

Activity

Find eight circular objects (tins, plates, buckets, wheels, etc.) For each object, measure the diameter and the circumference and write the results in a table. Use a flexible tape measure for the circumference or wrap a piece of string around the object and then measure the string with a ruler. For each pair of readings, work out the ratio (*circumference ÷ diameter*).

You should find that the number in the $\frac{c}{d}$ column is about the same each time.

Work out the mean value of the eight numbers in the $\frac{c}{d}$ column.

Object	Circumference c	diameter d	$\frac{c}{d}$
Tin of tuna	28.6 cm	8.8 cm	3.25
...			
...			

22 cm

A piece of string 22 cm long will make:

About 7 cm

A circle whose diameter is just over 7 cm

If you divide the circumference of a circle by its diameter, the number you obtain is always just over three.

This means $\dfrac{\text{circumference}}{\text{diameter}} \approx 3$ Circumference ≈ 3 × diameter

This provides a fairly good *estimate* for the circumference of any circle.

170

Pi

For any circle, the exact value of the ratio $\left(\dfrac{\text{circumference}}{\text{diameter}}\right)$ is π. We say 'pi'.

Since $\dfrac{\text{circumference}}{\text{diameter}} = \pi$, we can write $\{$ Circumference $= \pi \times$ diameter $\}$

π is a Greek letter. Most calculators have a $\boxed{\pi}$ button, which will give the value of π to at least 7 significant figures: 3.141593

Find the circumference of the circle.

Radius = 4 cm, so diameter = 8 cm

Circumference = $\pi \times 8$

$\qquad$ = 25.13274123... cm

$\qquad$ = 25.1 cm correct to one decimal place

Exercise 2M

Make a table and complete it for questions ① to ⑧ . Make sure you write the correct units. For the calculated circumference, give answers correct to one decimal place.

Number	Radius r	Diameter d	Estimated circumference	Calculated circumference
1	2 cm			
2				

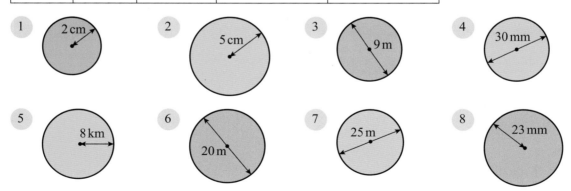

⑨ A circular mirror has diameter 50 cm. Work out its circumference, correct to one decimal place.

⑩ The head of a drawing pin is circular with radius 3.6 mm. Find its circumference.

11  The knuckle of a bride's ring finger has width 19 mm.
Find the internal circumference of the ring which will just fit.

12 Which has the longer perimeter and by how much: an equilateral triangle of side 10 cm or a circle of diameter 10 cm?

13 The diameter of the Earth is 12 742 km. How far would a person travel in total if they went around the circumference of the Earth four times?

14 In 1897, politicians in Indiana, USA, displayed a complete lack of mathematical understanding when they passed a local law stating that the value of pi was to be taken as 4

(a) Calculate the circumference of a circle of radius 3.5 cm in Indiana.

(b) Calculate the circumference of the same circle everywhere else in the world.

P.S. The law was soon discarded!

Perimeters

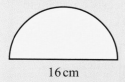

Calculate the perimeter of this semi circle.

circumference of whole circle $= \pi \times 16$
$= 50.27$ cm

curved perimeter of semi circle $= 50.27 \div 2$
$= 25.1$ cm

perimeter of semi circle = curved part + straight part $= 25.1 + 16$
$= 41.1$ cm (to 1 d.p.)

16 cm

Exercise 3M

Calculate the perimeter of each shape. All shapes are either semicircles or quarter circles.
Give answers correct to 1 decimal place.

1
8 cm

2
13 cm

3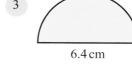
6.4 cm

4
7.4 cm

5 18.6 cm
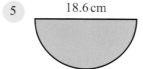

6
3.6 cm

7   A semi circle is attached to a rectangle as shown to make a window. What is the perimeter of the frame required for this window?

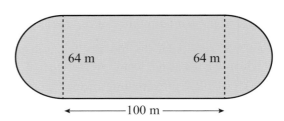

0.3 m

0.8 m

8   This running track is made from two semi circles and a rectangle. Calculate the perimeter of this shape (i.e. the length of the running track).

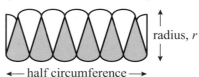

64 m   64 m

100 m

Area of a circle

(a) The circle below is divided into 12 equal sectors.

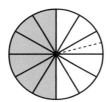

(b) The sectors are cut and arranged to make a shape which is nearly a rectangle (one sector is cut in half).

radius, r

← half circumference →

(c) The approximate area can be found as follows:

length of rectangle ≈ half circumference of circle

$$\approx \frac{\pi \times 2r}{2}$$

$$\approx \pi r$$

width of rectangle ≈ r

∴ area of rectangle ≈ $\pi r \times r$

$$\approx \pi r^2$$

If larger and larger numbers of sectors were used, this approximation would become more and more accurate.

This is a demonstration of an important result.

Area of a circle = πr^2 *Learn* this formula.

Note: πr^2 means $\pi(r^2)$. i.e. π multiplied by r^2

Find the area of each shape.

(a)

26 cm

radius = 13 cm

area = πr^2

= 530.9 cm² (1 d.p.)

(b)

←3.2 cm→

The shape is a quarter circle

area = $\dfrac{\pi(3.2)^2}{4}$

= 8.0 cm² (1 d.p.)

Exercise 4M

Calculate the area of each circle and give your answers correct to one decimal place.

1

11 mm

2

12 cm

3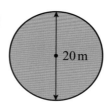

20 m

4

13 cm

5 The dart board shown has a diameter of 53 cm. Calculate the area of the dart board.

6 Work out the area of a circular lawn which has a radius of 4.2 m

7 The top of a mixing bowl is a circle with diameter 33 cm. Find the area of this circle.

8 Work out the area of each shape and give your answers correct to one decimal place.

(a)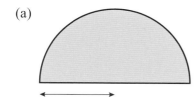

8 cm

(b)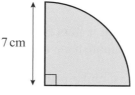

7 cm

(c)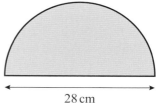

28 cm

9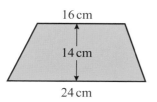

16 cm

14 cm

24 cm

Which shape has the greater area and by how much?

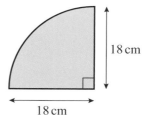

18 cm

18 cm

174

10 Find the shaded area.

Lengths are in cm.

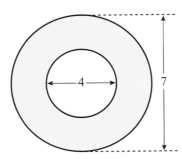

11 Work out the area of the shape shown opposite.

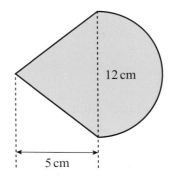

12 cm

5 cm

Need more practice with circles?

1 Calculate (i) the circumference and (ii) the area of each circle. Give each answer correct to one decimal place.

(a)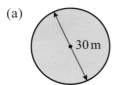
30 m

(b)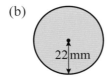
22 mm

(c)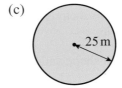
25 m

(d)
64 km

2 The tip of the minute hand of a clock is 8 cm from the centre of the clock face. Calculate the distance moved by the tip of the minute hand in one hour.

3 Olivia walks three times around a circular path. Elliot walks four times around a path in the shape of the trapezium shown below. Who walks further and by how much?

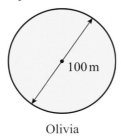
100 m

Olivia

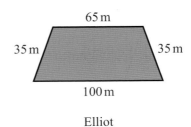
65 m
35 m   35 m
100 m

Elliot

4  Discs numbered 1 to 100 are used for bingo. Each disc has diameter 3.2 cm. Calculate the total area of the top faces of all the discs.

5 Calculate the shaded area shown opposite.

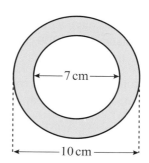

6 A carton of 'Verdone' weedkiller contains enough weedkiller to treat an area of 100 m². A circular lawn at Hampton Court has a radius of 16.5 m. How many cartons of weedkiller are needed to treat this lawn?

7 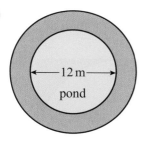 A 1 metre path surrounds a pond, as shown. Calculate the area of the path.

8 A car tyre has a radius of 37 cm.

(a) How long is its circumference in cm?

(b) How far does the car travel (in km) if the tyre makes 1000 rotations?

Extension questions with circles

In questions **1** to **3**, calculate (a) the perimeter and (b) the area of each shape.
Give the answers to 1 decimal place.

1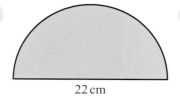
22 cm

2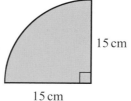
15 cm

15 cm

3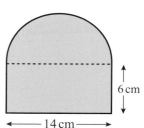
6 cm

14 cm

4 In this stained glass window the circle has diameter 3 m and the outer square is of side 4.5 m. Calculate the area which is outside the circle.

5 The diameters of 1p, 5p and 10p coins are 2 cm, 1.8 cm and 2.4 cm respectively. Calculate the total area of the top faces of the five coins used to make 18p.

6 The wheels on Gill's bike have a diameter of 62 cm. Gill rolls forward a distance of 1200 cm. Calculate how many times the wheels go round *completely*.

7 In a coin rolling competition Gemma rolls a one pound coin on its edge a distance of 4.2 m. A one pound coin has diameter 2.2 cm. How many times did the coin rotate completely?

8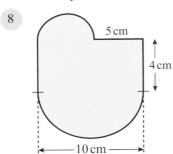

Work out the area of this shape which is made from two semicircles and a rectangle.

9 A semi circle is drawn within a rectangle as shown. What percentage of the rectangle is red?

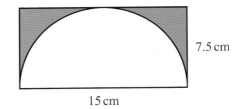

CHECK YOURSELF ON SECTIONS 3.1 and 3.2

1   Finding areas and perimeters using rectangles and triangles

Calculate the area of each shape. The lengths are in cm.

(a)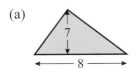

(b)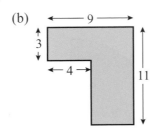

(c)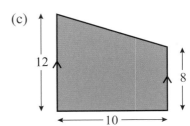

(d) A square has a perimeter of 24 cm. Find the area of the square.

2 Finding areas of parallelograms and trapeziums

Calculate the area of each shape. The lengths are in cm.

(a)

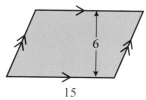

6

15

(b)

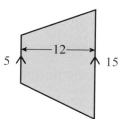

5   —12—   15

(c) Part of a wall is shown opposite.
Will takes 12 minutes on average to paint 1 m²

How many minutes will he take
to paint the entire wall?

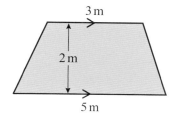

3 m

2 m

5 m

3 Finding the circumference of a circle

(a)

19 cm

Find the circumference of this circle, correct to 1 decimal place.

(b) A car tyre has a radius of 39 cm. How long is its circumference in cm, correct
to 1 decimal place?

(c) Calculate the perimeter of
this shape. Give the answer
correct to 1 decimal place.

8 cm

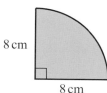

8 cm

4 Finding the area of a circle

The diameter of the top of the larger drum is 34 cm and
the radius of the top of the smaller drum is 8.5 cm

(a) Find the area of the top of the smaller drum.

(b) Find the area of the top of the larger drum.

(c) How many smaller drums would you need to have
the same top surface area as one larger drum?

3.3 Number – calculations review

In section 3.3 you will:

- review calculations with whole numbers and decimals
- practise reading number scales
- review calculations with fractions
- multiply and divide decimals

Calculations with decimals

(a) $5.6 + 12.32$

$$\begin{array}{r} 5.60 \quad \leftarrow \text{add zero} \\ + 12.32 \\ \hline 17.92 \end{array}$$

[Line up the decimal points]

(b) 5.26×10

$= 52.6$

Move the digits one place
to the left

(c) $28.1 \div 100$

$= 0.281$

Move the digits two
places to the right

(d) 0.38×1000

$= 380$

(e) $79.2 \div 6$

$$6\overline{)7^19.^12}\;\;\overset{13.2}{}$$

(f) $17 - 5.4$

$$\begin{array}{r} \overset{6}{1}\overset{1}{7}.0 \\ - \;\;5.4 \\ \hline 11.6 \end{array}$$

Exercise 1M

Work out, without a calculator.

1. 5.62×10
2. $59 \div 10$
3. $647 \div 100$
4. $8.3 \div 10$

5. $219 \div 1000$
6. $19.2 - 5.8$
7. $11 + 5.2$
8. $98.7 \div 7$

9. $0.38 - 0.252$
10. $73.2 \div 100$
11. 5.1×100
12. $5.48 \div 4$

13. $8.52 \div 4$
14. $234 + 23.4$
15. $0.612 \div 6$
16. $7.1 + 16$

17. $0.72 - 0.065$
18. $5.7 \div 100$
19. $0.83 - 0.059$
20. 0.06×1000

21. Which is larger $\boxed{0.832 - 0.75}$ or $\boxed{0.047 + 0.034}$ and by how much?

22. Ordinary pencils cost 35p but a special 'knotted' pencil costs £1.50.
Cherie buys eleven ordinary pencils and five knotted pencils.
How much change does she get from £20?

23. How many of the 'knotted' pencils in question 22 could you buy with £100?

24 | Photocopy prices |
|---|
| A4 sheet 6.9p per sheet |
| A3 sheet 12.4p per sheet |

Amy copies 1000 A4 sheets and 100 A3 sheets.
Use the prices in the table to find the total cost.

25 Copy and complete

(a) $0.38 \times \square = 38$ (b) $\square + 1.4 = 7.63$

(c) $4.76 \div \square = 0.476$ (d) $\square - 0.35 = 0.08$

26 Write the number half way between 4.6 and 4.7

27

Value of bike	Cost of service
£0 – £150	£15.70
£151 – £300	£19.35
£301 – £500	£21.54
£501 – £1000	£25.60
over £1000	£32.45

Hayley's bike shop will service bikes
(i.e. make sure everything is working properly).
The cost of the service depends on the value of
the bike, as shown in the table. Angus has
three bikes serviced. The values of the bikes
are £485, £1209 and £264
How much does Angus pay to have all three
bikes serviced?

More calculations and ordering decimals

(a) 34×200
  $= 34 \times 2 \times 100$
  $= 6800$

(b) $406 \div 14$

$$14\overline{)40^{12}6}\ \ \frac{2\ 9}{}$$

(c) Write *3.6, 3.56, 3.62, 3.074*
  in ascending order.

Remember: For ordering, put in zeros first

These are   *3.600, 3.560, 3.620, 3.074*
In order: *3.074, 3.56, 3.6, 3.62*

Exercise 2M

Work out, without a calculator.

1   26×300 2 124×200 3 $5615 - 3916$ 4 $56\,000 \div 20$

5   52×400 6 173×84 7 $576 \div 16$ 8 $1128 \div 24$

9   17×300 10 $4464 \div 36$ 11 738×48 12 $4000 - 264$

13　An astronaut spends 67 hours on the moon. How many minutes did the astronaut spend on the moon?

14　A factory has made 4416 baseball caps. An equal number of caps are to be delivered to 12 stores. How many caps does each store receive?

15　Four people walk across a tightrope. The time taken for each person is shown below.

Maurice	78.4	seconds
Cheryl	79.2	seconds
Ashley	78.38	seconds
Deb	79.09	seconds

Write down the names in order of the time taken, starting with the quickest.

16　A farmer plants 68 rows of cabbages. Each row contains 34 cabbages. It takes an average of 12 seconds to pick a cabbage and place it in a box. How many seconds will it take to pick and box all the cabbages?

17　The weights of five babies are shown below:

Ryan	Beth	Tania	David	Alex
3.94 kg	3.08 kg	3.6 kg	3.9 kg	3.07 kg

Write down the names in order of weight, starting with the heaviest.

18　Which is larger?　$0.74 + 8 + 4.6$　or　$15.8 - 2.56$

19　Maggie and her three friends have won £2943.
The money is split equally.
How much does each person get?

Reading number scales

Exercise 3M

For each of the scales, work out the measurement shown by each arrow.

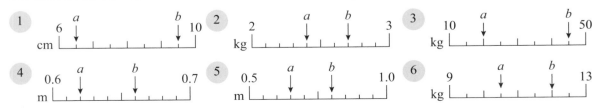

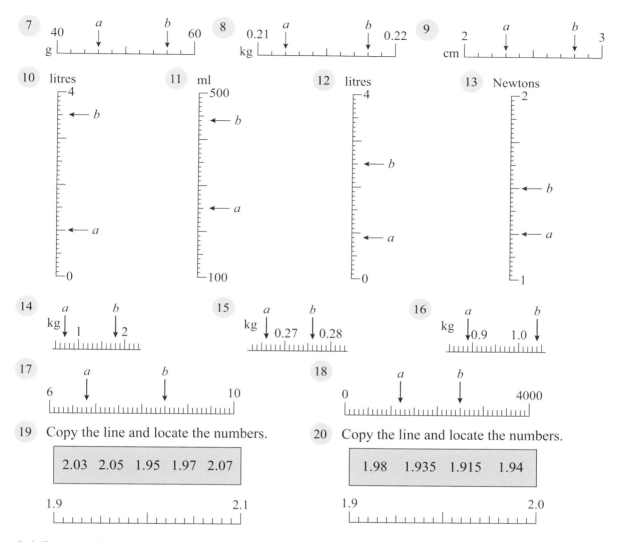

7 40   *a*   *b*   60
   g

8 0.21   *a*   *b*   0.22
   kg

9 2   *a*   *b*   3
   cm

10 litres
   4
   ← *b*
   ← *a*
   0

11 ml
   500
   ← *b*
   ← *a*
   100

12 litres
   4
   ← *b*
   ← *a*
   0

13 Newtons
   2
   ← *b*
   ← *a*
   1

14   *a*   *b*
   kg   1   2

15   *a*   *b*
   kg   0.27   0.28

16   *a*   *b*
   kg   0.9   1.0

17   *a*   *b*
   6   10

18   *a*   *b*
   0   4000

19 Copy the line and locate the numbers.

   | 2.03   2.05   1.95   1.97   2.07 |

   1.9   2.1

20 Copy the line and locate the numbers.

   | 1.98   1.935   1.915   1.94 |

   1.9   2.0

Adding and subtracting fractions

Exercise 4M

1

A	C	D	E	F	I	M	N	O	R	S	T	W	Y
$\frac{2}{5}$	$\frac{1}{4}$	$\frac{3}{8}$	$\frac{7}{10}$	$\frac{5}{9}$	$\frac{1}{2}$	$\frac{1}{10}$	$\frac{2}{3}$	$\frac{3}{7}$	$\frac{2}{9}$	$\frac{3}{10}$	$\frac{3}{4}$	$\frac{5}{6}$	$\frac{3}{20}$

Cancel down each fraction below as far as possible. Find the matching letter in the table above. Rearrange the first four letters to make one word and the remaining letters to make another word.

| $\frac{18}{60}$ | $\frac{6}{15}$ | $\frac{6}{40}$ | $\frac{21}{30}$ | | $\frac{27}{36}$ | $\frac{9}{21}$ | $\frac{35}{63}$ | $\frac{13}{26}$ | $\frac{45}{150}$ | $\frac{12}{30}$ | $\frac{9}{36}$ | $\frac{10}{15}$ | $\frac{16}{72}$ |

2 Answer true or false.

(a) $\frac{2}{3} + \frac{1}{4} = \frac{3}{7}$ (b) $\frac{3}{5} - \frac{3}{8} = \frac{9}{40}$

3 Work out the following, cancelling answers where possible.

(a) $\frac{1}{4} + \frac{2}{7}$ (b) $\frac{3}{8} + \frac{1}{6}$ (c) $\frac{5}{9} - \frac{2}{5}$ (d) $\frac{3}{4} - \frac{2}{9}$

(e) $\frac{7}{10} - \frac{3}{8}$ (f) $\frac{3}{20} + \frac{7}{10}$ (g) $\frac{8}{9} - \frac{3}{7}$ (h) $\frac{1}{8} + \frac{3}{11}$

4 Pete eats $\frac{1}{5}$ of a box of chocolates and his sister eats $\frac{3}{7}$ of the box of chocolates. What fraction of the box of chocolates has *not* been eaten?

5 Liz eats $\frac{4}{15}$ of a pear then her brother eats $\frac{5}{9}$ of the same pear. What fraction of the pear is left?

6 Josh and Lee each weigh the same amount. In April, Josh puts on $\frac{5}{8}$ of a stone and Lee puts on $\frac{1}{4}$ of a stone. In May, Josh loses $\frac{1}{3}$ of a stone and Lee puts on $\frac{1}{6}$ of a stone. Who weighs more by the end of May and by how much?

7 Work out, leaving each answer as a mixed number.

(a) $2\frac{1}{2} + \frac{3}{4}$ (b) $1\frac{1}{2} + \frac{2}{3}$ (c) $3\frac{1}{2} - 1\frac{3}{4}$

(d) $1\frac{1}{3} + 1\frac{1}{2}$ (e) $2\frac{1}{4} - \frac{3}{5}$ (f) $2\frac{2}{3} - 1\frac{3}{4}$

8 Four of the fractions below have a total of $2\frac{1}{2}$. Write down the four fractions.

| $\frac{3}{4}$ | $\frac{5}{8}$ | $1\frac{1}{3}$ | $\frac{5}{6}$ | $\frac{1}{12}$ | $\frac{1}{3}$ | $\frac{2}{5}$ |

Multiplying and dividing fractions

Exercise 5M

1 There are 360° in a circle. If you turn from north to south-east in a clockwise direction, what angle do you turn?

2

£48

Shirt

$\frac{2}{3}$ off

£40

Trousers

$\frac{1}{4}$ off

£49

Skirt

$\frac{2}{7}$ off

Jane buys the cheapest item from those listed above. How much money will she have left over from £50?

3 How many days are there in $\frac{4}{7}$ of a fortnight?

4 Work out, cancelling when possible.

(a) $\frac{3}{8} \times \frac{1}{5}$ (b) $\frac{5}{6} \times \frac{5}{7}$ (c) $\frac{4}{9} \times \frac{2}{5}$

(d) $\frac{6}{7} \times \frac{2}{3}$ (e) $\frac{1}{2} \div \frac{3}{5}$ (f) $\frac{3}{7} \div \frac{5}{8}$

(g) $\frac{1}{7} \times \frac{2}{5}$ (h) $\frac{3}{4} \div \frac{8}{9}$ (i) $\frac{3}{10} \div \frac{5}{6}$

(j) $\frac{2}{9} \div \frac{3}{4}$ (k) $\frac{7}{10} \div \frac{7}{8}$ (l) $\frac{3}{8} \times \frac{2}{9}$

> Remember: To divide by a fraction, turn the fraction you are dividing by upside down and then multiply.

5 Which is larger? $\frac{2}{3}$ of 36 or $\frac{3}{5}$ of 35

6 Which is smaller? $\frac{5}{8}$ of 40 or $\frac{5}{6}$ of 30

7 What angle does the minute hand turn through from 10:15 to 10:35?

8 Which is larger? $\frac{4}{5} \times 15$ or $\frac{3}{7} \times 35$

Exercise 6M

1 Arna has a piece of cloth $\frac{8}{9}$ m long. She cuts off $\frac{3}{4}$ of this length of cloth. How long is the left over piece of cloth?

2 $\leftarrow \frac{2}{5}$ cm $\rightarrow$

$\frac{1}{2}$ cm

$\frac{4}{5}$ cm

$\frac{7}{8}$ cm

Find the total area of this shape by finding the area of each rectangle and adding them together.

3 Copy and complete

(a) $3\frac{1}{2} \times \frac{2}{5}$

$= \frac{\square}{2} \times \frac{2}{5}$

$= \frac{\square}{10}$

$= \frac{\square}{5}$

$= \square\frac{\square}{5}$

(b) $2\frac{2}{3} \times 1\frac{1}{4}$

$= \frac{\square}{3} \times \frac{\square}{4}$

$= \frac{\square}{12}$

$= \frac{\square}{3}$

$= \square\frac{\square}{3}$

4 Marney had $2\frac{1}{2}$ loaves of bread. $\frac{3}{10}$ of this bread went rotten.

How many loaves of bread were fit to be eaten?

5 Work out

(a) $1\frac{3}{4} \times \frac{2}{3}$

(b) $2\frac{1}{2} \times \frac{3}{5}$

(c) $1\frac{2}{3} \times 2\frac{1}{4}$

(d) $3\frac{1}{4} \times 1\frac{1}{5}$

(e) $2\frac{1}{4} \div 1\frac{1}{2}$

(f) $3\frac{2}{3} \div \frac{2}{5}$

(g) $2\frac{4}{5} \div \frac{7}{10}$

(h) $1\frac{1}{2} \div 2\frac{1}{3}$

6

The area of this rectangle is $4\frac{1}{8}$ cm².

Work out the width of the rectangle.

? (rectangle) $2\frac{3}{4}$ cm

Multiplying decimal numbers – reminder

When we multiply two decimal numbers together, the answer has the same number of figures to the right of the decimal point as the total number of figures to the right of the decimal point in the question.

Examples:

(a) 0.6×0.7

$(6 \times 7 = 42)$

So $0.\underline{6} \times 0.\underline{7} = 0.\underline{42}$

(b) 0.08×0.6

$(8 \times 6 = 48)$

So $0.\underline{08} \times 0.\underline{6} = 0.\underline{048}$

Exercise 7M

Work out

1. 3×0.1
2. 26×0.1
3. 7×0.01
4. 15×0.01
5. 0.7×0.1
6. 63×0.01
7. 0.5×0.1
8. 5.2×0.01
9. 0.4×0.2
10. 0.6×0.3
11. 0.8×0.2
12. 0.4×0.03
13. 0.7×3
14. 0.7×0.02
15. 0.9×0.5
16. 6×0.04
17. 15×0.03
18. 0.4×0.04
19. 0.001×0.6
20. 33×0.02

21. Work out the area of each shape.

(a) 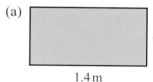 0.6 m, 1.4 m

(b) 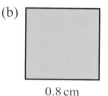 0.8 cm, 0.8 cm

(c) 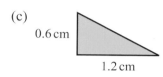 0.6 cm, 1.2 cm

22. Phone cable costs £0.55 per metre. Calculate the cost of 2.6 m of cable.

23. Work out

(a) 0.3^2 (b) 0.5^2 (c) 0.9^2 (d) 1.2^2

24. Copy and complete

(a) $6 \times 0.2 = \square$ (b) $0.4 \times \square = 0.04$ (c) $1.5 \times \square = 150$

25. Copy and complete the multiplication square.

×	0.1	0.02		8
0.2			0.1	
2.1				
				24
10				

26. The length of a rectangle is 1.5 m and its perimeter is 4 m. Find the area of the rectangle.

27.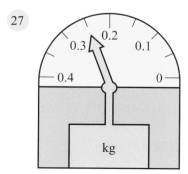

kg

Mary buys some Pik'n Mix sweets at the cinema. The weight of the sweets is shown opposite. How much does Mary pay for her sweets if 1 kilogram costs £9.80?

Dividing by 0.1 and 0.01

- $1 \div 0.1 = 1 \div \frac{1}{10} \ldots$ How many $\frac{1}{10}$s are there in 1?   Answer: 10

  $7 \div 0.1 = 7 \div \frac{1}{10} \ldots$ How many $\frac{1}{10}$s are there in 7?   Answer: 70

  $5.2 \div 0.1 = 5.2 \div \frac{1}{10} \ldots$ How many $\frac{1}{10}$s are there in 5.2?   Answer: 52

  $1 \div 0.01 = 1 \div \frac{1}{100} \ldots$ How many $\frac{1}{100}$s are there in 1?   Answer: 100

  $13 \div 0.01 = 13 \div \frac{1}{100} \ldots$ How many $\frac{1}{100}$s are there in 13?   Answer: 1300

- We see that:

> dividing by 0.1 is the same as multiplying by 10,
> dividing by 0.01 is the same as multiplying by 100

$$3 \div 0.1 = 3 \times 10 = 30$$

$$14 \div 0.1 = 14 \times 10 = 140$$

$$0.4 \div 0.1 = 0.4 \times 10 = 4$$

$$7 \div 0.01 = 7 \times 100 = 700$$

$$52 \div 0.01 = 52 \times 100 = 5200$$

$$0.7 \div 0.01 = 0.7 \times 100 = 70$$

Exercise 8M

1. $5 \div 0.1$
2. $9 \div 0.1$
3. $11 \div 0.1$
4. $6 \div 0.1$
5. $32 \div 0.1$
6. $0.7 \div 0.1$
7. $0.9 \div 0.1$
8. $1.3 \div 0.1$
9. $3 \div 0.01$
10. $11 \div 0.01$
11. $4 \div 0.01$
12. $0.3 \div 0.01$
13. $0.8 \div 0.01$
14. $57 \div 0.01$
15. $1.9 \div 0.01$
16. $0.42 \div 0.01$

17. Find the missing numbers.

    (a) $12 \div 0.1 = \square$ (b) $7 \div \square = 70$ (c) $3 \div \square = 300$

    (d) $\square \div 0.1 = 20$ (e) $1.2 \div 0.01 = \square$ (f) $1.7 \div \square = 17$

18. What numbers belong in each empty box?

    (a) $4.8 \overset{\div}{\longrightarrow} \square \longrightarrow 48 \overset{\div}{\longrightarrow} \square \longrightarrow 0.48 \overset{\div}{\longrightarrow} \square \longrightarrow 480 \overset{\div}{\longrightarrow} \square \longrightarrow 4800$

    (b) $390 \overset{\div}{\longrightarrow} \square \longrightarrow 3.9 \overset{\div}{\longrightarrow} \square \longrightarrow 39 \overset{\div}{\longrightarrow} \square \longrightarrow 0.39 \overset{\div}{\longrightarrow} \square \longrightarrow 39$

    (c) $0.4 \overset{\div}{\longrightarrow} \square \longrightarrow 4 \overset{\div}{\longrightarrow} \square \longrightarrow 400 \overset{\div}{\longrightarrow} \square \longrightarrow 40 \overset{\div}{\longrightarrow} \square \longrightarrow 0.04$

19. (a) Write 1 penny in pounds as a decimal.

    (b) How many 1ps are there in £8.05?

20. How many 0.1 metre pieces of wood can be cut from a 1.6 metre length of wood?

Dividing decimal numbers

To divide by any decimal number we transform the calculation into a division by a *whole number*.

Consider $1.5 \div 0.03$

Write the division as a fraction $\dfrac{1.5}{0.03}$

Multiply the top and bottom by a power of 10 so that both become whole numbers.

$\dfrac{1.5}{0.03} = \dfrac{150}{3}$

Now work out $150 \div 3$, which equals 50

$1.5 \div 0.03 = 50$

Both numbers were multiplied by 100, so the division answer remains the same.

(a) $3.6 \div 0.2 = \dfrac{3.6}{0.2}$

$\overset{\times 10}{\underset{\times 10}{\dfrac{3.6}{0.2}}} = \dfrac{36}{2} = 18$

(b) $1.8 \div 0.002 = \dfrac{1.8}{0.002}$

$\overset{\times 1000}{\underset{\times 1000}{\dfrac{1.8}{0.002}}} = \dfrac{1800}{2} = 900$

Exercise 8E

1 Work out the following decimal divisions.

(a) $0.6 \div 0.02 = \dfrac{0.6}{0.02} = \dfrac{60}{2} = ?$

(b) $8 \div 0.4 = \dfrac{8}{0.4} = \dfrac{80}{4} = ?$

(c) $2.8 \div 0.05 = \dfrac{2.8}{0.05} = \dfrac{280}{5} = ?$

(d) $6.9 \div 0.003 = \dfrac{6.9}{0.003} = \dfrac{6900}{?} = ?$

2 Work out

(a) $6 \div 0.05$

(b) $9.2 \div 0.04$

(c) $12 \div 0.005$

(d) $0.58 \div 0.02$

(e) $4.8 \div 0.06$

(f) $0.63 \div 0.009$

3 $2.52 \div 0.4 = \overset{\times 10}{\underset{\times 10}{\dfrac{2.52}{0.4}}} = \dfrac{25.2}{4} = 25.2 \div 4$

Work out $4\overline{)25.2}$ to get the final answer.

4 Work out

(a) $0.712 \div 0.2$

(b) $0.375 \div 0.5$

(c) $6.54 \div 0.2$

(d) $0.0585 \div 0.09$

(e) $5.04 \div 0.7$

(f) $0.2846 \div 0.2$

(g) $0.42 \div 0.03$

(h) $7.041 \div 0.01$

(i) $0.993 \div 0.3$

(j) $7.52 \div 0.4$

(k) $8.4 \div 0.02$

(l) $0.1638 \div 0.001$

5 A bottle of milk contains 1 litre. How many glasses can be filled from this bottle if each glass holds 0.2 litres?

6 A supermarket sells 200 g bags of redcurrants. An average redcurrant weighs 0.8 g. How many redcurrants are there in a 200 g bag?

7 $86.45 \div 35 = 2.47$

Use the calculation above to work out

(a) $864.5 \div 35$

(b) $0.8645 \div 35$

(c) $8.645 \div 3.5$

8 Arrange these divisions in order of size of their answers, starting with the smallest.

A $0.62 \div 0.04$

B $62 \div 0.04$

C $0.62 \div 0.4$

Need more practice with calculations?

Hidden words

(a) Start in the top left box in the first grid on the next page.

(b) Work out the answer to the calculation in the box.

(c) Find the answer in the top corner of another box.

(d) Write down the letter in that box.

(e) Repeat steps (b), (c) and (d) until you arrive back at the top left box.
     What is the message?

1

6.4 L 5×15	66 L $2^3 + 3^3$	274 N 20% of 50	985 E 15×100	12 S $756 \div 9$
422 N 10^3	75 S $150 - 67$	1.68 R 8×22	10 C $8.7 \div 10$	2.4 I $37 + 385$
3.85 U 0.16×10	176 E $421 - 147$	0.87 H $5 + 1.4$	1000 F $8.4 \div 5$	83 O $385 \div 7$
55 L $1000 - 15$	1500 I $\frac{2}{3}$ of 99	1.6 N 0.4×6	35 I 25% of 48	84 S $5.32 - 1.47$

2

612 $1.8 + 8.2$	0.8 T 5% of 400	0.77 W $2^3 \times 6$	0.2 V 5×69	0.62 T 20% of 65
32 C $50\,000 \div 200$	10 B $\frac{2}{5}$ of 450	13 R 0.6×2.6	18 E 80% of 80	250 U $0.9^2 - 0.1^2$
1.56 E $\frac{3}{8}$ of 48	0.6 R $\frac{1}{2}$ of 0.3	180 E $(0.2)^2$	0.15 S 0.32×10^2	64 S $806 - 194$
0.04 A 10% of 2	0.27 O $770 \div 1000$	20 D $0.3 - 0.03$	48 N 3.1×0.2	345 E $4.2 \div 7$

3

45	4	371	21	0.51
H	C	A	S	S
$\frac{1}{2} + \frac{1}{4}$	2^4	$10 \div 1000$	$62.5 \div 100$	$21 - 5 \times 4$
896	0.06	0.05	0.01	34
M	E	L	E	Y
$1^2 + 2^2 + 3^3$	$51 \div 100$	$25 \div 10$	$5 \times (5 - 2)^2$	5.1×100
0.625	1	$\frac{3}{4}$	$\frac{3}{8}$	32
T	O	M	S	I
$\frac{2}{3} \times \frac{1}{5}$	$6000 \div 20$	$4 + 5 \times 6$	0.3×0.2	53×7
510	16	2.5	300	$\frac{2}{15}$
C	A	Y	N	C
$\frac{3}{5}$ of 35	$\frac{1}{2} - \frac{1}{8}$	$8 + 888$	$\frac{1}{4} - 0.2$	$20 \div (12 - 7)$

Extension questions with calculations

1. Work out $\frac{3}{4} \times \frac{2}{5} \times \frac{8}{9}$

2. A charity is raising money for child eye operations in another country. Each eye operation costs £20. During June, 36 people each donate £25 and 89 people each donate £40. How many eye operations can the charity fund with this money?

3. Harry is on holiday and needs to change £80 into dollars. If £1 can be changed for $1.60, how many dollars will Harry get?

4. How many 0.2 m pieces of wood can be cut from a 3 metre length of wood?

5. Wire netting costs £0.88 per metre. What is the cost of 4.5 m of wire netting?

6. What fraction of this UK flag is white if $\frac{3}{8}$ of the flag is red and $\frac{1}{3}$ is blue?

7 Work out

   (a) $2\frac{1}{2} + 1\frac{5}{6}$
   (b) $3\frac{1}{3} - 1\frac{4}{5}$
   (c) $1\frac{2}{3} \times 2\frac{1}{4}$

8 Copy and complete the multiplication square.

×		0.6	0.07
0.4			
0.03	0.09		
	1.8		

9 6.2×2.1 is approximately $6 \times 2 = 12$

   6.2×2.1 gives the answer 13.02

   The actual answer is close to the approximate answer so is probably correct.

   Work out, after finding an approximate answer first.

   (a) 5.3×32 (b) 2.3×1.2 (c) 3.8×17 (d) 7.9×4.1

   (e) 6.2×4.2 (f) 35.1×0.9 (g) 0.32×5.8 (h) 1.9×1.8

10 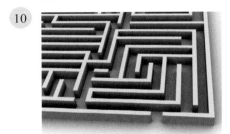 Six people have to get out of a maze. Each time taken to get out of the maze is shown below.

Carl	12.73 mins	Sam	12.6 mins
Julie	12.8 mins	Ben	13.08 mins
Arwen	13.14 mins	Melinda	12.75 mins

   If they all started at the same time, write down the order in which they got out of the maze.

11 Work out

   (a) $17.4 \div 0.2$ (b) $4.006 \div 0.002$ (c) $54 \div 0.3$ (d) $0.1685 \div 0.005$

12 £1 = $1.32 and £1 = €1.15

   Ben buys a radio for €115 in France. The radio is 10% more expensive to buy in the USA. How many dollars will the radio cost in the USA?

✗ **Spot the mistakes 5** ✗

Area, perimeter, circles and number calculations

Work through each question below and *explain clearly* what mistakes have been made. Beware – some questions are correctly done.

1 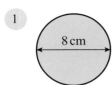 Work out the area of this circle.
Give the answers to 1 decimal place.

Answer: Area $= \pi \times 8^2$

$= 201.1$ cm^2

2 Work out 0.16×0.7

Answer:
$$\begin{array}{r} 16 \\ \times\ 7 \\ \hline 112 \\ \hline {}_4 \end{array}$$ so $0.16 \times 0.7 = 1.12$

3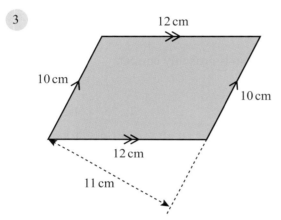

12 cm

10 cm

10 cm

12 cm

11 cm

Work out the area of this parallelogram.

Answer: Area $= 12 \times 10$

$= 120$ cm^2

4 Carol has three 2 litre bottles of water. She wants to fill as many 0.4 litre glasses as possible. How many glasses can she fill using all the water?

Answer: $6 \div 0.4 = \dfrac{6}{0.4} = \dfrac{60}{4}$

$60 \div 4 = 15$ glasses

5 Work out $4\frac{2}{9} \div 2\frac{2}{3}$

Answer: $4 \div 2 = 2$ and $\dfrac{2}{9} \div \dfrac{2}{3} = \dfrac{2 \div 2}{9 \div 3} = \dfrac{1}{3}$

so $4\frac{2}{9} \div 2\frac{2}{3} = 2\frac{1}{3}$

6 Calculate the area of this trapezium.

Answer:

Area of trapezium $= \frac{1}{2}h(a + b)$

$= \frac{1}{2}(5)(7 + 13) = 2.5 \times 20$

$= 50$ cm^2

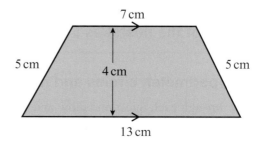

7 cm

5 cm

4 cm

5 cm

13 cm

7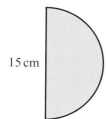

Work out the perimeter of this semicircle.
Give the answers to 1 decimal place.

15 cm

Answer: Perimeter $= \dfrac{\pi \times 15}{2} = 23.6$ cm

8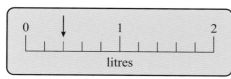

litres

The arrow shows how much petrol is left in a car's petrol tank. How much petrol must be added so that the petrol tank contains 10 litres of petrol?

Answer: There are 0.2 litres of petrol in the tank so another 9.8 litres of petrol are needed to fill the tank.

9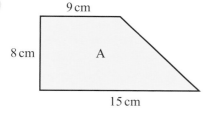

9 cm

8 cm   A

15 cm

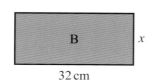

B x

32 cm

Shapes A and B have the same area. Work out the value of x.

Answer: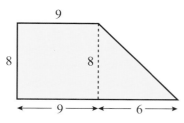

Area A $= (8 \times 9) + \left(\dfrac{8 \times 6}{2}\right)$

$= 72 + 24 = 96$ cm^2

Area B $= 32x = 96$

$x = 3$ cm

10 A circular lawn has a 1 metre path around it, as shown.
The radius of the lawn is 6 m.
Calculate the area of the path.
Give the answer to 1 decimal place.

Lawn

Answer: radius of lawn $= 6$

area of lawn $= \pi \times 6^2 = 113.1$ m^2

1 m extra path on each side, so radius of large circle $= 1 + 6 + 1 = 8$

area of large circle $= \pi \times 8^2 = 201.1$ m^2

area of path $= 201.1 - 113.1 = 88.0$ m^2

3.4 Using a calculator

In section 3.4 you will:

- review the correct order of operations in calculations
- use a calculator efficiently
- deal with negative numbers on a calculator

Order of operations – reminder

Brackets
Indices
Divide
Multiply
Add
Subtract

The word 'BIDMAS' is used to remember the correct order of operations.

Examples

$20 - 8 \times 2 = 20 - 16 = 4$

$20 - 8 \div (5 + 3) = 20 - 8 \div 8 = 20 - 1 = 19$

Exercise 1M

Work out, without a calculator. Show every step in your working.

1. $6 + 3 \times 4$
2. $8 - 2 \times 3$
3. $(9 - 2) \times 4$
4. $16 \div 4 - 1$
5. $17 + 12 \div 3$
6. $7 + 16 \div 8$
7. $12 + 4 \times 10$
8. $36 - 11 \times 3$
9. $27 \div (13 - 4)$
10. $(17 + 5) \times 3$
11. $9 + 9 \times 9$
12. $36 - 6 - 20$
13. $8 + 3 \times 3 - 5$
14. $18 - (8 \times 1) + 4$
15. $2 + 16 \div (5 + 3)$
16. $(6 \times 5) \div (12 \div 2)$
17. $80 - (44 \div 2)$
18. $(50 \times 4) \div (201 - 199)$
19. $8 + 24 \div 6 - 2$
20. $40 \div 8 - 12 \div 3$
21. $3 \times (4 \times 2 - 3)$
22. $\dfrac{17 + 3}{2}$
23. $\dfrac{45}{12 + 3}$
24. $\dfrac{45 + 5}{8 - 6}$

25. Work out 4×5^2 [Remember: work out 5^2 and then multiply by 4]

26. Work out

(a) $8 + 4^2$

(b) $20 - 3^2$

(c) $6^2 - 10$

(d) $5^2 + 7^2$

(e) $(2 + 2)^2$

(f) $4 \times (4^2 - 1)$

(g) $(12 - 8)^2 \div 2$

(h) $(6^2 + 8^2) \div 50$

(i) $56 \div 7 - 2^2$

(j) $\dfrac{8^2 - 4}{20}$

(k) $\dfrac{5^2}{4 + 1}$

(l) $\dfrac{(2 + 3)^2 + 15}{10}$

Exercise 2M

Copy each question and write brackets so that each calculation gives the correct answer.

1 $4 + 2 \times 3 = 18$

2 $6 + 3 \times 4 = 36$

3 $2 \times 3 + 5 = 16$

4 $3 \times 10 - 5 = 15$

5 $20 - 8 \times 3 = 36$

6 $28 \div 2 + 5 = 4$

7 $13 + 7 \div 5 = 4$

8 $9 + 1 \times 8 - 6 = 20$

9 $7 + 4 \times 5 = 55$

10 $16 - 3 + 3^2 = 4$

11 $8 + 3 + 9 \div 2 = 10$

12 $7 + 2 \times 8 - 7 = 9$

13 $9 - 3^2 + 3 = 3$

14 $8 + 3 - 5 \times 0 = 0$

15 $8 + 2^2 \times 10 - 3^2 = 12$

In questions 16 to 24 , find the missing signs ($+$, $-$, $\times$, $\div$). There are no brackets.

16 9   3   3 = 18

17 7   3   11 = 32

18 6   12   3 = 10

19 11   4   4 = 10

20 15   4   5 = 35

21 8   3   6 = 30

22 7   6   2 = 10

23 8   4   4   4 = 18

24 9   2   2   5 = 10

Using a calculator – reminder

The fraction button on a calculator is and above it is for mixed numbers.

Press SHIFT first before using the key for mixed numbers.

Exercise 3M

Use a calculator and give the answer correct to two decimal places.

1 3.4×1.23

2 $20.4 - 5.7412$

3 0.341^2

4 $0.17 + 2.89 - 1.514$

5 $3.2^2 - 2.8$

6 $4.6 \times 1.9 + 8.05$

7 $0.54 \times 0.87 - 0.1$

8 $8.7 \div 2.73$

9 $12.5 - 0.516 + 1.2$

10 $\dfrac{8.9}{7.4}$

11 $\dfrac{20.2}{5.6} + 8.2$

12 $\dfrac{8.65}{6} - 0.12$

In questions 13 to 30 , remember 'BIDMAS'.

13 $2.6 + 2.7 \times 1.9$

14 $8.01 + 0.8 \times 3.2$

15 $7.93 + 5 \div 12$

16 $8.6 \div 0.7 - 5.55$

17 $8 \div 0.55 + 2.33$

18 $8.06 + 1.4 \times 1.5$

19 $3.5 + \dfrac{8.5}{1.34}$

20 $1.53^2 + 2.53$

21 $6.4 + \dfrac{1.7}{0.85}$

22 $8.65 + 30 \div 8.2$

23 $5.44 + 1.37^2$

24 $6.4^2 \div 19$

25 $0.751 - 0.14 \times 0.9$

26 2.3^3

27 $10 + 10 \times 10$

28 $8.9 + \dfrac{19.6}{15}$

29 $\dfrac{2.7 + 5.65}{3.3}$

30 $\dfrac{11.2 - 5.67}{1.9}$

31 Matt sends 529 texts during June. Each text costs 11p. He has to pay £14 for his June phone calls. What is his total June bill for texts and phone calls?

32 If a farmer sells a cow, he makes a profit of £110. If he cannot sell a cow, he loses £45. If the farmer sells a pig, he makes a profit of £33 but loses £18 if he cannot sell the pig. One year the farmer has 45 cows and manages to sell 34 of them. He has 59 pigs and is able to sell 41 of them. Calculate the farmer's total profit.

Exercise 4M

1 Use a calculator to work out

(a) $\frac{9}{10} + \frac{1}{20}$ (b) $\frac{11}{12} - \frac{3}{4}$ (c) $\frac{4}{9} \times \frac{1}{2}$ (d) $\frac{3}{11} \times \frac{1}{4}$

(e) $2\frac{1}{4} + \frac{1}{3}$ (f) $3\frac{2}{3} - 1\frac{1}{2}$ (g) $4\frac{1}{2} + \frac{5}{8}$ (h) $\frac{1}{6} + 3\frac{3}{4}$

2 Jenny works out $6 + \frac{4}{2}$ and says the answer is 5

What mistake has she made? Write down the correct answer.

3 Work out and give each answer correct to 2 decimal places.

(a) $11.52 - (3.14 \times 2.6)$ (b) $12.5 + (3.8 \div 6)$ (c) $(5.27 + 8.2) \div 2.7$

(d) $9.6 + (8.7 \div 11)$ (e) $(9.5 \div 7) - 0.44$ (f) $13.7 - (8.2 \times 1.31)$

(g) $6.31 - \left(\frac{8.2}{1.9}\right)$ (h) $\left(\frac{7.65}{1.5}\right) - 3.06$ (i) $\frac{3.63}{(3.9 + 0.121)}$

(j) $(11.2 \div 7) \times 2.43$ (k) $(3.65 + 1.4 - 2.34) \times 2.6$ (l) $35 - (8.7 \times 2.65)$

(m) $\frac{9.37 + 8.222}{2.47}$ (n) $\frac{4.5}{8} + \frac{4.7}{7}$ (o) $3.2^2 - \frac{4.2}{3.7}$

4 Which gives the larger answer and by how much?

$$\frac{4}{9} - \left(\frac{1}{8} - \frac{2}{5}\right) \quad \text{or} \quad \left(\frac{4}{9} - \frac{1}{8}\right) - \frac{2}{5}$$

5 Copy and complete

(a)

+		$\frac{3}{5}$		$1\frac{3}{4}$
	$\frac{5}{8}$		$\frac{5}{6}$	
$\frac{1}{4}$				
$2\frac{1}{2}$	$2\frac{5}{8}$			
			$\frac{11}{15}$	

(b)

×			$\frac{5}{8}$	$2\frac{1}{5}$
$\frac{4}{5}$	$\frac{2}{5}$			
		$\frac{5}{24}$		
	$\frac{1}{8}$	$\frac{1}{6}$		
$1\frac{1}{2}$				

6 Work out

(a) $\left(\frac{1}{3} - \frac{1}{4}\right) \times \frac{6}{7}$

(b) $\dfrac{\left(2\frac{3}{5} - 1\frac{3}{4}\right)}{\left(\frac{1}{5} - \frac{1}{6}\right)}$

(c) $\frac{14}{15} \times \frac{3}{7} - \frac{7}{10} + \frac{1}{15}$

Negative numbers on a calculator

On a calculator, the $\boxed{(-)}$ button is used for negative numbers.

(a) $-5.2 + 7.81$

Press the keys

$\boxed{(-)}$ $\boxed{5.2}$ $\boxed{+}$ $\boxed{7.81}$ $\boxed{=}$

Answer $= 2.61$

(b) $7.5 \div (-0.04)$

$\boxed{7.5}$ $\boxed{\div}$ $\boxed{(-)}$ $\boxed{0.04}$ $\boxed{=}$

Answer $= -187.5$

Notice that we do not *need* the brackets buttons. You may use them if you prefer.

Exercise 5M

Work out the following. Give the answer correct to one decimal place where appropriate.

1 -7×3

2 $-5 \times (-2)$

3 $8 \div (-4)$

4 $10 \times (-4)$

5 $-2 \times (-2)$

6 $-12 \div 3$

7 $-5 \times (-4)$

8 $-8 - 11$

9 $-7 + 2$

10 $-9 + 30$

11 $-20 \div 4$

12 $-16 - 15$

13 $-3.4 \times (-2.5)$

14 -0.5×6.8

15 $12.5 - (-2.5)$

16 $-1.1 \times (-1.1)$

17 $-8 \div (-0.25)$

18 $-6.8 \div 0.1$

19 $\dfrac{-8 \times (-3)}{4}$

20 $\dfrac{12}{(3 \times (-2))}$

21 $\dfrac{20}{(-2)} + 8$

22 $-11.4 + 1.71$

23 $-9.2 - 7.4 + 15.2$

24 $-4.74 - (-13.08)$

25 Answer true or false.

(a) $(-22)^2 = 484$

(b) $-3^2 = 9$

(c) $-5.1^2 = 26.01$

(d) $-20 \div -2.5 = 8$

(e) $8 - 9.5^2 = -82.25$

(f) $\dfrac{8 - (-3.2)}{-0.1} = -112$

26 Copy and complete

(a) $4.6 - \square = 11.61$

(b) $-8.4 \times \square = 27.72$

(c) $6.3 + \square = -14.29$

(d) $\dfrac{-16.34}{\square} = -4.3$

Need more practice with using a calculator?

Calculator words

- When you hold a calculator display upside down some numbers

appear to form words: | 4506 | spells "Gosh"

| 0.70 | spells "Old"
(ignoring the decimal point)

Warning

The letters on some calculators are not so easy to make out. Agree with your teacher which number gives which letter.

Translate this passage using a calculator and the clues below: " (1) !" shouted Olag out of the window of his (2) . "I need some (3) / (4) for my dinner. Do you (5) them?" " (6) did"

(7) / (8) "I even took off the (9) for free. (10) / (11) / (12) they were. The problem is that all the (13) were eaten in the (14) ,

mostly by (15) . (16) / (17) such a (18) / (19) lately. (20) and (21) are always

(22) because of the amount of (23) they drink every night" " (24) well,

he is the (25) I suppose", Olag grumbled "Roast (26) again tonight then…"

Clues to passage

(1) $(2.37 + 2.53) \div 0.7^2$

(2) $(3 \div 40) + 0.0011$

(3) 0.09277×4

(4) $5 \times 12 \times 100 - 7$

(5) $(90 \times 80) + (107 \times 5)$

(6) $\sqrt{0.01} \times 10$

(7) $(68 + 1.23) \div 200$

(8) $101^2 - (5 \times 13) - 2$

(9) $750^2 + (296\,900 \div 20)$

(10) $2^2 \times 5^2 \times 6 + 16.3 + 1.7$

(11) $(70\,000 \div 2) + (3 \times 2)$

(12) $11\,986 \div 2$

(13) $(600^2 - 6640) \div 10$

(14) $200^2 - 685$

(15) $(0.5^2 \times 0.6)$

16 $\sqrt{289} \times 2$

17 $836.4 \div 17 + 1.8$

18 $30^2 + 18$

19 64.6×125

20 $(63\,508 \times 5) - 3$

21 $\sqrt{(1160 - 4)}$

22 1.3803×0.25

23 $(32 \times 1000) + 8$

24 $2^2 \times 10$

25 $(5^2 \times 2^2 \times 55) + 8$

26 $7000 \times 10^2 \times 10^2 - 956\,3966$

Extension questions with using a calculator

1 Work out and give each answer correct to 2 decimal places.

   (a) $\dfrac{11.23}{9.7 - 6.66}$

   (b) $\dfrac{114 - 95.6}{14}$

   (c) $\dfrac{6.9}{1.4} + \dfrac{3.2}{0.8}$

   (d) $2.7^2 - 1.56$

   (e) $(8.2 - 6.93)^2$

   (f) $(2.9^2 - 1.8) \div 5$

   (g) $\dfrac{5.48 + 7.63}{9.74 - 2.99}$

   (h) $\dfrac{\sqrt{7.4}}{2.86 - 1.9}$

   (i) $\sqrt{\dfrac{6.2}{3.4 + 0.83}}$

2 Find the total bill for
   6 avocados at 92p each
   4 grapefruit at 59p each
   48 eggs at £2.58 per dozen
   3 packets of tea at £3.26 each
   200 g of cheese at £6.80 per kg
   20 oranges at £1.80 for 5

3 Work out

   (a) $\left(\dfrac{3}{5} + \dfrac{1}{8}\right) \times \dfrac{1}{2}$

   (b) $\left(\dfrac{5}{6} - \dfrac{1}{9}\right) \times \dfrac{3}{4}$

   (c) $\dfrac{3}{8} \times \left(\dfrac{2}{3} + \dfrac{1}{5}\right)$

   (d) $\left(1\dfrac{2}{3} + \dfrac{1}{4}\right) \div \dfrac{2}{3}$

   (e) $\dfrac{5}{8} \div \left(\dfrac{1}{3} + \dfrac{1}{2}\right)$

   (f) $2\dfrac{3}{4} \times \left(\dfrac{2}{5} + \dfrac{1}{10}\right)$

4 Amos uses a calculator to work out the square of -4. He types -4^2 into a calculator and gets the answer -16. This is not correct. The answer should be 16. What buttons should Amos press to make sure that he gets the correct answer 16?

5 Work out, giving answers to one decimal place.

   (a) $\dfrac{(-8.23) \times (-1.24)}{3.6}$

   (b) $\dfrac{5.1 \times (-1.42)}{(-1.7)}$

   (c) $-6.2 + (-8.4)$

   (d) $-7.2 + \left(\dfrac{4.3}{1.5}\right)$

   (e) $-8.7 \times \left(\dfrac{7.2}{11}\right)$

   (f) $(-7.2 + 4)^2$

6 A shop sells carrots in $\frac{2}{5}$ kg bags and $1\frac{1}{2}$ kg bags.
   Hal needs to buy *exactly* $2\frac{7}{10}$ kg carrots.
   How many of each bag must he buy?

7   A leap year is divisible by 4. Which years are leap years between 2021 and 2035?

8   Huan works out $\dfrac{5.9 + 3.16}{2.62 - 0.97}$ by typing into a calculator $5.9 + 3.16 \div 2.62 - 0.97$.

Does Huan get the correct answer? Justify your answer.

CHECK YOURSELF ON SECTIONS 3.3 and 3.4

1   Calculations with whole numbers and decimals

Work out, without a calculator.

(a) 184×38 (b) $0.082 + 17 + 5.09$ (c) $2516 \div 37$

2   Reading number scales

In each question, work out the difference between the two values shown by the arrows.

3   Calculations with fractions

Work out

(a) $\dfrac{3}{7} - \dfrac{1}{5}$ (b) $2\dfrac{1}{4} + 1\dfrac{2}{3}$ (c) $\dfrac{3}{4} \times \dfrac{2}{9}$ (d) $3\dfrac{1}{3} \div \dfrac{5}{6}$

4   Multiplying and dividing decimals

Work out, without a calculator

(a) 0.7×0.08 (b) $12 \div 0.1$ (c) 0.32×0.03 (d) $2.8 \div 0.04$

5   Order of operations

Work out, without a calculator

(a) $9 + 2 \times 4$ (b) $5 \times (6 + 2) - 4$ (c) $30 - 16 \div 4$

Use a calculator and give the answers below correct to two decimal places.

(d) $6.14 + 3 \div 11$ (e) $0.826 - 0.27 \times 0.4$ (f) $5.7 + \dfrac{13.6}{14}$

6   Using a calculator efficiently

Work out and give your answers correct to one decimal place.

(a) $\dfrac{17.1}{8.2 - 7.57}$ (b) $\dfrac{8.7}{1.4} + \dfrac{11.92}{2.6}$ (c) $27.7 \div (0.97 \times 35.4)$

7 Using negative numbers on a calculator

Use a calculator to work out

(a) $9 \times (-14)$

(b) $-16 - (-30)$

(c) $\dfrac{-8 \times 4}{-2}$

3.5 Fractions, decimals and percentages

In section 3.5 you will:

- convert between fractions, decimals and percentages
- change fractions to recurring decimals

Changing fractions to decimals and vice versa – reminder

Fractions to decimals – convert denominator to 10, 100, etc.

$\dfrac{3}{20} = \dfrac{15}{100} = 0.15$ $\qquad\qquad$ $\dfrac{9}{25} = \dfrac{36}{100} = 0.36$

If too 'tricky', divide the two numbers.

$\dfrac{5}{8} = 5 \div 8$ $\qquad$ $8\overline{)5.{}^{5}0{}^{2}0{}^{4}0}^{0.625}$ $\qquad$ so $\dfrac{5}{8} = 0.625$

Decimals to fractions – always cancel the fraction if possible.

$0.4 = \dfrac{4}{10} = \dfrac{2}{5}$ $\qquad\qquad$ $0.35 = \dfrac{35}{100} = \dfrac{7}{20}$

Exercise 1M

1 Without using a calculator, change the following fractions to decimals. Afterwards divide with a calculator to check your answer.

(a) $\dfrac{1}{5}$ $\qquad$ (b) $\dfrac{7}{10}$ $\qquad$ (c) $\dfrac{4}{5}$ $\qquad$ (d) $\dfrac{9}{20}$ $\qquad$ (e) $\dfrac{7}{25}$

(f) $\dfrac{13}{20}$ $\qquad$ (g) $\dfrac{3}{4}$ $\qquad$ (h) $\dfrac{6}{8}$ $\qquad$ (i) $\dfrac{35}{500}$ $\qquad$ (j) $\dfrac{7}{8}$

2 Use a calculator to convert the fractions to decimals. Write in order of size, smallest first.

(a) $\dfrac{7}{8}, 0.85, \dfrac{9}{10}$ $\qquad$ (b) $\dfrac{13}{20}, 0.645, \dfrac{31}{50}$ $\qquad$ (c) $\dfrac{3}{4}, 0.715, \dfrac{29}{40}$ $\qquad$ (d) $\dfrac{3}{16}, 0.18, \dfrac{1}{5}$

3 0.56 of the people on a crowded beach are female. What fraction of the people are male?

4 Austin has eaten 0.8 of his pizza and Mika has eaten $\frac{17}{20}$ of her pizza. Who has eaten the most pizza? Give a reason for your answer.

5 Change the following decimals to fractions, cancelling when possible.

(a) 0.6   (b) 0.7   (c) 0.07   (d) 0.08   (e) 0.003

(f) 0.004   (g) 0.06   (h) 0.24   (i)   0.42   (j) 0.25

(k) 0.015   (l)   0.85   (m) 0.025   (n) 0.57   (o) 0.325

6 Change these mixed numbers to decimals.

(a) $3\frac{2}{5}$ (b) $5\frac{1}{2}$ (c) $2\frac{3}{4}$ (d) $2\frac{7}{8}$ (e) $6\frac{3}{100}$

7 Copy and fill in each box with one of $<$, $>$ or $=$.

(a) $\frac{1}{5}$ ☐ 0.5   (b) $\frac{9}{25}$ ☐ 0.36   (c) 0.8 ☐ $\frac{4}{5}$

(d) $\frac{3}{20}$ ☐ 0.1   (e) 0.3 ☐ $\frac{7}{20}$ (f) $\frac{27}{50}$ ☐ 0.5

Changing to a percentage and vice versa

> To change a fraction or a decimal to a percentage, multiply by 100

(a) To change $\frac{2}{5}$ to a percentage, multiply by 100

$$\frac{2}{5} \times \frac{100}{1} = \frac{200}{5}$$
$$= 40\%$$

(b) To change $\frac{1}{8}$ to a percentage, multiply by 100

$$\frac{1}{8} \times \frac{100}{1} = \frac{100}{8}$$
$$= 12\frac{1}{2}\%$$

(c) To change $\frac{3}{7}$ to a percentage, multiply by 100

$$\frac{3}{7} \times \frac{100}{1} = \frac{300}{7}$$
$$= 42.857...\%$$
$$= 43\%, \text{ to the nearest whole number.}$$

(d) To change 0.37 to a percentage, multiply by 100

$$0.37 \times 100 = 37\%$$

Exercise 2M

1. Change these fractions to percentages.

   (a) $\dfrac{1}{4}$ (b) $\dfrac{3}{5}$ (c) $\dfrac{9}{10}$ (d) $\dfrac{73}{100}$ (e) $\dfrac{3}{8}$

   (f) $\dfrac{7}{20}$ (g) $\dfrac{8}{25}$ (h) $\dfrac{7}{8}$ (i) $\dfrac{3}{4}$ (j) $\dfrac{19}{20}$

2. In an archery competition, Phoenix hits the bullseye with 16 of his 25 arrows. Amina hits the bullseye with 60% of her arrows. Who has the best rate of hitting the bullseye? Give a reason for your answer.

3. A group of people were asked if they had been to the fair in the last year. $\dfrac{3}{25}$ of these people said 'yes'. What *percentage* of these people said 'no'?

4. Change these decimals to percentages.

   (a) 0.16 (b) 0.57 (c) 0.09 (d) 0.78 (e) 1.6

5. $\frac{1}{2}$ to 1 hour $\left(\dfrac{9}{150}\right)$

   $\frac{1}{2}$ hour or less $\left(\dfrac{15}{150}\right)$

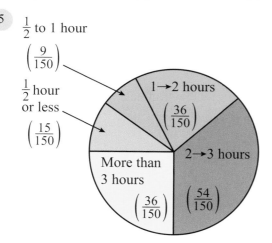

   The chart opposite shows the TV viewing habits of 150 people in a survey. What percentage watch

   (a) $\frac{1}{2}$ hour or less

   (b) more than 3 hours

   (c) 2 → 3 hours?

6. Here are four children's test results.

Clive	Abbie	Molly	Ron
$\dfrac{17}{20}$	$\dfrac{42}{60}$	$\dfrac{27}{40}$	$\dfrac{49}{140}$

   Change them to percentages then write the names in order of percentage marks obtained, starting with the largest.

7. Change these percentages to decimals.

   (a) 29% (b) 47% (c) 1% (d) 98% (e) 7.5%

204

8   The chart opposite shows the favourite foods of 80 people.

     What percentage prefer

     (a) Italian   (b) Asian

     (c) French   (d) Anything but Chinese?

     (e) Marcus plans to open a restaurant specialising in one
         type of food shown. He will only choose a type of food
         if *more than* 20% of the people prefer it.
         What type of food might Marcus serve in his restaurant?

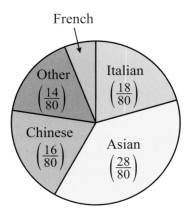

Recurring decimals

Some fractions give rise to decimals which repeat themselves forever. We call these recurring
decimals, and use the notation below to save us from writing out the number until our ink runs out!

(a) 0.555…   We write $0.\dot{5}$

(b) 0.434343…   We write $0.\dot{4}\dot{3}$

(c) 0.5265265…   We write $0.5\dot{2}6\dot{6}$

Changing fractions to recurring decimals

(a) Change $\frac{1}{3}$ to a decimal. $$3\overline{)1.^{1}0^{1}0^{1}0^{1}0^{1}0…} \quad 0.\,3\,3\,3\,3\,3…$$

The calculation is never going to end.

We write $\frac{1}{3} = 0.\dot{3}$. We say 'nought point three recurring'.

(b) Change $\frac{3}{11}$ to a decimal.

$$11\overline{)3.^{3}0^{8}0^{3}0^{8}0^{3}0^{8}0…} \quad 0.\,2\,7\,2\,7\,2\,7…$$

This time a *pair* of figures recurs.

We write $\frac{3}{11} = 0.\dot{2}\dot{7}$

(c) Change $\frac{1}{7}$ to a decimal.

$$7\overline{)1.^{1}0^{3}0^{2}0^{6}0^{4}0^{5}0^{1}0^{3}00…} \quad 0.\,1\,4\,2\,8\,5\,7\,1\,42…$$

The sequence '142857' recurs.

We write $\frac{1}{7} = 0.\dot{1}4285\dot{7}$

Exercise 3M

Change the following fractions to decimals.

1   $\frac{5}{9}$ 2 $\frac{2}{3}$ 3 $\frac{1}{6}$ 4 $\frac{3}{7}$ 5 $\frac{7}{9}$

6   $\frac{5}{7}$ 7 $\frac{2}{11}$ 8 $\frac{4}{9}$ 9 $\frac{7}{11}$ 10 $\frac{5}{6}$

11 (a) Work out each of the following as a decimal: $\frac{1}{7}, \frac{2}{7}, \frac{3}{7}, \frac{4}{7}, \frac{5}{7}, \frac{6}{7}$

     (b) What do you notice about the answers?

Need more practice with fractions, decimals and percentages?

1. Change the following numbers into decimals.

   (a) $\dfrac{19}{20}$
   (b) 42%
   (c) $\dfrac{38}{200}$
   (d) 30%

2. Change the following numbers into percentages.

   (a) 0.8
   (b) 0.08
   (c) $\dfrac{7}{10}$
   (d) $\dfrac{11}{20}$

3.
   The table below shows what we throw away and scope for recycling. Change each percentage to a fraction, cancelling down when possible.

Food waste	Plastic	Glass	Paper and card	Metals	Textiles	Other
24%	10%	8%	26%	4%	3%	25%

4. Gary has scored 0.7 in a test. His parents feel that a test result of 7% is not Gary's best ever mark and that he will have to work hard to improve this. *Explain* what mistake his parents have made.

5. Write down true or false for each statement below.

   (a) $0.35 > \dfrac{4}{10}$
   (b) $\dfrac{96}{300} < 36\%$
   (c) $0.9 < 80\%$

   (d) $\dfrac{18}{25} = 90\%$
   (e) $0.62 > \dfrac{31}{50}$
   (f) $40\% > \dfrac{10}{40}$

6. Change $\dfrac{5}{11}$ to a recurring decimal.

7. $\dfrac{3}{8}$ of a group of people are American and 0.2 of the people are African. The remaining people are European. What percentage of the people are European?

8. Copy and complete the table.

	fraction	decimal	percentage
(a)		0.09	
(b)			36%
(c)		0.28	
(d)	$\dfrac{11}{20}$		
(e)			7%

Extension questions with fractions, decimals and percentages

1 The letters shown on the right are each given a number as a fraction, a decimal or a percentage.

In (a), (b), (c) below, the numbers 1, 2, 3, … give the positions of the letters in a sentence. So 1 is the first letter, 2 is the second letter and so on.

Find the letter whose value is the same as the number given, and write it in the correct position.

For example, in part (a) number 1 is $\frac{3}{5}$

Since $\frac{3}{5} = 0.6$, letter R goes in the first box.

A	24%	N	0.9
E	0.05	O	0.625
F	0.32	R	0.6
G	$\frac{3}{20}$	S	$\frac{7}{20}$
H	0.36	T	0.02
I	3%	U	$\frac{3}{25}$
L	0.49	V	0.1%
M	$\frac{3}{4}$	Y	99%

Find the sentence in each part.

(a)

1	2	3	4	5	6	7	8	9	10	11	12
R											

1. $\frac{3}{5}$ 2. 0.24   3. 2%   4. 0.03   5. $\frac{5}{8}$ 6. 0.35

7. $\frac{6}{25}$ 8. 60%   9. $\frac{1}{20}$ 10. 32%   11. 0.12   12. $\frac{9}{10}$

(b) 1. 15%   2. $62\frac{1}{2}\%$ 3. 49%   4. $\frac{8}{25}$ 5. $\frac{3}{100}$ 6. 35%

7. 0.75   8. 0.99   9. 0.15   10. 0.24   11. 75%   12. 5%

(c) 1. $(0.6)^2$ 2. 0.2 + 0.04   3. $\frac{1}{2}$ of 0.98   4. 32%   5. $\frac{5}{8}$ 6. $\frac{8}{25}$

7. 0.2 ÷ 10   8. 5%   9. 90%   10. $\frac{15}{500}$ 11. 50% of $\frac{7}{10}$ 12. $\frac{64}{200}$

13. 3 ÷ 100   14. $\frac{1}{1000}$ 15. $(0.2)^2 + (0.1)^2$

2 Make up a sentence of your own using the letters given in question **1** . Write clues and try it out on a friend.

3 24% of the grid opposite is shaded. (Of the 100 squares on the grid, exactly 24 are shaded.)

Draw a grid like this one and draw a number of your choice. For example, if you choose '16', make sure you shade in 16 out of the 100 squares. Try to make both digits the same size!

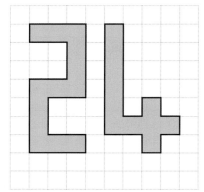

3.6 Brackets and equations

In section 3.6 you will:

- multiply out single brackets and simplify expressions
- solve linear equations
- solve linear equations involving brackets
- solve problems by forming equations

Multiplying out single brackets – reminder

A number or symbol outside the brackets multiplies each number or symbol inside the brackets.

$5(x + 2) = 5x + 10$

$2(1 + 3x) = 2 + 6x$

$3(x - 2) = 3x - 6$

$a(x + b) = ax + ab$

Find expressions for the area and the perimeter of the photo.

$\text{Area} = 7(x + 5)$

$\qquad = 7x + 35$

$\text{Perimeter} = x + 5 + x + 5 + 7 + 7$

$\qquad\qquad = 2x + 24$

7

$x + 5$

Exercise 1M

Multiply out

1   $5(x + 3)$ 2 $2(x + 6)$ 3 $3(x + 4)$

4   $7(x - 2)$ 5 $3(x - 5)$ 6 $4(x + 6)$

7   $2(x - 1)$ 8 $3(2x + 3)$ 9 $5(2x - 5)$

10   $4(2x + 1)$ 11 $6(3x - 4)$ 12 $3(2x + 4)$

13   $5(3x - 6)$ 14 $8(3x - 2)$ 15 $7(4x + 3)$

16   $6(2 + 5x)$ 17 $3(5 + 3x)$ 18 $2(6x - 4)$

19 (a) Write an expression for the area of
        the picture.

    (b) Write an expression for the perimeter
        of the picture.

7

$x + 3$

Expand (multiply out) the following expressions.

20 $a(x + y)$

21 $a(b + c)$

22 $b(m - n)$

23 $m(p - q)$

24 $y(x + m)$

25 $n(p + 4)$

26 $x(y + 3)$

27 $p(q - 7)$

28 $m(3 + n)$

29 $n(n + 2)$

30 $4(m + 6)$

31 $p(p - 9)$

32 $2(x + y)$

33 $x(x - 3)$

34 $a(5 + a)$

35 $y(4x + 2)$

36 $3(5a - 2)$

37 $6(10 - 3n)$

38 Copy and complete

    (a) $3(2x + \boxed{}) = 6x + 21$

    (b) $4(\boxed{} + \boxed{}) = 12x + 20$

    (c) $\boxed{}(6 - 3x) = 36 - 18x$

    (d) $\boxed{}(9 - \boxed{}) = 27 - 24x$

39 Amelia says that $8(2x - 3)$ is the same as $4(4x - 6)$.
    Show clearly whether Amelia is correct or not.

Remove the brackets and simplify.

(a) $3(x + 2) + 2(x + 1)$

    $= 3x + 6 + 2x + 2$

    $= 5x + 8$

(b) $4(x + 1) + 2(2x + 3)$

    $= 4x + 4 + 4x + 6$

    $= 8x + 10$

Remember: First remove the brackets then collect the like terms.

Exercise 2M

Remove the brackets and simplify.

1   $2(x + 1) + 3(x + 3)$

2   $3(x + 4) + 2(x + 1)$

3   $4(x + 2) + 2(x + 2)$

4   $5(x + 1) + 3(x + 2)$

5    $5(x + 1) + 4(x + 3)$

6    $6(x + 3) + 4(x + 3)$

7    $2(4x + 3) + 4(3x + 4)$

8    $3(4x + 5) + 2(x + 5)$

9    $6(2x + 1) + 3(1 + 2x)$

10    $2(3x + 2) + 6(2x + 3)$

11

Find an expression for the total area of the three rectangles. Simplify your answer.

In questions 12 to 21 , remove the brackets and simplify.

12    $3(2x + 4) + 2(x + 1)$

13    $5(3 + 2x) + 10x$

14    $6x + 3(2x + 3)$

15    $9 + 3(3x + 1)$

16    $5 + 4(2 + 3x)$

17    $5(3x + 2) + 3(x + 1) + 4x$

18    $x + 6(3x + 2)$

19    $4(x + 1) + 2x + 4(2x + 4)$

20    $6(2x + 3) + 3(3x + 4)$

21    $5x + 2(3x + 7) + 9$

22   Josie earns £$(2n + 1)$ each week and her partner earns £$(n + 4)$ each week. Write down and simplify an expression for how much Josie and her partner earn in total during 15 weeks.

Remove the brackets and simplify.

(a) $3(n + 3) - 2(n + 1)$

    $= 3n + 9 - 2n - 2$

    $= n + 7$

(b) $3(a + b) - 2(a - 2b)$

    $= 3a + 3b - 2a + 4b$

    $= a + 7b$

Exercise 2E

Remove the brackets and simplify.

1    $5(x + 2) + 3(x - 2)$

2    $4(3x + 1) + 2(2x - 1)$

3    $5(3x - 1) + 6(2x + 1)$

4    $4(n + 3) - 2(n + 1)$

5    $8(a + 1) - 3(a + 2)$

6    $7(m + 3) - 2(m - 1)$

7    $3(a + b) + 5(2a + b)$

8    $3(3a + b) - 2(a + b)$

9    $4(2a + b) - 2(a - b)$

10    $5(a - b) - 3(a - 2b)$

11 Jack has $3(2a + 4)$ coins. He spends $2(3 - a)$ coins. Write down and simplify an expression for the number of coins he now has.

Remove the brackets and simplify.

12 $5(2n + 1) - 3(n + 1)$

13 $7(3n + 2) - 2(4n - 3)$

14 $6(3m + 4) - 4(2 - m)$

15 $8(2y + 6) - 5(3y + 4)$

16 $4(6a + 4) - 2(7 - 3a)$

17 $6(4x + 9) - 2(5x + 4)$

18 Remove the brackets and simplify $8(2n + 6) - (3n - 1) + 2(3n - 4)$

Rules for solving equations – reminder

The main rule when solving equations is

'Do the same to both sides'

You may *add* the same thing to both sides.
You may *subtract* the same thing from both sides.
You may *multiply* both sides by the same thing.
You may *divide* both sides by the same thing.

Solve the equations. The circles show what is done to both sides of the equation.

(a) $n + 5 = 12$
$-5 \quad -5$
$n = 7$

(b) $n - 7 = 11$
$+7 \quad +7$
$n = 18$

(c) $2n + 3 = 15$
$-3 \quad -3$
$2n = 12$
$\div 2 \quad \div 2$
$n = 6$

(d) $3n - 5 = 16$
$+5 \quad +5$
$3n = 21$
$\div 3 \quad \div 3$
$n = 7$

Exercise 3M

Solve the equations.

1 $3a = 21$

2 $5m = 35$

3 $2n + 1 = 7$

4 $3x + 2 = 14$

5 $5y + 3 = 33$

6 $3m + 2 = 17$

7   $4p + 7 = 19$

8   $4n + 6 = 30$

9   $6y + 5 = 41$

10   $6n + 4 = 22$

11   $3m + 9 = 24$

12   $5a + 16 = 36$

13   $6n - 7 = 17$

14   $5x - 3 = 7$

15   $4p - 9 = 23$

16   $3m - 4 = 11$

17   $2m - 11 = 9$

18   $3a - 5 = 10$

19   $31 = 7y + 3$

20   $14 = 3a - 1$

21   $5 + 3n = 11$

22   $21 = 9a - 6$

23   $8 + 4m = 8$

24   $30 = 6y - 12$

25   If $\dfrac{n}{6} = 5$ then $n = 30$, which is 5×6

Find the value of n if $\dfrac{n}{8} = 3$

Solve

26   $\dfrac{n}{5} = 8$

27   $\dfrac{x}{7} = 6$

28   $\dfrac{a}{9} = 7$

29   $\dfrac{m}{10} = 6$

30   $8 = \dfrac{n}{9}$

31   $12 = \dfrac{m}{5}$

32   $\dfrac{n}{4} + 3 = 7$

33   $\dfrac{x}{5} - 2 = 3$

34   $\dfrac{m}{2} - 11 = 5$

Equations with the unknown on both sides

(a) $2n + 3 = n + 7$

    $\overset{\ominus n}{}\quad\overset{\ominus n}{}$

    $n + 3 = 7$

    $\overset{\ominus 3}{}\quad\overset{\ominus 3}{}$

    $n = 4$

(b) $5n - 3 = 2n + 9$

    $\overset{\ominus 2n}{}\quad\overset{\ominus 2n}{}$

    $3n - 3 = 9$

    $\overset{\oplus 3}{}\quad\overset{\oplus 3}{}$

    $3n = 12$

    $n = 4$

Exercise 4M

Solve the equations.

1   $6n + 4 = 3n + 19$

2   $4n + 2 = 2n + 8$

3   $7n + 1 = 4n + 13$

4   $10n - 3 = 7n + 21$

5   $8n + 6 = 4n + 30$

6   $6n - 5 = 4n + 15$

7   $5n - 4 = 2n + 2$

8   $9n - 10 = 4n + 10$

9   $4n - 17 = n + 10$

10   $7n + 9 = 5n + 21$

11 Ben has $(3n + 12)$ books and Megan has $(n + 52)$ books. If they have an equal number of books, find the value of n. How many books does Ben have?

Now solve these equations.

12 $7x + 1 = 6x + 8$

13 $4x + 3 = x + 9$

14 $6x - 1 = 3x + 8$

15 $3x + 7 = x + 15$

16 $5x - 4 = 2x + 5$

17 $1 + 3x = x + 2$

18 $4x - 11 = 2x + 11$

19 $6x = 3x + 24$

20 $5x - 4 = x$

21 $1 + 5x = 3x + 13$

22 $8x - 2 = 2x + 28$

23 $9x + 8 = x$

24

$6n - 7$

$3n + 17$

The opposite sides of a rectangle are equal in length. Write down an equation then find the value of n.

Equations involving brackets

Remove the brackets first.

(a) $3(2x + 1) = 15$

$\qquad 6x + 3 = 15$

$\qquad \quad (-3) \qquad (-3)$

$\qquad \quad 6x = 12$

$\qquad \quad (\div 6) \quad (\div 6)$

$\qquad \quad x = 2$

(b) $4(3x - 1) = 8$

$\qquad 12x - 4 = 8$

$\qquad \quad (+4) \qquad (+4)$

$\qquad \quad 12x = 12$

$\qquad \quad (\div 12) \quad (\div 12)$

$\qquad \quad x = 1$

Exercise 5M

1 Copy and complete

(a) $3(n + 2) = 21$

$\qquad 3n + \square = 21$

$\qquad \quad 3n = \square$

$\qquad \quad n = \square$

(b) $5(2n - 6) = 30$

$\qquad 10n - \square = 30$

$\qquad \quad 10n = \square$

$\qquad \quad n = \square$

Solve these equations.

2 $2(n + 1) = 10$ 3 $2(n + 3) = 12$ 4 $3(n + 4) = 21$

5 $3(n - 2) = 12$ 6 $3(2n + 1) = 9$ 7 $4(n - 2) = 8$

8 $5(n + 1) = 5$ 9 $2(3n - 1) = 10$ 10 $2(3n + 2) = 10$

11 $2(n + 3) = 12$ 12 $4(n + 1) = 24$ 13 $6(n + 2) = 54$

Now solve these.

14 $5(a + 1) = 20$ 15 $3(m - 1) = 18$ 16 $4(b + 3) = 20$

17 $3(2n + 3) = 39$ 18 $14 = 2(3y + 1)$ 19 $16 = 4(p - 2)$

20 $18 = 2(2m + 3)$ 21 $5(2a + 2) = 10$ 22 $3(2w - 7) = 3$

23 Make up an equation with brackets which will give the answer $x = 4$.
Ask a friend to solve the equation to see if it works.

24 Make up any equation which gives the same x-value as the equation $4(3x - 2) = 76$.
Ask a friend to solve the equation to see if it works.

25 The area of this rectangle is $92 \, cm^2$.
Write down an equation then find the value of n.

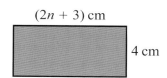

$(2n + 3) \, cm$

$4 \, cm$

Solving problems by forming equations

The length of a rectangle is three times its width. The perimeter is 40 cm.
Find the width of the rectangle.

Let the width be x.
So the length is $3x$.
Form the equation:

$3x + x + 3x + x = 40$
$8x = 40$
$x = 5$

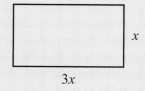

x

$3x$

So the width is 5 cm. [Check $5 + 15 + 5 + 15 = 40$ ✓]

Exercise 6M

In each question, use the information to form an equation and then solve the problem.

1 If we multiply the number by 4 and then subtract 3, the answer is 13

2 If we double the number and add 7, the answer is 23

3 If we treble the number and subtract 7, the answer is 14

4 In the triangle, BC is twice as long as AB.
AC is 9 cm long.
If the perimeter is 24 cm, form an equation
and solve it to find x.

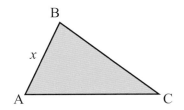

5 The length of a photo is twice its width.
The perimeter is 30 cm. Find the width.

6 The length of a rectangle is three times its width. If the perimeter is 32 cm, find its width.
(Hint: let the width be x)

7 Form equations to find x.

(a)

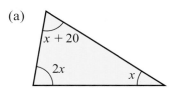

(b)

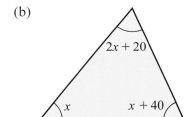

8 7, 8 and 9 are consecutive numbers.
The sum of three different consecutive numbers is 63. Let the first number be n.
The second number will then be $n + 1$ and the third number will be $n + 2$.
Form an equation then find the values of the three numbers.

9 If AB is a straight line, form an equation
involving x and solve it to find x.

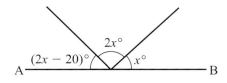

10

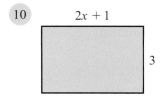

The rectangle has an area of 27 square units.
Form an equation and solve it to find x.

Need more practice with expanding brackets and equations?

Expand

1   $3(n + 6)$

2   $7(2n - 3)$

3   $8(2a + 5)$

4   $6(4p - 7)$

5   $a(x + p)$

6   $m(n - 4)$

7   $n(a - m)$

8   $7(4a + 3n)$

9   $p(2x - 1)$

Remove the brackets and simplify.

10   $4(2x + 3) + 5(x + 6)$

11   $7(3n + 4) + 2(5n + 1)$

12   $8(5a + 2) + 3(2a + 7)$

13   $6(4p + 3) + 7p + 2(3p + 2)$

Solve these equations.

14   $7n = 28$

15   $3y - 2 = 10$

16   $4m + 1 = 33$

17   $5x + 9 = 49$

18   $52 = 6a - 8$

19   $\dfrac{n}{8} = 3$

20   $8w + 10 = 4w + 22$

21   $10x - 9 = 8x + 9$

22   $7y - 4 = 4y + 23$

23   Each side of a square is equal. All lengths are given in cm.

(a) Form an equation then find the value of n.

(b) Write down the actual area of the square.

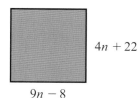

$4n + 22$

$9n - 8$

24   Hattie has to solve $3(2n - 3) = 4n + 15$

She writes: $3(2n - 3) = 4n + 15$
$6n - 9 = 4n + 15$
$2n - 9 = 15$
$2n = 6$
$n = 3$

Explain clearly what mistake Hattie has made.

25

$x + 1$

$3x - 1$

The perimeter of this rectangle is 40 cm.
Find x and hence find the area of the rectangle.

Solve these equations.

26   $5(n + 3) = 35$

27   $7(2n - 1) = 21$

28   $3(2m + 5) = 27$

29   $30 = 6(4w - 7)$

30   $40 = 2(9x + 2)$

31   $4(2n - 9) = 12$

32   8 bags of flour weigh 160 kg. Each bag weighs $(3n + 2)$ kg. Work out the value of n.

Extension questions with expanding brackets and equations

1   Copy and complete

   (a) $-2(m + 4) = -2m - \square$

   (b) $-4(n - 3) = -4n + \square$

   (c) $-2(x - 3) = -2x \square 6$

   (d) $-5(y + 3) = -5y \square 15$

   Remember:
   $-2 \times (-3) = 6$
   $-2 \times (+3) = -6$

Expand (multiply out) the following expressions.

2   $-4(a - 2)$

3   $-6(m - 3)$

4   $-3(n + 4)$

5   $-2(y + 8)$

6   $-4(3 + w)$

7   $7(6 - 2x)$

8   $-8(n - 4)$

9   $3(3y + 7)$

10   $-5(4 - 2m)$

11   $-6(4w - 2)$

12   $-7(4 + 2n)$

13   $3(2 + 7a)$

Remove the brackets and simplify.

14   $5(n + 4) - 2(n - 3)$

15   $4(2m + 7) - 3(2m + 3)$

16   $8(3n + 5) - 4(4n + 7)$

17   $9(4p + 5) - 6(3p - 2)$

18   $5(6w + 3a) - 2(5w - 4a)$

19   $7(5m + 3p) - 4(2m + 5p)$

20   The sum of three consecutive numbers is 165. Find the three numbers.

21   The total mass of three stones A, B and C is 60 kg.
     Stone B is twice as heavy as stone A.
     Stone C is 30 kg heavier than stone A.
     Find the mass of stone A. [Call it x kg.]

A   B   C

22   The angles in a triangle are $x°$, $(2x + 50)°$ and $70°$. Find the angles in the triangle.

23

B

$2n + 15$ $5n - 3$

A   C
   $2n + 4$

Triangle ABC is isosceles where AB = BC.

   (a) Form an equation and solve it to find n.

   (b) What is the actual perimeter of the triangle?
        Assume all lengths are given in cm.

24   Copy and complete

(a) $4(n + 3) = 2(n + 11)$
$4n + \square = 2n + \square$
$2n = \square$
$n = \square$

(b) $3(3x - 2) = 2(2x + 7)$
$9x - \square = 4x + \square$
$5x = \square$
$x = \square$

Solve these equations.

25   $3(n + 2) = 2(n + 5)$

26   $4(n + 1) = 3(n + 3)$

27   $2(n + 5) = n + 13$

28   $5(2n + 3) = 3(3n + 7)$

29   $6n - 10 = 2(n + 7)$

30   $3(n - 1) = 2(n + 6)$

31   $5(x - 2) = 3(x + 2)$

32   $2(2x - 3) = 3(x + 7)$

33   $6(2x + 1) = 10x + 22$

34   $7(3x - 5) = 5(2x + 4)$

35   $5(5x + 2) = 2(3x + 5)$

36   $7(2x - 1) = 7$

✖ Spot the mistakes 6 ✖

Using a calculator; converting between fractions, decimals and percentages; expanding brackets and equations

Work through each question below and *explain clearly* what mistakes have been made.
Beware – some questions are correctly done.

1   Work out $3 + 2 \times 6 - 1$

Answer: $3 + 2 = 5$ then $5 \times 6 = 30$
then $30 - 1 = 29$
so $3 + 2 \times 6 - 1 = 29$

2   Solve $\dfrac{n}{4} = 12$

Answer: $n = 12 \div 4 = 3$

3   Use a calculator to work out $\dfrac{7.2}{4} + \dfrac{3.19}{0.2}$

Answer: Press

Final answer = 17.75

4   Solve $20x - 9 = 6(3x + 1)$

Answer: $20x - 9 = 6(3x + 1)$
$20x - 9 = 18x + 1$
$20x - 18x = 1 + 9$
$2x = 10$
$x = 5$

5   The perimeter of the rectangle is 64 cm.
Form an equation and work out the value of x.

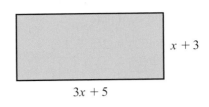

$x + 3$

$3x + 5$

Answer: Perimeter $= 3x + 5 + x + 3 = 64$

$$4x + 8 = 64$$
$$4x = 56$$
$$x = 14 \text{ cm}$$

6   Write these numbers in order of size, starting with the smallest.

8% $\dfrac{9}{20}$ 0.25

Answer: $8\% = 0.8$ and $\dfrac{9}{20} = \dfrac{45}{100} = 0.45$

The order is $0.25, 0.45, 0.8$

Final answer is $0.25, \dfrac{9}{20}, 8\%$

7   Use a calculator to work out $(-3)^2 + 1$

Answer: Press $\boxed{(-)}$ $\boxed{3}$ $\boxed{x^2}$ $\boxed{+}$ $\boxed{1}$ $\boxed{=}$

Final answer is $= -8$

8   $\dfrac{7}{16}$ of the students in Year 8 in Hutton High School are
given awards for hard work.

What percentage of the students are not given awards?

Answer: $\dfrac{7}{16} = \dfrac{7}{16} \times 100\% = 43.75\%$

$100\% - 43.75\% = 56.25\%$

So, 56.25% of the students are not given awards.

9   Remove the brackets and simplify $4(3x + 5) - 2(x + 6)$

Answer: $4(3x + 5) - 2(x + 6) = 12x + 20 - 2x + 12$
$$= 10x + 32$$

10

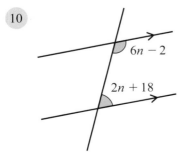

$6n - 2$

$2n + 18$

Form an equation then find the value of n.
Answer: Angles are equal, so

$$6n - 2 = 2n + 18$$
$$4n - 2 = 18$$
$$4n = 20$$
$$n = 5°$$

CHECK YOURSELF ON SECTIONS 3.5 and 3.6

1 Converting between fractions, decimals and percentages

(a) Copy and complete this table.

Fraction	$\frac{3}{5}$	$\frac{7}{20}$		$\frac{3}{8}$		
Decimal			0.03		0.12	0.8

(b) Change 34% into a decimal.

(c) Change $\frac{11}{25}$ into a percentage.

(d) $65\% = \frac{13}{20}$. True or false?

(e) Fran scores $\frac{18}{25}$ in an exam and Roy scores 74% in the same exam. Who scores the higher percentage and by how much?

2 Changing fractions to recurring decimals

(a) Change $\frac{8}{9}$ to a recurring decimal.

(b) Change $\frac{5}{11}$ to a recurring decimal.

3 Multiplying out single brackets and simplifying expressions

Expand (multiply out) and simplify when possible

(a) $5(x - 4)$ (b) $3(4x + 2)$ (c) $n(n - 8)$

(d) $4(x + 3) + 7(x + 2)$ (e) $3(2x + 7) + 2(4x - 1)$

4 Solving linear equations

Solve these equations.

(a) $5n - 3 = 27$ (b) $4x + 3 = 2x + 15$ (c) $7n - 5 = 3n + 15$

5 Solving linear equations involving brackets

Solve these equations.

(a) $4(n + 3) = 36$ (b) $3(2x - 3) = 21$ (c) $6(2x + 3) = 2(5x + 13)$

6   Solving problems by forming equations

(a)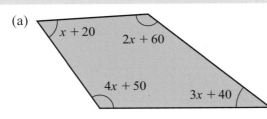

The angles in a quadrilateral add up to 360°.
Form an equation then use it to find the value of x.

(b) If I treble a number, take away 6 and then multiply the result by 2, the answer is 18.
Find the number.

(c)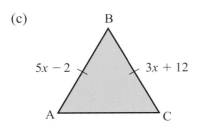

Triangle ABC is isosceles, so the sides AB and BC are equal.
Form an equation then use it to find the value of x.
How long is side BC if all the measurements are in cm?

3.7 Applying mathematics 3

In section 3.7 you will apply maths in a variety of situations.

1   Mark earns £1800 each month from which he pays £580 rent.
Susie earns £1900 each month from which she pays £660 rent.
Mark gets a 4% pay rise but his rent increases by 5%.
Susie gets a 3% pay rise but her rent increases by 4%.
Who now has more money left each month after paying rent?
How much more money does this person have?

2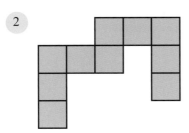

Imagine the area of this shape is 360 cm².
Work out the length of the perimeter
of this shape.

3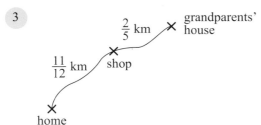

Anya walks from her home to the shop and then
walks on towards her grandparents' house.

How far has she walked in total when she is $\frac{1}{4}$ km
away from her grandparents' house?

4 Des scores $\frac{17}{25}$ in a maths test, $\frac{13}{20}$ in a science test and $\frac{33}{50}$ in an English test.
   In which test did Des get the highest mark? Give reasons for your answer.

5 This graph shows the amount of oil used by a central-heating boiler for the month of
   November (30 days).

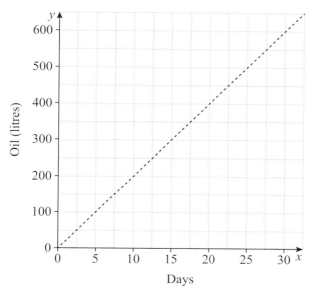

(a) What do 2 small squares on the horizontal axis show?
(b) How much oil was used in (i) 25 days (ii) 17 days?
(c) How long was the boiler running if it used
     (i) 180 litres   (ii) 420 litres   (iii) 240 litres?
(d) Barney has 300 litres of oil. Is this enough to use the boiler for a fortnight?

6 Will the triangle fit perfectly into the gap as shown?
   Give clear reasons for your answer.

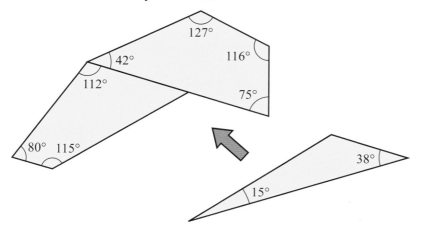

7   Emma has £n. Rayan has three times
    as much money as Emma.
    Hayley has £16 less than Rayan.

    (a) Write down algebraic expressions for how
        much money Rayan and Hayley each have.

    (b) They have £159 in total. Form an equation
        then work out the value of *n*.

    (c) How much money does Hayley have?

8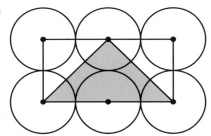

    Six touching circles of radius 5 cm are shown.
    Calculate the area of the triangle shaded green.

9   Sequence A begins   3, 8, 13, 18, …
    Sequence B begins   59, 56, 53, 50, …

    The same number is given at the same point in both sequences.
    Which term is this, e.g. 2nd term, 3rd term or …?

10 A pack of 52 cards has 4 cards of each number and 4 of each picture card
    (a king, queen or jack).

    Mark played a card game with Paul. The cards were dealt so that both players received
    two cards. Mark's cards were a five and a four. Paul's first card was a six.

Mark

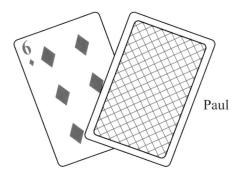

Paul

Find the probability that Paul's second card was

(a) a five

(b) a picture card.

UNIT 3   MIXED REVIEW

Part one

1   Work out the following (remember 'BIDMAS').

(a) $30 - 6 \times 4$ (b) $17 + 5^2$ (c) $20 - 16 \div 4$

(d) $(8 - 2)^2$ (e) $13 + 2 \times 3$ (f) $(13 + 2) \times 3$

2   Expand (multiply out)

(a) $4(n + 3)$ (b) $m(n - 5)$ (c) $x(x + 2)$

3   Work out

(a) $\dfrac{5}{7} - \dfrac{1}{4}$ (b) $\dfrac{3}{8} + \dfrac{3}{5}$ (c) $\dfrac{2}{3} + \dfrac{2}{9}$

4   Ben and Elaine each have 30 sweets.

(a) Ben eats $\frac{2}{5}$ of his sweets. How many does he eat?

(b) Elaine eats 5 of her sweets. What *fraction* of her sweets does she eat?

5   Find the area of each shape. All lengths are in cm.

(a)

(b)

(c)
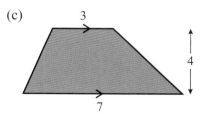

6   Work out, without a calculator.

(a) $7.46 + 5$ (b) 25×0.3 (c) $678.4 \div 100$

(d) 0.8×0.04 (e) 1.2×0.6 (f) $9 \div 5$

7   Solve

(a) $4(x + 1) = 20$ (b) $4(x - 2) = 20$ (c) $8(x + 5) = 56$

8   Work out the missing numbers.

(a) $0.1 \times 100 = \square$ (b) $(\square)^2 = 225$ (c) $\square \times 3 = 192$

(d) $35 \div 100 = \square$ (e) $0.3 \times 0.9 = \square$ (f) $4 \times \square = 2.8$

9 

Dennis is very sad. He used to have a diameter of 15 cm but after a heavy wash, he now has a radius of 5 cm.

Calculate, to one decimal place, by how much his circumference has decreased.

10 Use a calculator to work out the following. Give your answers correct to 1 decimal place or as a fraction.

(a) $16.9 - (2.48 \times 2.37)$

(b) $\dfrac{6.19}{(8.6 - 6.18)}$

(c) $4\frac{1}{3} - \frac{2}{5}$

(d) $\left(\dfrac{7.9}{1.46}\right)^2$

(e) $\left(\dfrac{9.25}{3.5}\right) - 1.43$

(f) $3\frac{1}{2} \div \frac{3}{8}$

11 Find the area of the yellow circle, giving your answer to one decimal place.

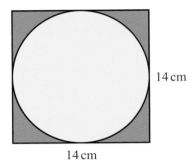

14 cm

14 cm

12 Solve

(a) $3x + 2 = 20$

(b) $6x - 1 = 29$

(c) $8 + 4x = 20$

13 Which of these numbers is the largest?

$\dfrac{7}{25}$ 26% $\dfrac{1}{4}$ 0.29

14 Find the shaded area.

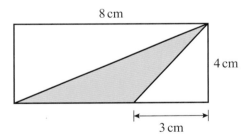

8 cm

4 cm

3 cm

15 Jim and Marie want to carpet their living room. The dimensions of the room are shown opposite. They can buy a piece of 'Munster Gold' carpet for £75 or 'Durban Twist' carpet. The 'Durban Twist' carpet is 4 m wide and costs £16.83 per metre length.

(a) How much will the 'Durban Twist' carpet cost for the living room?

(b) What area of 'Durban Twist' carpet would be wasted?

(c) Which is the cheaper to buy – Munster Gold or Durban Twist? Write down the difference in the cost.

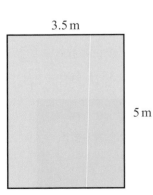

3.5 m

5 m

Part two

1. Work out, without a calculator
   (a) 4×0.1
   (b) 1.7×10
   (c) 12.738×100
   (d) $428.6 \div 100$
   (e) 428.6×0.01
   (f) $8 \div 0.1$

2. Put these numbers in order of size, starting with the smallest.

   $0.4, \ \dfrac{3}{5}, \ \dfrac{1}{4}, \ 45\%$

3. Solve
   (a) $4n + 3 = 2n + 15$
   (b) $5n - 1 = 2n + 17$
   (c) $3(2n + 3) = 4n + 25$

4. Work out
   (a) $\dfrac{1}{4} \times \dfrac{3}{5}$
   (b) $\dfrac{2}{3} \times 12$
   (c) $\dfrac{3}{7} \times \dfrac{1}{6}$

5. The square ACDE is cut into seven pieces. Find the area, in square units, of
   (a) triangle EDI
   (b) square BJIG
   (c) parallelogram FGHE.

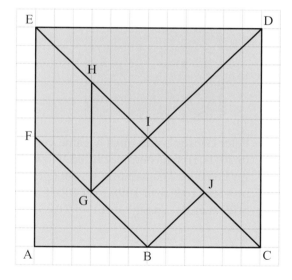

6. Write brackets to make the calculations correct.
   (a) $7 + 3 \times 6 = 60$
   (b) $20 - 4 \div 2 = 18$
   (c) $8 \times 2 + 3 - 2 = 38$
   (d) $19 \times 5 - 2 = 3 \times 14 + 17$

7. Richard is three times as old as Frances. If Richard is also 30 years older than Frances, how old is Frances? (Hint: Let n be the age of Frances and form an equation)

8. Write down two possible answers for the missing digits. Ask a friend to check your solutions.

   $$3 \ \boxed{} \ 0 \ \times \ \boxed{} \ \boxed{} \ \div \ \boxed{} \ = 60$$

9 The floor of a room was covered with
black and white square tiles of side 30 cm.
The rectangular room measured 27 m by 36 m.
How many tiles were there on the floor?

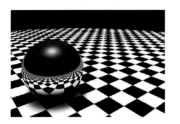

10 Expand and simplify

(a) $4(n + 2) + 3(2n + 5)$ (b) $4(2n + 5) - 3(n - 3)$

11 Which is larger? $\frac{1}{2} + \frac{1}{5}$ or 0.8

12 The perimeter of this triangle is 38 cm. Form an equation
involving x then use it to find the length of AC
(all lengths are in cm).

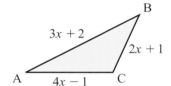

13 A box of seeds costs £8.75 and will cover 50 m². How much will it cost to seed the entire lawn shown opposite?

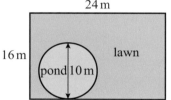

14 Peter Gibson's paintings became very fashionable
in 2020. His masterpiece titled 'Now' was sold
for €65 000. The painting was bought by its
previous owner in 1998 for £400. Calculate the
price increase in euros. [£1 = €1.25]

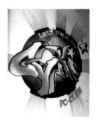

15 Work out the following with a calculator, giving each answer correct to 2 decimal places.

(a) $(4.17 + 2.6) \div 1.89$ (b) $\dfrac{(-7)^2}{2.43}$ (c) $\dfrac{7.4}{(2.63 + 1.76)}$

16 As part of an advertising campaign, the message 'Exercise is good for you' is taped individually
right around 500 000 tennis balls, each of diameter 6.5 cm. Find the total cost of the tape for the
campaign, given that a 33 m roll of tape costs 96p. (Give your answers to the nearest pound)

17 The radius of this circle is 7 cm. Calculate the area of the region
shaded red. Give your answer correct to 1 decimal place.

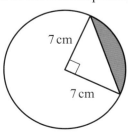

Puzzles and problems 3

Coordinate puzzles

1 Draw a pair of axes with the values shown.

Plot the points below and join them up with a ruler in the order given.

$(11, 4\frac{1}{2})$	$(11, 17)$	$(10, 21)$	$(4, 21)$	$(2, 17)$
$(2, 14)$	$(1\frac{1}{2}, 13)$	$(1\frac{1}{2}, 11\frac{1}{2})$	$(2, 11)$	

On the same grid, plot the points below and join them up with a ruler in the order given.
Do not join the last point in the box above with the first point in the new box.

$(5, 21)$	$(6, 22)$	$(8, 21)$	$(8, 20)$

On the same grid, plot the points below and join them up with a ruler in the order given.

$(6, 21)$	$(7, 22)$	$(8, 22)$	$(9, 21)$	$(9, 20)$

On the same grid, plot the points below and join them up with a ruler in the order given.

$(2\frac{1}{2}, 3)$	$(5, 3)$	$(6\frac{1}{2}, 5)$	$(6\frac{1}{2}, 9)$	$(4, 10)$	$(2, 10)$	$(1, 8)$
$(4, 8)$	$(5, 7)$	$(5\frac{1}{2}, 6)$	$(5\frac{1}{2}, 5)$	$(5, 4)$	$(3, 4)$	$(3, 3)$

On the same grid, plot the points below and join them up with a ruler in the order given.

$(3, 1\frac{1}{2})$	$(1\frac{1}{2}, \frac{1}{2})$	$(2\frac{1}{2}, 3)$	$(4, \frac{1}{2})$	$(5, 2\frac{1}{2})$	$(7, \frac{1}{2})$	$(11\frac{1}{2}, 2\frac{1}{2})$	$(11\frac{1}{2}, 4\frac{1}{2})$	$(5, 2\frac{1}{2})$

On the same grid, plot the points below and join them up with a ruler in the order given.

$(2, 14)$	$(3, 14)$	$(4, 13)$	$(4, 12)$	$(4, 13)$	$(5, 14)$	$(7, 14)$	$(8, 13)$
$(8, 11)$	$(7, 10)$	$(5, 10)$	$(4, 11)$	$(4, 12)$	$(1\frac{1}{2}, 10\frac{1}{2})$	$(1\frac{1}{2}, 10)$	$(2, 10)$

On the same grid, plot the points below and join them up with a ruler in the order given.

$(10, 11)$	$(11\frac{1}{2}, 11)$	$(11\frac{1}{2}, 12)$	$(10, 12)$	$(10, 14)$	$(11, 12)$	$(11\frac{1}{2}, 14)$	$(12, 12)$

228

On the same grid, plot the points below and join them up with a ruler in the order given.

| (2, 8) | $(3\frac{1}{2}, 5)$ | $(3\frac{1}{2}, 4)$ | (5, 5) | $(5\frac{1}{2}, 5)$ | (5, 5) | $(4\frac{1}{2}, 4)$ |

Draw a • at (2, 12) and a • at (6, 12)

Colour me in.

2 Draw a pair of axes with the values shown.

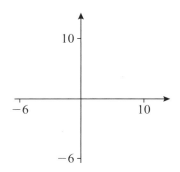

Plot the points below and join them up with a ruler in the order given.

| (2, 0) | $(2\frac{1}{2}, 1)$ | $(5\frac{1}{2}, 1)$ | (6, 0) | (6, −2) | $(5\frac{1}{2}, -3)$ | $(2\frac{1}{2}, -3)$ | (2, −2) | (2, 0) |

On the same grid plot the points below and join them up with a ruler in the order given.
Do not join the last point in the box above with the first point in the new box.

| (3, 1) | (3, 2) | (1, 2) | (0, 3) | (0, 4) | (1, 5) | (3, 5) | (4, 4) | (5, 5) | (6, 5) |
| (7, 4) | (7, 3) | (6, 2) | (5, 2) | (5, 1) | (5, 2) | (4, 3) | (4, 4) | (4, 3) | (3, 2) |

On the same grid, plot the points below and join them up with a ruler in the order given.

| (3, 7) | (3, 8) | (4, 8) | $(5\frac{1}{2}, 8\frac{1}{2})$ | $(5\frac{1}{2}, 6\frac{1}{2})$ | (4, 7) | (4, 8) |

On the same grid, plot the points below and join them up with a ruler in the order given.

| $(5\frac{1}{2}, 0)$ | $(5\frac{1}{2}, -2)$ | $(3\frac{1}{2}, -2)$ | $(3\frac{1}{2}, -1\frac{1}{2})$ | $(5, -1\frac{1}{2})$ | $(5, -\frac{1}{2})$ | $(3\frac{1}{2}, -\frac{1}{2})$ | $(3\frac{1}{2}, 0)$ | $(5\frac{1}{2}, 0)$ |

On the same grid, plot the points below and join them up with a ruler in the order given.

| (4, 7) | (3, 7) | $(1\frac{1}{2}, 6\frac{1}{2})$ | $(1\frac{1}{2}, 8\frac{1}{2})$ | (3, 8) |

On the same grid, plot the points below and join them up with a ruler in the order given.

(6, −1)	(8, −1)	(7, 2)	(10, 5)	(7, 6)	(6, 10)	(3, 8)
(1, 10)	(−1, 7)	(−4, 7)	(−3, 4)	(−5, 2)	(−3, 1)	(−3, −2)
(−1, −1)	(0, −4)	$(4\frac{1}{2}, -4)$	(5, −3)

On the same grid, plot the points below and join them up with a ruler in the order given.

$(-2, 2)$ $(-3, 2)$ $(-3, 3)$ $(-2, 3)$

On the same grid, plot the points below and join them up with a ruler in the order given.

$(-2, 2\frac{1}{2})$ $(-2\frac{1}{2}, 2\frac{1}{2})$

Draw a • at $(1, 3)$ and a • at $(6, 3)$

Colour me in.

Mental arithmetic practice 3

Ideally a teacher will read out each question twice, with pupils' books closed.

Test 1

1. By how much is three kilos more than 800 grams?

2. How many 20p coins do I need to make £400?

3. How many square centimetres are there in one square metre?

4. How much more than £108 is £300?

5. Two angles of a triangle are 44° and 54°. What is the third angle?

6. Work out 10% of £5000

7. My watch reads ten past eight. It is 15 minutes fast. What is the correct time?

8. A 50p coin is 2 mm thick. What is the value of a pile of 50p coins 2 cm high?

9. Add together £2.35 and £4.15

10. A ship was due at noon on Friday but arrived at 8.00 a.m. on Saturday. How many hours late was the ship?

11. By how much is half a metre longer than 1 millimetre? (answer in mm).

12. What number is thirty-five more than eighty?

13. How many minutes are there in two and a half hours?

14. From nine times seven, take away five.

15. A TV show lasting 45 minutes starts at 10 minutes to eight. When does it finish?

16. A train travels at an average speed of 48 mph. How far does it travel in 2 hours?

17. What is the perimeter of a square of side 14 cm?

18. A string of length 390 cm is cut in half. How long is each piece?

19. A half is a quarter of a certain number. What is the number?

20. A man died in 1993 aged 58. In what year was he born?

21. *Roughly* how many millimetres are there in one foot?

22. Write down ten thousand pence in pounds.

23. What is a quarter of 210?

24. Find two ways of making 66p using five coins.

25. John weighs 8 stones and Jim weighs 80 kg. Who is heavier?

230

Test 2

1. What number is 10 less than 9000?

2. I want to buy 4 books, each costing £4.49. To the nearest pound, how much will my bill be?

3. How many magazines costing 95p can I buy with £10?

4. What is the total of 57 and 963?

5. What is a half of a half of 10?

6. True or false: 3 feet are slightly longer than 1 metre.

7. A triangle has a base 4 cm and a height of 10 cm. What is its area?

8. What number is exactly mid-way between 3.7 and 3.8?

9. Work out two squared plus three squared.

10. The pupils in Darren's class are given lockers numbered from 32 to 54. How many pupils are there in Darren's class?

11. Write 7 divided by 100 as a decimal.

12. Jane is 35 cm taller than William, who is 1.34 metres tall. How tall is Jane?

13. A toy train travels 6 metres in one second. How far will it go in one minute?

14. Which is larger: 2 cubed or 3 squared?

15. What number is next in the series 1, 2, 4, 8, …?

16. Write the number '$2\frac{1}{2}$ million' in figures.

17. Joe borrowed £4.68 from his father. He paid him back with a £10 note. How much change did he receive?

18. What is a tenth of 2.4?

19. I think of a number and subtract 6. The result is equal to 7 times 3. What is the number?

20. Write down the next prime number after 32

21. How much longer is 7.5 metres than 725 centimetres?

22. How many lines of symmetry does a square have?

23. What is a quarter of a half?

24. Work out 200 times 300

25. How many edges does a cube have?

A long time ago! 3

The Fibonacci sequence

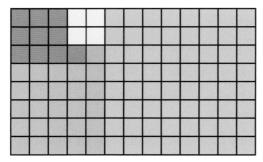

Scale: 1 square = 1 cm²

This rectangle is made from six squares. Write down the length of one side in each of the squares.

Can you arrange the numbers to make a pattern?

What would be the next number in your pattern?

Write down a rule for your pattern.

Fibonacci was born in Pisa, Italy. He lived in the 13th century.

He worked on the pattern 1, 1, 2, 3, 5, 8, ...

Each number is found by adding the two terms immediately before it.

The next number is 13 from $5 + 8$

Fibonacci found that these numbers helped to explain things to do with spirals in flowers, shells, the breeding of rabbits, pine cones, the family tree of honeybees and many other cases.

Exercise

1   Write down the first 22 numbers in the Fibonacci sequence 1, 1, 2, 3, 5, 8, ...

2   **Assembly rules**

In Hatford High School, two boys are *not* allowed to sit next to each other in any single row of chairs in assembly.

- If a row has 1 chair only, either a boy or a girl sits on the chair, so there are 2 ways of filling the chair – B or G (B for Boy, G for Girl)
- If a row has 2 chairs only, there are 3 ways of filling the chairs – BG or GB or GG
- If a row has 3 chairs only, there are 5 ways of filling the chairs – BGG or BGB or GBG or GGB or GGG (remember: BB *not* allowed next to each other)

(a) Show all the different ways of filling the chairs if a row has 4 chairs only.

(b) How many different ways are there of filling the chairs if a row has 10 chairs only?

(c) How many different ways are there of filling the chairs if a row has 20 chairs only?

3   **RESEARCH:**

(a) Find out more about Fibonacci's life.

(b) List as many things as you can which are connected to Fibonacci numbers.

(c) Find a picture which shows how rabbits breeding give Fibonacci numbers.

4.1 Averages and range

In section 4.1 you will:

- review the mean, median, mode and range of a set of data
- compare sets of data
- find averages from frequency tables

The mean

All the data is added and the total is divided by the number of items.
In everyday language, the word 'average' usually stands for the mean.

The median

When the data is arranged in order of size, the median is the
one in the middle. If there are two 'middle' numbers,
the median is in the middle of these two numbers.

> The word
> 'average' is used
> to describe a
> *typical* member
> of a set of data.

The mode

The mode is the number or quality (such as a colour) which occurs
most often. Sometimes a set of data will have no mode, two modes
or even more, and this is a problem which we cannot avoid.

Range

The range is not an average but is the difference between the
largest value and the smallest value in a set of data. It is useful
in comparing sets of data when the spread of the data is important.

The marks in a spelling test were: 7, 8, 6, 6, 5, 3, 9, 8

(a) mean mark $= \dfrac{7 + 8 + 6 + 6 + 5 + 3 + 9 + 8}{8} = \dfrac{52}{8} = 6.5$

(b) arrange the marks in order: 3 5 6 6 7 8 8 9

the median is the half way number $= \dfrac{6 + 7}{2} = 6.5$

(c) there are two modes, 6 and 8

(d) range $= 9 - 3 = 6$

Exercise 1M

1. (a) Find the mean of 2, 4, 5, 9, 10
   (b) Find the median of 1, 3, 3, 4, 5, 7, 8, 11, 14, 14, 16
   (c) Find the mode of 3, 3, 3, 3, 4, 4, 5, 6, 6, 6, 7, 7
   (d) Find the range of 7, 8, 11, 14, 26, 30

2. Six girls have heights of 1.48 m, 1.51 m, 1.47 m, 1.55 m, 1.40 m and 1.59 m
   (a) Find the mean height of the six girls.
   (b) Find the mean height of the remaining five girls when the tallest girl leaves.

3. The temperatures at midnight in nine towns were, in °C,
   $$1°, 0°, -3°, -4°, 3°, -6°, 2°, -2°, -1°$$
   What was the median temperature?

4. The heights of the people shown are, in m,
   1.82   1.71   1.74   1.69   1.73
   1.64   1.8   1.77   1.84

   (a) Find the median height of these people.
   (b) Two more people of heights 1.61 m and
   1.7 m join this group. What is the median
   height of this new group of eleven people?

5. In a history test, Andrew got 62%. For the whole class, the mean mark was 64% and the median mark was 59%. Which 'average' tells Andrew whether he is in the 'top' half or the 'bottom' half of the class?

6. Lauren has five cards. The five cards have a mean of 7 and a range of 4. What are the missing numbers?

   | 7 | 7 | 7 | | |

7. There were ten children on a coach journey. The mean age of the children was 11 and the range of their ages was 4. Write each statement below and then write next to it whether it is *True*, *Possible* or *False*.
   (a) The youngest child was 9 years old.
   (b) Every child was 11 years old.
   (c) All the children were at least 10 years old.

8. The range for nine numbers on a card is 60.
   One number is covered by a sticker.
   What could that number be?
   [There are two possible answers.]

56	43	15
48	61	10
24	34	

9   The mean of the numbers 2, 6, 8, 5 and n is 6. Find the value of n.

10   Becky throws a dice eight times and wins 50p if the mean score is more than 3.
The dice shows 6, 1, 2, 5, 6, 4, 5, 3. Find the mean score. Does Becky win 50p?

11   Ed has five cards. The mean for four of the cards is 8. When the fifth card is included, the
mean for all five cards is 7. Write down the number on the fifth card.

12   For the set of numbers below, find the mean and the median.

$$\boxed{1, \ 3, \ 3, \ 3, \ 4, \ 6, \ 99}$$

Which average best describes the set of numbers?

Comparing sets of data

To compare two sets of data, always write at least two things.
1 Compare an average (i.e. mean, median or mode).
2 Compare the range of each set of data (this shows how spread out the data is).

Exercise 2M

1   The Comets and the Typhoons are two athletics teams. They each have runners in the
100 m races.
Their best times (in seconds) are listed below.
Comets: 10.7   10.5   11   10.8   11.2   11.1   10.9
Typhoons: 10.9   10.4   11.1   10.7   10.6
Use the median and range to write a sentence to compare the times taken by the runners for the
Comets and the Typhoons in the 100 m race.

2   The weights of the tigers in a safari park in Spain
are as follows:

     65 kg, 71 kg, 72 kg, 85 kg, 91 kg, 92 kg, 94 kg, 101 kg

(a) Find the mean weight of these tigers and the range of
their weights.

(b) At another safari park in Portugal the mean weight of the
tigers is 96 kg and the range of their weights is 120 kg.
Write one or two sentences to compare the weights of the
tigers at these two safari parks.

3   The heights in metres of the children in Year 8 classes in two schools were recorded.

| School A | 1.60 | 1.59 | 1.63 | 1.57 | 1.64 | 1.58 | 1.57 | 1.62 | 1.57 | 1.64 |
| School B | 1.55 | 1.42 | 1.65 | 1.48 | 1.50 | 1.64 | 1.44 | 1.69 | 1.41 | 1.40 |

(a) Work out the mean height and the range for school A.

(b) Work out the mean height and the range for school B.

(c) Write a sentence to compare the heights of the children in the two schools.

4   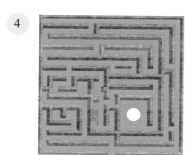 In an experiment, firstly red ants and then black ants were released at the dot in a maze. The time they took to escape was recorded. Here are the results. The times are in seconds.

Red ants: 7   9   10   13   13   22   23   26   30

Black ants: 8   8   11   12   13   13   14   15   17

Write a sentence to compare the times taken to escape for the red ants and black ants.

Finding averages from frequency tables

Twenty children were asked how many computer games they had bought during one year. The results are below.

5   4   4   0   1   2   2   6   1   2
3   5   2   5   1   0   3   3   5   2

This data can be recorded in a frequency table.

| number of computer games | 0 | 1 | 2 | 3 | 4 | 5 | 6 |
| frequency (number of children) | 2 | 3 | 5 | 3 | 2 | 4 | 1 |

Use the table to work out the mean number of computer games.

$$\text{mean} = \frac{(2 \times 0) + (3 \times 1) + (5 \times 2) + (3 \times 3) + (2 \times 4) + (4 \times 5) + (1 \times 6)}{20}$$

↗ total number of children

$$\text{mean} = \frac{56}{20} = 2.8$$

Note: The **modal** number of computer games is 2, since more people bought 2 computer games than any other number of computer games.

Exercise 3M

1   The table below shows the number of children in each of 100 families.

number of children	0	1	2	3	4	5	6	7
frequency	4	24	22	19	15	7	7	2

Copy and complete: mean number of children $= \dfrac{(4 \times 0) + (24 \times 1) + (\dots)}{100} = \dfrac{\square}{100} = \square$

2   The table below shows the number of cars for each house on Carter Road in Romford.

number of cars	0	1	2	3
frequency	7	12	11	10

Copy and complete: mean number of cars $= \dfrac{(7 \times 0) + (12 \times 1) + (\dots) + (\dots)}{40}$

$$= \dfrac{\square}{40} = \square$$

3   The frequency table shows the weights of 30 eggs laid by the hens on a free range farm.

weight	44 g	48 g	52 g	56 g	60 g
frequency	5	6	7	9	3

Find the mean weight of the eggs, giving your answer to 1 decimal place.

4   The frequency table shows the weights of the 40 pears sold in a shop.

weight	70 g	80 g	90 g	100 g	110 g	120 g
frequency	2	7	9	11	8	3

Calculate the mean weight of the pears.

5   The marks, out of 10, achieved by 25 teachers in a spelling test were as follows:

mark	5	6	7	8	9	10
frequency	8	7	4	2	3	1

Find   (a) the mean mark

(b) the modal mark (this means the 'mode',
i.e. which test mark did more teachers get than any other).

mite	✗
might	✓
goal	✓
gole	✗
paralel	✗
thay	✗

6   The number of daily portions of fruit and vegetables eaten by 30 people is shown in the table below

number of portions	0	1	2	3	4	5	6
frequency	2	3	3	7	3	9	3

(a) Find the mean number of portions eaten each day.

(b) Find the modal number of portions eaten each day (i.e. the 'mode', the number of portions eaten by more people than any other).

Need more practice with averages and range?

1   (a) Find the mean of the numbers 4, 13, 5, 7, 9, 6, 5

   (b) Find the median of the numbers 6, 20, 1, 16, 2, 12, 6, 3, 8, 6, 8

   (c) Find the mode of the numbers 13, 2, 11, 2, 10, 4, 5, 10, 8, 10

2   These digits are made using 5p coins.

   (a) Count the number of coins in each of the digits from 1 to 9

   (b) What is the median number of coins used in a digit?

   (c) Work out the mean value of the coins used in a digit when the number 654 is formed.

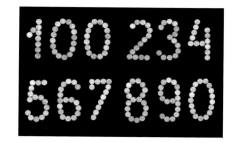

3   In several different shops the price of a certain DVD was £5.95, £3.99, £2.99, £4.75, £3.50, £2.95, £6.50. What is the median price of the DVD?

4   Find the range of the following sets of numbers.

   (a) 4, 11, 3, 8, 22, 5, 7, 30, 18

   (b) 9, 18, 100, 64, 11, 26

   (c) 4, −2, 6, 4, 5, 10, 3

5   Twelve skydivers take part in a jump.
They were born in the following years:

1987   1983   1965   1971   1970   1980
1956   1967   1984   1985   1962   1978

Work out the mean age of the skydivers   (a) in 2009

                                            (b) in 2025

6   The mean average pocket money for six children is £7. Olivia joins these six children. What is the mean average pocket money for all seven children if Olivia gets £14 pocket money each week?

7   The median of the numbers 5, 7, 2, 12, 11 and x is 8. Find the value of x.

8   Write down five numbers so that

the mean is 7

the median is 6

the mode is 4

9   David throws a dice five times and the mean score on the dice is 4. What was his last score if the first four scores were 5, 3, 4 and 6?

Extension questions with averages and range

1   The yearly salaries of eight people who work in Karen's business are shown below. Karen's salary is the largest.

£10 000	£12 000	£12 000	£76 000
£11 000	£12 000	£14 000	£13 000

  (a) Work out the mean, mode and median salary.

  (b) Karen wants to attract people to work for her business.
Which average should she use to most help her to attract people?
Give a reason for your answer.

2   3   4   9   ?

If the median of the four numbers above is 4, work out the mean average of the four numbers.

3   The ages of four people are n, $5n$, $4n$ and $2n$.
Write down an algebraic expression for the mean age of the four people.

4. Leila did a survey of the number of people living in the houses in a street in Luton.

(a) Write down the modal number of people in these houses.

People in house	Tally	Frequency
0	I	1
1	⅃卌 I	6
2	卌 卌	
3	卌 卌 II	
4	卌 卌 卌	
5	卌 III	
6	II	

Stephen did a similar survey in a street in Stevenage. His results are below.

number of people	0	1	2	3	4	5	6
frequency	0	13	11	5	1	0	1

(b) Write a sentence to compare the number of people living in the houses in these two towns. (Remember to compare an average and to compare the ranges (spread) of the two sets of data.)

(c) Suggest a possible reason for the difference you observe.

5. Max and his dad go fishing twice every month. The tables below show how many fish each of them caught every time they went fishing one year.

(a) Find the mean number of fish caught by Max and the mean number of fish caught by his dad.

(b) On an 'average' fishing trip, who caught more fish?

Max

number of fish	0	1	2	3	4	5	6	7
frequency	3	4	2	1	5	2	6	1

Dad

number of fish	0	1	2	3	4	5	6	7
frequency	2	5	3	4	5	3	0	2

6. Nine people have a mean weight of 68 kg.
A tenth person joins the group and the mean weight of all ten people is 69 kg. How much does this tenth person weigh?

4.2 Charts, including scatter graphs

In section 4.2 you will:

- draw and interpret scatter graphs
- use two-way tables, frequency diagrams, pie charts, and stem and leaf diagrams

Scatter graphs

Sometimes it is important to discover if there is a connection or relationship between two sets of data.

Examples
- Do tall people weigh more than short people?
- If you spend longer revising for a test, will you get a higher mark?
- Do tall parents have tall children?
- Do older people have higher pulse rates?

If there is a relationship, it will be easy to spot if your data is plotted on a scatter diagram – that is a graph in which one set of data is plotted on the horizontal axis and the other is plotted on the vertical axis.

- Here is a scatter graph showing the test marks of some pupils in a maths test and a science test.

- We can see a connection: the pupils who got a high mark in science generally got a high mark in maths.

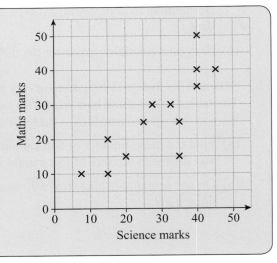

Exercise 1M

1. The scatter graph shows the number of hot drinks sold by a café and the outside temperature.
   (a) On how many days was it less than 12°C?
   (b) How many hot drinks were sold when it was 35°C?
   (c) On how many days were 40 or more hot drinks sold?
   (d) Fill the blank with either 'increases' or 'decreases': As temperature *increases*, the number of drinks sold _____ .

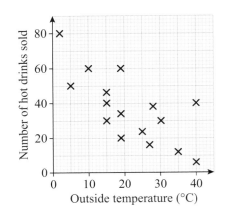

2. Here are the heights and masses of 9 people. Draw the axes shown and complete the scatter graph.

Name	Mass (kg)	Height (cm)
Alice	45	115
Fred	60	160
Jack	65	155
John	55	125
Percy	75	160
Hugh	75	170
Mabel	65	140
Diana	85	180
Cyril	52	146

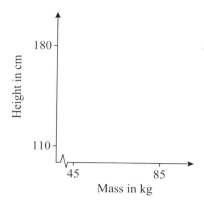

3. The graph shows the scores in a spelling test and the shoe sizes of 14 children.

(a) How many take size 6 or less?

(b) The pass mark is 4 or more. How many children failed?

(c) Is there a connection between a child's shoe size and test score?

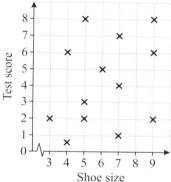

Correlation

The word correlation describes how things *co-relate*. There is correlation between two sets of data if there is a connection or relationship.

The correlation between two sets of data can be positive or negative and it can be strong or weak, as indicated by the scatter graphs below.

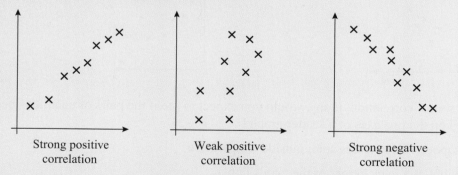

When the correlation is positive, the points are around a line which slopes upwards to the right. When the correlation is negative, the 'line' slopes downwards to the right.

When the correlation is strong, the points are bunched close to a line through their midst. When the correlation is weak, the points are more scattered.

It is important to realise that often there is *no* correlation between two sets of data.

If, for example, we take a group of students and plot their maths test results against their time to run 800 m, the graph might look like the one on the right. A common mistake in this topic is to 'see' a correlation on a scatter graph where none exists.

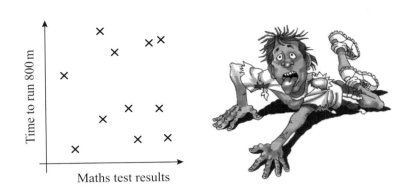

Exercise 2M

1   Plot the points given on a scatter graph, with *s* across the page and *p* up the page. Draw axes with values from 0 to 20

Describe the correlation, if any, between the values of *s* and *p*. [i.e. 'strong negative', 'weak positive', etc.]

(a)

s	7	16	4	12	18	6	20	4	10	13
p	8	15	6	12	17	9	18	7	10	14

(b)

s	11	1	16	7	2	19	8	4	13	18
p	5	12	7	14	17	1	11	8	11	5

2   Describe the correlation, if any, in these scatter graphs.

(a)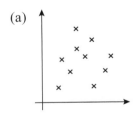

(b)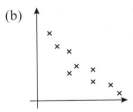

3   What sort of correlation, if any, would you expect to see if the pairs of quantities below were plotted on the two axes of a scatter graph?

(a) number of ice creams sold; outside temperature

(b) height of a man; height of the man's father

(c) outside temperature; amount of energy used to heat a home

4   The table shows the marks of 7 students in the two papers of a science examination.

Paper 1	35	10	60	17	43	55	49
Paper 2	26	15	40	15	30	34	35

(a) Plot the marks on a scatter diagram, using a scale of 1 cm to 5 marks.

(b) A student got a mark of 25 on paper 1 but missed paper 2. What would you expect her to get on paper 2?

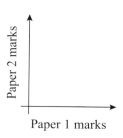

5   Decide on two pieces of data to get from each person in the class (agree this with your teacher). Draw a scatter graph to show this information. Can you see a connection between the two pieces of data?

Two-way tables

Exercise 3M

1

JANUARY	Max. temperature (°F)	Hours of sunshine	Rainfall in mm
Vancouver	42	2	8
Rio de Janeiro	84	7	2
London	45	2	2

The table gives the expected weather in January for Vancouver, Rio de Janeiro and London.

(a) Which city expects the most rainfall?

(b) Which city expects the most sunshine?

(c) What is the expected maximum temperature in London?

2   Jane, John and Joan all work in a restaurant. The tips they receive one week are recorded below.

	Jane	John	Joan
Under £3	8	12	6
£3 to £5	17	14	20
Over £5	10	18	8

(a) How many tips between £3 and £5 did Joan receive?

(b) Who received the most tips this week?

(c) What percentage of Jane's tips were under £3? Give the answer to 1 decimal place.

244

3 The table shows the age at which one hundred mothers had their first child in 1950 and 2000

	1950	2000
under 18	16	12
18 to 24	44	23
25 to 30	27	35
Over 30	13	30

How many mothers had their first child

(a) between the ages of 18 and 24 in 2000

(b) between the ages of 25 and 30 in 1950?

(c) What fraction of the mothers in 1950 were over 30 years old?

(d) Write a sentence about any differences you notice between 1950 and 2000

4 International dialling codes.

From \ To	France	Germany	UK	USA
France	—	1949	1944	191
Germany	0033	—	0044	001
UK	0033	0049	—	001
USA	01133	01149	01144	—

What code would you need to dial

(a) from the UK to Germany

(b) from France to the USA

(c) from the USA to the UK?

5 How far is it from

(a) Berlin to Helsinki

(b) Amsterdam to Paris?

(c) What would be the total distance of the round trip from Berlin to Paris on to Rome and back to Berlin?

(d) How much further is it from Berlin to Rome compared with Amsterdam to Paris?

Road distance in km

Amsterdam				
665	Berlin			
1205	505	Helsinki		
487	1047	1605	Paris	
1653	1476	2041	1399	Rome

Frequency diagrams, and stem and leaf diagrams

Stem and leaf diagrams – reminder

Here are the ages of 20 people.

16	23	21	17	32	21	37	45	39	42
36	29	37	41	45	19	32	23	28	18

Put the ages into groups 10–19, 20–29, 30–39 and 40–49

Choose the tens digit as the 'stem' and the units digit as the 'leaf'.

Stem	Leaf
1	6 7 9 8
2	3 1 1 9 3 8
3	2 7 9 6 7 2
4	5 2 1 5

Now order
the leaf numbers.

Stem	Leaf
1	6 7 8 9
2	1 1 3 3 8 9
3	2 2 6 7 7 9
4	1 2 5 5

Add a key to show what the numbers mean:

2|3 means 23 years old

Exercise 4M

1 Classes 8C and 8D both take the same maths test. The maximum mark in the test is 60.
   The frequency diagrams below show the results in the test.

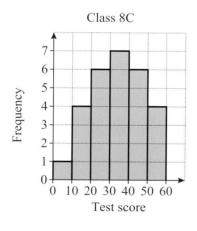

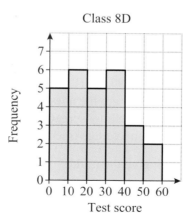

Which class generally did better in this maths test?
Give a reason for your answer.

246

2 Here are the heights, in cm, of the 21 members of a school swimming team.

136.8, 146.2, 141.2, 147.2, 151.3, 145.0, 155.0,
149.9, 138.0, 146.8, 157.4, 143.1, 143.5, 147.2,
147.5, 158.6, 154.7, 144.6, 152.4, 144.0, 151.0

(a) Put the heights into groups.

(b) Draw a frequency diagram like those in question 1 .

class interval	frequency
$135 \leqslant h < 140$	
$140 \leqslant h < 145$	
$145 \leqslant h < 150$	
$\vdots$	

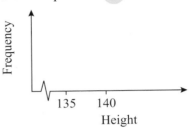

(c) What fraction of the members were 155.0 cm tall or more?

3 The stem and leaf diagrams below show the ages of patients in two hospital wards, the Carlton Ward and the Holbrook Ward.

The Carlton Ward

Stem	Leaf
2	1 4
3	0 3 6
4	4 4 7 9
5	3 6

Key
3|6 means 36 years old

The Holbrook Ward

Stem	Leaf
5	1 4
6	3 5 8
7	0 1 6 8
8	2 4 7
9	5

Key
7|8 means 78 years old

(a) Find the range and the median age of the patients for each ward.

(b) Write two sentences to compare the ages of the patients in the two wards (one sentence should include how spread out the ages are (range) and the second sentence should include an average (median)).

4 The numbers shown below give the midday temperatures in June for a local farm.
Draw an ordered stem and leaf diagram to show this data.

18	23	24	22	19	17	16	21	23	25
21	19	17	18	22	21	24	20	23	21
25	28	27	30	27	23	19	18	23	25

5   The times, in seconds, of some athletes in a 100 m race are shown below.

| 10.1 | 10.3 | 10.3 | 9.8 | 10.7 | 11.1 | 11.5 | 10.2 | 10.6 | 11.0 |
| 10.3 | 12.1 | 11.3 | 11.1 | 10.4 | 9.9 | 10.6 | 11.1 | 11.8 | 10.2 |

(a) Draw a stem and leaf diagram to show the times, using the key as below:

Stem	Leaf
9	
10	
11	
12	

10|3 means 10.3 seconds

The stem is shown opposite.

(b) What was the median time?

(c) What percentage of the athletes took less than 10 seconds?

Pie charts

Each week Maurice spends £8 on newspapers, £6 on magazines and £4 on lottery tickets. Draw a pie chart to show this spending.

(a) Add the 3 parts: $8 + 6 + 4 = 18$

(b) £18 = 360°

$$£1 = \frac{360}{18} = 20°$$

(c) For newspapers,   £8 = 8 × 20 = 160°
    For magazines,   £6 = 6 × 20 = 120°
    For lottery tickets, £4 = 4 × 20 = 80°

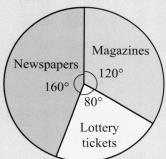

Exercise 5M

1   A 'Chewit' bar contains these four ingredients:

Oats   6 g
Barley   9 g
Sugar   3 g
Rye   18 g

(a) Work out the total weight of the ingredients.

(b) Work out the angle on a pie chart for 1 g of the ingredients [i.e. 360° ÷ (total weight)].

(c) Work out the angle for each ingredient and draw a pie chart.

248

In questions ② , ③ and ④ work out the angle for each sector and draw a pie chart.

② Type of vehicle
on the road

Type	Frequency
car	30
van	3
lorry	8
other	4

③ Pupils' favourite
colour

Colour	Frequency
red	15
green	12
blue	16
yellow	11
other	6

④ Activities each
day

Activity	Frequency
work	7
eat	1
sleep	8
exercise	2
other	6

⑤ In a survey, 320 people on an aircraft and 800 people on a ferry were asked to state their country of origin.

Aircraft: 320 people

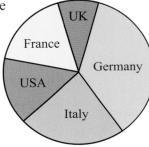

Ferry: 800 people

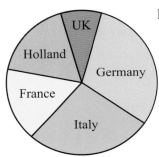

Jill looked at the charts and said 'There were about the same number of people from Italy on the aircraft and on the ferry'. Explain why Jill is wrong.

⑥ At the 'Crooked Corkscrew' last Friday, 120 customers ordered meals.

40 ordered beefburger
20 ordered ham salad
25 ordered cod
16 ordered curry
19 ordered chicken.

(a) Draw a pie chart to show this information.

(b) What percentage of the ordered meals were cod?
Give the answer to 1 decimal place.

7 Eurostar did a survey of over a thousand passengers on one of its trains. Here are the passengers' nationalities:

British 30%
French 20%
German 15%
Dutch 35%

On a pie chart, the angle for British passengers is found by working out 30% of 360°

Find the angle on a pie chart representing

(a) French passengers

(b) Dutch passengers.

8 Some people were asked what their favourite fruit was from apples, peaches, pears and bananas.

80 people chose peaches. The results are shown in the pie chart opposite.

(a) How many people chose bananas?

(b) How many people chose apples?

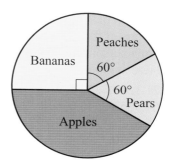

Need more practice with charts, including scatter graphs?

1 The table below shows how many people went to university each year in a certain country.

	2018	2019	2020
male	168 500	147 316	148 716
female	129 498	152 859	160 832

(a) How many females went to university in 2019?

(b) How many fewer males went to university in 2019 compared with 2018?

(c) What percentage of the people going to university in 2020 were female?
Give your answer to the nearest percentage.

2 Plot the points given on a scatter graph, with s across the page and p up the page.
Draw axes with values from 0 to 20

Describe the correlation, if any, between the values of s and p (i.e. 'strong negative',
'weak positive', etc.).

(a)

s	3	8	12	15	16	5	6	17	9
p	4	2	10	17	5	10	17	11	15

(b)

s	18	6	8	4	12	16	2	20	10	13
p	6	12	12	15	10	8	16	4	10	8

3 A group of 7 year olds were each accompanied
by one of their parents on a coach trip to a zoo.
Each person on the coach was weighed in kg.
Here are the weights:

21.1, 45.7, 22.3, 26.3, 50.1, 24.3, 44.2,
54.3, 53.2, 46.0, 51.0, 24.2, 56.4, 20.6,
25.5, 22.8, 52.0, 26.5, 41.8, 27.5, 29.7,
55.1, 30.7, 47.4, 23.5, 59.8, 49.3, 23.4,
21.7, 57.6, 22.6, 58.7, 28.6, 54.1

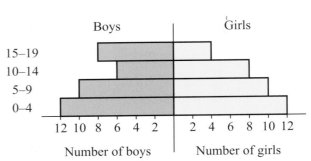

(a) Put the weights into groups.

class interval	frequency
$20 \leqslant w < 25$	
$25 \leqslant w < 30$	
$30 \leqslant w < 35$	
⋮	

(b) Draw a frequency diagram.

(c) What percentage of the group weighed $20\,\text{kg} \leqslant w < 25\,\text{kg}$?
Give your answer to 1 decimal place.

4 Here is an age distribution pyramid
for the children at a Center Parcs resort.

(a) How many girls were there
aged 5–9?

(b) How many children were there
altogether in the 0–4 age range?

(c) How many girls were at the resort?

Boys   Girls

15–19
10–14
5–9
0–4

12 10 8 6 4 2   2 4 6 8 10 12

Number of boys   Number of girls

5   The stem and leaf diagram shows the marks
    for each student in a maths test.

    (a) How many students took the maths test?

    (b) Write down the range of the marks.

    (c) The pass mark was 45. How many students
        passed the test?

    (d) What was the median mark?

Stem	Leaf
4	2 3 3 6 9
5	0 0 0 1 2 8 9
6	1 2 5 5 6 7 7 8
7	2 3 3 5 7 8 8
8	0 6 6 8

Key: 5|8 means 58 marks

6   The students in Year 8 are given the PE options: rugby, dance, soccer or gymnastics.
    The number of students choosing each option is shown below.

Option	rugby	dance	soccer	gymnastics
Frequency	28	38	34	20

Draw a pie chart to show this information.

Extension questions with charts, including scatter graphs

1   The table below shows details of the number of rooms and the number of occupants
    of 11 houses in a street.

Number of rooms	2	3	7	11	7	5	5	11	5	6	4
Number of occupants	2	8	5	2	6	2	7	7	4	0	1

    (a) Draw a scatter graph.

    (b) Can you estimate the likely number of people living in a house with 9 rooms?
        If so, what is the number? Explain your answer.

2   The pie chart illustrates the sales of
    four flavours of crisps.

    (a) If cheese and onion accounts
        for $\frac{1}{3}$ of total sales, calculate
        the angles x and y.

    (b) What percentage of total sales
        does plain have?

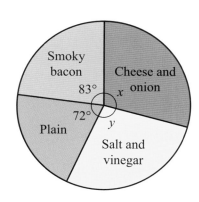

3 Four people intend to go snowboarding at Christmas. They cannot decide where to go. They have this information about two possible places.

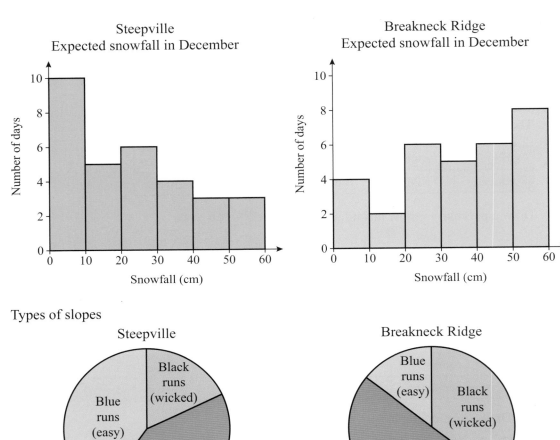

Decide where you think they should go. It doesn't matter where you decide, but you *must* say why, using the two types of diagram to help you explain.

4   Explain how each of the diagrams below is misleading in some way.

(a)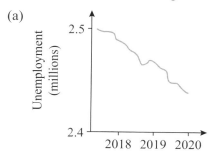

(b)   Sales of apples

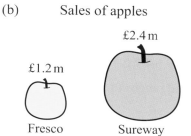

5   The weights, in kg, of two groups of people are recorded below

Group A

57	63	63	79	55	82	73	87	61
62	77	76	85	68	70	93	74	
77	88	57	52	88	74	63	86	

Group B

72	83	87	74	69	66	92	85	77	69
81	93	85	72	64	74	89	94	90	82
77	85	69	94	73	69	90	81	86	66

(a) Draw an ordered stem and leaf diagram for each group of people.
    You must include a key for each.

(b) Which group of people were generally heavier?
    You must use medians and ranges to support your answer.

CHECK YOURSELF ON SECTIONS 4.1 and 4.2

1   Reviewing the mean, median, mode and range of a set of data

6   3   9   2   9   8   2   9

For the numbers above, find

(a) the mode   (b) the mean   (c) the range   (d) the median.

(e) The five cards below have a mean of 6 and a median of 6.
    What are the two missing numbers?

2   Comparing sets of data

Children in class 8B and 8C have a spelling test. The marks for 10 children from each class are shown below.

Class 8B: 8 7 6 6 9 6 4 7 2 5   Class 8C: 4 7 3 9 9 8 6 9 8 7

Use the means and ranges to write two sentences to compare the marks for each class.

3   Finding averages from frequency tables

A golfer played the same hole 30 times with the following results.

score	3	4	5	6	7	8
frequency	3	13	5	3	2	4

(a) Find her mean score.

(b) Find her modal score (mode).

4   Interpreting scatter graphs

The scatter graph shows the heights and masses of some people.

(a) How many people were more than 150 cm tall?

(b) How many people weighed 60 kg or less?

(c) Answer *true* or *false*: 'In general as height increases, mass increases'.

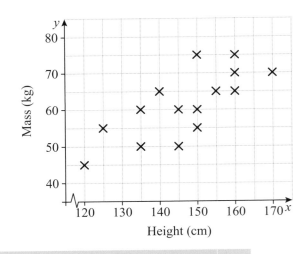

5   Using two-way tables, frequency diagrams, pie charts, and stem and leaf diagrams

The table shows how many children are in Years 7, 8 and 9 in Henton High School.

(a) How many children are there in Year 9?

(b) How many girls are there in total?

	Year 7	Year 8	Year 9
boys	102	119	97
girls	106	94	110

(c) What percentage of the Year 8 children are boys?
     Give your answer to 1 decimal place.

(d) Meg asked 40 people what their favourite fruit was. The table shows the information. Work out the angle for each sector and then draw a pie chart to show the results.

(e) What percentage of the people chose 'apple'?

Fruit	Frequency
peach	3
apple	8
strawberry	13
banana	5
pear	7
orange	4

(f)

Stem	Leaf
3	5
4	2 3 4
5	1 5 7
6	8 8 9
7	5

This stem and leaf diagram shows the ages of some people at a birthday party. Find the range of the ages and the median for the ages.

Key:
5|7 means 57 years old

4.3 Pythagoras' theorem

In section 4.3 you will calculate the length of a side in a right-angled triangle using Pythagoras' theorem

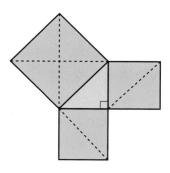

The sum of the areas of the two small squares is equal to the area of the large square.

This result was proved in about 550 BCE by a famous Greek mathematician called Pythagoras.

Pythagoras' theorem

'In a right-angled triangle, the square on the hypotenuse is equal to the sum of the squares on the other two sides.'

The 'hypotenuse' is the longest side in a right-angled triangle.

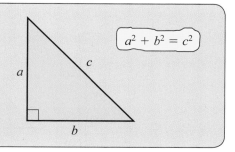

$$a^2 + b^2 = c^2$$

The theorem can be used to calculate the third side of a right-angled triangle when two sides are known.

Find the length x.

(a)

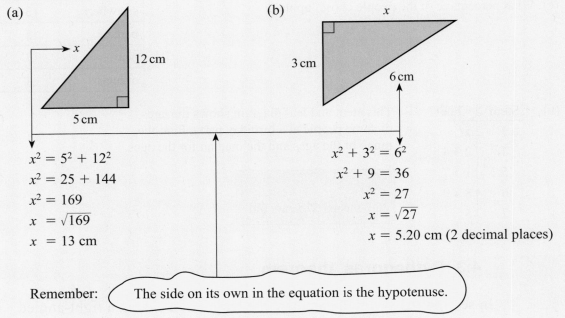

(b)

$x^2 = 5^2 + 12^2$

$x^2 = 25 + 144$

$x^2 = 169$

$x = \sqrt{169}$

$x = 13$ cm

$x^2 + 3^2 = 6^2$

$x^2 + 9 = 36$

$x^2 = 27$

$x = \sqrt{27}$

$x = 5.20$ cm (2 decimal places)

Remember: (The side on its own in the equation is the hypotenuse.)

Exercise 1M

In this exercise, give answers correct to 2 decimal places if they are not whole numbers.
The units are cm unless you are told otherwise.

1 Copy and fill in the boxes.

(a)

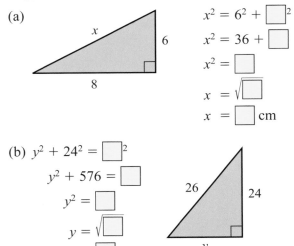

$x^2 = 6^2 + \boxed{}^2$

$x^2 = 36 + \boxed{}$

$x^2 = \boxed{}$

$x = \sqrt{\boxed{}}$

$x = \boxed{}$ cm

(b) $y^2 + 24^2 = \boxed{}^2$

$y^2 + 576 = \boxed{}$

$y^2 = \boxed{}$

$y = \sqrt{\boxed{}}$

$y = \boxed{}$ cm

(c)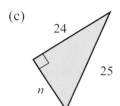

$$n^2 + \boxed{}^2 = 25^2$$
$$n^2 + \boxed{} = 625$$
$$n^2 = \boxed{}$$
$$n = \sqrt{\boxed{}}$$
$$n = \boxed{} \text{ cm}$$

2 Find the value of x in each triangle.

(a)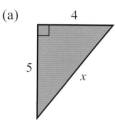

(b)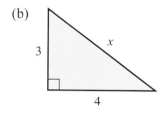

(c)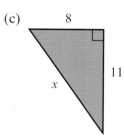

3 Find the value of y in each triangle.

(a)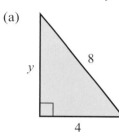

(b)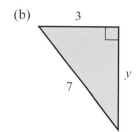

(c)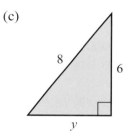

4 Find the side marked with a letter. It may be the hypotenuse or one of the other sides.

(a)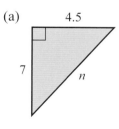

(b)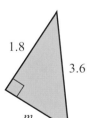

(c)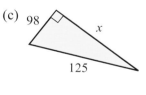

(d)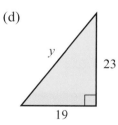

(e)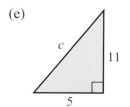

(f)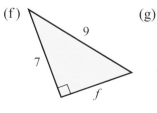

(g)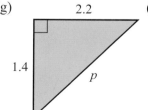

(h)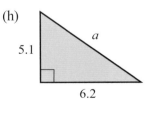

258

Give answers correct to 2 decimal places where necessary.

1

A ladder of length 5 m rests against a vertical wall.
The bottom of the ladder is 2 m from the wall.
How far up the wall does the ladder reach?

Wall

5 m

2 m

Ground

2 A ladder of length 4.5 m rests against a vertical wall. The bottom of the ladder is 1.8 m from the wall. How far up the wall does the ladder reach?

3 A ladder reaches 3.6 m up a vertical wall. The bottom of the ladder is 1.75 m from the wall. How long is the ladder?

4 Work out the length of the diagonal AC.

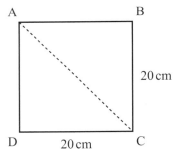

A   B

20 cm

D   20 cm   C

5

A chess board measures 32 cm by 32 cm. Calculate the length of a diagonal drawn across the whole board.

6   Alexander is 3 km due east of Evan.
    Sapphire is due south of Evan.
    Sapphire is 7 km away from Alexander.
    How far apart are Sapphire and Evan?

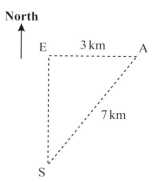

7   A ship sails 40 km due south and then a further 65 km due east.
    How far is the ship from its starting point?

8   The square and the rectangle have the
    same perimeter. Which has the longer
    diagonal and by how much?

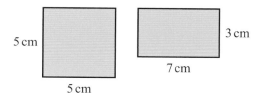

Need more practice with Pythagoras' theorem?

Give your answers correct to 2 decimal places where necessary. The units are cm unless you are told otherwise.

1   Find the side marked with a letter.

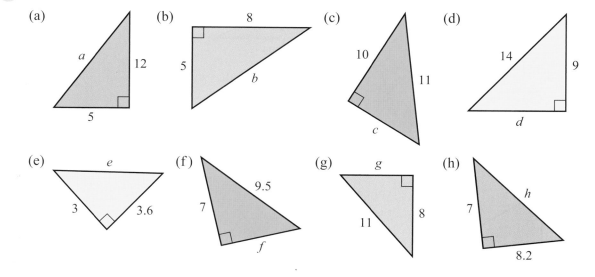

2 A rope attached to a flagpole is 10 m long. The rope is fixed to the ground 5 m from the foot of the flagpole. How tall is the flagpole?

10 m

5 m

3 A ladder of length 4 m reaches 3.2 m up a vertical wall. How far is the bottom of the ladder from the wall?

4 A ship is 8 km due north of an oil tanker. The ship is also 5 km due east of a lighthouse. How far is the oil tanker from the lighthouse?

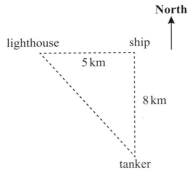

North

lighthouse   ship

5 km

8 km

tanker

5 Work out the length of a diagonal in a 10 cm by 10 cm square.

Extension questions with Pythagoras' theorem

Give your answers correct to 2 decimal places where necessary.

1 Calculate the perimeter of this triangle.

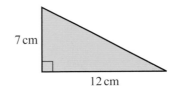

7 cm

12 cm

2 A ship sails 30 km due north and then a further 18 km due west. How far directly is the ship now from its starting position?

3 How much further would you travel from A to C then C to B compared with travelling directly from A to B?

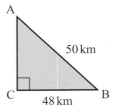

A

50 km

C   48 km   B

4 Which triangle has the greater area and by how much?

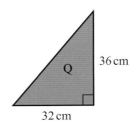

52 cm

P

48 cm

36 cm

Q

32 cm

5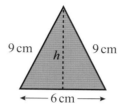

The diagram shows how the height line cuts the base line in half. The height line is the 'perpendicular bisector' of the base. Calculate the value of h.

11 cm   11 cm
h
← 4 cm →←— 4 cm →

6   Calculate the height of the isosceles triangle shown.

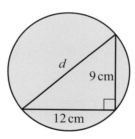

9 cm   9 cm
h
←— 6 cm —→

7   12 cm
8 cm
12 cm

Work out the area of this isosceles triangle.

8   A circle has diameter d.
Calculate the circumference of the circle
(remember: circumference $= \pi d$).

d
9 cm
12 cm

✗ Spot the mistakes 7 ✗

Averages and range, charts and Pythagoras' theorem

Work through each question below and *explain clearly* what mistakes have been made.
Beware – some questions are correctly done.

1   Work out the median of the numbers

        8, 11, 5, 15, 9, 8, 14, 6

    Answer: Write out the numbers in order of size.

            5, 6, 8, 8, 9, 11, 14, 15

            There are 8 numbers and the median is the
            middle number, so the 4th number

                median = 8

2 Calculate the value of x.

Answer: $24^2 + 30^2 = x^2$ (Pythagoras' theorem)

$$x^2 = 1476$$
$$x = \sqrt{1476} = 38.4 \text{ cm}$$

30 cm

24 cm

x

3 The volume, V, and mass, m, are recorded in a science experiment. The results are shown in the table below.

V (cm³)	20	27	10	30	40	15	20	38	18	30
m (g)	150	175	50	200	250	100	75	225	100	150

Describe how V and m are related.

Answer:

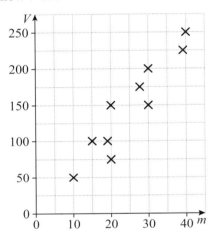

There is positive correlation.

4

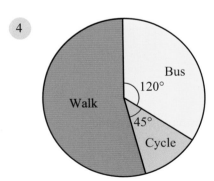

The pie chart shows how children get to school in the morning. What fraction of the children walk?

Answer: bus fraction $= \dfrac{120}{360} = \dfrac{1}{3}$

cycle fraction $= \dfrac{45}{360} = \dfrac{1}{8}$

bus and cycle fraction $= \dfrac{1}{3} + \dfrac{1}{8} = \dfrac{2}{11}$

fraction of children who walk $= 1 - \dfrac{2}{11}$

$= \dfrac{9}{11}$

5 The stem and leaf diagram shows the ages of some people in a shop at a certain time. Work out the difference between the median and the mode.

Answer: 28 people so median is 14th person, i.e. median = 22
mode = 36
difference = 36 − 22 = 14

Stem	Leaf
0	2 3 5 7 7
1	0 1 3 3 3 5 9
2	1 2 3 6 7 8 8 9
3	1 4 6 6 6 6
4	0 2

Key: 2|6 means 26 years old

6

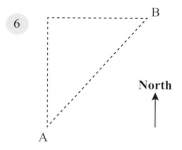

A ship sails 14 km due north from A then 6 km due east to B. How far is it directly from A to B?

Answer: AB = 6^2 + 14^2
AB = 36 + 196
AB = 232 km

7 Five cards have median 7, range 12 and mean 9. Write down the two missing values.

Answer: Missing values are 13 and 15

8 The table shows the number of cars for each house on a road. Calculate the mean number of cars per house.

Answer: Total frequency = 3 + 8 + 22 + 4 + 3
= 40
Total number of cars = 0 + 1 + 2 + 3 + 4 = 10
mean = 40 ÷ 10 = 4 cars per house

Number of cars	Frequency
0	3
1	8
2	22
3	4
4	3

9

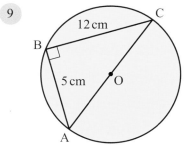

O is the centre of the circle. Calculate the area of this circle.

Answer: AC^2 = 5^2 + 12^2 (Pythagoras' theorem)
AC^2 = 169
AC = 13 cm

Area of circle = πr^2 = $\pi \times 13^2$
= 530.9 cm^2 (to 1 d.p.)

10   The pie charts below show the proportion of students who study certain languages at two schools.

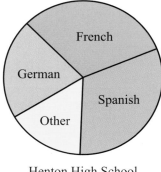

Henton High School

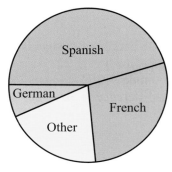

Dorminster School

At which school do more students study Spanish?

Answer: More students study Spanish at Dorminster school.

4.4 Bearings and scale drawing

In section 4.4 you will:

- use bearings
- make scale drawings to solve problems

Bearings are used by navigators on ships and aircraft and by people travelling in open country.

Bearings are measured from north in a *clockwise* direction.

A bearing is always given as a three-digit number.

A bearing of 090° is due east. If you are going south-west, you are on a bearing of 225°

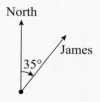

North

James is walking on
a bearing of 035°

North

146°

Mary

Mary is walking on
a bearing of 146°

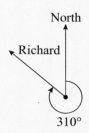

North

Richard

310°

Richard is walking on
a bearing of 310°

Exercise 1M

1   Ten children on a treasure hunt start in
the middle of a field and begin walking
in the directions shown below.
On what bearing is each child walking?

2   Ten pigeons are released and they fly in
the directions shown below. On what
bearing is each pigeon flying?

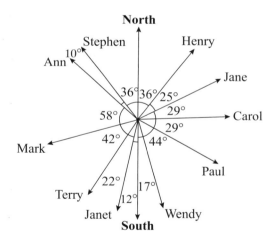

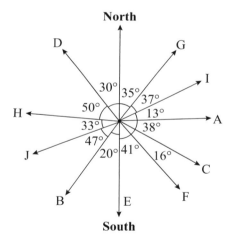

3   For each diagram, write down the bearing of C from D.

(a)
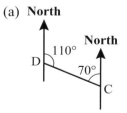

(b)
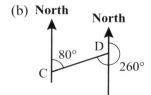

(c)
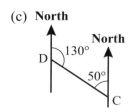

4   Draw lines to show the following bearings. Remember to start from a North line.

(a) 040°   (b) 075°   (c) 120°   (d) 200°   (e) 300°

5 Use a protractor to measure the bearing on which each person is moving.

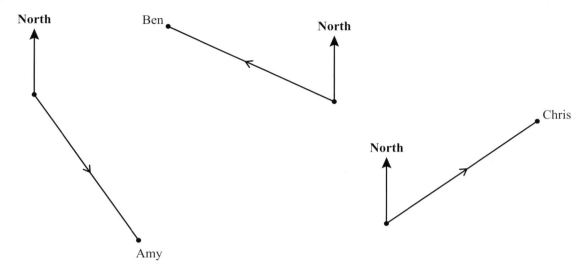

Scale drawing

A rectangle has length 12 m and width 8 m

Draw an accurate scale drawing of the rectangle using a scale of 1 cm for every 4 m

Length 12 m will be 12 ÷ 4 = 3 cm on the drawing.

Width 8 m will be 8 ÷ 4 = 2 cm on the drawing.

Scale drawing:

3 cm

2 cm

Exercise 2M

Draw an accurate scale drawing of each shape below using the scale shown.

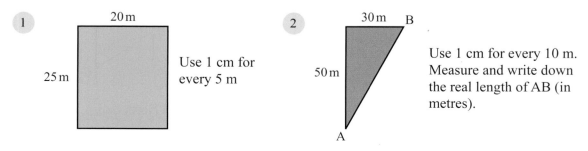

1   20 m

25 m

Use 1 cm for every 5 m

2   30 m   B

50 m

A

Use 1 cm for every 10 m. Measure and write down the real length of AB (in metres).

3

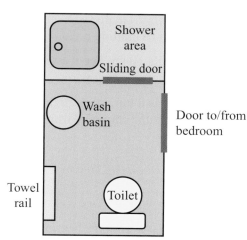

← 2.2 cm →

Wall unit Door 1 Wall unit

Pantry Fridge

Sink

3.5 cm

Unit

Door 2

1.5 cm Radiator

Work surface

Cooker

Work surface

Work surface

←— 3 cm —→←—2.5 cm —→←— 3 cm —→◄1.5 cm►

This is a plan of Mrs Smith's kitchen. It has been drawn to a scale of 1 cm for every 40 cm (often written as 1 : 40).

(a) In Mrs Smith's house, how wide is

(i) the cooker (ii) the sink unit (iii) the radiator (iv) door 1?

(b) If the work surface next to the radiator is 160 cm long, what length would it be on the plan?

(c) If door 2 is 92 cm wide, what width should it be on the plan?

This is a plan of Mr Hazel's bathroom. It is drawn to a scale of 1 cm for every 50 cm (often written as 1 : 50).

(d) Measure the length and width of the floor on the plan.

(e) Calculate the real length and width of the bathroom.

(f) The door to the bedroom is 80 cm wide. How wide should it be on the plan? Measure and check your answer.

(g) The towel rail measures 1.4 cm on the plan. How long is the real one?

(h) Measure the width of the sliding door on the plan. How wide is the real one?

Shower area

Sliding door

Wash basin

Door to/from bedroom

Towel rail

Toilet

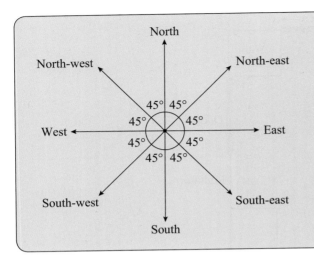

With questions about compass directions, it is helpful to begin by drawing a small sketch to get an idea of where the lines will go. Choose as large a scale as possible for greater accuracy.

A ship sails 7 km north-east and then a further 10 km due south. How far is the ship from its starting point?

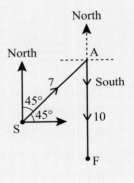

We will use a scale of 1 cm to 1 km

(a) Mark a starting point S and draw a line at 45° to the lines on the page.

(b) Mark a point A, 7 cm from S.

(c) Draw a line vertically through A and mark a point F, 10 cm from A.

(d) Measure the distance SF.
    Answer: The ship is 7.1 km from its starting point.
    (An answer between 7.0 km and 7.2 km would be acceptable.)

Exercise 3M

In questions 1 to 7 use a scale of 1 cm to represent 1 km

1. A ship sails 7 km due east and then a further 5 km due south. Find the distance of the ship from its starting point.

2. A ship sails 10 km due west and then a further 4 km due south-east. Find the distance of the ship from its starting point.

3. A ship sails 8 km due north and then a further 7 km on a bearing of 080°. How far is the ship now from its starting point?

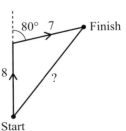

4. A ship sails 6 km on a bearing of 120° and then a further 4 km due south. How far is the ship from its starting point?

5   A ship sails 7 km on a bearing of 075° and then a further 5 km on a bearing of 130°.
    How far is the ship from its starting point?

6   A bird leaves its nest and flies around its
    territory in three stages.

    (a) Make a scale drawing to show the journey.

    (b) How far does the bird have to fly to return to
        its nest?

	Direction	Distance
1st stage	west	5 km
2nd stage	south-east	6 km
3rd stage	east	12 km

7   The diagram shows ports P and Q where P is
    10 km west of Q. An aircraft carrier A is 9 km
    north-east of P. An enemy submarine S is 4 km
    north-west of Q. The torpedoes on the submarine
    have a range of 4 km. Is the aircraft carrier in range
    of the torpedoes?

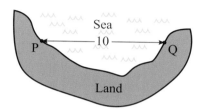

Need more practice with bearings and scale drawing?

1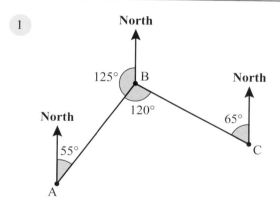

    Write down the bearing of

    (a) B from C

    (b) A from B

    (c) B from A.

2   Measure the bearings of these
    journeys.

    (a) A to B

    (b) B to C

    (c) A to C

    (d) A to D

    (e) C to D

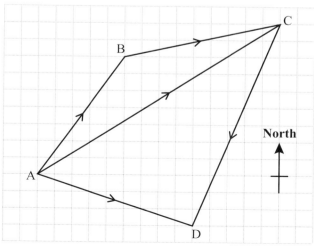

270

3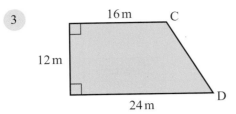

Draw an accurate scale diagram. Use 1 cm for every 4 m.
Measure and write down the real length of CD (in metres).

4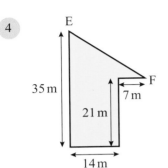

Drw an accurate scale diagram. Use 1 cm for every 7 m. Measure
and write down the real length of EF (in metres).

5 The map shows several features on
and around an island. Axes are drawn
to identify positions.
[e.g. The coordinates of the cave
are (9, 3).]

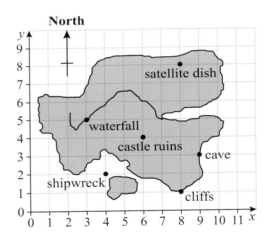

Four commandos, Piers, Quintin, Razak and Smudger, are in hiding on the island.
Find the coordinates of the commandos, using the following information.

(a) The castle ruins are due south of Piers and the waterfall is due west of him.

(b) From Quintin, the bearing of the satellite dish is 045° and the shipwreck is due
south of him.

(c) From Razak, the bearing of the waterfall is 315° and the bearing of the castle
ruins is 045°

(d) From Smudger, the bearing of the cave is 135° and the bearing of the waterfall is 225°

(e) The leader of the commandos is hiding somewhere due north of the shipwreck
in a hollow tree. From this tree, the castle ruins and the cliffs are both on the same
bearing. Find the coordinates of this hollow tree.

Extension questions with bearings and scale drawing

1   Here is a sketch of a company logo which is to be
    painted full size on the side of a ship.
    The designer needs to know the total height of the logo.
    Make a scale drawing of the logo with a scale of 1 cm
    to 1 m and find the height of the logo.

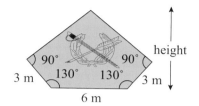

2   Use a scale of 1 cm to represent 1 km. A ship sails 12 km due east and then a further 7 km due
    south-west. Make a scale drawing then find the distance of the ship from its starting point.

3

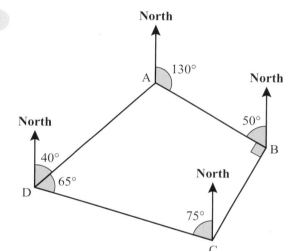

Edith walks directly from A to B then B to
C then C to D and finally back to A again.
Write down each bearing that Edith walks
on before returning to A.

4   Use a scale of 1 cm to represent 1 km. A ship sails 8 km on a bearing of 125° and then a
    further 4 km on a bearing of 040°. Make a scale drawing then find out how far the ship is
    from its starting point.

5   Draw a point F with a cross. Use a scale of 1 cm to 1 km to show
    the points G and H described below.

    Point G is 9 km from F on a bearing of 130° from F.
    Point H is 10 km from F on a bearing of 212° from F.
    What is the bearing of G from H?

6   Make a scale drawing of a room in your house.
    Design a layout for the furniture you would like
    to have in the room.

CHECK YOURSELF ON SECTIONS 4.3 and 4.4

1 Using Pythagoras' theorem

Find the length of the sides marked with letters. All lengths are in cm.

(a)

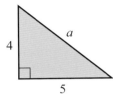

4

a

5

(b)

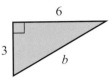

6

3

b

(c)

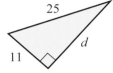

25

d

11

(d) Work out the perimeter of this triangle.

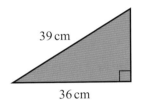

39 cm

36 cm

2 Using bearings

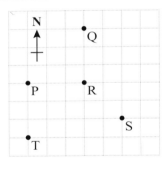

State the bearings of

(a) Q from P

(b) R from P

(c) S from R

(d) R from Q

(e) P from R

(f) T from R.

3 Making scale drawings

(a)

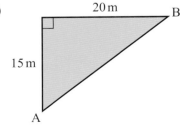

20 m

B

15 m

A

Make an accurate scale drawing of this triangle using a scale of 1 cm for every 5 m. Measure and write down the real length of AB (in metres).

(b) A plane flies 70 km on a bearing of 040° and then a further 50 km due south. Make a scale drawing using a scale of 1 cm for every 10 km. Find the distance of the plane from its starting point.

4.5 Congruent shapes and tessellation

In section 4.5 you will:

- use congruent shapes
- draw tessellations

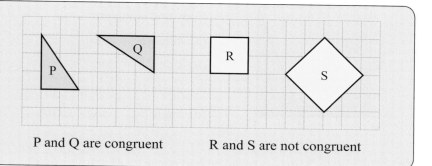

Congruent shapes are exactly the same in shape and size. Shapes are congruent if one shape can be fitted exactly over the other.

P and Q are congruent   R and S are not congruent

Exercise 1M

1. Decide which shapes are congruent pairs. [You can use tracing paper]

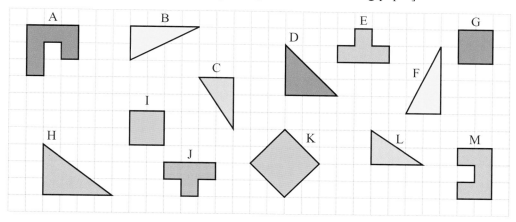

2. Copy the diagram and colour in congruent shapes with the same colour.

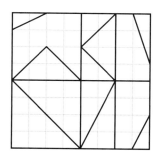

3 Two congruent right-angled triangles are
   joined together along equal sides.

   (a) How many shapes are possible?

   (b) How many shapes are possible if the
       congruent triangles are equilateral?

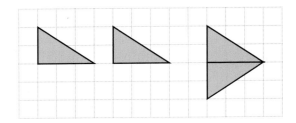

4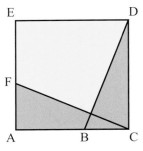

You are told that triangles DBC and CFA are congruent.
Copy and complete:

(a) side AF = side ☐

(b) side CF = side ☐

(c) angle CFA = angle ☐

(d) angle ☐ = angle CDB.

5 Use square dotty paper or squared paper.
   Draw 4 × 4 grids as shown.

   The 4 × 4 grids are divided into two
   congruent shapes.

   Divide 4 × 4 grids into two congruent
   shapes in as many different ways as
   possible.

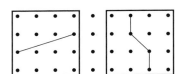

Tessellation

In tessellation we study the different ways we can regularly tile any flat surface, no matter how
large. The examples below show tessellation using quadrilaterals.

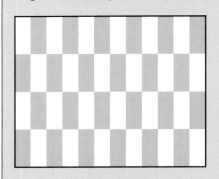

(Rectangles)

(Kites)

Any quadrilateral can be drawn on card and used to make a tessellation.

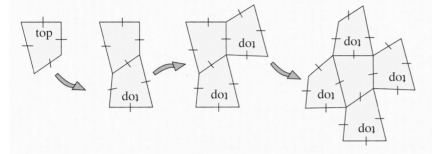

- Interesting tessellations may be formed using sets of different shapes, provided the lengths of their sides are compatible.

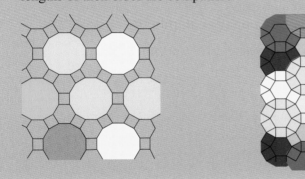

Exercise 2M

1 Draw and cut out a template on card for each of the shapes below.
(You can trace the shapes below to save time. All their sides are compatible.)

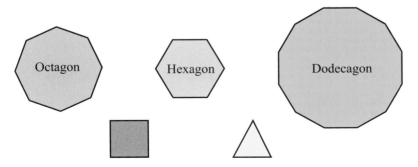

2   Either (i) draw a tessellation on plain paper or (ii) draw a tessellation directly onto tracing paper, using

(a) only hexagons

(b) only octagons and squares

(c) only dodecagons and equilateral triangles

(d) only hexagons, squares and equilateral triangles

(e) only dodecagons, hexagons and squares

(f) only squares and equilateral triangles.

3   For each tessellation in 2 , colour the pattern in an interesting way.

4.6 Negative numbers

In section 4.6 you will:

- review adding and subtracting negative numbers
- review multiplying and dividing negative numbers

Adding and subtracting negative numbers

For adding and subtracting negative numbers a number line is very useful.

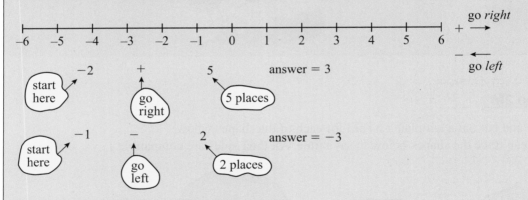

Two signs together

Remember: It is possible to replace two signs next to each other by one sign, as follows:

$$+ + = +$$
$$- - = +$$ 'add' if you have the same signs
$$- + = -$$
$$+ - = -$$ 'subtract' if you have different signs

When two signs next to each other have been replaced by one sign in this way, the calculation is completed using the number line as before.

Work out the following

(a) $-7 + (-4)$
$= -7 - 4$
$= -11$

(b) $8 + (-14)$
$= 8 - 14$
$= -6$

(c) $5 - (+9)$
$= 5 - 9$
$= -4$

(d) $6 - (-2)$
$= 6 + 2$
$= 8$

Exercise 1M

1   Use a number line to work out

(a) $3 - 4$
(b) $-3 + 5$
(c) $-2 + 7$
(d) $-3 - 1$

(e) $1 - 6$
(f) $-4 + 6$
(g) $3 - 8$
(h) $-4 + 3$

(i) $-3 - 2$
(j) $6 - 7$
(k) $2 - 4$
(l) $-5 + 9$

2   Work out

(a) $5 - 10$
(b) $-4 - 4$
(c) $-3 + 1$
(d) $-2 + 2$

(e) $7 - 11$
(f) $9 - 12$
(g) $-2 - 2$
(h) $5 - 15$

(i) $-6 - 9$
(j) $-2 - 12$
(k) $7 - 10$
(l) $-4 + 10$

3   Copy each sequence and fill in the missing numbers.

(a) $12, 8, 4, \boxed{}, \boxed{}$

(b) $\boxed{}, -2, 1, 4, 7$

(c) $\boxed{}, \boxed{}, -20, -10, 0$

4   Copy and complete the addition squares.

(a)

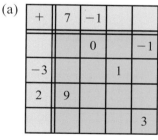

+	7	-1		
		0		-1
-3			1	
2	9			
				3

(b)

+	-5	3		
-1		2		0
			10	
4				
			6	-1

5   Use a number line to *explain clearly* why
$-4 + 2$ is *not* -6

Exercise 2M

1   Work out

(a) $6 + (-3)$
(b) $3 + (-4)$
(c) $5 + (-5)$
(d) $3 + (-7)$

(e) $7 - (+2)$
(f) $4 - (+5)$
(g) $6 - (-2)$
(h) $3 - (-4)$

(i) $2 - (-4)$
(j) $5 - (-1)$
(k) $8 - (+3)$
(l) $10 - (+7)$

2 Work out

(a) $1 - (-3)$ (b) $7 - (-4)$ (c) $6 + (-8)$ (d) $4 + (-3)$

(e) $7 + (+2)$ (f) $5 - (+3)$ (g) $4 - (-6)$ (h) $3 - (-2)$

(i) $6 + (-9)$ (j) $10 + (-11)$ (k) $7 + (-10)$ (l) $-5 - (-7)$

3 At 25 000 feet on a mountain the air temperature is $-23°C$ and because of the low air pressure water boils at $71°C$ (which makes it difficult to make a nice cup of tea).

What is the difference between the air temperature and the temperature of the water?

4 Nadia says that $-5 - 3$ is equal to 8 because 'two negative signs' mean 'add'. Is she correct? Give reasons for your answer.

5 You can choose any three numbers from

-4 5 6 2 -1

Here is a calculation $\boxed{} + \boxed{} - \boxed{} =$

(a) What is the largest answer you can get?

(b) What is the smallest answer you can get?

6 Copy and complete the tables.

a	9	3	8	3	2	5	4	7			
b	5	5	3	7	-2	-2				4	2
$a - b$	4	-2					-2	-3		-3	-1

a	-3	4	3	5	7	4	6			
b			-3	-1				5	-1	2
$a - b$	-3	-5			8	10	6	2	3	-2

7 Pat has $-£40$ in his bank account (this means he owes the bank £40).

During the next week he spends £15, £60 and £35. He pays in £30 and £75. How much money does Pat now have in his bank account and what does this mean?

8   A golfer has the following scores at 6 holes.

$-1, +1, +1, 0, -2, -1$

What is the total score for this golfer?

9   Work out the calculation in each box and put the answers in order of size, smallest first, to make a word.

R
$-1 - 2$

E
$-2 - (-2)$

O
$-6 + (-1)$

D
$-5 + 6$

S
$-9 - (-1)$

T
$-1 + (-1)$

10   In a 'magic square' you get the same number when you add across each row, add down each column and add diagonally. Copy and complete the following magic squares.

(a)
0		
-1		
4	-3	

(b)
1	-6	-1
-3		

(c)
	-1		-3
3		9	
		-5	
-6	5	0	7

Multiplying and dividing negative numbers

Remember:

> When two numbers with the *same sign* are multiplied together, the answer is *positive*

> When two numbers with *different signs* are multiplied together, the answer is *negative*

For division, the rules are the same as for multiplication.

$-3 \times (-2) = 6$ $6 \times (-4) = -24$ $-12 \div 4 = -3$

$30 \div (-3) = -10$ $-80 \div (-10) = 8$ $-2 \times (-4) \times (-2) = -16$

Exercise 3M

1. Copy and complete the multiplication square below. Some numbers inside the square are shown as an explanation.

×	−5	−4	−3	−2	−1	0	+1	+2	+3	+4	+5
+5						0					
+4						0					
+3		−12				0					
+2						0				8	
+1						0					
0	0	0	0	0	0	0	0	0	0	0	0
−1						0					
−2						0	−4				
−3				6		0					
−4						0					
−5						0					

Exercise 4M

Work out

1. $6 \times (-2)$
2. -3×3
3. $8 \times (-2)$
4. $-5 \times (-3)$

5. $14 \div (-2)$
6. $12 \div (-3)$
7. $6 \div (-1)$
8. $-10 \div (-2)$

9. $-4 \div (-1)$
10. $16 \div (-8)$
11. $-20 \div (-5)$
12. $-18 \div (-6)$

13. $-25 \div 5$
14. $-30 \div (-6)$
15. $12 \div (-6)$
16. $-50 \div 10$

17. $28 \div (-4)$
18. $-36 \div 9$
19. $-24 \div (-8)$
20. $30 \div (-15)$

21. Find two numbers that multiply to give −20 and add together to make −8

22. Work out the value of $(-5)^2$

23. Find two numbers that multiply to give −36 and add together to make −5

24 The temperature in London one night is $-3°C$ and in Toronto it is $-8°C$. The temperature in Moscow is five times as cold as in London. The temperature in Kiev is twice as cold as in Toronto.

Which is colder – Moscow or Kiev – and by how much?

25 Find the missing numbers.

(a) $-4 \times \boxed{} = 12$ (b) $3 \times \boxed{} = -12$ (c) $-8 \div -4 = \boxed{}$ (d) $5 \times \boxed{} = -5$

(e) $\boxed{} \times (-3) = 9$ (f) $12 \div \boxed{} = -6$ (g) $\boxed{} \div (-3) = 2$ (h) $\boxed{} \div 5 = -4$

(i) $-2 \times \boxed{} = 20$ (j) $-3 \times \boxed{} = 6$ (k) $-2 \times \boxed{} = 4$ (l) $(-1)^2 = \boxed{}$

26 The next number in each table is found by multiplying the two numbers before it.

For example | -3 | -2 | 6 | -12 | -72 |

Copy and complete each table.

(a)  | 3 | -1 | | |

(b) 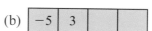 | -5 | 3 | | |

(c)  | -1 | -2 | | |

(d) | 3 | -2 | | |

(e)  | -2 | -2 | | |

(f)  | 2 | | -6 | |

(g) | | | 3 | -9 |

(h) 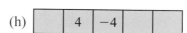 | | 4 | -4 | |

(i)  | | | | -10 | 100 |

27 Answer true or false.

(a) $7 \div (-7) = -1$ (b) $(-4)^2 = -16$ (c) $0 \times -5 = -5$

(d) $(-3)^2 = 9$ (e) $4 \times (-2) \times (-3) = 24$ (f) $3 \times (-3)^2 = -18$

28 Copy and complete the number wall. The number in each box is found by *multiplying* the two numbers below it.

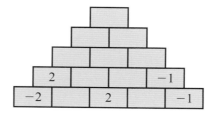

Need more practice with negative numbers?

Work out the following questions.

Part A

1. $-8 - 8$
2. $-8 \times (-8)$
3. -5×3
4. $-5 + 3$
5. $8 - (-7)$
6. $20 - 2$
7. $-18 \div (-6)$
8. $4 + (-10)$
9. $-2 + 13$
10. $+8 \times (-6)$
11. $-9 + (+2)$
12. $-2 - (-11)$
13. $-6 \times (-1)$
14. $2 - 20$
15. $-14 - (-4)$
16. $-40 \div (-5)$
17. $5 - 11$
18. -3×10
19. $9 + (-5)$
20. $7 \div (-7)$

Part B

1. $-10 \times (-10)$
2. $-10 - 10$
3. $-8 \times (+1)$
4. $-8 + 1$
5. $5 + (-9)$
6. $15 - 5$
7. $-72 \div (-8)$
8. $-12 - (-2)$
9. $-1 + 8$
10. $-5 \times (-7)$
11. $-10 + (-10)$
12. $-6 \times (+4)$
13. $6 - 16$
14. $-42 \div (+6)$
15. $-13 + (-6)$
16. $-8 - (-7)$
17. $5 \times (-1)$
18. $2 - 15$
19. $21 + (-21)$
20. $-16 \div (-2)$

Part C

1. $-2 \times (+8)$
2. $-2 + 8$
3. $-7 - 6$
4. $-7 \times (-6)$
5. $+36 \div (-9)$
6. $-8 - (-4)$
7. $-14 + 2$
8. $5 \times (-4)$
9. $11 + (-5)$
10. $11 - 11$
11. $-9 \times (-4)$
12. $-6 + (-4)$
13. $3 - 10$
14. $-20 \div (-2)$
15. $16 + (-10)$
16. $-4 - (+14)$
17. $-45 \div 5$
18. $18 - 3$
19. $-1 \times (-1)$
20. $-3 - (-3)$

Part D

1. $-4 + 4$
2. $-4 \times (+4)$
3. $-2 - 12$
4. $-2 \times (-12)$
5. $3 + (-4)$
6. $4 - (-10)$
7. $-22 \div 11$
8. $-9 + 7$
9. $-6 - (-13)$
10. $-3 \times (-11)$
11. $4 - 5$
12. $-20 - (+10)$
13. $4 \times (-7)$
14. $7 - (-12)$
15. $9 - 18$
16. $56 \div (-7)$
17. $7 - 6$
18. $-11 + (+2)$
19. $-2 \times (+8)$
20. $-8 \div (-2)$

Extension questions with negative numbers

1. Copy and complete this addition square.

+	−3			−5
−2			−3	
		5		
−4		2		
				2

2. Find the value of each expression below if $m = -4$

$$n = 5$$
$$p = -6$$

(a) $m + n$ (b) $m - p$ (c) $n - m$ (d) $m + p$ (e) $n - p + m$

3. The midnight temperatures during one week on a mountain road are shown below

$-6°C, -3°C, -5°C, -1°C, -6°C, -8°C, -6°C$

Find the mean average temperature.

4. Answer true or false.

(a) $4 \times (-5) = -20$ (b) $-3 \times (-6) = -18$ (c) $-2 \times (-4) = 8$

(d) $-5 \times 2 = -10$ (e) $4 \times (-8) = 32$ (f) $-3 \times (-5) = 15$

5. Copy and complete this multiplication square.

×		−5	6	
−3				
		−20		−28
8				
−9	18			

6. Find the value of each expression below if $w = -3, x = -7, y = 0$

(a) wx (b) $4x$ (c) $6w$ (d) w^2 (e) $3w + x$

(f) $2x - w$ (g) xy (h) x^2 (i) $w + 3x$ (j) wxy

284

7 Copy and complete each number chain.

(a)
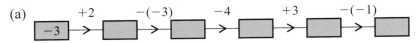

(b)
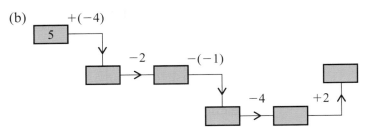

(c)
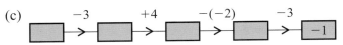

8 Which answer is greater and by how much?

$$4 \times -0.1$$

$$-\frac{1}{2} \times \frac{1}{2}$$

9 Find the missing numbers.

(a) $5 \times \boxed{} = -50$

(b) $30 \div (-5) = \boxed{}$

(c) $\boxed{} \times (-6) = 42$

(d) $-36 \div 9 = \boxed{}$

(e) $-60 \div \boxed{} = -6$

(f) $\boxed{} \div (-3) = -2$

(g) $-54 \div (-6) = \boxed{}$

(h) $-4 \times \boxed{} = 28$

(i) $48 \div \boxed{} = -6$

10 Find the missing value in the box if

$$-3 \times 5 - 3 \times \boxed{?} = -3$$

✖ Spot the mistakes 8 ✖

Bearings, scale drawing, congruent shapes and negative numbers

Work through each question below and *explain clearly* what mistakes have been made.
Beware – some questions are correctly done.

1 Work out $-7 + 3$

Answer: -10

2 Work out $(-5)^2$

Answer: -25

3

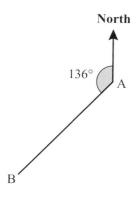

North

136°

A

B

A cyclist cycles from A to B.
On what bearing does the cyclist travel?

Answer: The cyclist travels on the
bearing 136°

4   Are triangles P and Q congruent? Give a reason for your answer.

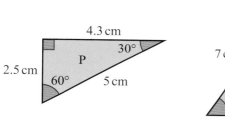

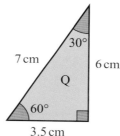

4.3 cm

30°

P

2.5 cm

60°   5 cm

7 cm   30°   6 cm

Q

60°

3.5 cm

Answer: Triangles P and Q are congruent because all the angles are the same.

5   A well known maths formula is $y = mx + c$.
Write down the value of y when $m = 7$, $c = -3$ and $x = -4$

Answer: $y = mx + c = 7 \times (-3) + (-4)$
$$= -21 - 4$$
$$= -25$$

6   Make a scale drawing of a rectangle with dimensions 16 m by 12 m.
Use 1 cm for every 4 m. Measure and write down the
real length of one of the diagonals of the rectangle.

Answer:

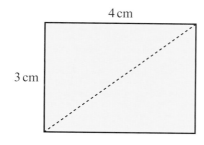

4 cm

3 cm

The diagonal is 5 cm long, so
the real length of the diagonal
is 20 m

7

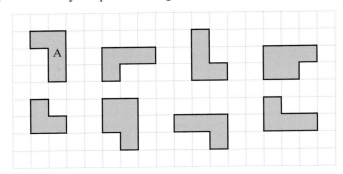

Write down the bearing of C from B.

Answer: 120°

8   Work out the value of $3a + 5b$ if $a = -4$ and $b = -3$

Answer: $3a + 5b = 3 \times (-4) + 5 \times (-3)$
$$= -12 + (-15)$$
$$= 27$$

9   How many shapes are congruent to shape A?

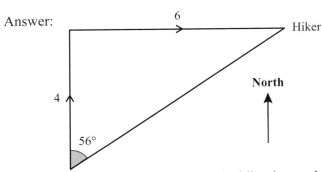

Answer: 3 shapes are congruent to shape A.

10   A hiker walks 4 km due north then 6 km due east.
Make a scale drawing using a scale of 1 cm for 1 km.
Measure the bearing of the hiker now from the
starting position.

Answer:

The hiker is on a bearing of 056° from the starting position.

CHECK YOURSELF ON SECTIONS 4.5 and 4.6

1   Using congruent shapes

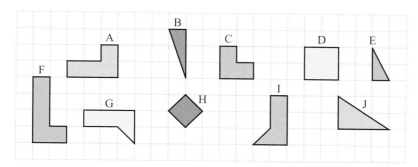

(a) Which shape is congruent to shape I?   (b) Which shape is congruent to shape B?

2   Drawing tessellations

Draw a tessellation using this shape *at least* 8 times.

3   Adding and subtracting negative numbers

Work out

(a) $3 + (-5)$ (b) $2 - (-4)$ (c) $-4 - (-2)$ (d) $-3 - 2$ (e) $-6 + 2$

(f) What number belongs in the box? $-8 - \square = -5$

4   Multiplying and dividing negative numbers

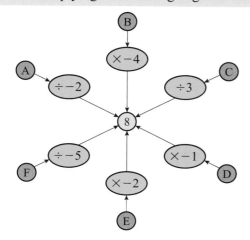

(a) Write down the value of each
of the letters A to F.

Work out

(b) $-7 \times (-4)$

(c) $20 \div (-2)$

(d) $-15 \div 3$

4.7 Applying mathematics 4

In section 4.7 you will apply maths in a variety of situations.

1   Juan needs to hire a large tile cutter for 12 weeks.

> 'Smartgear' charge a fixed cost of £35 plus £42 for each week.

> 'Heavy tools' charge a fixed cost of £22 plus £5.50 for each day.

Which firm will be cheaper and by how much?

2   A floor plan of a room is shown.
Mel wants a polished concrete floor
which costs £95 per m².
How much will it cost to cover the
whole floor with polished concrete?

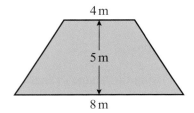

3   The times taken for each of three security guards to leave
the main office to check things and then return to the main
office are shown opposite. The guards do this continually.
If all three guards leave the main office at 09:30, when
will all three of them arrive back at the main office at
the same time?

Guard 1	20 minutes
Guard 2	35 minutes
Guard 3	40 minutes

4

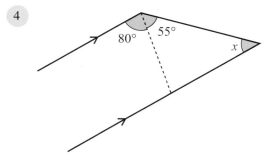

A designer needs to know the value of angle x.
Write down this value.

5   Calculate the total surface area of a solid wooden cuboid with dimensions 5 cm × 8 cm × 3 cm.

6   A 200 cm piece of wood is cut as shown. Work out the value of x.

$$\longleftarrow x \longrightarrow \longleftarrow x + 60 \longrightarrow \longleftarrow 2x \longrightarrow$$

7   Zak has a piece of fabric which is $2\frac{1}{2}$ m long. A customer wants a $1\frac{2}{3}$ m piece of the fabric. Zak cuts off $\frac{2}{3}$ m but still has too much fabric.

How much more fabric must he cut off to get the correct length for the customer?

8   The diameter of this circle is 15 cm

   (a) Work out the area of the triangle.

   (b) Work out the red area inside the circle but outside the triangle.

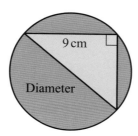

9 cm

Diameter

9   A TV is on sale for £800. At the end of May, the shop reduces the price of the TV by 20%. At the end of June, the shop reduces the price by 20% of the new price. At the end of July, the shop increases the price of the TV by 40%. How much does the TV cost now?

10 The probability of Agnes being late to work or not on a Monday for two consecutive weeks is shown in the table below.

	late both Mondays	late on one Monday but not the other	not late on either Monday
probability	$\frac{1}{10}$	$\frac{2}{5}$	?

What is the probability that Agnes will not be late on either Monday?

UNIT 4   MIXED REVIEW

Part one

1   Work out

   (a) $-9 + 4$

   (b) $-5 \times (-4)$

   (c) $-7 - 9$

   (d) $4 \times (-4)$

   (e) $-6 \div 2$

   (f) $-5 \times (-6)$

2 Look at these number cards.

| −3 | 0 | +2 | −5 | +4 | −6 | +3 |

(a) Choose a card to give the answer 2

+4 + −5 + ☐ = 2

(b) Choose a card to give the lowest possible answer.

−3 + ☐ = ?

(c) Choose a card to give the highest possible answer.

−5 − ☐ = ?

3 These cards show the scores awarded by four judges in a diving contest.

(a) Find the mean score.

(b) Find the median score.

| 6 | 3 | 7 | 4 |

(c) Write down the range of scores.

4

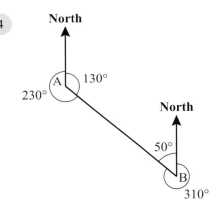

Write down the bearing of A *from* B.

5 The pupils in a school were given a spelling test. Some of the results are given in the table.

(a) Copy and complete the table with the missing entries.

(b) How many pupils passed the test in total?

(c) What percentage of the pupils who passed the test were girls?
Give your answer to 1 decimal place.

	Passed	Failed	Total
Boys		311	589
Girls		257	
Total		568	914

6 Copy and complete this addition square.

+		−3	
−2			−1
	−4	−1	
	−7		

7  Draw a tessellation using this shape *at least* 8 times.

8 The marks of 24 children in a test are shown.

32	15	43	20	47	55	63	51
47	22	49	58	37	12	68	26
35	38	31	19	26	52	49	19

Stem	Leaf
1	5
2	
3	2
4	3
5	
6	

Key:
5|7 means 57

(a) Draw a stem and leaf diagram. The first three entries are shown.

(b) What is the range of the marks?

(c) What is the median mark?

9  The coins in a box have the following values in pence.

| 5 | 1 | 2 | 10 | 50 | 20 | 5 | 5 | 1 | 1 |
| 100 | 2 | 10 | 5 | 5 | 2 | 2 | 2 | 200 | 50 |

For these coins, which is greater and by how much: the mean value or the median value?

10 Kerry and Felix arrange a charity concert. They charge £3.50 per person. The graph below shows the times at which people arrive at the concert.

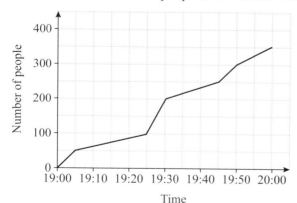

(a) How much money has been taken by 19:45?

(b) Kerry and Felix want to collect £700 for their charity. The cost of the concert is £500. Do they collect enough money to meet their target?

11 Some children collect 1500 sea shells. The shells weigh
    15.3 kg. Calculate the mean weight of a shell.

12 Find the value of the letter in each question.
    Give each answer to 1 decimal place.

(a)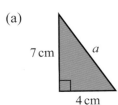
    7 cm   *a*   4 cm

(b)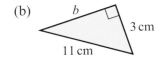
    b   3 cm   11 cm

(c)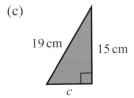
    19 cm   15 cm   *c*

13 Write a sentence to explain what 'congruent shapes' mean.

14 In this number wall each brick is made by adding
    the two bricks underneath it. Copy and complete
    the wall.

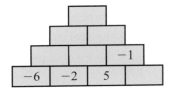

-1

-6 -2 5

Part two

1 Work out
   (a) $(-2) + (-5)$ (b) $3 \times (-4)$ (c) $(-6)^2$ (d) $32 \div (-8)$

2 This pie chart shows the energy resources available
   for a particular country.

   (a) If $\frac{2}{9}$ of the resources are nuclear, what angle will
       be needed for nuclear in the pie chart?

   (b) What angle will be needed for gas?

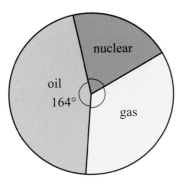

nuclear

oil
164°

gas

3 Find the missing numbers.
   (a) $6 \times \boxed{} = -30$ (b) $-48 \div \boxed{} = -8$ (c) $-7 - \boxed{} = -4$

4   The scatter graphs show the sales of ice cream,
soup and sandwiches on different days.
Describe the connection, if any, between the
sales of each product and the temperature.

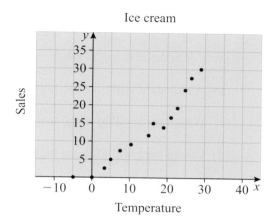

Ice cream

5   The total mass of five greyhounds is 76 kg. Calculate the mean mass of the dogs.

6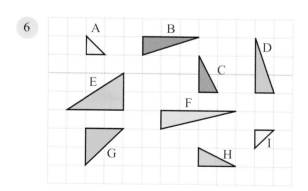

Which triangle is congruent to triangle B?

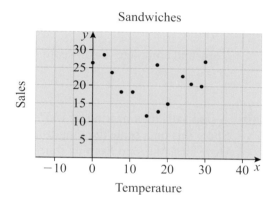

Soup

Sandwiches

7   A 4.3 m ladder rests against a vertical wall so that the bottom of
the ladder is 1.9 m from the wall. How far up the wall does the ladder reach?
Give your answer to 1 decimal place.

8 Look at these number cards: $\boxed{5}$ $\boxed{-2}$ $\boxed{0}$ $\boxed{7}$ $\boxed{-6}$ $\boxed{3}$ $\boxed{2}$ $\boxed{-4}$

(a) Fill in the missing number: $-2 + \boxed{} = 5$

(b) Which card will give the highest possible answer here: $-2 \times \boxed{} = ?$

(c) Which card will give the lowest possible answer here: $-4 - \boxed{} = ?$

(d) Which card will give the highest possible answer here: $3 - \boxed{} = ?$

9 A dice was thrown 20 times. Here are the results.

Score on dice	1	2	3	4	5	6
Number of throws	3	1	5	5	2	4

Copy and complete: mean score $= \dfrac{(1 \times 3) + (2 \times 1) + (3 \times 5) + \dots}{20}$

$= \boxed{}$

10 A ship sails on a bearing of 135° for 5 km and then a further 6 km due south. Show this on a scale drawing using a scale of 1 cm to represent 1 km. How far is the ship from its starting point?

11 Which is greater and by how much: $(-2)^2$ or $2 \times (-2)$?

12 A pie chart shows the contents of a transport museum.

(a) The sector for trams has an angle of 36°. What percentage of the whole pie chart is this sector?

(b) The sector for steam trains has an angle of 144°. What percentage of the whole pie chart is this sector?

13 Copy and complete the magic squares. (a)

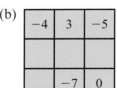

6		2
	5	
8		

(b)

−4	3	−5
	−7	0

14 13 cm 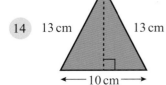 13 cm   Work out the area of this isosceles triangle.

10 cm

Puzzles and problems 4

1 The totals for the rows and columns are given. Find the values of the letters.

(a)

W	Y	X	Z	24
Y	Y	Y	Y	36
Z	Y	X	X	26
X	Z	Y	W	24
24	30	32	24	

(b)

E	D	E	C	E	45
A	B	D	C	E	41
E	C	E	C	E	41
D	A	C	C	A	33
E	E	D	C	C	43
42	41	47	35	38	

(c) Find P, Q, R, S and find the letter hidden by an ink blot.

S	Q	R	S	42
Q	Q	Q	Q	36
Q	Q	●	S	44
S	Q	P	R	41
44	36	41	42	

(d) This one is more difficult.

A	B	B	A	38
A	A	B	B	38
A	B	A	B	38
B	B	A	B	49
27	49	38	49	

2 The symbols γ, ↑, !, ⊖, ⊥ each stand for one of the digits 1, 2, 3, 5 or 9 but not in that order. Use the clues below to work out what number each symbol stands for.

(a) ↑ × ↑ = ⊥

(b) ⊖ × ↑ = ↑

(c) ⊖ + ⊖ = γ

(d) γ + ↑ = !

3   The ten symbols below each stand for one of the digits 0, 1, 2, 3, 4, 5, 6, 7, 8 or 9 but not in that order.

♂ ᙎ □ ⊙ ↑ ∗ ⧄ △ ⧆ ⊠

Use the clues below to work out what number each symbol stands for.

(a) ♂ + ♂ + ♂ + ♂ + ♂ = ᙎ

(b) ᙎ + ⊠ = ᙎ

(c) ᙎ + ♂ = ⊙

(d) ⧆ + ⧆ + ⧆ + ⧆ = ↑

(e) ∗ × ∗ = ⧄

(f) ⊙ − ⧆ = △

(g) ∗ + △ = □

4   Here is a 5 × 5 square cut into 8 smaller squares.

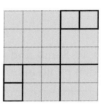

(a) Cut up a 7 × 7 square into 9 smaller squares.

(b) Cut up a 9 × 9 square into 10 smaller squares but you can use only one 3 × 3 square.

5   Fill up the square with the numbers 1, 2, 3, 4 so that each number appears only once in every row and column.

[You can have the same numbers in any diagonals.]

6   Fill up the square with the numbers 1, 2, 3, 4, 5 so that each number appears only once in every row, column and *main* diagonal.

The main diagonals are marked: AC and BD.

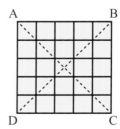

Mental arithmetic practice 4

Ideally a teacher will read out each question twice, with pupils' books closed.

- *Allow 5 seconds to answer each of questions 1 to 6*

1 What is half of the total of 18 and 22?

2 Change one hundred and forty millimetres into centimetres.

3 What is sixty-three divided by nine?

4 If $3n = 12$, write down the value for n.

5 Write $\frac{14}{21}$ in its simplest form.

6 Write four fifths as a decimal number.

- *Allow 10 seconds to answer each of questions 7 to 20*

7 What is the value of $5x$ when x equals six?

8 A film starts at five minutes to seven. It lasts forty-five minutes. At what time does the film finish?

9 What is one hundred and forty minus eighty?

10 On a coach there are fifty pupils. Thirty of the pupils are girls. A pupil is chosen at random. What is the probability that a girl is chosen?

11 What is 5% of 260?

12 Ten per cent of a number is eight. What is the number?

13 A pond is fifteen feet long. About how many metres is that?

14 Write the number two and a half million in figures.

15 If $x - 3 = 30$, work out the value of $2x$.

16 Two angles in a triangle are 80° and 55°. How large is the other angle in the triangle?

17 Estimate the value of fifty-two per cent of sixteen pounds ninety pence.

18 How many halves are there altogether in four and a half?

19 What is five hundred minus forty-five?

20 n stands for a number. Write an expression for the following: 'add six to n, then multiply the result by three'.

- *Allow 15 seconds to answer each of questions 21 to 30*

21 Pete and Bob share some money in the ratio of one to two. Pete's share is fifteen pounds. How much money is Bob's share?

22 What is one quarter of two hundred thousand?

23 Write two consecutive numbers that add up to thirty-five.

24 What is the value of eleven squared plus three squared?

25 Divide twenty-two pounds between four people. How much money does each person get?

26 Work out an approximate answer for 41.22×9.87

27 Find n if two times n minus one equals eleven.

28 The marks for four pupils in a test are 1, 3, 4 and 4. What is the mean mark?

29 Work out three plus four plus five, all squared.

30 A man's heart beats 80 times in 1 minute. How many times does it beat in one hour?

A long time ago! 4

Perfect numbers

| 496 | What a perfect number! |

The factor pairs of 496 are   1, 496

$$2, 248$$
$$4, 124$$
$$8, 62$$
$$16, 31$$

Ignore the number ⟨496⟩ itself. Add up all the other factors.

$$1 + 2 + 4 + 8 + 16 + 31 + 62 + 124 + 248 = ⟨496⟩$$

A number is perfect if it is equal to the sum of its factors (excluding itself).

The ancient Greeks looked very closely at perfect numbers to help them although there are not many perfect numbers which have been found.

Exercise

1 Find all the factors of 6 then show that 6 is a perfect number.

2 Find out if any of the numbers 24, 25, 26, 27, 28 or 29 are perfect by finding factors and adding them up.

Your answer to this question should be the number of days between a new full moon. Hundreds of years ago people felt that the *perfection* of the universe was shown by this period for the moon.

3 Find out if any of the numbers between 10 and 20 are perfect.

4 **RESEARCH:**

    (a) The number 33550336 is a perfect number. Find at least two more perfect numbers.

    (b) Find out what is meant by 'abundant' and 'deficient' numbers.

UNIT 5

5.1 Sequences 2

In section 5.1 you will find the nth term of an arithmetic sequence

---

Finding the nth term of an arithmetic sequence

In an *arithmetic* sequence the difference between each pair of terms is always the same number.

3, 11, 19, 27, 35, …

the difference between each pair of terms is 8

each number is called a term

The nth term is always of the form $an + b$
where a is the *difference* between each pair of terms.

The difference here is 8, so $a = 8$

Put the sequence in a table and write a column for $8n$.

We can see that the term is always 5 less than $8n$, so $b = -5$

The nth term is $8n - 5$

n	$8n$	term
1	8	3
2	16	11
3	24	19
4	32	27

Exercise 1M

1   The nth term of an arithmetic sequence is $3n + 7$
    (a) Use $n = 1$ to find the value of the 1st term.
    (b) Use $n = 2$ to find the value of the 2nd term.
    (c) Find the values of the 3rd term, 4th term and 5th term.

2   Write down the first 5 terms of an arithmetic sequence with
    (a) nth term $= 2n + 9$ (b) nth term $= 5n - 2$
    (c) nth term $= 4n - 1$ (d) nth term $= 7n + 10$

3   Look at the sequence 5, 9, 13, 17, …

The difference between terms is 4

Copy the table, which has a column for $4n$.

Copy and complete: 'The nth term of the

sequence is $4n + \square$.'

n	$4n$	term
1	4	5
2	8	9
3	12	13
4	16	17

4   Look at the sequence and the table underneath. Find the nth term in each case.

(a) Sequence 7, 10, 13, 16, …

n	$3n$	term
1	3	7
2	6	10
3	9	13
4	12	16

nth term = $\boxed{}$

(b) Sequence 4, 9, 14, 19, …

n	$5n$	term
1	5	4
2	10	9
3	15	14
4	20	19

nth term = $\boxed{}$

5   In the sequence 6, 10, 14, 18, …
the difference between terms is 4.
Copy and complete the table and write
an expression for the nth term of the sequence.

n	$\square$	term
1	$\square$	6
2	$\square$	10
3	$\square$	14
4	$\square$	18

6   Look at the sequence 5, 8, 11, 14, …

Write down the difference between terms.

Make a table like the one in question 5 and use it to find an expression for the nth term.

7   Write down each sequence in a table and then find the nth term.

(a) 8, 10, 12, 14, 16, …   (b) 3, 7, 11, 15, …

(c) 8, 13, 18, 23, …   (d) 15, 21, 27, 33, …

(e) 7, 15, 23, 31, …

8   Here is a sequence of shapes made from sticks.

      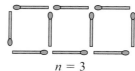

Shape number: $n = 1$ $n = 2$ $n = 3$
Number of sticks: 4   7   10

The number of sticks makes the sequence 4, 7, 10, 13, …
Make a table for the sequence and find the nth term.

Exercise 2M

1   Look at the sequence and the table underneath. Find the nth term in each case.

(a) Sequence 3, 5, 7, 9, ...

n	$2n$	term
1	2	3
2	4	5
3	6	7
4	8	9

nth term = ☐

(b) Sequence 7, 12, 17, 22, ...

n	$5n$	term
1	5	7
2	10	12
3	15	17
4	20	22

nth term = ☐

2   The sequence 8, 11, 14, 17, ... has nth term = $3n +$ ☐. What number belongs in the box?

3   The sequence 1, 6, 11, 16, ... has nth term = $5n -$ ☐. What number belongs in the box?

4   Find the nth term for the sequence 3, 10, 17, 24, ...

In questions 5 to 10 you are given a sequence of shapes made from sticks or dots.

If you need to, make a table to help you find the nth term of the sequence.

5   Here is a sequence of triangles made from dots. Draw the next diagram in the sequence.
How many dots are there in the nth term?

Shape number:	$n = 1$	$n = 2$	$n = 3$
Number of dots:	3	6	9

6   Louise makes a pattern of triangles from sticks.

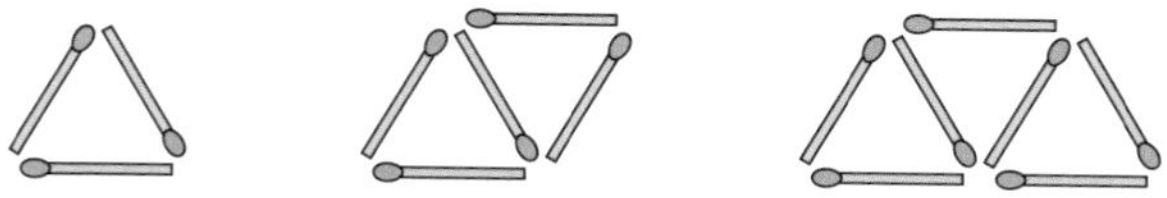

Shape number:	$n = 1$	$n = 2$	$n = 3$
Number of sticks:	3	5	7

Draw shape number 4 and shape number 5
How many sticks are there in the nth term?

7 Here is a sequence of 'steps' made from sticks. Draw the next diagram in the sequence.
How many sticks are there in the nth term?

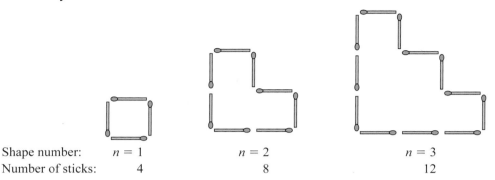

Shape number: $n = 1$ $n = 2$ $n = 3$
Number of sticks: 4   8   12

8 Here is a sequence of houses made from sticks.

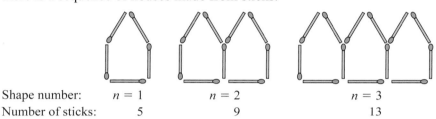

Shape number: $n = 1$ $n = 2$ $n = 3$
Number of sticks: 5   9   13

Draw shape number 4. How many sticks are there in the nth term?

9 Paul makes a pattern of squares from dots.

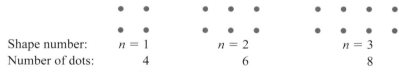

Shape number: $n = 1$ $n = 2$ $n = 3$
Number of dots: 4   6   8

(a) Draw shape number 4 and shape number 5

(b) How many dots are there in the nth term?

(c) How many dots are there in shape number 20?

10 Here is another sequence made from dots.

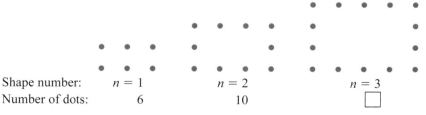

Shape number: $n = 1$ $n = 2$ $n = 3$
Number of dots: 6   10   ☐

(a) Draw shape numbers 4 and 5

(b) How many dots are there in the nth term?

(c) How many dots are there in shape number 12?

Need more practice with sequences?

1. The nth term of a sequence is $5n + 11$

   Write down (a) the 1st term (b) the 2nd term (c) the 10th term.

2. The nth term of a sequence is $3n - 1$

   Write down (a) the 1st term (b) the 10th term (c) the 100th term.

3. Write down the first five terms of the sequence where the nth term is
   (a) $10n - 1$ (b) $n + 2$ (c) $5n$ (d) $3n + 6$ (e) $n - 2$

4. Look at the sequence and the table underneath. Find the nth term in each case.

   (a) Sequence 3, 12, 21, 30, ...

   The differences are equal to 9

n	$9n$	term
1	9	3
2	18	12
3	27	21
4	36	30

   nth term = ☐

   (b) Sequence 2, 7, 12, 17, ...

   The differences are equal to 5

n	$5n$	term
1	5	2
2	10	7
3	15	12
4	20	17

   nth term = ☐

5. Copy and complete
   (a) 5, 9, 13, 17, ... nth term = $4n +$ ☐
   (b) 3, 5, 7, 9, ... nth term = $2n +$ ☐
   (c) 0, 5, 10, 15, ... nth term = $5n -$ ☐
   (d) 4, 11, 18, 25, ... nth term = $7n -$ ☐
   (e) 7, 10, 13, 16, ... nth term = $3n +$ ☐

6. An arithmetic sequence is shown below.

   | 12 | | | 27 | | 37 |

   (a) Write down the missing values in the sequence.

   (b) Write down the nth term for this sequence.

7. Find the nth term of each sequence below.
   (a) 13, 16, 19, 22, ...
   (b) 3, 13, 23, 33, ...
   (c) 9, 14, 19, 24, ...
   (d) 20, 24, 28, 32, ...

8   This table can seat 6 people.

The diagrams below show how many people can be seated when tables are joined together.

    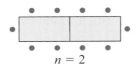   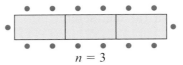

$n = 1$ $n = 2$ $n = 3$

(a) Draw the diagram for 4 tables.

(b) Write down how many people sit at 1 table, 2 tables, 3 tables and 4 tables.

(c) How many people would sit at 5 tables?

(d) Copy and fill in the empty box:

'The number of people sitting at n tables is $4n + \boxed{}$'

(e) *Discuss* with your teacher *why* the rule in part (d) works.

Extension questions with sequences

1   Write down each sequence and select the correct expression for the nth term from the list given.

(a) 3, 6, 9, 12, …

(b) 5, 10, 15, 20, …

(c) $1^2, 2^2, 3^2, 4^2, \ldots$

(d) 7, 14, 21, 28, …

(e) 2, 3, 4, 5, 6, …

(f) 5, 8, 11, 14, 17, …

(g) 1, 3, 5, 7, 9, …

$\boxed{3n}$ $\boxed{n + 1}$

$\boxed{7n}$ $\boxed{2n - 1}$

$\boxed{n^2}$ $\boxed{5n}$ $\boxed{3n + 2}$

2   Groups of people form a circle.

After 1 minute there are 6 people.

After 2 minutes there are 11 people.

After 3 minutes there are 16 people.

After 4 minutes there are 21 people.

(a) How many people do you expect in the circle after 5 minutes?

(b) Which of the following is true?
'After n minutes there will be $(5n + 4)$ people' *or*
'After n minutes there will be $(5n + 1)$ people'

3 Make a table for each sequence and write the *n*th term.

(a) $2\frac{1}{2}, 4\frac{1}{2}, 6\frac{1}{2}, 8\frac{1}{2}, \ldots$ (b) $-7, -4, -1, 2, 5, \ldots$ (c) $0.15, 0.45, 0.75, 1.05, \ldots$

4 Tables can be pushed together to seat people as shown below.

  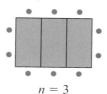

$n = 1$ $n = 2$ $n = 3$

(a) How many people sit at the table in the *n*th diagram?

(b) How many people sit at the table in the 10th diagram?

(c) In which diagram are 28 people seated?

5 The differences for the sequence 25, 22, 19, 16, … are -3

This is *negative* because the numbers are getting smaller each time.
We can make a table using $-3n$.

n	$-3n$	term
1	-3	25
2	-6	22
3	-9	19
4	-12	16

$-3 + 28 = 25$
$-6 + 28 = 22$
$-9 + 28 = 19$
$-12 + 28 = 16$ so *n*th term $= -3n + 28$

Use a table for each sequence below to find a formula for the *n*th term.

(a) 40, 35, 30, 25, …   (b) 33, 29, 25, 21, …

(c) 51, 45, 39, 33, …   (d) 17, 15, 13, 11, …

(e) 11, 8, 5, 2, …   (f) 36, 29, 22, 15, …

6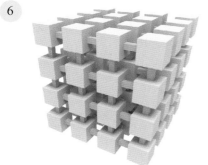

A mesh is made from cubes as shown. Several different sizes are made. The number of cubes used each time is shown below.

1, 8, 27, 64, 125, …

Which of the rules below works for this sequence?

$n + 7$ $n^2 + 4$ n^3 $n^2 - 1$

5.2 More algebra

In section 5.2 you will:

- review section 1 algebra
- substitute numbers into formulae
- work out values of expressions

Review of section 1 algebra

An algebraic expression is formed from letter symbols and numbers.
For example: $2n - 3$, $5y$, $7 - 3x$.

$8 \times y = 8y$

$\dfrac{5n^2}{n} = \dfrac{5 \times n \times \cancel{n}}{\cancel{n}} = 5n$

$abc = a \times b \times c$

$3a + 4b - a + 3b = 2a + 7b$

$\dfrac{m}{n} = m \div n$

$4n^2 + 2n^2 = 6n^2$

Exercise 1M

1. Answer 'true' or 'false'.

   (a) $2m \times 3n = 5mn$
   (b) $8m + 2 = 10m$
   (c) $n \times n = n^2$

   (d) $6x + 3y - 2x = 4x + 3y$
   (e) $5m + 2m - m = 7m$
   (f) $3a \times 5a = 15a^2$

   (g) $m + m = m^2$
   (h) $\dfrac{6n}{n} = 6$
   (i) $\dfrac{8a^2}{2} = 4a$

2. A magazine costs £3. Heather buys n magazines.
   Write down an expression for the total cost of the magazines.

3. The number of cards in 3 piles is shown.

   (a) How many cards are left in pile A
   if $(n + 5)$ cards are removed?

   (b) How many more cards are in pile A than pile B?

   (c) All the cards in piles A and C are divided equally between 3 people.
   How many cards does each person get?

   Pile A
   $4n + 12$

   Pile B
   $n + 6$

   Pile C
   $2n + 3$

4. Simplify

   (a) $6m \times 4n$
   (b) $2y \times 5p \times 3q$
   (c) $4m \times 4m$

   (d) $4m \times 7n \times 2p$
   (e) $5a \times 4$
   (f) $2 \times 8n$

   (g) $\dfrac{8m}{m}$
   (h) $\dfrac{a^2}{a}$
   (i) $\dfrac{4n^2}{n}$

5   Donna gets off the bus then takes n minutes to walk to the bank. She is in the bank for 8 minutes, then walks for $3n$ minutes to a supermarket. She spends m minutes in the supermarket, then takes 7 minutes to walk to a coffee shop to meet a friend. She stays for $5n$ minutes in the coffee shop. She then walks back to the bus stop, which takes 12 minutes. How long was it between Donna getting off the bus and then returning to the bus stop?

6   Mason says that $7n + 3n = 10n^2$. *Explain clearly* the mistake that Mason has made.

7   Kyle is three times older than Liz. Violet is 8 years younger than Kyle. How old is Violet if Liz is n years old?

8   Which shape has the longer perimeter and by how much? All lengths are in cm.

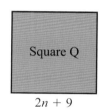

$n + 4$ | Rectangle P

$3n + 15$

Square Q

$2n + 9$

9   A chocolate bar costs a pence and a bottle of water costs b pence. How much change from £5 does Ryan get if he buys one bar of chocolate and two bottles of water?
Note that the answer is not £$(5 - a - 2b)$.

Substituting into a formula

(a) In the formula $s = ut$,

   s is for distance

   u is for speed

   t is for time

When $u = 9$ and $t = 10$, $s = ut = 9 \times 10 = 90$

(b) The mass m of a person of height h is given by the formula

   $m = 90h + 13$

   When $h = 1.7$,

   $m = 90h + 13 = 90 \times 1.7 + 13$

   $m = 166$

308

Exercise 2M

In questions ① to ⑩ you are given a formula. Find the value of the letter required in each case.

① $m = 4p + 6$

Find m when $p = 3$

② $x = 7y + 3$

Find x when $y = 5$

③ $a = \dfrac{b}{6} + 2$

Find a when $b = 18$

④ $c = \dfrac{d}{4} - 5$

Find c when $d = 20$

⑤ $q = 9w + 4$

Find q when $w = 7$

⑥ $m = 2n - 8$

Find m when $n = 10$

⑦ $y = \dfrac{x}{8} - 3$

Find y when $x = 48$

⑧ $v = 4(3w - 4)$

Find v when $w = 9$

⑨ $a = 5(2b + 1)$

Find a when $b = 6$

⑩ $g = \dfrac{6h + 4}{2}$

Find g when $h = 5$

⑪ The area of a triangle is given by $A = \dfrac{1}{2}bh$.

Find A when $b = 16$ and $h = 7$

⑫ The perimeter of a hexagon is given by the formula $p = 3x + 2y + w$.
Find p when $x = 5$, $y = 4$ and $w = 9$

⑬ Below are several different formulae for y in terms of x.
Find the value of y in each case.

(a) $y = 4x - 9$ $x = 2.5$

(b) $y = \dfrac{3x + 1}{2}$ $x = 3$

(c) $y = 6(5x + 3)$ $x = 1$

⑭ Here are some polygons.

Number of sides: 3   4   5
Sum of angles: 180°   360°   540°

The sum of the angles in a polygon with n sides is given by the

formula $\{$ sum of angles $= (n - 2) \times 180°$ $\}$

(a) Find the sum of the angles in a hexagon (6 sides).

(b) Find the sum of the angles in a polygon with 102 sides.

(c) Show that the formula gives the correct answer for the sum of the angles in a pentagon (5 sides).

15 The total surface area A of the solid cuboid
    shown is given by the formula

    $A = 2bc + 2ab + 2ac$

    Find the value of A when $a = 2, b = 3, c = 4$

Values of expressions

Below are three expressions involving a, b, c and d.
Find the value of each expression given that $a = 3, b = 2, c = 5, d = -1$

(i) $5a + 7$

$= 5 \times 3 + 7$

$= 15 + 7$

$= 22$

(ii) $2b + d$

$= 2 \times 2 + (-1)$

$= 4 - 1$

$= 3$

(iii) $ab + 5c$

$= (3 \times 2) + (5 \times 5)$

$= 6 + 25$

$= 31$

Notice that the working goes down the page, not across. This helps to avoid errors.

Exercise 3M

In questions 1 to 10 , find the value of each expression.

1 $3x + 2$ if $x = 5$

2 $4x - 3$ if $x = 2$

3 $6x - 5$ if $x = 2$

4 $8y + 7$ if $y = 4$

5 $23 + p$ if $p = 8$

6 $13 - m$ if $m = 6$

7 $6 + 4n$ if $n = 3$

8 $12 + 3q$ if $q = 7$

9 $32 - 5y$ if $y = 4$

10 $40 - 8x$ if $x = 3$

11 Find the value of these expressions when $n = 6$

(a) $6n + 2$ (b) $50 - n^2$ (c) $4(2n - 7)$

In questions 12 to 23 , find the value of the expressions given that $x = 4$ and $y = -2$

12 $x + 3$

13 $3(x + 2)$

14 x^2

15 $2(x - 2)$

16 $x + y$

17 $3y$

18 $2y + 1$

19 $x^2 - 9$

20 $\dfrac{x + 2}{x - 1}$

21 $8 - y$

22 y^2

23 $\dfrac{2 + y}{y}$

24 Given that $p = 40$ and $n = -10$, find the value of each of the following expressions.

(a) $2p + n$ (b) n^2 (c) $p - n$

(d) $n^2 - 2p$ (e) np (f) $p(p + 3n)$

25 Henry needs to work out the value of $8n - 3p$ when $n = 4$ and $p = -2$.
He writes $8n - 3p = 8 \times 4 - 3 \times (-2) = 32 - 6 = 26$.
Is he correct? If not, describe his mistake.

26 If $w = -9$, which expression has the larger value?

$w^2 + w$ or $7w + w$

Need more practice with algebra?

1 Using the formula $y = 70 + 3x$, find the value of y when

  (a) $x = 6$ (b) $x = 100$ (c) $x = 0.1$

2 In the formulae below, t is given in terms of n and a. Find the value of t in each case.

  (a) $t = 5a + 2n$ $a = 3,$ $n = 4$

  (b) $t = 6a + 3n - 10$ $a = 2,$ $n = 1$

  (c) $t = an + 7$ $a = 5,$ $n = 2$

3 When the wind velocity is v, the cost of damage, £C, is given by the formula
$C = 500v + 20\,000$

Find the cost of damage when $v = 100$

4 $p = \dfrac{9m + 3}{10}$

  Find p when $m = 3$

5 $y = 6(4x - 3)$

  Find y when $x = 7$

6 $a = b^2 + 17$

  Find a when $b = 5$

7 A father weighs n kg. His son weighs $\frac{3}{4}n$ kg and his daughter weighs $\frac{1}{2}n$ kg. How much more do the son and daughter weigh in total compared with the father's weight?

8 Which of the cards below have a value of 9 when $n = 3$?

$(6 - n)^2$ $8n - 14$ n^2 $3 + 2n$

$(2n - 1)^2$ $\dfrac{27}{n}$ $17 - 3n$

9 Using the formula $m = 35 + 2n$, find the value of m when

  (a) $n = -2$ (b) $n = -10$ (c) $n = \dfrac{1}{2}$

10 A pizza costs £m and a drink costs £3. Mandy and Gavin buy one pizza and two drinks in total. They split the cost. Write down an expression for how much Mandy pays.

11 Find the value of these expressions when $m = 0$

(a) $m^2 + 3$

(b) $\dfrac{5m}{2}$

(c) $18 - 3m$

12 Which expression below is the odd one out?

m^2n mnm nm^2 nmn mmn

Extension questions with algebra

1 Find the value of these expressions when $x = 4$

(a) $\dfrac{x + 8}{x}$

(b) $\dfrac{x + 5}{x - 3}$

(c) $\dfrac{1}{x} + \dfrac{3}{x}$

2 For each statement, answer 'true' or 'false'.

(a) $6 \times m = m \times 6$

(b) $2 \div n = n \div 2$

(c) $m + m = m^2$

(d) $a - b = -b + a$

(e) $3t - t = 2t$

(f) $n \times n \times n = n^3$

3 Suppose you add the numbers from 1 to 50: $1 + 2 + 3 + \ldots + 49 + 50$

The answer is $\dfrac{50 \times 51}{2} = 1275$

If you add the numbers from 1 to any number n, the answer is given by

the formula $\text{sum} = \dfrac{n(n + 1)}{2}$

(a) Use the formula to find the sum of the numbers from 1 to 10 (i.e. $1 + 2 + 3 + \ldots + 9 + 10$).

(b) Check your answer by adding the numbers in the normal way.

(c) Use the formula to find the sum of the numbers from 1 to 99

4 Gareth is n years old. Carol is four times older than Gareth and Ellie is 7 years older than Carol. Write down an expression for how much older Ellie is than Gareth.

5 Using the formula $h = 6(15 - y)$, find the value of h when

(a) $y = -5$

(b) $y = 10$

(c) $y = -10$

6 The area A of a red circle is given by the formula $A = 3r^2$.
Find the total area of 75 red circles if the value of r for each circle is 5

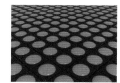

In questions ⑦ to ㉗ , find the value of the expressions, given that $a = 6$
$b = 5$
$c = 1$
$d = -3$

7 $4a - c$

8 $3b + a$

9 $b + d$

10 $4c - b$

11 $5b + c$

12 $a - d$

13 $7b + 8$

14 $a + b + d$

15 $c - 5$

16 $4a + d$

17 $a^2 + b^2$

18 $ab + c$

19 d^2

20 $3a + b + d$

21 $d^2 + 8$

22 $3d + c$

23 $d + 4b$

24 $4(a - c)$

25 $bc - d$

26 $b(b + c)$

27 $\dfrac{2a}{d}$

Race game

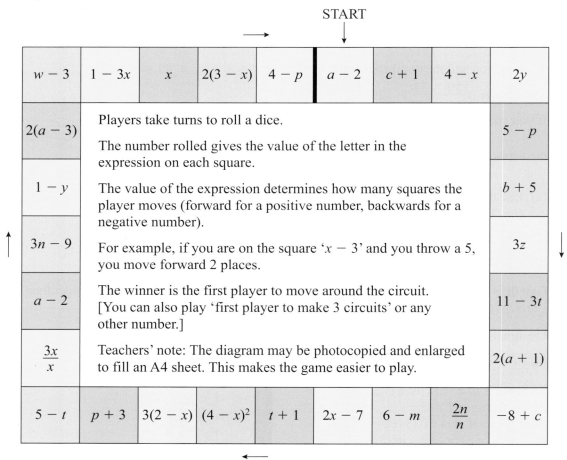

START

| $w - 3$ | $1 - 3x$ | x | $2(3 - x)$ | $4 - p$ | $a - 2$ | $c + 1$ | $4 - x$ | $2y$ |

$2(a - 3)$

Players take turns to roll a dice.

The number rolled gives the value of the letter in the expression on each square.

$5 - p$

$1 - y$

The value of the expression determines how many squares the player moves (forward for a positive number, backwards for a negative number).

$b + 5$

$3n - 9$

For example, if you are on the square '$x - 3$' and you throw a 5, you move forward 2 places.

$3z$

$a - 2$

The winner is the first player to move around the circuit. [You can also play 'first player to make 3 circuits' or any other number.]

$11 - 3t$

$\dfrac{3x}{x}$

Teachers' note: The diagram may be photocopied and enlarged to fill an A4 sheet. This makes the game easier to play.

$2(a + 1)$

| $5 - t$ | $p + 3$ | $3(2 - x)$ | $(4 - x)^2$ | $t + 1$ | $2x - 7$ | $6 - m$ | $\dfrac{2n}{n}$ | $-8 + c$ |

CHECK YOURSELF ON SECTIONS 5.1 and 5.2

1   Finding the *n*th term of an arithmetic sequence

(a) Look at the sequence and the table.
Find an expression for the *n*th term.

8, 13, 18, 23, ...

Difference between terms = 5

*n*th term = ☐

n	5*n*	term
1	5	8
2	10	13
3	15	18
4	20	23

(b) Look at the sequence 2, 9, 16, 23, ...
Write down the difference between terms. Use this to find an expression for the *n*th term.

2   Reviewing section 1 algebra

Simplify

(a) $4m + 3n + n - 2m$ (b) $5n \times 7n$ (c) $n^2 + n^2$

(d) A bag of nuts weighs 125 g. What is the weight of *m* bags?

(e) Is $\dfrac{m}{n}$ always equal to $\dfrac{n}{m}$?

3   Substituting numbers into formulae

(a) $m = \dfrac{n + 10}{2}$

Find *m* when $n = 20$

(b) $y = 4(3x - 1)$

Find *y* when $x = 7$

(c) Mark sells computers. The more computers he sells, the more money he is paid.

If he sells *n* computers in any month, his pay *P* (in pounds) for that month is given by the formula

$P = 800 + 50n$

The table below shows how many computers he sold in February.
How much was his pay for February?

week	number of computers sold
1	3
2	5
3	2
4	4

4   Working out values of expressions

Find the value of each expression.

(a) $7 - 3y$ if $y = 2$ (b) $3(x + 6)$ if $x = 3$

(c) $4p - 1$ if $p = -2$ (d) $5m - n$ if $m = 6$ and $n = -3$

5.3 Interpreting and sketching real-life graphs

In section 5.3 you will interpret and sketch a range of graphs

Exercise 1M

1   Which of the graphs **A** to **D** best fits each of the following statements?

(a) 'The price of petrol was steady for several years but has fallen recently.'

(b) 'The cost of air flights was falling slowly until 2020, but is now rising.'

(c) 'The birthrate in Italy has fallen steadily over the last decade.'

(d) 'The weight of the bird increased steadily after hatching.'

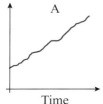
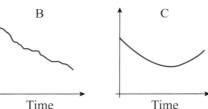
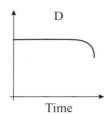

2   A scientist records the height of a growing plant every day for 20 days. The results are shown opposite.

(a) What was the height of the plant after 5 days?

(b) After how many days was the height

   (i) 70 cm   (ii) 105 cm?

(c) What was the greatest increase in height in one day?

(d) What was the full-grown height of the plant?

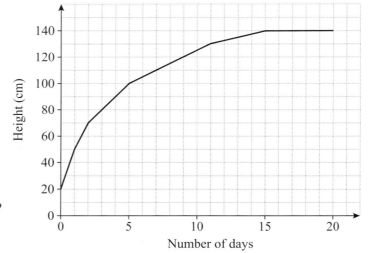

3 The graph shows the mass of crisps in a packet during the time after opening the packet.

(a) Were all the crisps eaten?

(b) What is the mass of a full packet of crisps?

(c) Explain the shape of the graph. Why are some vertical lines on the graph longer than others?

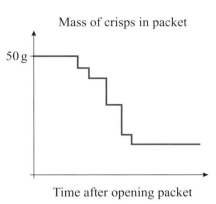

Mass of crisps in packet

50 g

Time after opening packet

4 A packet of frozen fish is taken out of a freezer and left on a kitchen table for 4 hours. The fish is then heated in a frying pan. Sketch a graph to show the temperature of the fish after it is taken from the freezer.

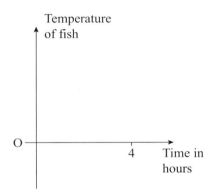

Temperature of fish

O   4   Time in hours

5 This diagram shows the temperature and rainfall readings in one week. The rainfall is shown as the bar chart. The temperature is shown as the line graph.

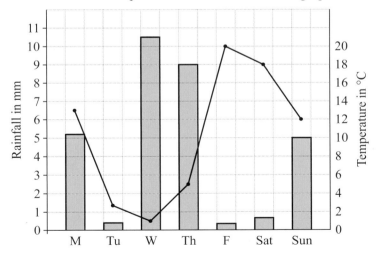

(a) Use *both* graphs to describe the weather on Wednesday.

(b) On which two days was the weather fairly wet and warm?

(c) Compare the weather on Tuesday and Saturday.

6 The graph shows a car journey from A to B and back to A.

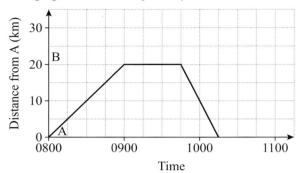

(a) How far is it from A to B?

(b) For how long does the car stop at B?

(c) At what two times is the car halfway between A and B?

7 This graph shows a car journey from London to Stevenage and back.

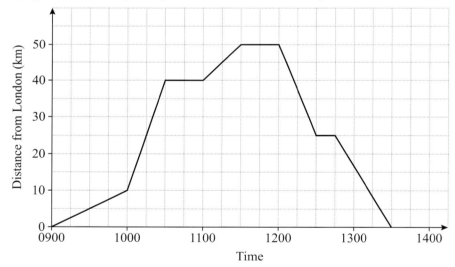

(a) For how long in the whole journey was the car at rest?

(b) At what time was the car half way to Stevenage on the outward journey?

(c) Between which two times was the car travelling at its highest speed?

Need more practice with interpreting and sketching real-life graphs?

1   The number of children inside a school is counted every ten minutes from 7.30 a.m. until 9.00 a.m., when the bell rings. The results are shown below.

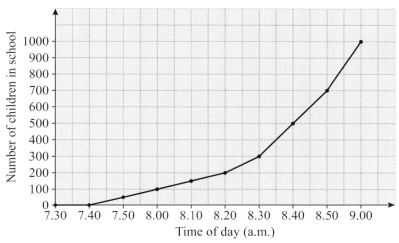

(a) How many children were inside the school at

    (i) 8.00 a.m.   (ii) 8.35 a.m.   (iii) 8.55 a.m.?

(b) How many children arrived between 7.30 a.m. and 8.30 a.m.?

(c) Estimate when the first children arrived.

(d) How many children arrived during the last 10 minutes before the bell rang at 9.00 a.m.?

(e) At what time were there 250 children in the school?

2   The graph shows the amount of petrol in the tank of a car.

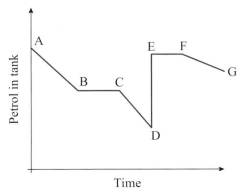

Explain briefly what you think is happening in each section of the graph:
AB, BC, CD, DE, EF, FG.

318

3  A graph is drawn to show the value of a car over a period of 4 years. The car was bought for £9000. At the end of the fourth year the car was in an accident. Sketch a graph to show how you think the value of the car might change over the years.

4 Water is poured at a constant rate into each of the containers A, B and C.
The graphs X, Y and Z show how the water level rises.
Decide which graph fits each container.
State your reasons.

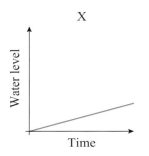
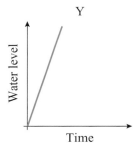
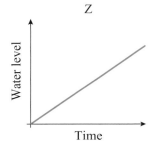

A   B   C

X   Y   Z

5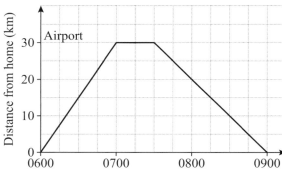

The graph above shows Sue's journey between home and the airport.

(a) When did she arrive at the airport?

(b) When did she arrive home?

(c) What happened between 0700 and 0730?

(d) At what speed did she travel

    (i) from home to the airport

    (ii) from the airport back to her home?

6   The graph shows a return journey from A.

(a) When is the car half way between A and C on the outward journey?

(b) Between what times does the car stop at B?

(c) When is the car half way between C and B on the return journey?

(d) Find the speed of the car

    (i)   from A to C

    (ii) from C back to B

    (iii) from B back to A.

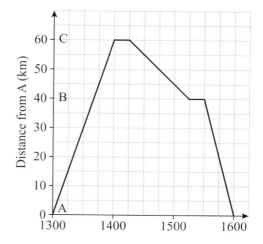

Extension questions with interpreting and sketching real-life graphs

1   (a) Draw axes that go up to 70 km on the vertical axis and up to 4 hours on the horizontal axis.

(b) Draw the graph for the following journey:

    Part 1. Car leaves home at 13:00 and travels at 40 km/h for 30 minutes.

    Part 2. Car stops for 45 minutes.

    Part 3. Car travels away from home at 50 km/h for one hour.

    Part 4. Car stops for 30 minutes.

    Part 5. Car returns home at 70 km/h.

(c) Answer the following questions.

    (i) How far from home is the car at 14:45?   (ii) At what time does the car return home?

2   The petrol consumption of a car depends on the speed, as shown opposite.

(a) What is the petrol consumption at a speed of

    (i)   30 km per hour

    (ii) 100 km per hour

    (iii) 180 km per hour?

(b) At what speed is the petrol consumption

    (i)   8 km per litre

    (ii) 12 km per litre

    (iii) 9 km per litre?

(c) At what speed should the car be driven in order to use the least amount of petrol?

(d) A car is driven at 160 km per hour. How far can it travel on 20 litres of petrol?

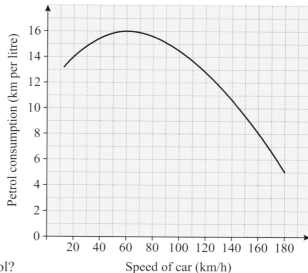

3 Draw a vertical axis which goes up to 50 km and a horizontal axis which goes up to 4 hours.

At 17 00 Lisa leaves her home and cycles at 20 km/h for 1 hour. She stops for $\frac{1}{4}$ hour and then continues her journey at a speed of 40 km/h for the next $\frac{1}{2}$ hour. She then stops for $\frac{3}{4}$ hour. Finally she returns home at a speed of 40 km/h.

Draw a travel graph to show Lisa's journey. When did she arrive home?

✖ Spot the mistakes 9 ✖

Sequences, simplifying algebraic terms, forming expressions, substituting into formulae and expressions, and using real-life graphs

Work through each question below and *explain clearly* what mistakes have been made.
Beware – some questions are correctly done.

1 Sophie has £n. Eva has five times as much money as Sophie and Eva has £25 more than Luke. Write down an expression for how much money Luke has.

Answer: Eva has £$(5n)$.

Luke has £$(5n + 25)$.

2 The nth term of a sequence is $4n - 3$. Write down the first 4 terms of the sequence.

Answer: 1st term $= 4 \times 1 - 3 = 1$
2nd term $= 4 \times 2 - 3 = 5$
3rd term $= 4 \times 3 - 3 = 9$
4th term $= 4 \times 4 - 3 = 13$

3 Simplify $5 \times m + 3 \times m \times p$
Answer: $8m^2p$

4 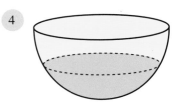 Some water is poured steadily into a hemispherical bowl. Sketch a graph to show how the height, h, of the water changes.

Answer: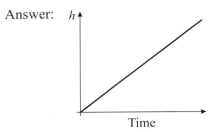

5

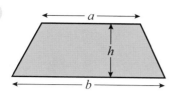

The formula for the area, A, of a trapezium is $A = \frac{1}{2}h(a + b)$.

Find the value of A when $h = 6$, $a = 3$ and $b = 7$

Answer: $A = \frac{1}{2}h(a + b)$

$A = \frac{1}{2} \times 6 \times (3 + 7)$

$A = 3 \times 5 = 15$

6 Find the value of $a^2 - ab$ if $a = -4$ and $b = -3$

Answer: $a^2 - ab = -4^2 - (-4) \times (-3)$

$= -16 - 12$

$= -28$

7 Here is a sequence made from sticks. How many sticks are in the nth diagram?

Answer: The number of sticks increases by 5 each time.

nth term $= n + 5$

   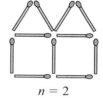   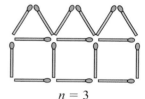

$n = 1$ $n = 2$ $n = 3$

8 Simplify $m^2 + m^2 + m^2$

Answer: m^6

9 Work out the nth term for the arithmetic sequence 25, 22, 19, 16, …

Answer: Difference between each pair of terms $= 3$

nth term $= 3n + 22$

10 The graph shows Amy's journey from home. At what time does Amy first stop?

Answer: 13:45

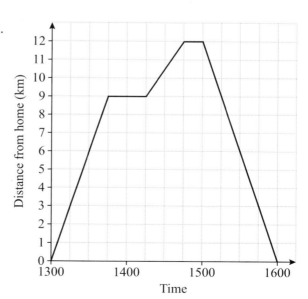

5.4 Ratio and proportion

In section 5.4 you will:

- tackle problems involving ratio and direct proportion
- share in ratios
- use map scales

Reminder: we use ratio to compare parts of a whole.

In a mixed class of 32 children, 17 are girls.

There must be 15 boys.

The ratio girls : boys is 17 : 15

Reminder: ratios can sometimes be written in a simpler form.

The ratios 6 : 10 and 3 : 5 are the same (divide by 2)

The ratios 15 : 20 : 30 and 3 : 4 : 6 are the same (divide by 5)

Exercise 1M

1. In a hall there are 45 chairs and 9 tables. Find the ratio of chairs to tables. Give your answer in its simplest form.

2. In an office there are twice as many men as women. Write down the ratio men : women.

3. In a group of people, the ratio of red umbrellas to other colours is 1 : 5. If there are 4 red umbrellas, how many umbrellas of a different colour are there?

4. Write these ratios in their simplest form.
   (a) 15 : 10   (b) 15 : 25   (c) 20 : 80   (d) 44 : 40   (e) 40 : 25   (f) 18 : 24

5. In a shop, the ratio of apples to pears is 5 : 2. If there are 200 pears, how many apples are there?

6. A factory produces mainly cars but also the occasional washing machine! The ratio of cars to washing machines is 5 : 1. One day 400 cars were made. How many washing machines were produced?

7   Magazines cost £20 for 8. Find the cost of 3 magazines. (Find the cost of 1 magazine first.)

8   If 5 hammers cost £23, find the cost of 7

9    During a snowstorm there are 474 cars in a 3 mile traffic jam. About how many cars are there in an 8 mile jam?

10 A worker takes 8 minutes to make 2 circuit boards.
    How long would it take to make 9 circuit boards?

11 The total weight of 8 tiles is 1720 g. How much do 17 tiles weigh?

12 On a Saturday the football results gave a ratio of home wins to away wins to draws of 6 : 2 : 1.
    If there were 10 away wins, how many home wins were there and how many draws were there?

13 Find the ratio (coloured area) : (uncoloured area) for each diagram.
    (a)   (b)   (c)
    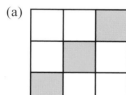 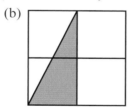 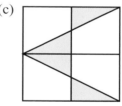

14 A group of people are asked what their favourite food is. $\frac{3}{7}$ of the people say curry and $\frac{1}{4}$ of the
    people say pizza. What proportion of the people do not say curry or pizza?

15 The ratio of dogs to cats in a village is 2 : 3. What fraction of these animals are dogs?

16
Christmas decorations	
baubles	£10.20 for 12
candles	£18.60 for 20
angels	£8 for 5

The prices of some Christmas decorations are shown opposite. Jim needs to buy 8 baubles and 12 candles. He also wants to buy as many angels as possible with the rest of his money. He has £20 to spend. How many angels can he buy with his left-over money?

Ratio and sharing

Share £63 between Ann, Ben and Carol in the ratio $2:3:4$. The ratio $2:3:4$ means we are dividing into '$2 + 3 + 4$' = 9 shares. £63 is split in to 9 shares, so 1 share = £63 ÷ 9 = £7

Ann gets 2 shares × £7 = £14

Ben gets 3 shares × £7 = £21

Carol gets 4 shares × £7 = £28

[Check: $14 + 21 + 28 = 63$✓]

Exercise 2M

1   Will and Chloe share a prize of £60 in the ratio $3:1$. How much does each person receive?

2   Alex and Debbie share a bag of 30 sweets in the ratio $3:2$.
    How many sweets does each person get?

3   Share each quantity in the ratio given.

    (a) 54 cm, $4:5$ (b) £99, $4:7$ (c) 132 km, $6:5$

    (d) £36, $2:3:4$ (e) 200 kg, $5:2:3$ (f) £2000, $1:9$

4   Two hungry dogs share a meal weighing
    650 g in the ratio $7:3$.
    Find the larger share.

5   Kate and Connor share 72 marbles in the ratio $4:5$.
    How many marbles does Connor get?

6   Find the largest share in each of these problems.

    (a) £56, ratio $3:5$

    (b) 90 kg, ratio $7:2$

    (c) 240 m, ratio $3:4:3$

7   The angles in a triangle are in the ratio $3:1:2$. Find the size of the three angles.

8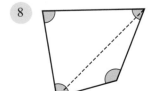
    The angles in a quadrilateral are in the ratio $2:2:3:2$.
    Find the largest angle in the quadrilateral.

9   In a kitchen, the ratio of forks to spoons is $7:9$.
    If there are 45 spoons, how many forks are there?

10   Gary and Ning share some sweets in the ratio 5 : 3. If Ning gets 21 sweets, how many sweets do they share out in total?

11   To make concrete you can mix 3 parts sand to 1 part cement.
How much sand do you need to make 8 tonnes of concrete?

12   The ratio of squash to water in a drink is 3 : 8. How much squash is used with 4 litres of water?

13   Some people play football on the beach.
The number of goals scored by Nick,
Savannah and Liam is in the ratio 3 : 4 : 1.
How many goals did Savannah score if
Nick scored 4 goals more than Liam?

14   Margo does a maths test. Her ratio of correct answers to incorrect answers is 3 : 2.
She gets 4 more answers right than wrong. How many questions does she get correct?

Map scales

On a map of scale 1 : 2 000 000,
Swansea and Cardiff appear
3 cm apart.

What is the actual distance between
the towns?

1 cm on map = 2 000 000 cm on land.

3 cm on map = 3 × 2 000 000 cm on land.

6 000 000 cm = 60 000 m
            = 60 km

Swansea is 60 km from Cardiff.

Exercise 3M

1   Convert each distance below into the suggested metric unit.
   (a) 650 cm → m
   (b) 900 cm → m
   (c) 5000 cm → m
   (d) 7200 cm → m
   (e) 7000 m → km
   (f) 12 500 m → km
   (g) 800 000 cm → km
   (h) 4 000 000 cm → km
   (i) 150 000 cm → km

2   On a map whose scale is 1 : 1000, the distance between two houses is 3 cm.
Find the actual distance between the two houses, giving your answer in metres.

3. The distance on a map between two points is 8 cm. Find the actual distance in metres between the two points, given that the scale of the map is 1 : 100

4. The scale of a certain map is 1 : 10 000. What is the actual distance in metres between two churches which are 4 cm apart on the map?

5. On a map whose scale is 1 : 100 000, the distance between two villages is 7 cm. What is the actual distance in kilometres between the two villages?

6. The distance on a map between two towns is 9 cm. Find the actual distance in kilometres between the two towns, given that the scale of the map is 1 : 1 000 000

7. Find the actual distance in metres between two towers which are 5 cm apart on a map whose scale is 1 : 10 000

8. A river is 5 cm long on a map whose scale is 1 : 20 000. Find the actual length of the river.

9. Andrew finds that the distance between two cities on a map whose scale is 1 : 5 000 000 is 12 cm. What is the actual distance in kilometres between the two cities?

10. If the distance between two places on a map is 10 cm, find the actual distance in kilometres between the two places, given that the scale of the map is 1 : 10 000

11. Sandra has two maps. There are train stations in Manley and Cowton. Map A has a scale of 1 : 20 000 and shows that Sandra is 17.5 cm from Manley. Map B has a scale of 1 : 50 000 and shows that Sandra is 6 cm from Cowton. Which train station should Sandra head for if she wants to walk the least distance? *Explain your answer.*

Need more practice with ratio and proportion?

1. Find the cost of 4 cakes if 7 cakes cost £10.50

2. In a room there are 18 women and 16 men. Find the ratio of women to men. Give your answer in its simplest form.

3. In a box, the ratio of apples to peaches to bananas is 3 : 1 : 2. If there are 8 peaches, how many apples are there and how many bananas are there?

4   Write these ratios in their simplest form.
   (a) $9:6:12$ (b) $40:5:15$ (c) $12:10:8$
   (d) $18:12:18$ (e) $70:10:50$ (f) $14:7:35$

5   In a firm, the ratio of women to men is $3:2$.
   If there are 14 men, how many women are there?

6   A machine can fill 3000 bottles in 15 minutes. How many bottles will it fill in 2 minutes?

7   Louis says that the ratio $3\,m:60\,cm$ can be simplified to $5:1$
   Xanthe does not agree. She says the simplified ratio will be $1:20$
   Who is correct? Give full reasons for your answer.

8
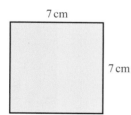

Two squares are shown.
   (a) Write down the ratio of the lengths of their sides.
   (b) Work out the ratio of their areas.

9   Two places are separated by a distance of 20 cm on a map with a scale of $1:6000$
   How far apart in reality are the two places?

10 The scale of a map is $1:200\,000$. What is the actual distance between two villages given that
   they are 8.5 cm apart on the map?

11 $\frac{7}{10}$ of the people who live in a village go to the village fête one July. Write down the ratio of the
   number of people from the village who went to the fête compared with the number of people
   who did not go.

12 Find the smallest share in each of these problems.
   (a) £60, ratio $1:11$
   (b) 48 cm, ratio $2:1$
   (c) 42 litres, ratio $2:3:2$

13 If two towns are 5.4 cm apart on a map and the scale of the map is $1:3\,000\,000$,
   what is the actual distance between the two towns?

14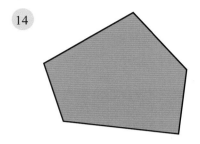

The sum of the interior angles of
a pentagon is 540°.
The ratio of the angles in the pentagon
is 2 : 3 : 4 : 4 : 5.
The ratio of the angles in a
quadrilateral is 1 : 2 : 2 : 4.
Which shape has the largest angle
and by how much is it greater than
the largest angle in the other shape?

Extension questions with ratio and proportion

1. £15 can be exchanged for 18 euros. How many euros can be exchanged for £37.50?

2. A car travels 280 km on 35 litres of petrol. How much petrol is needed for a journey of 440 km?

3. $\frac{2}{9}$ of a stretch of motorway has roadworks. Write down the ratio of motorway with roadworks
   to motorway with no roadworks.

4. The distance on a map between
   buildings A and B is 3 cm
   The scale of the map is 1 : 50 000
   Another map has scale 1 : 80 000
   Buildings C and D are 2 cm apart on this map.

   Which actual distance is greater and by how much:

   the distance between A and B or the distance between C and D?

5. All the numbers in a ratio can be multiplied by the same number, for example: $\frac{1}{2} : 3 = 1 : 6$
   (both the numbers $\frac{1}{2}$ and 3 are multiplied by 2).

   Multiply so that the ratios below only contain whole numbers.
   Write the ratios in their simplest form.

   (a) $\frac{1}{3} : 4$ (b) $\frac{1}{4} : \frac{1}{2}$ (c) $0.3 : 0.8$

   (d) $0.02 : 0.3$ (e) $\frac{2}{5} : \frac{7}{10}$ (f) $0.01 : 2$

   (g) $0.2 : 0.06$ (h) $\frac{1}{8} : \frac{7}{8}$ (i) $0.5 : \frac{3}{4}$

6. If 4 grapefruit can be bought for £2.96, how many can be bought for £8.14?

7  Carl and Simone jet ski 25 km in 30 minutes.
How long will they take to jet ski 40 km at the same speed?

8 The ratio $m : n = 1 : 2$ and the ratio $n : p = 4 : 5$.
Write down the ratio $m : p$.

9 Which box of biscuits
offers the best value?
Explain your answer fully.

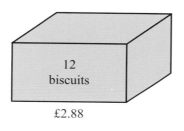

12
biscuits

£2.88

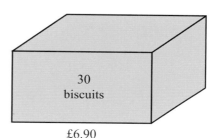

30
biscuits

£6.90

10 Mrs Turner gives Sam and Robyn £360
in the ratio 1 : 3.
Mr Harris gives Alana, Bill and Julie £320
in the ratio 2 : 1 : 5.
A digital camera costs £197.50.
Sam and Alana want to put their money together
to buy the camera.
They do not have enough money so Robyn
gives them the rest of the money for the camera.
How much money does Robyn have to give them?

11 Tom has some mints, toffees and chocolates. The ratio of mints to toffees is 4 : 7 and the ratio
of toffees to chocolates is 3 : 5. How many chocolates does Tom have if he has 12 mints?

12 £1200 is shared between Aaliyah, Alex and Vanya in the ratio 5 : 3 : 2.
Some other money is shared in the ratio 4 : 3 : 8 between Jocelyn, Asha and Christian.
Jocelyn gets £600.
Which two people get a total of £810 between them?

CHECK YOURSELF ON SECTIONS 5.3 and 5.4

1   Interpreting and sketching a range of graphs

(a) The graph shows the water level when Simon has a bath.

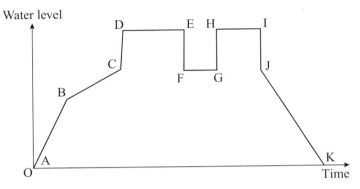

For JK the 'bath is being emptied'. Describe what is happening for each part of the graph. Here are some possibilities:

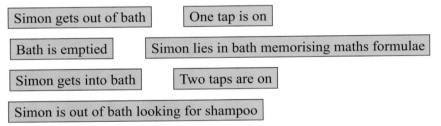

Simon gets out of bath   One tap is on

Bath is emptied   Simon lies in bath memorising maths formulae

Simon gets into bath   Two taps are on

Simon is out of bath looking for shampoo

(b) Draw a vertical axis which goes from 0 km to 60 km. Draw a horizontal axis which goes from the time 12:00 up to 16:00

Draw a travel graph to show Helen's journey below.

'At 12:00 Helen leaves home and travels at a speed of 30 km/h. At 13:00 she stops for $\frac{1}{2}$ hour and then continues her journey at a speed of 60 km/h for the next $\frac{1}{2}$ hour. She then stops for $\frac{1}{4}$ hour. Finally she returns home at a speed of 60 km/h.'

(c) At what time did Helen arrive home?

2   Tackling problems involving ratio and direct proportion

(a) In a cinema there are 45 adults and 27 children.
Write down the ratio of adults to children in its simplest form.

(b) Find the cost of 2 footballs if 7 footballs cost £37.80

(c) Some hikers take 6 hours to walk 21 km.
At the same pace of walking, how long would it take them to travel 35 km?

3 Sharing in ratios

(a) The ratio of red cubes to white cubes is 1 : 26.
Another solid is made using the same ratio of cubes.
How many white cubes are used if 6 red cubes are used?

(b) £360 is shared in the ratio 4 : 2 : 3.
How much is the largest share?

4 Using map scales

(a) The distance on a map between two houses is 4 cm. The scale of the map is 1 : 50 000
What is the actual distance in kilometres between the two houses?

(b) On a map whose scale is 1 : 20 000, the length of a field is 3 cm.
What is the actual length of the field in metres?

5.5 Percentages 2

In section 5.5 you will:

- review section 2 percentages
- calculate simple interest
- find percentage profit and loss

Decrease £60 by 5%

10% of 60 = $\frac{1}{10}$ of 60 = 6

5% of 60 = 3

Answer = 60 − 3 = £57

Exercise 1M

Do not use a calculator in this exercise.

1 A factory employs 1600 people. On one day 8% of the people are absent.
How many people work in the factory on that day?

2 Jackie does a test which is marked out of 40. If she gets a score of 65%, how many marks out of 40 did she get?

3 Work out the price of each item in the sale.

(a)
Jacket
£140
35% off

(b)
Shirt
£25
20% off

(c)
Shoes
£50
30% off

(d)
Umbrella
£15
40% off

4 There are 16 biscuits in a box. Mervyn eats 4 of the biscuits. What percentage of all the biscuits has Mervyn eaten?

5 11 out of 25 people who live on Broad Street go on a foreign holiday one year. 9 out of 20 people who live on Narrow Lane also go on a foreign holiday one year. What is the difference in the percentage of people who go on a foreign holiday between the 2 roads?

6 All train prices are increased by 5%. A train ticket costs £110. What is the new price after the increase?

7 Charlie scored $\frac{16}{25}$ in a science test and Holly scored 62%. Who scored the higher mark and by how much?

8 Penny is to have her loft insulated. A contractor makes an estimate of £320 and offers a 15% discount for prompt payment. What would this reduced price be?

9 Which answer is the odd one out?

30% of £80   35% of £70   20% of £120

10 Wesley weighs 90 kg and Edgar weighs 85 kg. They both eat more sensibly and exercise more. Wesley loses 10% weight and Edgar loses 15% weight. How much more does Wesley now weigh than Edgar?

Remember: a calculator has a % button. Use it when you can!

Exercise 2M

You may use a calculator.

1 (a) Increase £238 by 8%   (b) Decrease £64 by 12%
  (c) Reduce £419 by 32%   (d) Increase £17 by 9%

2   Tyler skips 400 times each day.
During one week he increases this by 12%.
How many times does Tyler skip during this entire week?

3   An electric cooker costs £425. Its price is reduced by 18%.
What is the new price of the cooker?

4

	swim	rounders	total
male	32	11	43
female	17	29	46
total	49	40	89

One afternoon on holiday, the people in a group either swim or play rounders. The table shows how many males and females did each activity.
(a) What percentage of the males played rounders?
(b) What percentage of the people were female?

5   An iron is priced at £42. Mr Denby works for the store and gets an 8% reduction on any item he buys from the store. How much would Mr Denby pay for the iron?

6   An auction house receives a 9% commission on everything it sells.
During February it sells the following amounts.

week 1	£7488
week 2	£12 650
week 3	£11 864
week 4	£6882

How much commission does the auction house receive in February?

7   Match each given fraction or decimal to one of the percentages below them.

| $\frac{9}{60}$ | 0.4 | $\frac{1}{4}$ | $\frac{54}{90}$ | $\frac{7}{40}$ | 0.04 |

| 17.5% | 15% | 4% | 60% | 25% | 40% |

8   Madeline earns £420 each week and Justin earns £446. Madeline is given a 7% pay rise. Does she now earn more or less than Justin and by how much?

9   During August a stationery shop sells £9200 of goods.
In September this amount increases by 23%.
In October the amount of sales decreases by 23% of the September sales.
How much money does the shop take in October?

10 Deals are offered on the same digital radio in two different stores. The VAT rate is 20%

> Electric House
> £90
> +VAT
> 15% reduction

> Sparks
> £115
> 20% reduction

In which store is the radio cheaper and by how much?

Simple interest

If people invest money, for example in a bank, they usually receive extra money, called *interest*.

If people borrow money, they may have to pay back extra money, called *interest*.

Simple interest is the interest calculated at a fixed yearly rate on the sum of money involved.

£3000 is invested at 10% per annum (year) simple interest.

How much money will there be after 4 years?

Simple interest for 1 year = 10% of £3000 = 300

Interest for 4 years   = 300 × 4 = 1200

Total money after 4 years = 3000 + 1200 = £4200

Exercise 3M

Use a calculator if needed.

1 £2500 is invested at 10% per annum (year) simple interest.
  (a) How much interest is made over 3 years?
  (b) Find the total amount of money invested after 3 years.

2 £8000 is invested at 6% per annum simple interest.
  (a) How much money is made over 5 years?
  (b) Find the total amount of money invested after 5 years.

3 Find the total amount of money invested after the number of years shown.

	Money invested	Simple interest rate	Number of years
(a)	£1000	7%	4
(b)	£7000	3%	3
(c)	£3600	9%	10
(d)	£750	5%	4
(e)	£20 000	4%	25
(f)	£1378	11%	5

4 Wasim borrows £1500 from a friend. He has to pay back the loan after 2 years.
His friend charges Wasim 5% per annum simple interest.
How much money does Wasim have to pay back in total?

5 A museum needs to borrow £15 000.
The museum is charged 4% per annum simple interest.
The museum pays back all the money after 5 years.
How much money does the museum pay back?

6 Helena invests £6500 in a bank at 4% per annum
simple interest. Guy invests £8200 at 3% per annum
simple interest. Who makes more interest after 3 years
and by how much?

7 Madeline borrows £85 000 to buy a hot air balloon. She is charged 3.5% per annum simple
interest. How much will she pay in total if she pays back all the money after 7 years?

8 Rohan invests £9000 in a building society at 2.5% per annum simple interest.
Naomi invests £8500 at 4% per annum simple interest.
Who has more money after 5 years and by how much?

9

Smart Bank	Sound Society
4.5% per annum simple interest	3.75% per annum simple interest

Alf has £4900 to invest in Smart Bank
or the Sound Society.
How much more interest will he make
each year if he puts his money in the
Smart Bank?

10 Julia borrows £12 200 at $6\frac{1}{4}$% per annum simple interest.
How much interest will she be charged if she repays the loan after 7 years?

Percentage profit and loss

The *original* price of an item is the *cost price*.

Actual profit = selling price − cost price

> Percentage profit = $\dfrac{\text{actual profit}}{\text{cost price}} \times 100\%$

If an item is sold at a loss,

> Percentage loss = $\dfrac{\text{actual loss}}{\text{cost price}} \times 100\%$

The cost price of fish and chips is £5. It costs £7 to buy the fish and chips in a restaurant. What percentage profit does the restaurant make on the fish and chips?

actual profit = 7 − 5 = £2

percentage profit = $\left(\dfrac{2}{5}\right) \times 100 = 40\%$

                   ↑
cost price

Exercise 4M

Use a calculator if needed.

1. Clement makes tables. It costs £60 to make a table. What percentage profit does Clement make if he sells a table for £114?

2. An antique dealer buys a piece of armour for £720.
   The dealer sells the armour for £972.
   What percentage profit does the dealer make?

3. Georgina buys shares in a company for £14 000.
   Two years later, she needs the money and sells the
   shares for £11 900.
   Work out the percentage loss in the value of the shares.

4

	Cost price	Selling price
(a)	£280	£350
(b)	£510	£663
(c)	£80	£108
(d)	£790	£726.26
(e)	£9	£7.20

Work out the percentage profit or loss in each case.

5 Mr Cumberwell invests £9200 in a bank. Five years later, his investment is worth £10 672. What percentage profit has he made?

6 A very wealthy person buys an island for £53 000 000.
During hard financial times, the person has to sell the island for £32 860 000.
What is the percentage loss?

7 In a supermarket, an orange costs 45p The supermarket buys the oranges at £25 per 100. What percentage profit does the supermarket make if every orange is sold?

8 A shop buys 40 magazines at £1.60 each. The shop sells 35 of these magazines at £3 each. What overall percentage profit does the shop make on these magazines? Give your answer to the nearest whole number.

9

A store buys light bulbs at £400 per 250.
Each light bulb is sold for £2.88 each.
What percentage profit does the store make if it sells all the light bulbs?

10 Frankie buys 3 bikes at £90 each, 5 pushchairs at £220 each and 2 swings at £45 each. She manages to sell 2 of the bikes for £170 each, 4 pushchairs for £350 each and both swings for £60 each. She keeps 1 bike and 1 pushchair for herself. Work out her overall percentage profit. Give your answer to the nearest whole number.

Need more practice with percentages?

1 Danny buys a house in 2017 for £210 000. In 2020 he sells the house and makes a 15% profit. How much does he sell the house for?

2 Change the following to percentages.
(a) 0.8   (b) 0.08   (c) $\frac{7}{20}$ (d) $\frac{1}{4}$ (e) 0.36   (f) $\frac{19}{25}$ (g) $\frac{1}{3}$ (h) 0.2

3 Which is greater: $\frac{17}{20}$ or 83%? Justify your answer.

4 A computer costs £880 plus VAT.
   How much does the computer cost if the VAT rate is 20%?

5 The 2019 price of a weekend trip to London was £520.
   Calculate the 2020 price, which is 5% higher.

6 The pass mark in an exam is 40%. Martina scores $\frac{11}{25}$.
   Does she pass the exam?
   Give a reason for your answer.

7 £4500 is invested in a bank at 4% per annum simple interest.
   How much money is in the bank after 3 years?

8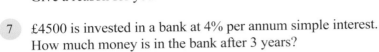

Tracksuit	Trainers	Golf balls	Sweatshirt
£58	£70	£28	£36
45% off	60% off	5% off	12% off

   Richard is in a sports shop. He has £30. Which of the above items could he afford to buy?
   Give reasons for your answer.

9 Nikolai buys a table for £85 and sells it for £153.
   What percentage profit does Nikolai make on the sale of the table?

10 The table shows the number of British passengers
   on 2 planes. What percentage of the passengers on
   both planes are British?
   Give the answer to 1 decimal place.

	Plane A	Plane B
British passengers	153	72
Total passengers	342	217

11 A TV costs £240 plus VAT (20%). Estelle pays for the TV in 12 equal monthly instalments.
   How much does Estelle pay each month?

12 Des buys 144 umbrellas for a total of £792.
   He sells 110 of the umbrellas for £12 each and the remaining umbrellas for £6 each.
   What percentage profit did Des make overall? Give the answer to 1 decimal place.

Extension questions with percentages

1 Decrease £16.50 by 8.2%. Give your answer to the nearest penny.

2 A meal costs £78.25. A service charge of 15% is added to the bill.
   Work out the total bill that needs to be paid.

3 Diya books a holiday for £418.85. Due to a fall in fuel prices, she is given an 8% discount. How much does her holiday now cost?

4 For each part of the question, work out the value of the savings after the amount of time shown.

	Investment	Simple interest	Time
(a)	£2500	3%	2 years 6 months
(b)	£7000	$2\frac{1}{2}$%	4 years 6 months
(c)	£1800	$5\frac{1}{2}$%	1 year 9 months
(d)	£340	$1\frac{3}{4}$%	3 years 3 months
(e)	£15 600	$7\frac{1}{4}$%	6 years 3 months

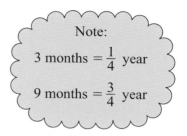

Note:

3 months = $\frac{1}{4}$ year

9 months = $\frac{3}{4}$ year

5 In a spelling test Aysha got 52 out of 80. What was her mark as a percentage?

6 Write in order of size, smallest first.

82% $\frac{17}{20}$ 0.8   0.09 $\frac{3}{5}$ $\frac{30}{40}$ 73%

7 Dai invests £5000 in a bank at $3\frac{1}{2}$% simple interest. After 1 year 6 months, Dai takes all his money out of this bank and puts it in a building society at $4\frac{1}{4}$% per annum simple interest. How much money will Dai have after a further 3 years 6 months?

8

Remember: percentage increase = $\left(\dfrac{\text{actual increase}}{\text{original value}}\right) \times 100$

percentage decrease = $\left(\dfrac{\text{actual decrease}}{\text{original value}}\right) \times 100$

A person changes diet and increases the amount of exercise undertaken.
This person's weight decreases from 74 kg to 69 kg.
Work out the percentage decrease in weight.

9 Lin plays the violin.
During one year she plays in 23 concerts.
During the next year she plays in 31 concerts.
What is the percentage increase in the number of concerts she plays in during the second year compared to the first year?

10 In April a landlord increases Freya's rent from £520 per month to £560.
The new rent is then increased by 5% in December.
What is now the overall percentage increase in Freya's rent from the original £520?

11 The price of an £80 chair is increased to £108 and the price of a £195 wardrobe is increased to £257.40. Which item has the greater percentage increase and by how much?

5.6 Statistics review

In section 5.6 you will review averages, range, charts and probability

Averages from a table – reminder

The frequency table shows the number of pieces of fruit eaten by some children one day.

number of pieces of fruit	0	1	2	3	4
frequency	6	17	11	4	2

(a) mean $= \dfrac{(0 \times 6) + (1 \times 17) + (2 \times 11) + (3 \times 4) + (4 \times 2)}{40}$

mean $= \dfrac{59}{40} = 1.475$

(b) The modal number of pieces of fruit is 1, since the frequency for 1 is highest (i.e. 17).

Exercise 1M

1. | 6 | | 3 | | 11 | | 2 | | 8 | | 9 | | 2 | | 7 |

Which is greater for the numbers above and by how much: the mean or the median?

2. The probability that John eats an egg in the morning is 0.85. What is the probability that John does not eat an egg?

3.

Stem	Leaf
4	1 2 4 9 9
5	0 3 3 6 7 8 8
6	1 4 5 5 5 6 7 9
7	0 0 4 5 7 7 9
8	1 3 3 6

Key 6|5 means 65%

Class 8C take a maths exam. Their marks are shown in the stem and leaf diagram.

(a) How many students scored more than 70%?

(b) What was the median mark for the class?

4.

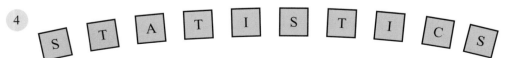

One card is chosen from above. Write down the probability that the card is

(a) the letter 'A'

(b) the letter 'S'

(c) a vowel.

5

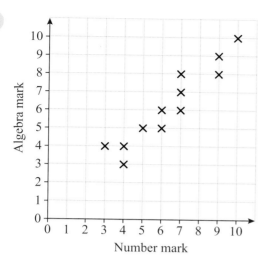

Some students do a number test and an algebra test.
Their marks out of 10 are shown on the scatter graph.

(a) Describe the correlation.

(b) What would you expect the algebra mark to be for a student who scored 8 in the number test?

6 This spinner is spun 480 times.
How often would you expect to spin

(a) an odd number

(b) a number less than 4

(c) a prime number

(d) a square number?

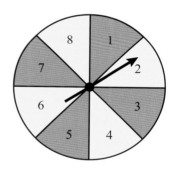

7

| 10 | | 2 | | 11 | | 10 | | ? | | ? |

The mode of the numbers above is 2. Write down the median value.

8 The goals scored by 20 teams in the football premiership one weekend are shown in the table opposite.

number of goals	0	1	2	3	4	5
frequency	6	5	4	3	1	1

(a) Work out the mean number of goals scored.

(b) Write down the modal number of goals scored.

9 The pie chart shows how Tina spends each 24 hours.
For how many hours is she not sleeping or cooking?

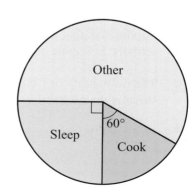

10   This two-way table shows how many boys and girls are in Years 8 and 9 in a school.

	Year 8	Year 9	Total
Boys		136	245
Girls	130		
Total			500

(a) Copy and complete the table.

(b) How many girls are in Year 9?

(c) What percentage of all the children are boys?

Need more practice with statistics?

1   The weights of 8 people are shown below.

| 58 kg | 73 kg | 72 kg | 68 kg |
| 79 kg | 52 kg | 64 kg | 73 kg |

The heaviest person and the lightest person leave.
What is the mean weight of the remaining people?

2   A bowl contains the fruit shown opposite. One piece of fruit is taken out at random. Which fruit has a probability of $\frac{3}{16}$ of being chosen? Justify your answer.

13 apples	4 peaches
9 oranges	6 pears

3   The pie charts below show what proportion of students went on Year 7 camp last year in three schools.

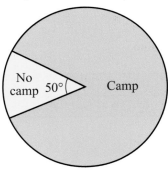

Marley High School

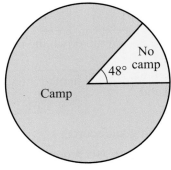

Beechwood School

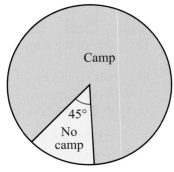

Hanly School

Sophie says that more people went to camp from Hanly School than from each of the other schools. Is Sophie correct? Justify your answer.

4   The probability of Denton scoring more than 50% in his next science test is 0.65.
What is the probability that Denton will score 50% or less in his next science test?

5   Work out the mean average score on one side of a dice.

6 Miya has the following cards to choose from:

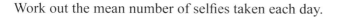

| 2 | 4 | 5 | 8 | 11 | 15 | 21 |

She removes all the prime numbers then chooses one card at random.
What is the probability that she will choose an odd number?

7 Melissa enjoys taking selfies. The number of selfies taken
each day last week is shown in the table.

number of selfies	10	15	20
frequency	2	3	2

Work out the mean number of selfies taken each day.

8 A scatter graph shows negative correlation. *Describe* what this scatter graph will look like.

9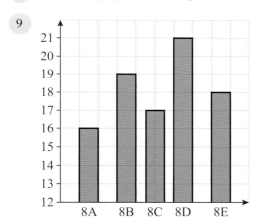

The bar chart shows how many students from each
of five Year 8 classes bring packed lunches.
Write down two things which are wrong with this
bar chart.

10
Stem	Leaf
2	2 6 6
3	1 5 9 9
4	0 1 1 2 5
5	3 3 3 4 8 8
6	0 4 7

Key 4 | 5 means 45 years old

The stem and leaf diagram shows the ages of
people in the Stowchester drama group.
The ages of people in the Avalon drama group are
listed below.

27	37	41	53	42	18
38	40	27	23	36	47
52	27	19	48	53	39
36	18	37	23	42	31

Write one or two sentences to compare the ages of the two drama clubs (i.e. compare an
average and the ranges to show how spread out the ages are).

Extension questions with statistics

1 The probability of a netball team winning the next game is 0.45 and the probability of drawing the next game is 0.2. What is the probability that the netball team loses the next game?

2 A group of people are asked what their favourite type of music is. The information is recorded in the table opposite.
Draw an accurate pie chart to show this information.

Type	Frequency
Blues	20
Classical	35
Hip hop	25
Jazz	10
Other	30

3

Stem	Leaf
3	2 2 3 5 7
4	0 1 3 3 5 6 6 8
5	1 2 2 2 3 8 9
6	3 4 4 7 9

Key 4|3 means 4.3 cm

The heights of some small plants are measured and recorded in the stem and leaf diagram.
Work out the mean height of the plants.

4 The table below shows how many counters of each colour are in a bag.

Colour	Red	Blue	Green	Yellow
Number of counters	7	3	6	4

A counter is repeatedly taken out of the bag then replaced. A counter is to be removed and replaced 200 times. How many times would the counter be expected to be red?

5

| 8 | 8 | 9 | 9 | ? | ? |

In the list of six positive numbers above, the mode is 9 and the range is 9.
Work out the mean for these six numbers.

6 The table below shows how many cups of tea are sold from a kiosk each day during a fortnight and the average temperature on each of these days.

Temperature (°C)	25	28	28	27	32	24	27	25	30	28	26	23	26	29
Number of cups of tea	45	30	15	40	5	60	25	55	15	20	35	60	40	20

(a) Draw a scatter graph to show this data.

(b) Describe the correlation.

(c) How many cups of tea might the kiosk expect to sell if the temperature was 31°C?

7 A bag contains yellow, white and pink balls. The table shows the probability of removing each colour when one ball is taken out of the bag at random.

Colour	Yellow	White	Pink
Probability	?	0.3	?

(a) What is the probability of removing a yellow ball if it is equal to the probability of removing a pink ball?

(b) If a ball is removed and replaced 50 times, how many times would it be expected to be white?

8 15 people have a mean weight of 60 kg.

(a) Work out the total weight of all the people.

(b) A new person, weighing 76 kg, joins the group. Work out the mean weight of all 16 people.

9 The pie charts show how Jordan and Madeline spend their money each month.

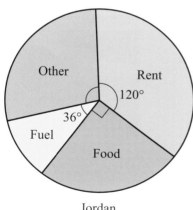

Jordan

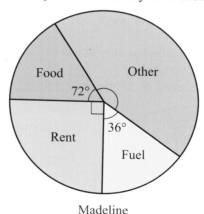

Madeline

Jordan earns £1200 each month and Madeline earns £1500

(a) Who spends more on food?

(b) Who has more money to spend on 'other' things and by how much?

10 The number of children in 50 families in a village is recorded below.

Number of children	0	1	2	3	4	5
Frequency	14	13	15	5	2	1

Which is greater and by how much: the mean number of children per family or the modal number of children per family?

✗ Spot the mistakes 10 ✗

Ratio, proportion, percentages and statistics

Work through each question below and *explain clearly* what mistakes have been made.
Beware – some questions are correctly done.

1   Simplify the ratio 50 cm : 2 m

Answer: Divide each part by 2
                50 : 2 = 25 : 1

2   Increase £74 by 4%

Answer: 1% of 74 = 7.4
        4% of 74 = 4 × 7.4 = 29.6
                         = £29.60
Final answer is £74 + £29.60 = £103.60

$$\begin{array}{r} 7\ 4 \\ \times \quad 4 \\ \hline 2\ 9\ 6 \\ {}^{1} \end{array}$$

3   The ratio of men to women in a cinema is 3 : 5
    What proportion of the people in the cinema are men?

Answer: 3 men in every 8 people, so $\frac{3}{8}$ of the people in the cinema are men.

4   300 people are asked what they like doing
    best at a swimming pool.
    The results are shown in the pie chart below.

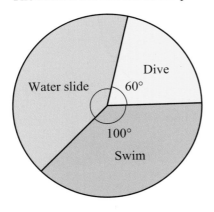

How many people
like diving best?

Answer: $\frac{60}{100} \times 300$

$= \frac{18\,000}{100} = 180$ people

5

Work out the median for the numbers above.

Answer: Write the numbers in order:

        1, 2, 2, 5, 8, 8

The median is half-way, so the median = 3

6   Some sweets are shared between Hattie and Ryan in the ratio 11 : 4
How many sweets does Hattie get if Ryan gets 60 sweets?

Answer: Total shares $= 11 + 4 = 15$

15 shares are 60 sweets

1 share is $\dfrac{60}{15} = 4$ sweets

Hattie gets $11 \times 4 = 44$ sweets.

7   The number of garages are counted at some houses.
The results are shown opposite.
Work out the mean number of garages per house.

Number of garages	Frequency
0	5
1	6
2	3
3	2

Answer: Total number of garages $= 0 + 1 + 2 + 3 = 6$

mean $= \dfrac{6}{4} = 1.5$ garages per house.

8   £3000 is invested at 6% per annum simple interest.
How much money will be invested after 3 years?

Answer: 1% of 3000 $= \dfrac{1}{100}$ of 3000 $= £30$

6% of 3000 $= £30 \times 6 = £180$

Interest for 3 years $= £180 \times 3 = £540$

Money invested $= £3000 + £540 = £3540$

9

A map has a scale 1 : 20 000
The distance from Hemp Wood to the village of
Malby is measured as 3 cm on the map.
What is the real distance from Hemp Wood to Malby?

Answer: $3 \times 20\,000 = 60\,000$ cm
$\qquad\qquad\qquad\quad = 6000$ m
$\qquad\qquad\qquad\quad = 6$ km

10   Arnold buys 20 jackets for £23 each. He sells 14 of the jackets for £48 each and the remaining
jackets for £20 each. What percentage profit does Arnold make on the jackets?

Answer: Cost price $= 20 \times 23 = £460$

Selling price $= (14 \times 48) + (6 \times 20)$
$\qquad\qquad\quad = 672 + 120$
$\qquad\qquad\quad = £792$

Profit $= 792 - 460 = £332$

Percentage profit $= \dfrac{332}{792} \times 100$

$\qquad\qquad\qquad\quad = 41.9\%$ (to 1 decimal place)

CHECK YOURSELF ON SECTIONS 5.5 and 5.6

1   Reviewing section 2 percentages

    (a) Esther has a 5% pay rise on her salary of £18 600.
        How much is her new salary?

    (b) Gavin scores $\frac{18}{25}$ in a test. What is his percentage mark?

    (c) Mr Harris manages to get an antique dealer to knock 18% off a £620 cabinet.
        How much does Mr Harris pay for the cabinet?

2   Calculating simple interest

    (a) £4000 is invested at 3% per annum simple interest. How much interest is made over 5 years?

    (b) Penny borrows £9500 to buy a car. She is charged 5% per annum simple interest.
        She pays back the loan after 2 years. How much money does she pay back in total?

3   Finding percentage profit and loss

    (a) Josephine buys a bike for £420. She sells it 2 years later for £294. What is the percentage loss?

    (b) A grocer buys bananas for £40 for 200. The grocer sells 150 bananas for £45 and each
        remaining banana is sold for 30p each.
        What percentage profit does the grocer make on these bananas?

4   Reviewing statistics

    (a) The table shows the number of bathrooms in various houses.

Number of bathrooms	1	2	3	4	5
Frequency	18	12	9	8	3

        Work out the mean number of bathrooms per house.

    (b)

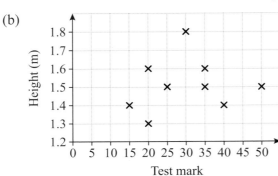

The scatter graph shows the heights and test marks of some students.

    (i) Describe the correlation.

    (ii) Work out the median test mark.

5.7 Applying mathematics 5

In section 5.7 you will apply maths in a variety of situations.

1   A 375 g packet of Greek currants costs £1.14.
    Calculate the cost of a 500 g packet if both packets represent the same value for money.

2   A computer costs £790 + VAT (20%). The overall cost of the computer is reduced by 35% in a
    sale. The computer still does not sell so the cost is further reduced by 15% of its current price.
    How much will it now cost to buy the computer?

3   Work out the area of this triangle.

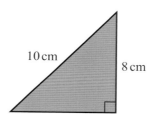

4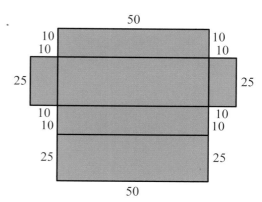

    The glass for a window is made from
    a rectangle and a semicircle, as shown.
    Calculate the area of this piece of glass.
    Give your answer to 1 decimal place.

5   Mrs Evans earns £3500 each month. She takes $\frac{2}{7}$ of this money to help her children,
    Agnes and Ben, save a deposit to buy a house. Mrs Evans splits this money in
    the ratio $11 : 9$ to give to Agnes and Ben. Using this monthly money only, how long
    will it take Ben to save up a £9000 deposit?

6   A company makes boxes from cardboard.
    The net for one box is shown opposite.
    All the measurements are in cm.
    Work out the volume of this box.

7

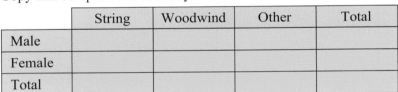

The pie chart shows vehicle sales by a garage last year.
Last year the garage sold 14 vans.
This year the garage sold 25% more cars.
How many cars did the garage sell this year?

8 Four 6s can be used to make 1: $6 + \dfrac{6}{6} - 6$

(a) Use three 9s to make 2   (b) Use three 7s to make 11   (c) Use four 5s to make 7

(d) Use four 5s to make 3   (e) Use four 8s to make 4

9 80 people are observed busking.
54 of the people are male.
32 people play string instruments, of which 25% are female.
20 males play woodwind instruments.
24 people play instruments other than woodwind or string.

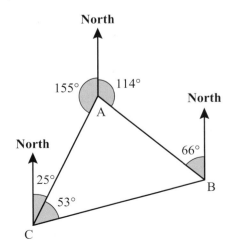

(a) Copy and complete the two-way table.

	String	Woodwind	Other	Total
Male				
Female				
Total				

(b) One of the females is chosen at random.
What is the probability that this female plays a woodwind instrument?

10 Write down the bearing that
a person at B must travel on
to go directly to A.

North

155°   114°

North

A

66°

B

North

25°

53°

C

UNIT 5   MIXED REVIEW

Part one

1   The floor area of Rachel's house is $80 \, m^2$. She has an extension built and the new floor area of her house is $96 \, m^2$. What is the percentage increase in the floor area?

2   Copy each sequence and find the missing terms.
   (a) ☐   4   4.01   4.02   ☐
   (b) ☐   ☐   5.05   5.1   ☐   5.2

3   Write the ratio $12 : 21 : 18$ in its simplest form.

4   The cost C of Carol's shopping is given by the formula

   $$C = n^2 + 8n$$

   where n is the number of hours she spends shopping.
   Find C when Carol spends 5 hours shopping.

5
Stem	Leaf
1	0 4 7 7
2	1 2 2 3 5 7 9 9
3	3 4 6 6 6 8 8
4	0 0 4 5

Key: 2|5 means 25 years old

The stem and leaf diagram shows the ages of some people at a cinema.
Is the median age greater or less than 30 and by how much?

6   Hayley says that $6m + 3 + m$ is $9m^2$. Is she correct? Justify your answer.

7   £6500 is invested at 6% per annum simple interest.
   (a) How much money is made after 4 years?
   (b) Find the total amount of money invested after 4 years.

8   2, 6, 10, 14, 18, ...
   Which expression below gives the nth term for this sequence?

   $n + 4$ $4n - 2$ $2n + 4$

9   £36 000 is shared between Ben and Lara in the ratio $5 : 4$
   How much money does Ben get?

10 The probability of Arun going to the cinema at the weekend is 0.3
   How many weekends would you expect Arun to go to the cinema during the next 20 weeks?

11 Find the value of each expression given that $a = 5$ and $b = -3$

(a) $4b$ (b) b^2 (c) $4a - 2$ (d) $a + b$

(e) $2(a - 1)$ (f) $4 - b$ (g) $a(a - b)$ (h) $\dfrac{10b}{a}$

12 Maria goes on a bike ride one day.
The graph shows her journey.

(a) When did she arrive at B?

(b) What happened between 1130 and 1200?

(c) At what speed did she cycle between
1030 and 1130?

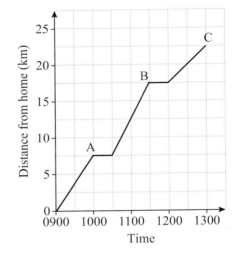

Part two

1 On a map of scale $1 : 20\,000$ a road is 2 cm long. How long is the actual road in metres?

2 A 350 g packet of almonds costs £2.10. How much does it cost for each 100 g of almonds?

3 Susie makes a pattern of rectangles from sticks.

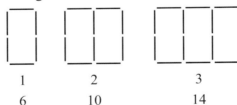

Shape-number, N	1	2	3
Number of sticks, S	6	10	14

Susie's rule is 'The number of sticks is four times the shape-number and then add 2.'

(a) Work out the number of sticks in shape-number 8

(b) One of the shapes needs 50 sticks. What is its shape-number?

(c) Write a formula, without words, to work out the number of sticks for any shape-number.
Use S for the number of sticks and N for the shape-number. Write '$S = \ldots\ldots$'.

4

The velocity, v, of a snowmobile
is given by the formula

$$v = u + at$$

Find v when $u = 0$, $a = 27$ and $t = 3$

5   A supermarket asked 500 people how many eggs they ate last week.
The results are shown in the table.

Number of eggs	0	1	2	3	4	5	6	7
Frequency	202	75	43	56	72	20	28	4

Work out the mean number of eggs eaten.

6   128 people apply for jobs at a company. 9 of these people are given a job. What percentage of
the people were given a job? Give your answer to the nearest whole number.

7   Find the nth term for each sequence below.

   (a) 2, 5, 8, 11, …

   (b) 8, 13, 18, 23, …

   (c) 4, 5, 6, 7, …

8   The maximum velocity v of a supermarket trolley
depends on the mass m of the person flying behind
the trolley and the saving s on a special offer.

$$v = \frac{s^2}{m - 10}$$

Find v when $s = 20$ and $m = 60$

9   Matt buys a motorbike for £2300 and a car for £7500.
Two years later he sells them both for a total of £8100.
Work out the percentage loss for Matt.
Give your answer to 1 decimal place.

10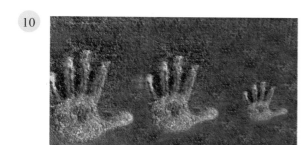

The thumbs on these handprints are
in the ratio $9 : 7 : 5$.
If the largest thumb is 63 mm long,
how long is the smallest thumb?

11 The pie charts below show the proportion of people in two musicals who sing, play instruments or do other tasks.

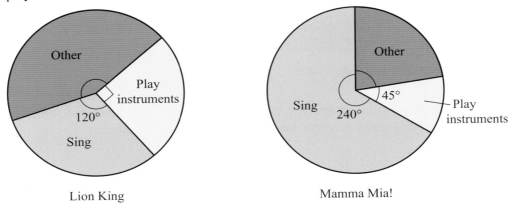

Lion King

Mamma Mia!

60 people are involved in the Lion King and 48 people are involved in Mamma Mia! How many more people play instruments in the Lion King than in Mamma Mia!?

12 On a map of scale 1 : 100 000 000 the distance from London to Athens is 2.5 cm. What is the actual distance in kilometres between these two cities?

Puzzles and problems 5

Crossnumbers

Make two copies of the pattern below and complete the puzzles using the clues given. To avoid confusion it is better not to write the small reference numbers 1–18 on your patterns.

1		2		3			4
				5			
	6		7			8	
9					10		
		11					12
				13	14		
15	16				17		
			18				

Part A [No calculators]

Across

1. 499 + 43

3. 216 × 7

5. 504 ÷ 9

6. 8214 − 3643

8. Half of 192

9. 20% of 365

10. Prime number between 30 and 36

11. 213 + 62 + 9

13. 406 ÷ 7

15. 0.7268 × 10 × 10 × 10 × 10

17. 1000 − 731

18. $2 \times 10^2 + 11$

Down

1. 1% of 5700
2. $600 - 365$
4. 6^3
7. $4488 \div 6$
8. $30^2 + 3 \times 6$

9. $10\,000 - 2003$
11. $4 \times 4 \times 4 \times 4$
12. $58.93 \times (67 + 33)$
14. $1136 - 315$
16. $11^2 - 10^2$

Part B [A calculator may be used. Write any decimal points on the lines between squares.]

Across

1. $9 \times 10 \times 11$
3. Ninety less than ten thousand
5. $\left(7\frac{1}{2}\right)^2$ to the nearest whole number
6. $140.52 \div 0.03$
8. Last two digits of 99^2
9. $3^2 + 4^2 + 5^2 + 6^2$
10. Angle between the hands of a clock at 2.00 pm
11. Eight pounds and eight pence
13. Next prime number after 89
15. 11% of 213
17. 3.1 m plus 43 cm, in cm
18. Area of a square of side 15 cm

Down

1. $\dfrac{5 \times 6 \times 7 \times 8}{2} - 11 \times 68$
2. 26% as a decimal
4. 0.1^2
7. Next in the sequence $102\frac{1}{2}$, 205, 410
8. $1 - 0.97$
9. 52% of £158.50
11. $0.0854 \div (7 - 6.99)$
12. $10^3 + 11^3$
14. $3 \times 5 \times 7^2$
16. Half of a third of 222

Mental arithmetic practice 5

Ideally a teacher will read out each question twice, with pupils' books closed.

Test 1

- *Allow 5 seconds to answer each of questions* 1 *to* 6

- *Allow 10 seconds to answer each of questions* 7 *to* 20

1 Write the number five hundred and sixty-seven to the nearest hundred.

2 What is five point two multiplied by one thousand?

3 Work out five per cent of four hundred.

4 Simplify the expression $a \times a \times a$.

5 What is the sum of 2.3, 2.7, 2.3 and 2.7?

6 What is one tenth of half a million?

7 What is the value of $2(x + 1)$ when x equals four?

8 Tim's height is one point seven metres. Greg's height is one hundredth of a metre more than Tim's height. What is Greg's height?

9 Twenty per cent of a number is eleven. What is the number?

10 Two angles in a triangle are each sixty-five degrees. What is the size of the third angle?

11 In a group of sixty-three children, twenty-eight are girls. How many are boys?

12 What is the area of a triangle with a base of 8 cm and a height of 7 cm?

13 The value of four x plus y is sixteen. Write the value of eight x plus two y.

14 Divide two by nought point one.

15 Michelle got thirty out of fifty on a test. What percentage did she get?

16 Work out one plus two plus three, all squared.

17 If '−4 less than x less than 0', write down one possible value of x.

18 How many eighths are there in one half?

19 Multiply six point nought two by one thousand.

20 Treble a number then subtract 1 gives the answer 65. What is the value of the number?

• *Allow 15 seconds to answer each of questions* 21 *to* 30

21 What is the cost of two items at two pounds ninety-nine pence each?

22 Which is the smaller of these three numbers?

0.2   0.18   0.332

23 Work out an approximate answer for 497.3 ÷ 1.97

24 Each side of a square is thirty-two centimetres. What is the perimeter of the square?

25 Between which pair of whole numbers does the square root of thirty-three lie?

26 If $32 \times 19 = 608$, what is sixteen multiplied by nineteen?

27 A map has a scale of one to one thousand. What is the actual length of a path which is 8 cm long on the map? Give your final answer in metres.

28 What is the value of $x^2 - 6$ when x equals nought?

29 Which has the longer perimeter: a square of side 10 cm or an equilateral triangle of side 15 cm?

30 A film started at eight fifty p.m. and ended two and a quarter hours later. When did it finish?

A long time ago! 5

The Tower of Hanoi

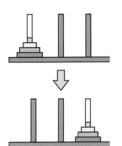

This puzzle was created by Eduard Lucas in the 19th century.
The task is to move a pile of different sized discs from one post to another.

There are three posts. Only one disc may be moved at any time and must be moved directly onto another post. A larger disc may never be placed onto a smaller disc.

The aim is to move all the discs to another post using the least number of moves.

Exercise

1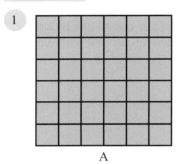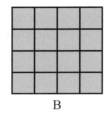

C

B

A

Cut out 3 squares as shown.

Use them in place of 3 discs.

Place C on top of B on top of A.

Place 3 crosses on a piece of paper in place of the posts.

Move A, B and C from one post onto another post using the Tower of Hanoi rules above.

What are the least number of moves needed?

Discuss with a partner. Could they do any better than you?

2 Now repeat with 4 discs.

3 Try with just 2 discs.

4 One disc would need one move.

Look at your answers for 1 disc, 2 discs, 3 discs and 4 discs.

Can you see a pattern for the least number of moves so far?

If you can see a pattern, what will be the least number of moves needed for 5 discs?

Now move 5 discs for real.

5 What is the least number of moves needed for 7 discs?

6 **RESEARCH:**

Check whether your answer for 7 discs is correct.

UNIT 6

6.1 Measures

In section 6.1 you will:

- convert metric units
- use imperial units

Converting between metric units

Length	Mass	Volume
1 cm = 10 mm	1 kg = 1000 g	1 millilitre (ml) = 1 cm^3
1 m = 100 cm	1 tonne = 1000 kg	1 litre = 1000 ml
1 km = 1000 m		

(a) 2.3 km = 2300 m
$\overset{\times 1000}{\curvearrowright}$

(b) 5600 g = 5.6 kg
$\overset{\div 1000}{\curvearrowright}$

(c) 4750 ml = 4.75 litres
$\overset{\div 1000}{\curvearrowright}$

Exercise 1M

Copy and complete

1. 2.75 m = _____ cm

2. 0.45 m = _____ cm

3. 5 m = _____ cm

4. 19 cm = _____ m

5. 350 m = _____ km

6. 15 cm = _____ m

7. 60 mm = _____ cm

8. 200 mm = _____ cm

9. 5 mm = _____ cm

10. 2500 m = _____ km

11. 3 kg = _____ g

12. 9.8 kg = _____ g

13. 450 g = _____ kg

14. 2 tonnes = _____ kg

15. 3500 ml = _____ litres

16 An alligator is crossing a 5.8 metre road. The alligator has 94 cm still to walk to get to the other side of the road. How far has the alligator walked across the road so far?

17 Ben weighs 52.4 kg. He puts on 1850 g weight during the next three weeks. How many kilograms does he now weigh?

18 A giant conveyer belt moves 100 kg of coal every minute. How many tonnes of coal will be moved in 1 hour?

19 Ellie walks 70 m in one minute. How many kilometres does she walk in half-an-hour?

20  A bottle of medicine contains 0.28 litres of cough mixture. How many 5 ml spoonfuls of medicine will the bottle provide?

21 A newspaper reported that a very rich American earned $30 every second of the day. How much did the rich American earn in one day?

22 Jack buys a 0.44 kg pack of bacon and 0.25 kg of butter. For breakfast he eats 75 g of bacon and 15 g of butter on his toast. How much bacon and how much butter does he have left?

23 Copy and complete each sentence.

(a) The width of the classroom is about ☐ m.

(b) The height of the door is about ☐ cm.

(c) A can of cola has a capacity of about ☐ ml.

(d) The width of a thumbnail is about ☐ mm.

Converting between metric and imperial units

1 m ≈ 3 feet   1 kg ≈ 2.2 pounds
8 km ≈ 5 miles   1 gallon ≈ 4.5 litres
1 litre is just less than 2 pints
1 foot = 12 inches
1 stone = 14 pounds   1 yard = 3 feet
     1 pound = 16 ounces

Exercise 2M

Some, though not all, of the measurements below are reasonable. Use your common sense to help you complete this table. Where the measurement given is obviously wrong, write a more sensible number.

Object	Measurement	Object	Measurement
Pound coin		Football	
Tennis ball		Family car	
This book		Newborn baby	
Chair height		Bag of sugar	
Tennis court		Biro	
Car speed		Labrador	
Pile of 100 pound coins		Badminton net	
12-year-old boy		50-seater coach	

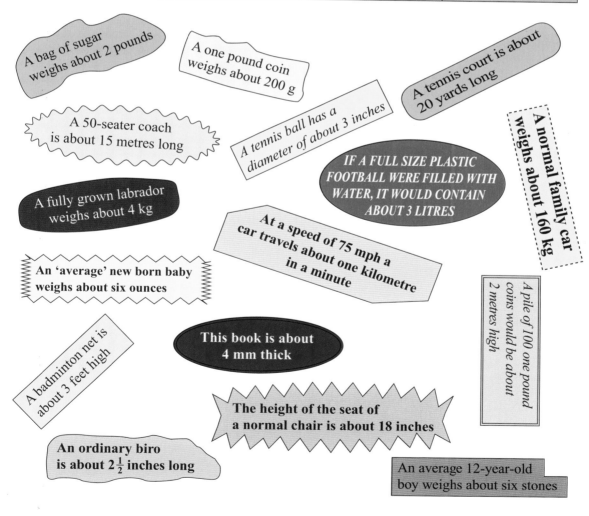

A bag of sugar weighs about 2 pounds

A one pound coin weighs about 200 g

A tennis court is about 20 yards long

A 50-seater coach is about 15 metres long

A tennis ball has a diameter of about 3 inches

IF A FULL SIZE PLASTIC FOOTBALL WERE FILLED WITH WATER, IT WOULD CONTAIN ABOUT 3 LITRES

A normal family car weighs about 160 kg

A fully grown labrador weighs about 4 kg

At a speed of 75 mph a car travels about one kilometre in a minute

An 'average' new born baby weighs about six ounces

A pile of 100 one pound coins would be about 2 metres high

A badminton net is about 3 feet high

This book is about 4 mm thick

The height of the seat of a normal chair is about 18 inches

An ordinary biro is about $2\frac{1}{2}$ inches long

An average 12-year-old boy weighs about six stones

Need more practice with measures?

Copy and complete

1. 0.7 m = _____ cm

2. 280 m = _____ km

3. 5.12 kg = _____ g

4. 6700 ml = _____ litres

5. 1.8 tonnes = _____ kg

6. 360 cm = _____ m

7. 5.9 m = _____ cm

8. 0.4 cm = _____ mm

9. 1.86 litres = _____ ml

10. A lorry weighs 2.6 tonnes. A load of 870 kg is put onto the lorry. What is the total weight (in tonnes) of the lorry and its load?

11. Harrison says that 320 cm is longer than 6.15 m. Explain clearly why Harrison is not correct.

12. A cake decorator puts 40 cm of icing onto a cake every minute. How many metres of icing does the cake decorator put on in 6 hours?

13. Sophie walks her dog 3.62 km. They now have another 768 m to walk before they get home. How far will Sophie and her dog have walked in total when they reach home?

14. Albert weighs 53.6 kg. He runs a marathon and loses 1940 g. How much does Albert weigh now?

15.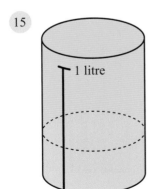

    40% of 1 litre of water is poured into this container. How much more water must be added to make one full litre of water?

16. At noon on April 1st a giant egg-timer was started. It was due to stop 1020 seconds later. At what time did it stop?

17 Work out
    (a) 5.3 tonnes − 2186 kg (in kg)   (b) 426 ml + 3.2 litres (in ml)
    (c) 2.47 km − 695 m (in km)   (d) 15 mm + 12 cm (in cm)

18 Which rectangle has the greatest area?

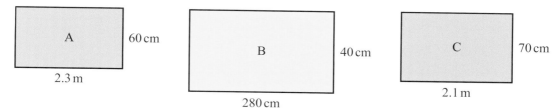

A   60 cm
2.3 m

B   40 cm
280 cm

C   70 cm
2.1 m

Extension questions with measures

1 Copy and complete
   (a) 4 m ≈ _____ feet   (b) 3 feet = _____ inches   (c) 5 pounds = _____ ounces
   (d) 4 gallons ≈ _____ litres   (e) 9 stones = _____ pounds   (f) 8.8 pounds ≈ _____ kg
   (g) 16 km ≈ _____ miles   (h) 45 litres ≈ _____ gallons   (i) 24 feet ≈ _____ m

2 Seth weighs 40 kg and Silas weighs 95 pounds.
   Who is heavier and approximately by how much?

3 A car has enough petrol to travel 40 km. The car is 28 miles from the driver's home.
   Will the car reach home without more petrol needing to be bought?

4 A lioness weighs 200 kg. Her cub weighs 88 pounds.
   How many times heavier is the lioness compared
   with her cub?

5 Write these distances in order of size, starting with the smallest.
       30 miles, 32 km, 45 miles, 64 000 m, 56 km

6
   Area
   = 9 m²

   Write down the perimeter of
   this square in centimetres.

364

7   The price of petrol is £1.40 per litre. Sandra puts 6 gallons of petrol into her car. How much does the petrol cost?

8   If 1 inch = 2.5 cm, work out the perimeter of this shape in centimetres.

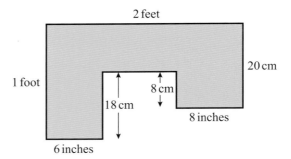

9   Which is heavier and by how much: 12 kg or 26 pounds?

10 Megan is 5 feet 6 inches tall. Chen is 5 cm taller than Megan and Kenny is 3 inches taller than Chen. How tall is Kenny in cm? (1 inch = 2.5 cm)

6.2 Volume

In section 6.2 you will find and use volumes of cuboids

Volume of a cuboid

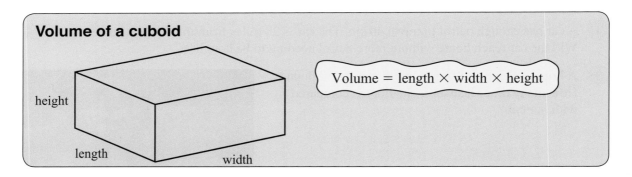

Volume = length × width × height

(a) Find the volume of the cuboid

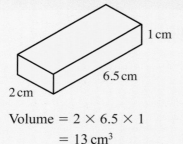

Volume = 2 × 6.5 × 1

= 13 cm³

(b) Find the volume of the cuboid

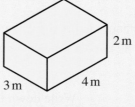

Volume = 3 × 4 × 2

= 24 m³   (note the units)

Exercise 1M

In questions 1 to 6 , work out the volume of each cuboid. Give your answer in the correct units.

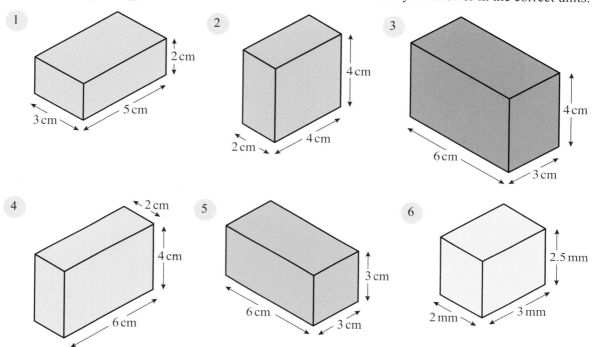

In questions 7 to 12 , write down the volume of the object. All the objects are made from centimetre cubes.

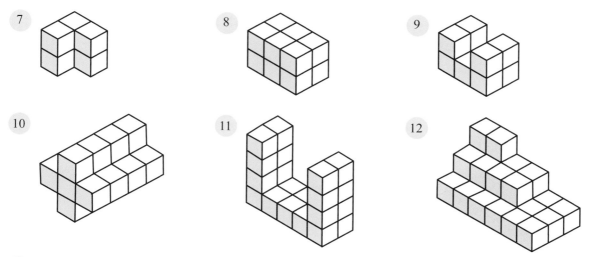

13 (a) Draw a sketch of a 4 m by 4 m by 2 m cuboid.
   (b) Calculate the volume of the cuboid.
   (c) Calculate the total surface area of the cuboid.

14 Calculate the volume of each girder by splitting it into cuboids. All lengths are in cm.

(a)

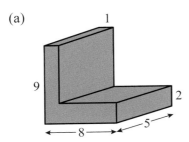

(b)

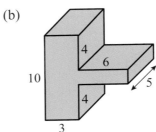

(c)

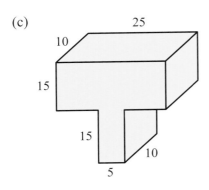

(d)

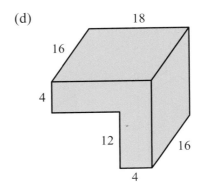

15

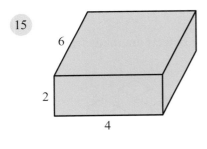

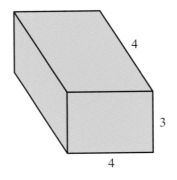

Both of these cuboids have a volume of 48 m³. What is the difference in their surface areas?

Exercise 2M

1

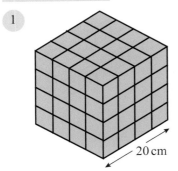

The large cube is cut into lots of identical small cubes, as shown. Calculate the volume of each small cube.

2 A cuboid P measures 10 cm by 2 cm by 3 cm. Write down the dimensions of at least two different cuboids which each have the same volume as cuboid P.

3 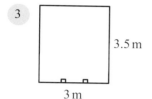 A mine shaft 400 m long is dug with the cross-section shown. Calculate the volume of earth which must be removed to make way for the shaft.

4 The diagram shows an empty swimming pool.
Water is pumped into the pool at a rate of 2 m³ per minute.
How long will it take to fill the pool?

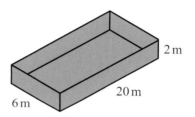

5 The shapes below are nets for closed boxes. Work out the volume of the box in each case, giving your answer in cubic cm.

(a)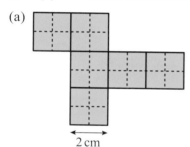

(b)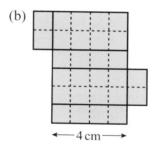

(c)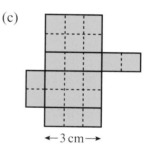

6 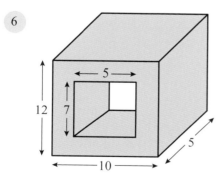 A wood carving is shown opposite.
A hole in the shape of a cuboid has been chiselled through the carving.
All lengths are in cm.
Work out the volume of the wood carving.

7 Find the length x.

(a)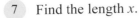

4 cm

x 7 cm

volume = 70 cm³

(b)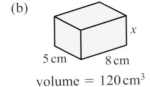

x

5 cm   8 cm

volume = 120 cm³

(c)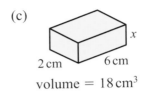

x

2 cm   6 cm

volume = 18 cm³

(d)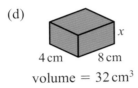

x

4 cm   8 cm

volume = 32 cm³

(e)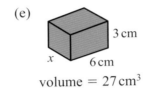

3 cm

x 6 cm

volume = 27 cm³

(f)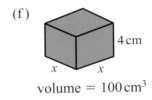

4 cm

x x

volume = 100 cm³

8 The diagram shows an object of volume 7 cm³.
Use isometric paper to draw the following objects:

(a) a cuboid with volume 45 cm³

(b) a T-shaped object with volume 15 cm³

(c) an L-shaped object with volume 20 cm³

(d) any object with a volume of 23 cm³

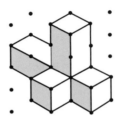

Need more practice with volume?

1

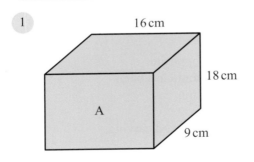

16 cm

18 cm

A

9 cm

Which cuboid has
the greater volume
and by how much?

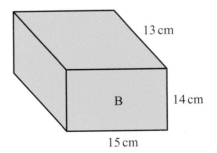

13 cm

B   14 cm

15 cm

2 Work out the volume of this solid. All lengths are in cm.

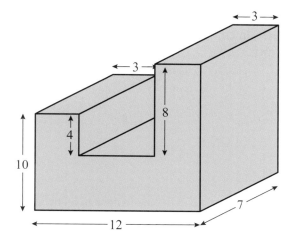

3 The inside of a spaceship orbiting the Earth is a cuboid measuring 200 cm by 300 cm by 200 cm. Unfortunately air is leaking from the spaceship at a rate of 1000 cm³/sec. How long will it take for all the air to leak out?

4

Gold cubes of side 3 cm are placed together in a flat square. The flat square has 30 cubes along each of its sides.

What is the volume of the gold used to make this shape?

5 Work out the total surface area of this cuboid.

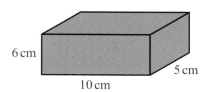

6 Two solid metal cuboids have dimensions, in cm, $2 \times 3 \times 2$ and $5 \times 3 \times 1$. The cuboids are melted down and formed into one large cube. Find the length of one side of the cube.

7. In a storm, 2 cm of rain fell in 1 hour. Calculate the volume of water, in cm³, which fell on the roof of the garage shown.

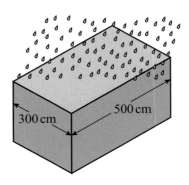

300 cm

500 cm

8.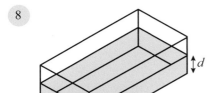

8 m

4 m

↕d

There is 64 m³ of water in this swimming pool.

Calculate the depth of water, *d*, in the pool.

9.

Farmers were asked to change the way they grew their melons so that they could fit more melons into delivery boxes. They grew melons as cubes of side 16 cm.

The melons are placed in boxes each of which is in the shape of a cube. Each side of the cube is 1.28 m. How many melons will fit into one of these boxes?

10. Sketch a cuboid *a* cm by *b* cm by *c* cm.

(a) Write an expression for the volume of the cuboid.

(b) Write an expression for the total surface area of the cuboid.

Extension questions with volume

Volume of a prism

A prism has the same cross-section throughout its length.

Volume of a prism
= (Area of cross-section) × (length)

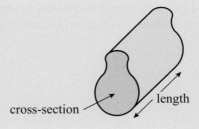

cross-section

length

Find the volume of this
triangular prism.

Area of cross-section $= \dfrac{4 \times 10}{2}$

$\qquad\qquad = 20\,\text{cm}^2$

Volume of prism = Area × length

$\qquad\qquad = 20 \times 7$

$\qquad\qquad = 140\,\text{cm}^3$

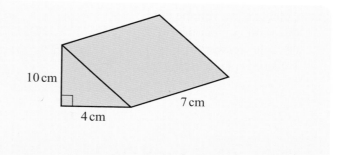

Find the volume of each prism.

1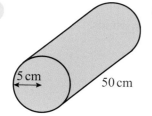

Area of end $= 7\,\text{m}^2$

11 m

2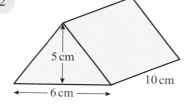

5 cm
6 cm
10 cm

3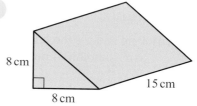

8 cm
8 cm
15 cm

4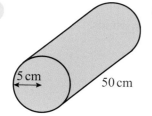

5 cm
50 cm

5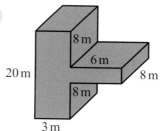

8 m
6 m
20 m
8 m
8 m
3 m

6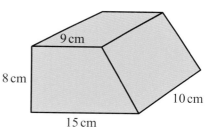

9 cm
8 cm
15 cm
10 cm

7   A prism has length 12 cm and volume 4500 cm³.
Find the area of the cross-section of the prism.

8   A triangular prism has a cross-sectional area of 38 cm² and a volume of 2356 cm³.
Find the length of the triangular prism.

9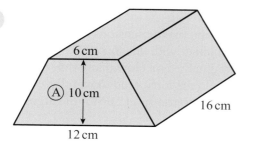

6 cm
(A) 10 cm
16 cm
12 cm

Which prism has
the greater volume
and by how much:
A or B?

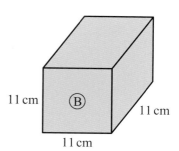

11 cm
(B)
11 cm
11 cm

10 Calculate the volume of
this semi circular prism.
Give the answer to
1 decimal place.

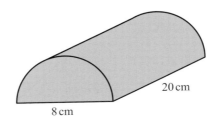

20 cm

8 cm

CHECK YOURSELF ON SECTIONS 6.1 and 6.2

1 Converting metric units

Copy and complete

(a) 6.7 kg = _____ g

(b) 5.89 litres = _____ ml

(c) 350 m = _____ km

(d) Pete and his three friends dig 2.4 tonnes of mud to clear a stream. If each person clears the same amount of mud, how many kilograms of mud does Pete clear?

2 Using imperial units

Answer true or false.

(a) A key measures about 3 inches.

(b) A teapot contains about 2 gallons when full.

(c) An average man will weigh about 13 pounds.

(d) A car is about 4 yards long.

3 Finding and using volumes of cuboids

Find the volume of each solid.

(a)

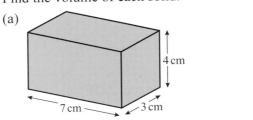

4 cm

7 cm   3 cm

(b)

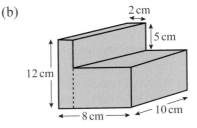

2 cm

5 cm

12 cm

8 cm   10 cm

(c)

The internal dimensions of the container with this lorry are 7 m by 3 m by 3 m. How many times would the lorry need to be fully loaded to transport 504 m³ of cargo?

6.3 Drawing three-dimensional objects

In section 6.3 you will:

- draw three-dimensional objects on isometric paper and solve problems with objects

- draw three different views of a three-dimensional object

Using isometric paper

A drawing of a solid is a 2D representation of a 3D object. Below are two pictures of the same object.

(a) On squared paper.

(b) On isometric dot paper.

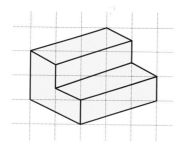
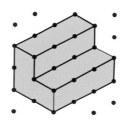

The dimensions of the object cannot be taken from the first picture but they can be taken from the second. Isometric paper can be used either as dots (as above) or as a grid of equilateral triangles. Either way, the paper must be the right way round (as shown here).

N.B. Most of the questions in this section are easier, and more fun to do, when you have an ample supply of 'unifix' or 'multilink' cubes.

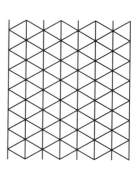

Exercise 1M

1   On isometric paper, make a copy of each object below. Underneath each drawing state the number of 'multilink' cubes needed to make the object. (Make sure you have the isometric paper the right way round!)

(a)

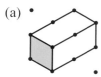

(b)

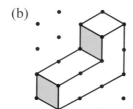

(c)

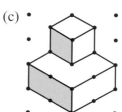

2 Using four cubes, you can make several shapes. A and B are different shapes but C is the same as A.

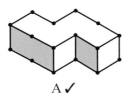

A ✓

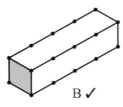

B ✓

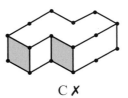

C ✗

Make as many different shapes as possible, using four cubes, and draw them all (including shapes A and B above) on isometric paper.

3 Make the object shown using cubes.
Now draw the object *from a different view*.

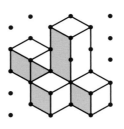

4 A
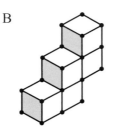

B

C
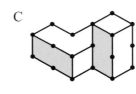

D
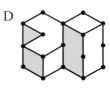

Build your own 3D models of shapes A, B, C and D above. If possible, use different coloured cubes for each model.

Decide which of the shapes below and on the next page are the same as shape A.

Repeat for shapes B, C and D.

Which shape is neither A, B, C nor D?

(a)
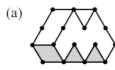

(b)
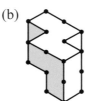

(c)
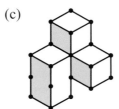

(d)
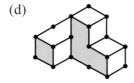

(e)
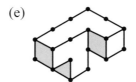

(f)
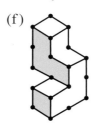

(g)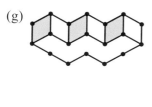

(h)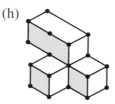

(i)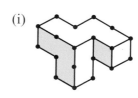

(j)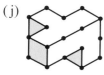

(k)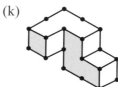

(l)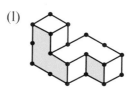

Need more practice with drawing three-dimensional objects?

1. You need 18 cubes.
Make the two shapes opposite.
Arrange them to make a $3 \times 3 \times 2$
cuboid by adding a third shape, which
you have to find. Draw the third shape
on isometric paper.

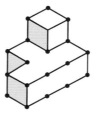 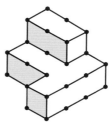

2. You need 27 small cubes for this question.
For each part, make the four shapes shown and arrange them into a $3 \times 3 \times 3$ cube by adding
a fifth shape, which you have to find. Draw the fifth shape on isometric paper. (The number
next to each shape indicates the number of small cubes in that shape.)

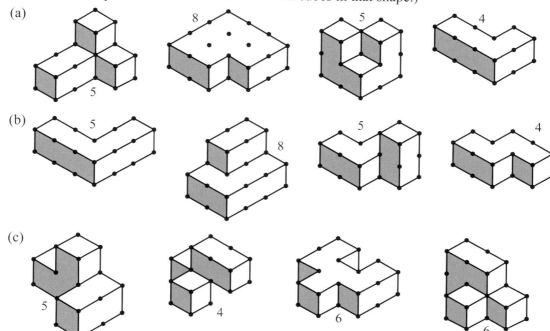

(a)

(b)

(c)

Extension questions with drawing three-dimensional objects

Three views of a shape

Here is a 3D object made from centimetre cubes. We can draw three views of the object on squared paper.

The front view and side view are known as the *front elevation* and *side elevation*.
The plan view is looking down on the object from above.

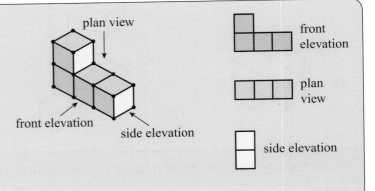

In questions ① to ⑥, draw the plan view, the front elevation and the side elevation of the object.

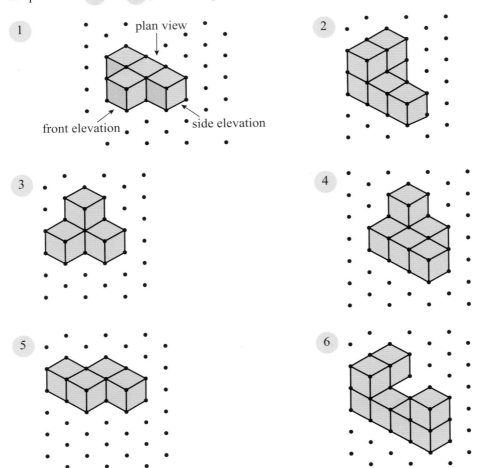

In questions ⑦ to ⑩ , you are given three views of a shape. Use the information to make the shape using centimetre cubes.

⑦

⑧

⑨

⑩

11 The plan view of an object is shown opposite. What could the object be?

12

front elevation

plan view

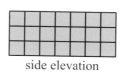

side elevation

A cuboid is made from cubes, as shown opposite. Supposing each cube is 1 cm³, what is the total surface area of the cuboid?

✗ Spot the mistakes 11 ✗

Measures, volume and drawing three-dimensional objects

Work through each question below and *explain clearly* what mistakes have been made. Beware – some questions are correctly done.

1 Convert 4.7 litres into millilitres.

Answer: 4.7 litres = 470 ml

2 Work out the volume of the cuboid.

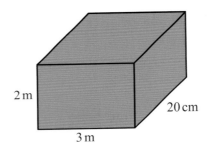

Answer: Volume = 2 × 3 × 20
                   = 6 × 20
                   = 120 m³

3 A swimming pool contains 18 000 gallons of water. How many litres of water does the swimming pool contain?

Answer: 1 gallon = 45 litres
           so 18 000 gallons = 18 000 × 45
                           = 810 000 litres

4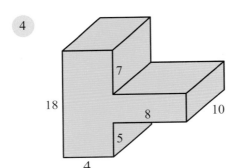

Work out the volume of this solid.
All lengths are in cm.

Answer:
Volume = (18 × 4 × 10) + (8 × 4 × 10)
       = 720 + 320
       = 1040 cm³

5 A lorry transports 8 crates, each weighing 375 kg. The total weight of the lorry and crates is 7.9 tonnes. How much does the lorry weigh when it has unloaded all 8 crates?

Answer: 8 crates weigh 8 × 375 kg = 3000 kg
                                    = 3 tonnes

       Unloaded lorry weighs 7.9 − 3 = 4.9 tonnes

6 Draw the plan view, front elevation and side elevation of this object.

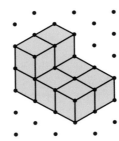

Answer:

front   side   plan
elevation   elevation   view

7

6 cm

9 cm

5 cm

Work out the total surface area of this cuboid.

Answer:

Area = $(6 \times 9) + (6 \times 5) + (9 \times 5)$

$= 54 + 30 + 45$

$= 129 \, \text{cm}^2$

8 The Harris family are travelling in France and are 88 km from Paris. How many miles from Paris are they?

Answer: 8 km = 5 miles

$88 \div 8 = 11$

so the Harris family are $11 \times 5 = 55$ miles from Paris.

9 Draw a plan view, front elevation and side elevation for the house shown.

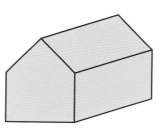

Answer:

front elevation

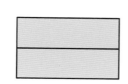

plan view

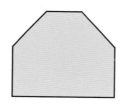

side elevation

10

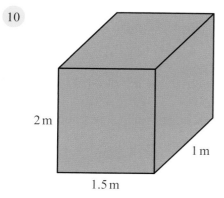

2 m

1.5 m

1 m

This water tank is completely full. Water leaks out of a hole in the bottom of the tank at a rate of 500 cm³/s. How many minutes does it take for the tank to completely empty?

Answer: Volume of tank = $200 \times 150 \times 100$

$= 30\,000 \times 100$

$= 3\,000\,000 \, \text{cm}^3$

Time taken to empty = $3\,000\,000 \div 500$

$= 6000$ seconds

$= 6000 \div 60$

$= 100$ minutes

6.4 Algebra review

In section 6.4 you will:

- simplify expressions
- substitute numbers for letters
- multiply out single brackets
- draw and use straight line graphs
- solve linear equations
- use the rules of indices

Simplifying expressions and substituting numbers for letters

$5 \times m = 5m$

$m \times m = m^2$

$\dfrac{m}{n} = m \div n$

If $m = 4$ and $n = 6$:

$m + 2n = 4 + (2 \times 6) = 4 + 12 = 16$

$\dfrac{n^2}{m} = \dfrac{6 \times 6}{4} = \dfrac{36}{4} = 9$

Like terms can be added:

$3a + 4b + 2a - 2b = 5a + 2b$

$7m + 3 + 2m = 9m + 3$

Exercise 1M

For questions **1** to **6**, answer true or false.

1 $3a + 5a + 3b - b = 8a + 3b$

2 $4x + 3y + 2x - 4x = 2x + 3y$

3 $9m - 3m + 5n + n = 6m + 6n$

4 $2p + 3q + 5q + 2 - 2q = 2p + 6q + 2$

5 $x + 3y + 4x + x + 5 = 6x + 8y$

6 $8a + 6 - 3a + 7 - a = 4a + 13$

For questions **7** to **18**, use $m = 7$, $n = 3$ and $w = 4$ to find the value of each expression.

7 $4m + n$

8 nw

9 $2w + 5n$

10 w^2

11 $2m - 2n$

12 $\dfrac{2m - 2n}{w}$

13 $\dfrac{8n}{w}$

14 $4m - w + n$

15 $w^2 - n^2$

16 $m^2 - 5w$

17 $mn + mw$

18 $\dfrac{m - w}{n}$

19

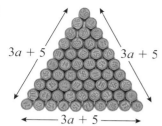

$3a + 5$ $3a + 5$

$3a + 5$

Write down an expression for the perimeter of this triangle. Collect like terms if possible.

20 Sammy has £36. He spends £m on a trip to the cinema. Write down an expression for the money he now has left.

21 Mia gets £x from her parents and £y from her grandparents. She spends £10. Write down an expression for the money she now has left.

22 A box of matches costs 43p. Dean buys n boxes. Write down an expression for the cost of the n boxes.

23 Copy and match up pairs of expressions shown below. The first one is done for you.

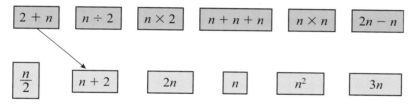

24 If $v = u + at$, find the value of v when $u = 18$, $a = 10$ and $t = 6$

25 If $m = 3(4n + 1)$, find the value of m if $n = 3$

26 If $p = \dfrac{w}{5} - 6$, find the value of p if $w = 40$

27 Simplify each expression.

(a) $5 \times m$

(b) $m \times 4 \times n$

(c) $m \times m$

(d) $6 \times n \times n$

(e) $\dfrac{8m}{2}$

(f) $\dfrac{10 \times n \times n}{5}$

28 Ali says that $n \times 2 \times m \times 3$ is equal to $6nm$. Evelyn does not agree and says the answer is $6mn$. Who is correct? Give a reason for your answer.

29 Which of the cards below have a value *less than* 8 when $n = 4$?

| $2n - 1$ | $\dfrac{40}{n}$ | $2 + 3n$ | $(n - 1)^2$ |

| $n^2 - 10$ | $5n - 11$ | $10 - n$ |

Multiplying out single brackets

Reminder: $4(n + 2) = 4n + 8$ $5(n - 3) = 5n - 15$

$4(2n + 3) = 8n + 12$ $m(n - 2) = mn - 2m$

Exercise 2M

Multiply out

1 $3(n + 5)$ **2** $6(n - 2)$ **3** $8(n + 4)$

4 $5(n - 5)$ **5** $4(2n + 2)$ **6** $2(7n + 3)$

7 $4(3n - 4)$ **8** $6(4n - 1)$ **9** $7(2 + 6n)$

10 $4(3 + 9n)$ **11** $3(6n - 8)$ **12** $9(5n + 1)$

13  Each person is given £$(2n + 1)$. Write down an expression for the total amount of money these people are given. Multiply out your answer if you need to.

Expand (multiply out) the following expressions.

14 $m(n + 3)$ **15** $p(n + m)$ **16** $a(b - c)$

17 $n(w + y)$ **18** $y(m - 4)$ **19** $x(y + 6)$

20 $f(2n + 4)$ **21** $m(n + 7)$ **22** $4(3m + 5)$

23 $7(2w - 5)$ **24** $n(n - 4)$ **25** $w(w + n)$

26 Harriet says that $3(2n + 1)$ is equal to $6n + 1$. *Explain clearly* the mistake she has made.

Remove brackets and simplify

(a) $5(n + 1) + 3(2n + 4)$

$\quad = 5n + 5 + 6n + 12$

$\quad = 11n + 17$

(b) $2(3a + 4) - 3(a - 5)$

$\quad = 6a + 8 - 3a + 15$

$\quad = 3a + 23$

Exercise 3M

Remove the brackets and simplify.

1 $4(n + 2) + 3(n + 4)$

2 $5(n + 3) + 2(n + 2)$

3 $6(a + 3) + 4(a + 1)$

4 $3(a + 6) + 4(a + 5)$

5 $3(2m + 4) + 3(m + 6)$

6 $4(3n + 2) + 7(2n + 3)$

7 $5(3a + 2) + 4(5a + 6)$

8 $6(2y + 1) + 5(3y + 5)$

9 Find an expression for the total area of these two rectangles. Simplify your answer.

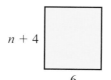
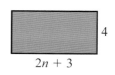

In questions **10** to **19** , remove the brackets and simplify.

10 $4(n + 3) + 5(n - 2)$

11 $3(2n + 1) - 4(n - 3)$

12 $5(a + 6) + 4(a - 3)$

13 $5(3m + 5) - 2(4m - 1)$

14 $6(3x + 5) - 3(4x - 2)$

15 $7(3a + 4) - 3(5a + 6)$

16 $5(4n + 2) + 2(2n - 3)$

17 $4(8n + 3) - 2(9n + 3)$

18 $4(6y + 9) - 3(4y - 1)$

19 $8(2x + 7) - 4(3x + 10)$

Drawing graphs – a reminder

Draw the graph of $y = 2x + 3$
for x-values from 0 to 4

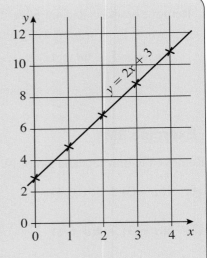

> Remember, this is done by first
> completing a table of values

$2x + 3$ means $x \rightarrow \boxed{\times 2} \rightarrow \boxed{+3}$

x	0	1	2	3	4
y	3	5	7	9	11
Coordinates	$(0, 3)$	$(1, 5)$	$(2, 7)$	$(3, 9)$	$(4, 11)$

Lines parallel to the axes

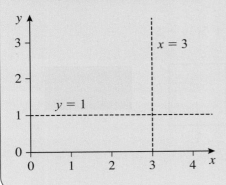

A line parallel to the y-axis has an equation
$x = $ 'a number'

A line parallel to the x-axis has an equation
$y = $ 'a number'

Exercise 4M

For each question, copy and complete the table then draw the graph using the scales given.

1 $y = x + 3$ for x-values from 0 to 5

x	0	1	2	3	4	5
y			5			
coordinates			$(2, 5)$			

(x-axis: use 1 cm for 1 unit
y-axis: use 1 cm for 1 unit)

2 $y = 2x + 2$ for x-values from 0 to 5

$2x + 2$ means $x \rightarrow \boxed{\times 2} \rightarrow \boxed{+2}$

x	0	1	2	3	4	5
y				8		
coordinates				$(3, 8)$		

(x-axis: use 1 cm for 1 unit
y-axis: use 1 cm for 2 units)

3 (a) Draw an x-axis from 0 to 6
   (b) Draw a y-axis from 0 to 6
   (c) Draw the line $y = 4$
   (d) Draw the line $y = 2$
   (e) Draw the line $x = 3$
   (f) Draw the line $y = x$
   (g) Write down the coordinates of the point where the line $y = x$ meets the line $x = 3$

4 Use a table of values to draw $y = 2x + 4$ for x-values from 0 to 5

5 Use a table of values to draw $y = x^2$ for x-values from -3 to 3

6 Use a table of values to draw $y = x^2 + 2$ for x-values from -3 to 3

7 (a) Use a table of values to draw $y = x - 1$ for x-values from 0 to 6
   (b) Draw the line $y = 5$
   (c) Write down the coordinates of the point where the line $y = x - 1$ meets the line $y = 5$

Finding the equation of a line

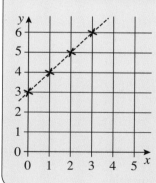

The line passes through:

$(0, 3), (1, 4), (2, 5), (3, 6)$

For each point, the y-coordinate is three more than the x-coordinate. The equation of the line is $y = x + 3$

Exercise 5M

In questions 1 to 10 you are given the coordinates of several points on a line. Find the equation of each line.

1

x	1	2	3	4	5
y	5	6	7	8	9

2

x	1	2	3	4	5	6
y	7	8	9	10	11	12

3

x	6	7	8	9	10
y	2	3	4	5	6

4

x	0	1	2	3	4	5
y	9	8	7	6	5	4

5

x	1	2	3	4	5
y	4	8	12	16	20

6

x	0	1	2	3	4
y	12	11	10	9	8

7

x	10	11	12	13	14
y	7	8	9	10	11

8

x	2	4	6	8	10
y	10	20	30	40	50

9

x	0	1	2	3	4
y	1	4	7	10	13

10

x	0	1	2	3	4
y	3	5	7	9	11

11

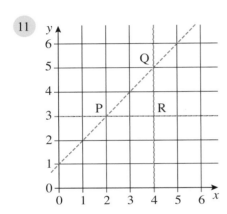

Find the equation of the line through

(a) P and Q

(b) P and R

(c) Q and R

Solving linear equations

Remember: The main rule when solving equations is:

'Do the same thing to both sides'

Solve the equations. The circles show what is done to both sides of the equation.

(a) $3n + 2 = 20$

    (-2) (-2)

    $3n = 18$

    $(\div 3)$ $(\div 3)$

    $n = 6$

(b) $2n - 7 = 21$

    $(+7)$ $(+7)$

    $2n = 28$

    $(\div 2)$ $(\div 2)$

    $n = 14$

(c) $3(2n - 4) = 18$

Remove brackets first

    $6n - 12 = 18$

    $(+12)$ $(+12)$

    $6n = 30$

    $(\div 6)$ $(\div 6)$

    $n = 5$

Exercise 6M

Solve the equations.

1. $6 + n = 40$
2. $n - 5 = 10$
3. $n - 8 = 0$
4. $4n = 24$
5. $3n + 2 = 20$
6. $4n + 7 = 23$
7. $5n - 13 = 27$
8. $9n - 50 = 40$
9. $3n + 8 = 29$
10. $\frac{n}{6} = 9$
11. $\frac{n}{3} - 2 = 2$
12. $\frac{n}{5} + 4 = 11$

13.
$$n + n + n = 18$$
and
$$m + m + n = 26$$
Find the value of m.

Now solve these equations.

14. $3(n + 2) = 21$
15. $5(n - 3) = 25$
16. $8(n - 1) = 8$
17. $4(n - 6) = 12$
18. $7(n + 10) = 210$
19. $3(3n + 2) = 42$
20. $5(2n - 4) = 50$
21. $180 = 2(2n - 10)$
22. $20 = 4(2n - 7)$

23. If I double a number n and then subtract 5, the answer is 17. Write down an equation and solve it to find the value of n.

24.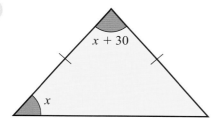

This triangle is isosceles. Write down an equation using x and then find the size of each angle in the triangle.

(a) $3x + 2 = x + 16$

$\quad \quad \boxed{-x} \quad \boxed{-x}$

$\quad 2x + 2 = 16$

$\quad \quad \boxed{-2} \quad \boxed{-2}$

$\quad \quad 2x = 14$

$\quad \quad \boxed{\div 2} \quad \boxed{\div 2}$

$\quad \quad \quad x = 7$

(b) $2(4x - 1) = 3(2x + 6)$

$\quad$ Remove brackets first

$\quad \quad 8x - 2 = 6x + 18$

$\quad \quad \quad \boxed{-6x} \quad \boxed{-6x}$

$\quad \quad \quad 2x - 2 = 18$

$\quad \quad \quad \quad \boxed{+2} \quad \boxed{+2}$

$\quad \quad \quad \quad 2x = 20$

$\quad \quad \quad \quad \quad \boxed{\div 2} \quad \boxed{\div 2}$

$\quad \quad \quad \quad \quad \quad x = 10$

Exercise 6E

Solve the equations.

1 $5x + 3 = 2x + 15$

2 $7x + 2 = 3x + 22$

3 $3x - 2 = x + 14$

4 $9x - 7 = 4x + 28$

5 $8x - 11 = 5x + 19$

6 $6x + 9 = 4x + 19$

7 $10x + 3 = 4x + 39$

8 $5x + 13 = 3x + 45$

9
A hat costs £$(5n - 3)$ and jeans cost £$(3n + 17)$. If the hat and jeans cost the same amount of money, find the value of n then work out how much the hat costs?

Now solve these equations.

10 $3(x + 2) = 2(x + 7)$

11 $5(2x - 1) = 3(2x + 5)$

12 $6(x + 3) = 2(2x + 15)$

13 $4(2x - 5) = 5(x + 8)$

14 $2(3x + 2) = 4(x + 6)$

15 $6(3x - 2) = 4(4x + 3)$

16 $3(2x - 4) = 2(2x + 9)$

17 $4(3x + 2) = 5(2x + 4)$

18 If I subtract 2 from the number n and then multiply the result by 5, the answer is 20. Write down an equation and solve it to find the value of n.

Rules of indices

Reminder: $a^m \times a^n = a^{m+n}$ $a^m \div a^n = a^{m-n}$

Exercise 7M

Simplify and write each answer in index form.

1 $m^7 \div m^3$

2 $m^2 \times m^4 \times m^2$

3 $m^7 \times m^2 \times m^2$

4 $\dfrac{m^{10}}{m^4}$

5 $\dfrac{m^5 \times m^4}{m^7}$

6 $m^6 \times m$

7 $\dfrac{m^6 \times m^3}{m^2 \times m^2}$

8 $\dfrac{m^{15}}{m^4 \times m^7}$

9 $\dfrac{m^{10} \times m^4}{m \times m^3 \times m}$

10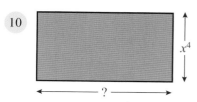

An expression for the area of this rectangle is x^9 cm². Write down an expression for the length of the rectangle in index form.

11 If $\dfrac{n^4}{n^x} = n$, write down the value of x.

12 If $\dfrac{n^6 \times n^x}{n^5} = n^8$, write down the value of x.

13 $5^6 \times 5 = 25^6$. True or false? Explain your answer.

14 Work out the actual value of $\dfrac{3^4}{3^2} - \dfrac{3^7}{3^6}$

15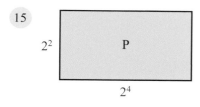

Which rectangle has the greater area and by how much? All lengths are cm.

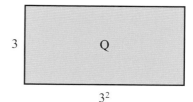

16 John says that $\dfrac{8^2 \times 8^5}{8^4}$ has the same value as $\dfrac{8^8}{8^2 \times 8^3}$

Is he correct or not? Explain your answer.

Need more practice with algebra?

1 If $V = IR$, find the value of V when $I = 20$ and $R = 4$

2 If $p = 2a + 2b$, find the value of p when $a = 7$ and $b = 12$

3 Use $m = 2$ and $n = 9$ to find the value of each expression.
   (a) $3(m + 1)$
   (b) $7(n - 4)$
   (c) $5(n - m)$
   (d) $4(m + n)$
   (e) $2(4m + n)$
   (f) $m(n + 3)$

4 Which of the following expressions are the same as $2n$?

| $3n - n$ | $n \times n$ | $5n - 4n$ | $n + n$ | $\dfrac{6n}{3}$ | $2 + n$ |

5 Bella has £$(3m + 7n)$. She spends £$3n$ but her mother gives her £m. Write down an expression for the money Bella now has.

6 Frank has made a clock using n nuts.

   (a) His sister eats 8 nuts. Write down an expression
      for how many nuts are still in the clock.

   (b) Next, Frank uses m nuts to make his clock look better.
      How many nuts are in the clock now?

   (c) Finally, Frank finishes his clock by using another m nuts.
      How many nuts are in the clock now?

7 Expand

   (a) $4(3n + 2)$ (b) $6(3m - 4)$ (c) $m(n + m)$

8 If $x = 3p + 4$, find the value of x when $p = -2$

9 Expand and simplify

   (a) $3(m + 2) + 5(2m + 1)$ (b) $4(3n + 7) - 2(4n - 3)$

10 (a) Copy and complete the table for $y = 5 - x$ for x-values from 0 to 5

x	0	1	2	3	4	5
y			3			
coordinates			(2, 3)			

   (b) Draw the graph of $y = 5 - x$ using 1 cm for 1 unit on both the x-axis and the y-axis.

11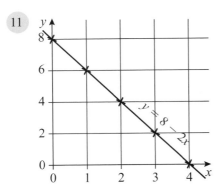

   (a) Copy this diagram showing the line $y = 8 - 2x$
   (b) Draw the line $x = 1$
   (c) Draw the line $x = 3$
   (d) Write down the coordinates of the point where the
      line $y = 8 - 2x$ meets the line $x = 1$

12 Margo says that $6a + 3b + a - 2b + 4 = 6a^2 + 5$.
Explain clearly whether Margo is correct or not.

13 Solve
(a) $7n - 6 = 36$ (b) $5(2n + 3) = 75$ (c) $\frac{n}{4} - 6 = 2$

(d) $8n - 2 = 5n + 19$ (e) $7n = 3$ (f) $3(3n - 2) = 7n + 10$

14 Work out the actual value of $\dfrac{5^2 \times 5^9}{5^8}$ without using a calculator.

15 What must be added to $5a + 3b - 4$ to make $9a + 2b - 1$?

Extension questions with algebra

1 For each statement, answer 'true' or 'false'.
(a) $8 \times m = m \times 8$ (b) $n + n^2 = n^3$ (c) $4y - y = 3y$
(d) $a + a + a = a^3$ (e) $4 \div n = n \div 4$ (f) $m - n = -n + m$

2 The perimeter p of a shape is given by the formula
$$p = 3a + 7b + 4c - 2$$
Find the value of p when $a = 6$, $b = 4$ and $c = -1$

3 Work out the actual value of $\dfrac{2^3 \times 2^7 \times 2^4}{2^8 \times 2^2} - \dfrac{2^5}{2^3}$

4 The perimeter of this rectangle is 32 cm.
Find x and hence find the area of the rectangle.

$x - 2$

$4x + 3$

5 In this number wall the number in each brick is found by
adding the numbers in the two bricks below.
Find the value of n.

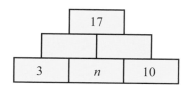

6 Expand and simplify $5(3x - 2) - 2(4x - 5) + 6(2x - 3)$.

7 Gwen says that $a^2 \times a^2 \times a^2 = a^8$. *Explain clearly* the mistake she has made.

8   Solve

(a) $3n + 7 = 8n + 2$

(b) $\dfrac{n}{7} = -2$

(c) $7n - 3 = 2$

(d) $3(2n + 5) = 16$

(e) $4n - 1 = 2n + 8$

(f) $6(3n - 4) = 2(7n + 6)$

9   All the sides of a square are equal.

(a) Look at the square opposite and write down an equation involving n.

(b) Solve the equation to find the value of n.

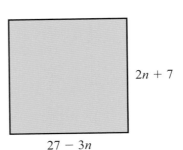

$2n + 7$

$27 - 3n$

10 Which three cards below have the same value when $n = 4$?
Write down what this value is.

| $3n - 12$ | $\dfrac{n^2 + 14}{6}$ | $(n + 1)^2$ | $13 - 2n$ | $\left(\dfrac{16}{n}\right)^2$ | $\dfrac{20}{n}$ |

11

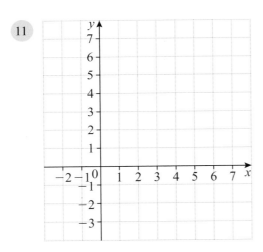

(a) Copy these axes.

(b) Using tables of values, draw the line with equation $y = 6 - x$ and the line with equation $y = 3x - 2$

(c) Write down the coordinates of the point where the two lines meet.

12 (a) Use a table of values to draw $y = x^2 + x$ for x-values from 0 to 4

(b) Use the curve to find the value of y when $x = 2.5$

Investigation – the painted cube

The diagrams below show five different sized cubes formed by unit cubes.

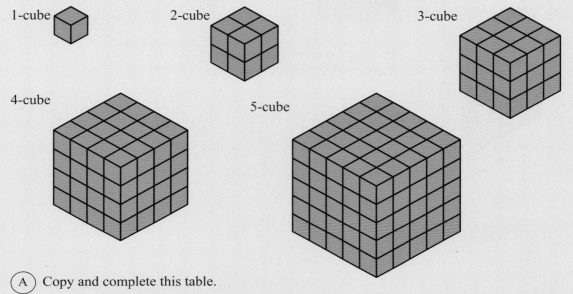

A Copy and complete this table.

Object	1-cube	2-cube	3-cube	4-cube	5-cube	6-cube	7-cube	8-cube
Number of unit cubes	1	8						

B The outside of each large cube is painted red. Some unit cubes will have 3 faces painted red, some will have 2 faces painted red, some will have only 1 face painted red and some unit cubes will stay completely unpainted.

Copy and complete the table below showing the number of unit cubes with 3, 2, 1 or 0 faces painted red.

Object	Number of unit cubes	Number of red faces			
		3	2	1	0
2-cube	8	8 cubes	0	0	0
3-cube					
4-cube					
5-cube					

C Use your table to help you predict the number of unit cubes with 3, 2, 1 or 0 faces coloured red for a 6-cube and for a 7-cube.

D How many unit cubes will have 1 red face for a 10-cube?

E How many unit cubes will have no red faces for a 20-cube?

CHECK YOURSELF ON SECTIONS 6.3 and 6.4

1 Drawing three-dimensional objects

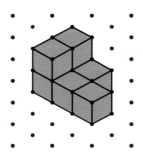

Draw a plan view, front elevation and side elevation for this object.

2 Simplifying expressions

(a) $3m + 6n - 4n + m = 4m + 2n$ True or false?

(b)

$4w + 3$

$n - 1$ $n - 1$

$2w + 1$

Write down an expression for the perimeter of this trapezium. Collect like terms if possible.

(c) Simplify $n^2 + n^2 + n^2$

3 Substituting numbers for letters

(a) If $n = 7$, which of the expressions below has the largest value?

$8n$ $n^2 + 9$ $60 - n$ $(n + 1)^2$

(b) If $y = mx + c$, find the value of y when $m = 6$, $x = 7$ and $c = -10$

4 Multiplying out single brackets

Multiply out   (a) $7(x + 4)$ (b) $6(2n - 1)$ (c) $m(m + n)$

Simplify   (d) $3(n + 5) + 8(n + 2)$ (e) $6(2x + 3) - 4(x - 2)$

5 Drawing and using straight line graphs

(a) Copy and complete the table for $y = 2x - 1$ then draw the graph using 1 cm for 1 unit on each axis.

x	0	1	2	3	4
y					
coordinates					

(b)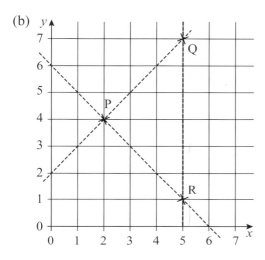

Look at the coordinates of the points on each line carefully. Find the equation of the line through

(i)   P and Q

(ii) P and R

(iii) Q and R

6 Solving linear equations

Solve   (a) $5x - 3 = 27$ (b) $3(2x + 5) = 33$ (c) $7x - 14 = 3x + 14$ (d) $\dfrac{x}{3} = 12$

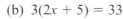

Rafa concentrates better with a box on his head.
He is n years old.

(e) Write down an expression for how old he will be in 34 years time.

(f) Rafa works out that in 34 years he will be three times as old as he is now. Write down an equation using n.

(g) Solve the equation to find out how old he is now.

7 Using the rules of indices

Simplify and write each answer in index form.

(a) $n^4 \times n^3$ (b) $\dfrac{n^9}{n^5}$ (c) $\dfrac{n^4 \times n^8}{n^{10}}$

(d) Find the value of x if $n \times n^x = n^7$

6.5 Probability 2

In section 6.5 you will:

- review unit 1 probability work
- find probabilities involving two events

Unit 1 probability review

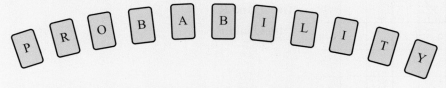

(a) A card is chosen at random from the cards above.
What is the probability of getting a vowel?

(b) A card is randomly removed then replaced 66 times.
How many times would you expect to get the letter 'B'?

(a) $p(\text{vowel}) = \dfrac{4}{11}$

(b) $p(\text{letter 'B'}) = \dfrac{2}{11}$

Letter 'B' expected $\dfrac{2}{11}$ of 66 times = 12 times

Exercise 1M

1 A bag contains 5 red balls, 3 blue balls and 2 green balls. One ball is selected at random.
Find the probability of selecting

  (a) a green ball   (b) not a blue ball   (c) a yellow ball.

2 A box of fruity chews contains the following flavours.

7 strawberry	4 blackcurrant
5 orange	7 lime
6 lemon	1 cherry

A chew is chosen at random. Which flavour has a probability of $\dfrac{1}{5}$ of being chosen?
Justify your answer.

3   3 out of 8 apples have gone rotten.
    One apple is chosen at random.
    What is the probability that
    this apple is *not* rotten?

4   The spinner is spun 225 times.
    How many times would you expect
    it to land on an even number?

5   Geraldine needs to throw a '6' to start a game. So far she has thrown 5, 1, 2, 2, 5, 3, 1, 4, 5, 4
    and 4. What is the probability that she will get a '6' with her next throw?

6   The probability of Jack getting a bike for Christmas is 0.28. What is the probability that Jack
    will not get a bike for Christmas?

7
    One ball is to be removed from
    bag A and one ball is to be
    removed from bag B.
    From which bag is it more
    likely a blue ball will be removed?
    Give a reason for your answer.

    Bag A   Bag B

8   Liliya scores 10 goals from 10 attempts during a netball game. Martha says that Liliya will
    definitely score a goal with her next attempt. Is Martha correct? Explain your answer fully.

9   What is the probability that a
    young child will randomly
    pick up a green cube from
    those shown opposite?

10 A coin is tossed 600 times. The number of heads and tails
    obtained is shown opposite.
    Do you think that the coin is fair? Justify your answer.

Heads	Tails
288	312

11 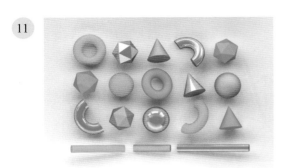 A solid is randomly removed from
    those shown opposite then replaced.
    This is done 90 times. How many
    times would you expect a cone to
    be removed?

12 Milo always does one lot of homework on a Sunday morning. It will always be science,
    history, maths or art. The probability of doing each homework is shown below.

subject	science	history	maths	art
probability	0.35	x	0.25	x

The probability of doing history or art is the same. Work out the probability of doing art.

Two events: listing possible outcomes

When an experiment involves two events, it is usually helpful to make a list of all the possible
outcomes. When there is a large number of outcomes, it is important to be systematic in making
the list.

- Coins
  Using H for 'head' and T for 'tail', two coins can land as:

H	H
H	T
T	H
T	T

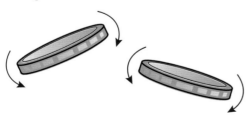

The probability of tossing two tails $= \dfrac{1}{4}$

- Two dice

  When a red dice is thrown with a white dice, the outcomes are (red dice first):

  (1, 1), (1, 2), (1, 3), (1, 4), (1, 5), (1, 6), (2, 1), (2, 2), (2, 3) … (6, 6).

  The 36 equally likely outcomes can be shown on a grid.
  Point A shows a 4 on the red dice and a 5 on the
  white dice. Point B shows a 2 on the red dice and
  a 4 on the white dice.
  The probability of rolling
  a 4 on the red dice and
  a 5 on the white dice is $\dfrac{1}{36}$

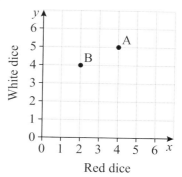

Exercise 2M

1   The four cards shown are shuffled and placed face down on a table.

Two cards are selected at random.

(a) List all the possible pairs of cards which could be selected.

(b) Find the probability that the total of the two cards is
   (i) 5
   (ii) 9

2   A red dice is thrown first and then a blue dice is thrown.
   Draw a grid like the earlier example.

(a) Find the probability that the score on the blue dice will be the same as the score on the red dice.

(b) Find the probability that the score on the blue dice will be one more than the score on the red dice.

3   A blue spinner and a yellow spinner are both spun. Draw a grid then work out the probability that the total score for both spinners will be 5

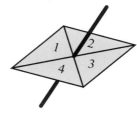

Blue spinner

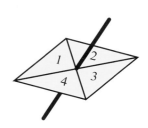

Yellow spinner

400

4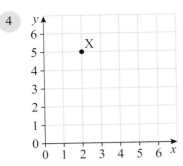

Two dice are rolled together and the *difference* is found.

In the grid, the point X has a difference of 3 obtained by rolling a 2 and a 5

Find the expected probability of obtaining a difference of

(a) 3

(b) 0

5 Roll a pair of dice 108 times and in a tally chart record the frequency of obtaining the totals from 2 to 12

Total	Frequency
2	
3	
⋮	
12	

6 (a) Work out the expected probability of getting a total of 5 when two dice are rolled together. Compare your answer with the experimental probability of getting a total of 5 obtained in the experiment in question 5.

(b) Work out the expected probability of other totals and compare them with the experimental results.

Need more practice with probability?

1 **G**₃ **A**₁ **R**₁ **A**₁ **G**₃ **E**₁

The word above is made during a game of Scrabble.
If one piece is chosen at random, what is the probability of getting
(a) an 'E'   (b) a tile that scores 1   (c) a vowel?

2 The probability of Kylo going to the cinema on a Friday evening is 0.3.
What is the probability of Kylo not going to the cinema next Friday evening?

3 **1** **2** **3** **4** **5** **6** **7** **8** **9**

All the square numbers are removed from above. One number is then randomly chosen from the numbers that remain.
What is the probability that this is a prime number?

4   The probability of Annie getting a
    times table question correct is 0.8.
    If Annie is asked to do 60
    times table questions, how many
    correct answers would Annie be
    expected to give?

5   Yara enjoys chicken curries.
    She has 4 favourite dishes.
    The probabilities of her choosing
    each one, when she has a curry,
    are shown in the table.

Bhuna	$\frac{1}{5}$
Dupiaza	?
Madras	$\frac{1}{10}$
Dhansak	$\frac{3}{10}$

    (a) Find the probability of Yara
         choosing a dupiaza.

    (b) Which dish does Yara choose most often?

6   A footballer scores a goal in 7 consecutive games. What is the probability that the footballer
    will score in the next game?

7

Main meal	Dessert
Lasagne	Ice cream
Cottage pie	Chocolate mousse
Fish pie	

Diners at a restaurant
have a main meal and
a dessert.

    (a) Write down all the different meals a diner might choose, e.g. fish pie, ice cream.

    (b) What is the probability that a diner will choose cottage pie with ice cream or
         chocolate mousse?

8   What is the probability of throwing 2 heads when tossing 2 coins?

9   A pack of 52 playing cards has 13 hearts. A card is randomly selected then returned to the pack
    96 times. How many times would you expect the card to be a heart?

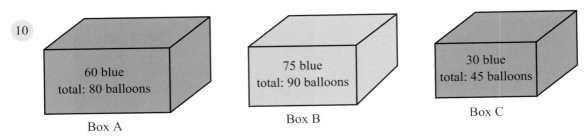

Box A Box B Box C

10   Three boxes of balloons contain the number of blue balloons shown above. If one balloon is removed from each box, which box gives the greatest chance of a blue balloon being picked? Give a reason for your answer.

Extension questions with probability

1   The spinner shown has six equal sections on the outside and three equal sections in the middle. The spinner shows a '5' and an 'A'.

Find the probability of spinning

(a) a 'C'

(b) a '7'

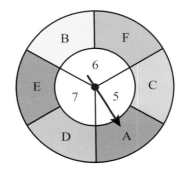

2   A coin and a dice are tossed together.

(a) List all the possible outcomes.

(b) Find the probability of getting

    (i)   a head on the coin and a 6 on the dice

    (ii) a tail on the coin and an even number on the dice.

3   Two bags contain numbered discs as shown. One disc is selected at random from each bag. The numbers on the two discs are added together.

(a) Draw a grid to show all 28 possible outcomes.

(b) Find the probability that

    (i)   the total of the two numbers is 6

    (ii) the total of the two numbers is less than 5

4　A bag contains a 1p coin, a 10p coin and a 20p coin. Two coins are selected at random.

　(a) List all the different ways in which two coins can be selected from the bag.

　(b) Find the probability that the total value of the two coins selected is

　　(i) 11p

　　(ii) 30p

5　(a) List all the outcomes when three coins are tossed together, for example: H T H.

　(b) Find the probability of getting

　　(i) exactly one head

　　(ii) three tails.

6　Find the probability of getting exactly one tail when four coins are tossed together.

6.6 Geometry review

In section 6.6 you will review angles, transformations, area, Pythagoras, bearings and volume

Reminder:

Area of a parallelogram = base × height

Area of a trapezium = $\frac{1}{2}$(sum of parallel sides) × height

Area of a circle = π × radius²

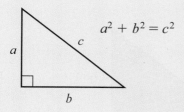

$a^2 + b^2 = c^2$

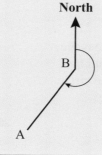

Bearing of A from B.
Bearings are
measured clockwise
from the North line.

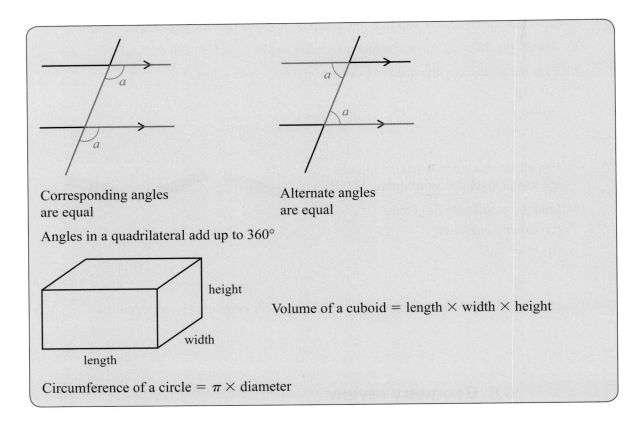

Corresponding angles
are equal

Alternate angles
are equal

Angles in a quadrilateral add up to 360°

Volume of a cuboid = length × width × height

Circumference of a circle = π × diameter

Exercise 1M

Give answers in this exercise to 1 decimal place if necessary.

1   Work out the value of x in each triangle below.

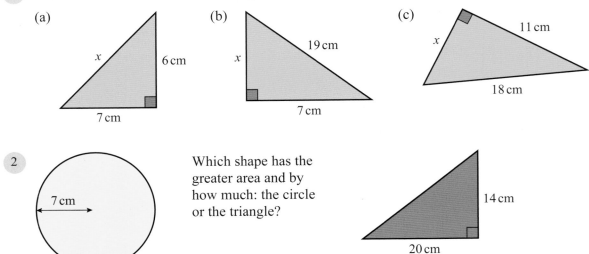

(a)
x
6 cm
7 cm

(b)
19 cm
x
7 cm

(c)
11 cm
x
18 cm

2   Which shape has the greater area and by how much: the circle or the triangle?

7 cm

14 cm
20 cm

3   One angle in a quadrilateral is 120°. The other three angles are all equal in size.
    What is the value of one of these angles?

4   Calculate the area of each shape. The lengths are in cm.

(a)   (b)   (c)

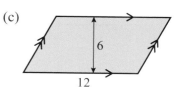

5   Copy this shape onto squared paper.

    (a) Translate this shape with $\begin{pmatrix} 4 \\ -2 \end{pmatrix}$.

    (b) Translate the new shape with $\begin{pmatrix} -4 \\ 2 \end{pmatrix}$.

        What do you notice.

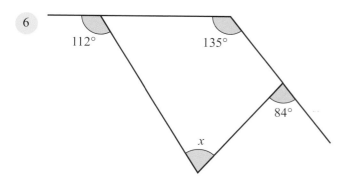

6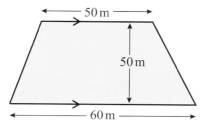

    Work out the
    value of angle x.

7   The basic plan of a castle is shown below.

    Work out the area of this plan.

8 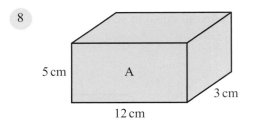 Write down the
ratio of the
volume of cuboid A
to the volume of
cuboid B. Give
your answer in
its simplest form.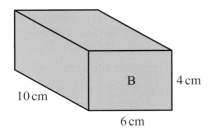

9  The end of each crayon is a circle with a radius of 4.5 mm.
Find the total area of the ends of all 34 crayons.
Give the answer to the nearest whole number.

10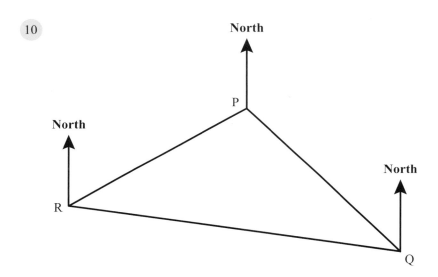

(a) Measure the bearing
of P from Q.
(b) Measure the bearing
of R from P.

Exercise 2M

Give answers in this exercise to 1 decimal place if necessary.

1 Work out the area of the lawn. The lengths are in metres.

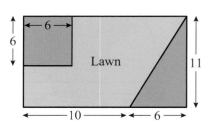

2

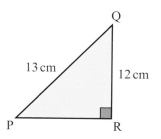

(a) Work out the value of PR.

(b) Work out the area of triangle PQR.

3 A square has a perimeter of 36 cm. Calculate the area of the square.

4

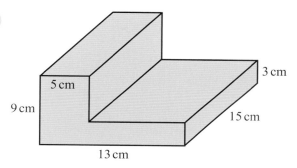

Work out the volume of this solid.

5

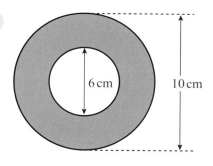

Find the purple area.

6 Work out the value of angle *x*.

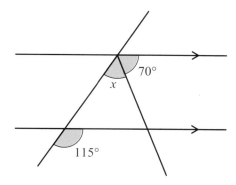

408

7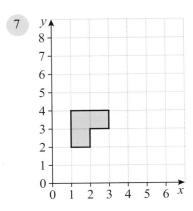

(a) Copy the diagram opposite.

(b) Enlarge the shape about (0, 0) with scale factor 2

(c) Enlarge the shape about (0, 3) with scale factor 2

8 Work out the area of this semicircle.

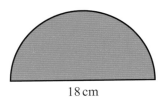

18 cm

9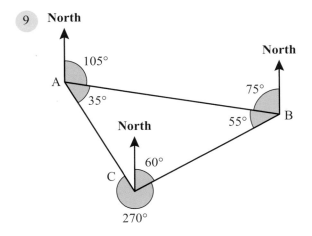

(a) Work out the bearing of C from A.

(b) Work out the bearing of C from B.

10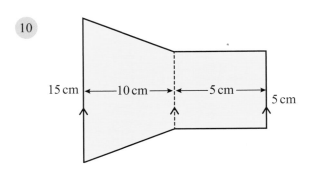

Work out the area of this shape.

15 cm   ←—10 cm—→ ←—5 cm—→   5 cm

Need more practice with geometry?

Give answers in this exercise to 1 decimal place if necessary.

1   Which area is
    the odd one out?

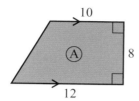 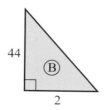 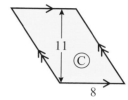

2   A piece of metal has
    a hole in the shape of
    a cuboid through its
    middle. All lengths
    are in cm.
    Work out the volume
    of the piece of metal.

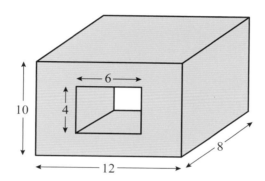

3

Prove that triangle ABD
is equilateral.

4   A shape is rotated 90° clockwise about (1, 3). *Describe fully* the clockwise rotation that will
    send the new shape back to its original position.

5   Find the area of the face of this clock if its diameter is 1.6 m

6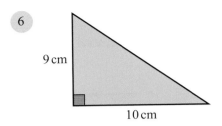

9 cm
10 cm

The area of the triangle is equal to the area of the parallelogram. What is the height of the parallelogram?

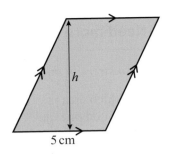

h
5 cm

7 A ship sails 6 km due north and then a further 8 km on a bearing of 075°. Make a scale drawing using a scale of 1 cm to represent 1 km. Use this scale drawing to work out how far the ship is now from its starting point.

8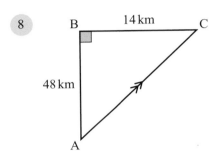

B   14 km   C

48 km

A

Anton travels from A to B then B to C.
Jess travels directly from A to C.
Who travels further and by how much?

9 Calculate the area of this shape.

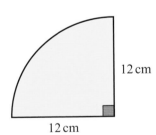

12 cm

12 cm

10

Copy the diagram opposite then reflect the shape in the line $x = 1$

Extension questions with geometry

Give answers in this exercise to 1 decimal place if necessary.

1

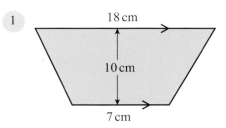

18 cm

10 cm

7 cm

The area of the parallelogram is equal to double the area of the trapezium. What is the perpendicular height of the parallelogram?

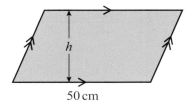

h

50 cm

2 A 4 metre ladder leans against a vertical wall. The base of the ladder is 1.5 metres from the wall. How high up the wall does the ladder reach?

3 Calculate the total area of this window, giving your answer to the nearest whole number.

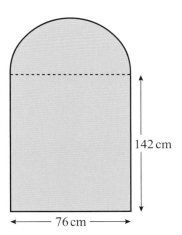

142 cm

76 cm

4

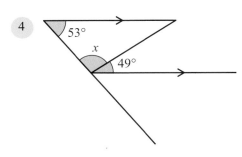

53°

x

49°

Work out the value of angle x.

5 Work out the value of x if the area of the triangle is 36 cm².

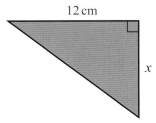

12 cm

x

412

6

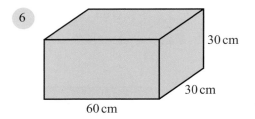

30 cm

30 cm

60 cm

Water is poured into this tank at a rate of 50 cm³ per second. How many minutes will it take to fill the tank completely?

7 A brother and sister argue because they both want the larger bedroom. Look at the plan opposite. Which bedroom do they both want? Show your working out. (You may use a calculator.)

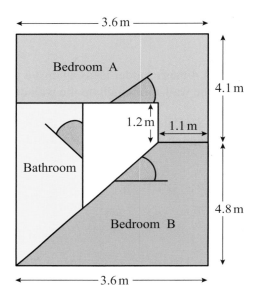

3.6 m

Bedroom A

4.1 m

1.2 m   1.1 m

Bathroom

4.8 m

Bedroom B

3.6 m

8

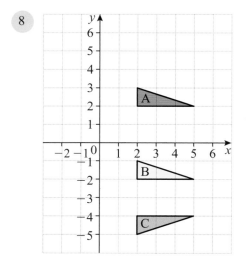

Describe fully the transformation of
(a) triangle A to triangle B
(b) triangle B to triangle C
(c) triangle C to triangle A.

9   The wheels on Vidal's bike have a diameter of 68 cm. Vidal cycles so that the bike wheels rotate 2500 times. How many km does Vidal cycle?

10   A large triangular prism is to be painted. The complete surface area is to be covered. One tin of paint covers 23 m². How many tins of paint will be needed to complete the painting?

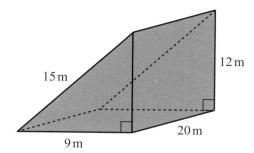

15 m

12 m

9 m

20 m

✖ Spot the mistakes 12 ✖

Algebra, probability and geometry

Work through each question below and *explain clearly* what mistakes have been made. Beware – some questions are correctly done.

1   Expand and simplify $4(2x + 3) + 5(3x + 1)$

     Answer: $4(2x + 3) + 5(3x + 1) = 8x + 12 + 15x + 1$
                                    $= 23x + 13$

2   Work out the area of the parallelogram.

     Answer: Area $= 15 \times 10$
                         $= 150 \, cm^2$

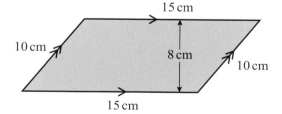

15 cm

10 cm

8 cm

10 cm

15 cm

3   Write this answer in index form: $\dfrac{n^3 \times n \times n^4}{n^2 \times n^2}$

     Answer: $\dfrac{n^3 \times n \times n^4}{n^2 \times n^2} = \dfrac{n^{12}}{n^4} = n^3$

4

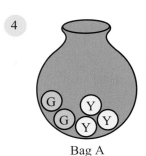

Bag A

Two bags each contain green and yellow balls, as shown. From which bag are you more likely to remove a yellow ball if one ball is randomly removed from each bag? Justify your answer.

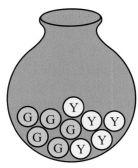

Bag B

Answer: You are more likely to remove a yellow ball from bag B because there are more yellow balls (5) in bag B than in bag A (3).

5 Solve $5(2n - 4) = 2(4n + 16)$

Answer: $5(2n - 4) = 2(4n + 16)$
$10n - 20 = 8n + 32$
$2n - 20 = 32$
$2n = 32 - 20$
$2n = 12$
$n = 6$

6

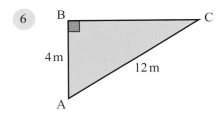

Work out the perimeter of this triangle.

Answer: $BC^2 = 4^2 + 12^2 = 160$
$BC = \sqrt{160} = 12.65 \text{ m (to 1 d.p.)}$
perimeter $= 12 + 4 + 12.65 = 28.65 \text{ m}$

7 The equation of a straight line is $y = mx + c$. Work out the value of y when $m = 4$, $x = -2$ and $c = 3$

Answer: $y = mx + c = 4 \times -2 + 3$
$= -8 + 3$
$= -5$

8 What is the bearing
   of P from Q?

   Answer:

   Bearing of P from Q
   $= 40° + 60° = 100°$

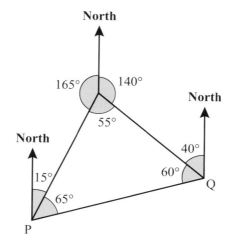

9

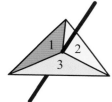

This spinner is spun twice. What is the
probability of getting a total of 4
from the two spins?

Answer: All possible outcomes:

A total of 4 appears
three times. There are
nine possible outcomes.

Probability of getting
a total of 4 is $\dfrac{3}{9} = \dfrac{1}{3}$

+	1	2	3
1	2	3	4
2	3	4	5
3	4	5	6

10

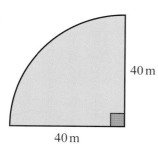

40 m

40 m

A quarter circle area within a
sports field is to be laid with
astroturf at £7.20 per square metre.
What will be the total cost of
the astroturf?

Answer: area $= \dfrac{\pi \times \text{diameter}}{4} = \dfrac{\pi \times 80}{4} = 62.83 \text{ m}^2$

cost $= 62.83 \times 7.20$
$= £452.38$

416

CHECK YOURSELF ON SECTIONS 6.5 and 6.6

1 Reviewing unit 1 probability work

(a) The probability of Rowena winning a swimming race is 0.15. Write down the probability of Rowena not winning the swimming race.

(b)

2	2	6	7	8	8	8	9

Eli removes the number '7' from the cards above. What is the probability that the next card he removes will be an '8'

(c) Jackie throws a fair dice 72 times. How many times would Jackie expect a square number?

2 Finding probabilities involving two events

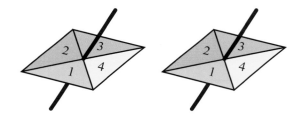

(a) Each spinner is used once. List all the possible outcomes.

   e.g. Spinner A   Spinner B

1	1
1	2
☐	☐

   (There are 16 different outcomes)

(b) What is the probability of getting a total score of 3?

(c) Two coins are thrown. What is the probability that one head and one tail are thrown?

3 Reviewing geometry

Calculate the area of each shape. The lengths are in cm.

(a)
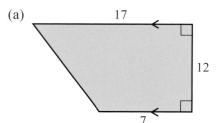

(b)
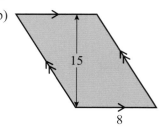

(c)
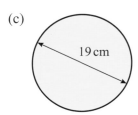

(d)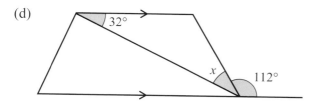

Write down the value of angle x.

(e) Which side is longer and by how much: BC or QR?

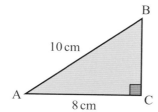

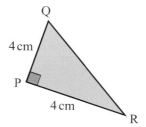

6.7 Applying mathematics 6

In section 6.7 you will apply maths in a variety of situations.

1   Three online stores have offers on the price of a jacket.

Jacks	Regal	Pantheon
£66 30% off	£70 $\frac{2}{5}$ off	£65 15% off plus a further 10% reduction

Which store price is the cheapest? Show all your working out.

2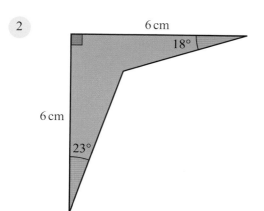

Suraj has the piece of wood shown opposite. He needs to cut another piece of wood to attach to this to make a 6 cm by 6 cm square.
Draw an accurate diagram of the piece of wood that Suraj needs to cut.

3   Galina spends 30% of her monthly money on rent and bills. She spends $\frac{2}{9}$ of the money on food. She also saves $\frac{1}{4}$ of the money for holidays. Each month she saves £450 for holidays.

(a) How much money does Galina earn each month?

(b) How much money does Galina have left over each month after paying for holidays, rent, bills and food?

4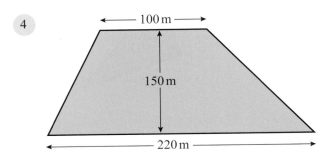

A farmer needs to spray this field. It costs £3 to spray each 1200 m². How much does it cost to spray the entire field?

5   There are dogs and cats in an animal rescue centre in the ratio 7 : 2. There are a total of 27 dogs and cats. If 9 more dogs and 4 more cats join the rescue centre, what does the ratio of dogs to cats become?

6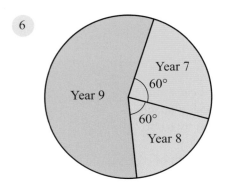

54 pupils in Years 7, 8 and 9 take part in the school play. The pie chart shows the proportion of pupils from each year group. $\frac{2}{3}$ of these Year 8 pupils are in the chorus. How many Year 8 pupils are in the chorus?

7   A chef has 5 litres of olive oil. During one day he uses 600 ml of the olive oil and also gives 1200 ml to another chef. During the following day he uses a quarter of the remaining olive oil. How much olive oil has the chef now got?

8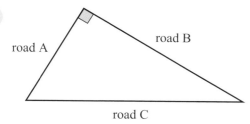

road A

road B

road C

Alan has to clean three roads every day for one whole week. The three roads are shown opposite. Road A is 1.2 km long and road B is 1.8 km long. Calculate the total length of road that Alan cleans in one whole week. Give the answer to 1 decimal place.

9 For one unit of electricity, which costs 12p, you can watch 18 episodes of EastEnders or heat water for 36 cups of tea. How much will it cost in electricity for Mr and Mrs Jamel to watch 54 episodes of EastEnders and each drink a cup of tea while doing so?

10 (a) Write down an expression for the volume of this box.

(b) Work out the value of x if the volume of the box is 180 cm³

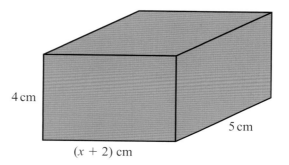

4 cm

5 cm

$(x + 2)$ cm

UNIT 6   MIXED REVIEW

Part one

1 Find the value of each expression when $n = 3$

(a) $n^2 - n$ (b) $4n + 2$ (c) $(5 - n)^2$ (d) $\dfrac{6}{n}$

2 Rewrite the expressions using algebra.

(a) Add four to m.

(b) Subtract p from six.

(c) Triple t then take away two.

3 Solve

(a) $5(2n - 3) = 25$ (b) $32 = 17 + 5n$ (c) $8n - 1 = 3n + 29$

4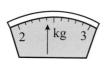

2 kg 3

Carrots cost 75p per kilogram. Some carrots weigh the amount shown opposite. How much will these carrots cost?

5   How many times can the small box be filled from the large container which is full of fertilizer?

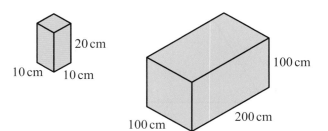

20 cm
10 cm   10 cm
100 cm
100 cm   200 cm

6   A spoon contains 20 ml of cough mixture. How many spoons can be filled from a one litre bottle of cough mixture?

7   If $m^2 \times m^x = m^7$, write down the value of x.

8   Calculate the pink area.

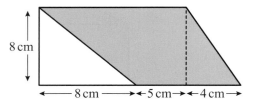

8 cm
8 cm   5 cm   4 cm

9   The cooks at a restaurant use 4000 ml of oil in 5 days. How many days will a 200 litre tank of oil last?

10   One card is picked at random from a pack of 52. There are 4 cards with each number or picture and there are 4 suits: hearts, diamonds, clubs and spades. Find the probability that the card is
(a) the queen of diamonds   (b) a ten   (c) a diamond.

11   The model is made from matchboxes.

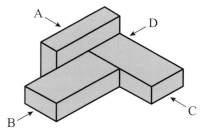

A
D
B
C

From which direction (A, B, C or D) are these views taken?

(a) 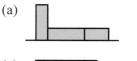   (b)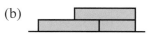

(c)    (d)

12 The probability of the Taylor family having fish for dinner is 0.27.
What is the probability that the Taylor family will not have fish for dinner?

13 Sam thinks of a number. He multiplies it by 3, adds 4 and then doubles the result.
The answer is 50. Form an equation and then solve it to find the number.

14 Asif is working on the top floor of a very tall
office building. He walks up 826 steps from
the ground floor to his office. Each step
is 24 cm.

(a) How high does he climb in cm?

(b) Change the height into km, correct
to one decimal place.

Part two

1 Darren says that $mn + nm$ is equal to $2mn$.
Is he correct or not? Give a reason for your answer.

2 Multiply out these brackets.

(a) $4(n + 6)$ (b) $5(3y - 7)$ (c) $m(m - p)$

3

Garden monster

Fang, with 27 000 teeth and
weighing in at 21.7 g and
5 inches long, beat 30
contenders for the heavy-
weight title of the slug world.
The event at a Bristol garden
centre raised several hundred
pounds for charity. Fang, a
common black slug, was
entered by Betty Baptiste, 60.

(a) How many kg does Fang weigh?

(b) Is Fang more or less than 20 cm long?

4 Anna has n marbles in a bag.

(a) She takes 3 marbles from the bag. Write an expression for the
number of marbles now in the bag.

(b) Steve has four bags, each containing n marbles. Write an expression
for the number of marbles there are altogether in the four bags.

(c) In a game Steve wins 10 more marbles. Write an expression for the number
of marbles he has now.

n
marbles

422

5 Write each sentence with the number you think is most likely.

   (a) The width of an adult hand is ☐. (4 inches, 4 cm, 0.5 m)

   (b) The classroom door is ☐ high. (80 cm, 2 m, 3 feet)

   (c) An adult man weighs about ☐. (75 g, 750 kg, 75 kg)

6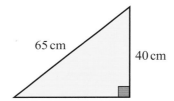

   Calculate the red area, giving the answer
   to 1 decimal place.

12 cm

12 cm

7 Calculate the perimeter of
   this triangle. Give the answer
   to 1 decimal place.

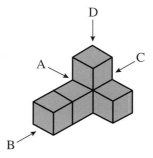

65 cm

40 cm

8 Draw this shape, on squared paper, as viewed from

   (a) A
   (b) B
   (c) C
   (d) D

   D

   A

   C

   B

9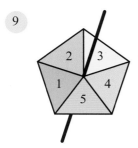

   This spinner is spun twice.
   Use a grid to work out the
   probability that the spinner
   will land on a 4 or 5 in
   either order.

   2   3
   1   4
     5

10 A bucket weighs 1.2 kg when it is empty, and 6.6 kg when it is full of water. What will it weigh when it is half full?

11 Part of a wall is painted yellow, as shown. On average it took Rio 12 minutes to paint 1 m² of the wall. How long did it take Rio to paint the yellow part of the wall?

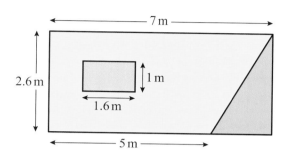

12 Four people are putting their suitcases on a plane. Each person is only allowed to take 22 kg on the plane.

(a) Whose luggage is too heavy and by how much?

	Weight of suitcases
Yasmin	7.83 kg, 12.14 kg
Eric	9.46 kg, 13.78 kg
Marie	6.19 kg, 8.37 kg, 5.2 kg
Matt	5.87 kg, 9.26 kg, 7.49 kg

Extra weight	Cost
0.01 kg to 0.5 kg	£13.68
0.51 kg to 1.5 kg	£29.17
1.51 kg to 3 kg	£42.13
3.01 kg to 5 kg	£57.45

(b) People can pay money to put extra weight on the plane. The costs are shown in the table above. How much extra will each of the people you chose in part (a) need to pay?

13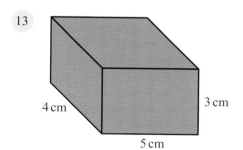

(a) Calculate the volume of this cuboid.

(b) Calculate the volume of the cuboid when each of the dimensions is increased by 10%.

14 The diagram shows two angles in an isosceles triangle. Form an equation involving x and solve it to find the angles of the triangle.

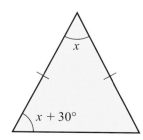

ANSWERS TO CHECK YOURSELF SECTIONS

Page 27 **Check yourself on sections 1.1, 1.2 and 1.3**

1. (a) 81 (b) 5^3

2. (a) 7^5 (b) 5^9 (c) 3^4

3. (a) 1, 28, 2, 14, 4, 7 (b) 60 (c) 15, 30, 45, 60, 75, 90

4. (a) $2 \times 3 \times 5 \times 5$ (b) $3 \times 3 \times 5 \times 7$

5. (a) HCF = 14, LCM = 1540 (b) HCF = 21, LCM = 1890

6. (a) $2m + 3n + 4$ (b) $x + 3y$ (c) $42mn$ (d) $5p - 4$ (e) $16n^2$

(f) $4m$ (g) A & C (h) False

7. (a) mp (b) $3n - 5$ (c) $70 + 4q$ (d) $5n + 14$

Page 45 **Check yourself on sections 1.4 and 1.5**

1. (a) 4.9 cm (b) 43° **2.** (a) 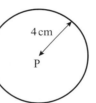 (b)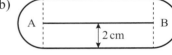

3. (a) 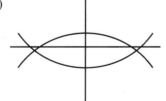 (b)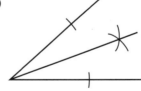

4. $a = 112°, b = 68°, c = 73°, d = 46°, e = 134°$

5.

$a + b + c = 180°$ (angles on a straight line)
so angles in a triangle add up to 180°

6. $a = 63°, b = 82°$ **7.** $a = 119°, b = 58°, c = 49°, d = 73°, e = 62°$

Page 69 **Check yourself on sections 1.6 and 1.7**

1. (a) $2\frac{1}{3}$ (b) $5\frac{5}{6}$ (c) $\frac{19}{5}$ (d) $\frac{11}{4}$

2. (a) $\dfrac{17}{30}$ (b) $\dfrac{5}{24}$ (c) $4\dfrac{1}{6}$ (d) $1\dfrac{9}{20}$

3. (a) $\dfrac{5}{14}$ (b) $2\dfrac{4}{5}$ (c) $\dfrac{5}{6}$ (d) $\dfrac{3}{5}$

4. (a) 0.1   (b) (i) $\dfrac{3}{8}$ (ii) $\dfrac{5}{8}$ (iii) $\dfrac{3}{8}$

5. (a) 120   (b) 24

6. (a) $\dfrac{18}{25} = 0.72$ (b) $\dfrac{7}{25} = 0.28$ (c) Yes

Page 97   **Check yourself on sections 2.1 and 2.2**

1. (a) 76%   (b) 17%   **2.** (a) £621   (b) (i) 144 cm²   (ii) 129.96 cm²

3. (a) 418.6   (b) 0.0811   (c) 3200   (d) 4000   (e) 22.47   (f) 437

4. (a) 800   (b) 200   (c) 36   (d) 2400

Page 119   **Check yourself on sections 2.3 and 2.4**

1. (a) $x = 4$ (b) $y = 3$ (c) $x = -2$ (d) line A $(x = 4)$

2. y: 4, 3, 2, 1, 0; coordinates: $(0, 4)$, $(1, 3)$, $(2, 2)$, $(3, 1)$, $(4, 0)$

3. (a) 7 km per litre   (b) 14 mpg   (c) 4 gallons

4. (a) $y = x + 6$ (b) A: $x + y = 3$, B: $y = x + 1$

5. (a) multiply by 4   (b) add 6   (c) subtract 3   (d) 9, 26, 77, 230

6. (a) 31, 39   (b) 39, 52

Page 147   **Check yourself on sections 2.5 and 2.6**

1. (a) 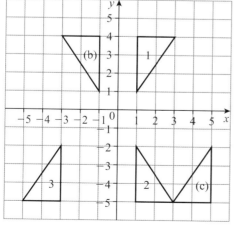   (d) $x = -1$

426

2.

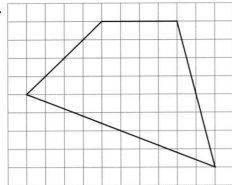

3. (a)

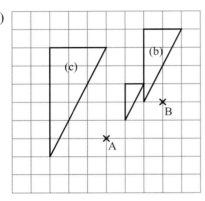

4.

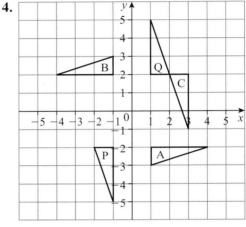

5. (a) $(0, -1)$ (b) $(-1, 0)$

6. (a) rotation 90° clockwise about $(-3, -1)$.

(b) e.g. rotation 90° clockwise about $(-3, -1)$
then translated 3 units right and 1 unit down.

(c) rotation 180° about $(0, 0)$

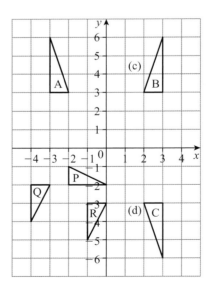

Page 176   **Check yourself on sections 3.1 and 3.2**

1. (a) 28 cm²   (b) 67 cm²   (c) 100 cm²   (d) 36 cm²

2. (a) 90 cm²   (b) 120 cm²   (c) 96 minutes

3. (a) 59.7 cm   (b) 245.0 cm   (c) 28.6 cm

4. (a) 227.0 cm²   (b) 907.9 cm²   (c) 4

Page 200   **Check yourself on sections 3.3 and 3.4**

1. (a) 6992   (b) 22.172   (c) 68

2. (a) 1.4   (b) 0.009

3. (a) $\dfrac{8}{35}$ (b) $3\dfrac{11}{12}$ (c) $\dfrac{1}{6}$ (d) 4

4. (a) 0.056   (b) 120   (c) 0.0096   (d) 70

5. (a) 17   (b) 36   (c) 26   (d) 6.41   (e) 0.72   (f) 6.67

6. (a) 27.1   (b) 10.8   (c) 0.8

7. (a) −126   (b) 14   (c) 16

Page 219   **Check yourself on sections 3.5 and 3.6**

1. (a)

$\dfrac{3}{5}$	$\dfrac{7}{20}$	$\dfrac{3}{100}$	$\dfrac{3}{8}$	$\dfrac{3}{25}$	$\dfrac{4}{5}$
0.6	0.35	0.03	0.375	0.12	0.8

(b) 0.34   (c) 44%

(d) True   (e) Roy by 2%

2. (a) $0.\dot{8}$ (b) $0.\dot{4}\dot{5}$ **3.** (a) $5x - 20$ (b) $12x + 6$

(c) $n^2 - 8n$ (d) $11x + 26$ (e) $14x + 19$ **4.** (a) $n = 6$

(b) $x = 6$ (c) $n = 5$ **5.** (a) $n = 6$ (b) $x = 5$

(c) $x = 4$ **6.** (a) 19°   (b) 5   (c) $x = 7$, BC = 33 cm

Page 253   **Check yourself on sections 4.1 and 4.2**

1. (a) 9   (b) 6   (c) 7   (d) 7   (e) 2 and 6

2. One sentence using Class 8B mean = 6 and Class 8C mean = 7, one sentence using
Class 8B range = 7, Class 8C range = 6

3. (a) 5   (b) 4

4. (a) 5   (b) 8   (c) True   **5.** (a) 207   (b) 310   (c) 55.9%

428

(d)

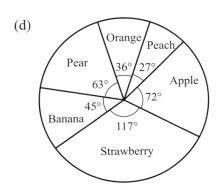

(e) 20%   (f) range = 40, median = 55

Page 272 *Check yourself on sections 4.3 and 4.4*

1. (a) $\sqrt{41}$ = 6.4 cm   (b) $\sqrt{45}$ = 6.7 cm   (c) $\sqrt{504}$ = 22.4 cm   (d) 90 cm

2. (a) 045°   (b) 090°   (c) 135°   (d) 180°   (e) 270°   (f) 225°

3. (a) 25 m   (b) $\approx$ 45 km

Page 287 *Check yourself on sections 4.5 and 4.6*

1. (a) G   (b) None   **2.** One possible tessellation:

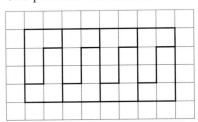

3. (a) −2   (b) 6   (c) −2   (d) −5   (e) −4   (f) −3

4. (a) A = −16, B = −2, C = 24, D = −8, E = −4, F = −40

(b) 28   (c) −10   (d) −5

Page 313 *Check yourself on sections 5.1 and 5.2*

1. (a) nth term = $5n + 3$ (b) Difference = 7, nth term = $7n − 5$

2. (a) $2m + 4n$ (b) $35n^2$ (c) $2n^2$ (d) $125m$ g   (e) No

3. (a) $m = 15$ (b) $y = 80$ (c) £1500

4. (a) 1   (b) 27   (c) −9   (d) 33

Page 330   **Check yourself on sections 5.3 and 5.4**

1. (a) AB−Two taps are on, BC−One tap is on, CD−Simon gets into bath,
DE−Simon lies in bath, EF−Simon gets out of bath, FG−Simon is out of bath looking for
shampoo, GH−Simon gets into bath, HI−Simon lies in bath, IJ−Simon gets out of bath,
JK−bath is emptied

(b)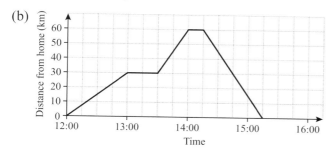

(c) 15:15

2. (a) 5 : 3   (b) £10.80   (c) 10 hours

3. (a) 156   (b) £160

4. (a) 2 km   (b) 600 m

Page 348   **Check yourself on sections 5.5 and 5.6**

1. (a) £19 530   (b) 72%   (c) £508.40

2. (a) £600   (b) £10 450   **3.** (a) 30% loss   (b) 50% profit

4. (a) 2.32   (b) (i) No correlation   (ii) 30

Page 372   **Check yourself on sections 6.1 and 6.2**

1. (a) 6700 g   (b) 5890 ml   (c) 0.35 km   (d) 600 kg

2. (a) True   (b) False   (c) False   (d) True

3. (a) 84 cm³   (b) 660 cm³   (c) 8

Page 394   **Check yourself on sections 6.3 and 6.4**

1.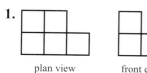

plan view   front elevation   side elevation

2. (a) True   (b) $6w + 2n + 2$ (c) $3n^2$ **3.** (a) $(n + 1)^2$ (b) $y = 32$

4. (a) $7x + 28$ (b) $12n − 6$ (c) $m^2 + mn$ (d) $11n + 31$ (e) $8x + 26$

5. (a) y: $−1, 1, 3, 5, 7$; coordinates: $(0, −1), (1, 1), (2, 3), (3, 5), (4, 7)$

(b) (i) $y = x + 2$ (ii) $x + y = 6$ or $y = 6 − x$ (iii) $x = 5$

430

6. (a) 6   (b) 3   (c) 7   (d) 36   (e) $n + 34$ (f) $n + 34 = 3n$ (g) $n = 17$

7. (a) n^7 (b) n^4 (c) n^2 (d) $x = 6$

Page 416   ***Check yourself on sections 6.5 and 6.6***

1. (a) 0.85   (b) $\dfrac{3}{7}$ (c) 24 times

2. (a) (1, 1), (1, 2), (1, 3), (1, 4), (2, 1), (2, 2), (2, 3), (2, 4), (3, 1), (3, 2), (3, 3), (3, 4), (4, 1), (4, 2), (4, 3), (4, 4)

    (b) $\dfrac{2}{16} = \dfrac{1}{8}$ (c) HH, HT, TH, TT   Answer $= \dfrac{1}{2}$

3. (a) 144 cm²   (b) 120 cm²   (c) 283.5 cm²   (d) 36°

    (e) BC (6 cm) is 0.34 cm longer than QR (5.66 cm).

INDEX